WILLIAM G. BROWNLOW

● TENNESSEANA EDITIONS ●

Very Respectfully, &c,

W. G. Brownlow

WILLIAM G. BROWNLOW
Fighting Parson of the Southern Highlands

BY E. MERTON COULTER

With an Introduction by
James W. Patton

THE UNIVERSITY OF TENNESSEE PRESS
KNOXVILLE

TENNESSEANA  EDITIONS

Nathalia Wright, General Editor

In the Tennessee Mountains by Mary Noailles Murfree (Charles Egbert Craddock), with an introduction by Nathalia Wright.

William G. Brownlow: Fighting Parson of the Southern Highlands by E. Merton Coulter, with an introduction by James W. Patton.

A Narrative of the Life of David Crockett of the State of Tennessee by David Crockett, with an introduction and annotation by Stanley J. Folmsbee. *In preparation.*

Frontispiece: The Parson at the age of about fifty-five. This steel engraving was used as the frontispiece for his *Sketches of the Rise, Progress, and Decline of Secession*, the famous *Parson Brownlow's Book.*

LIBRARY OF CONGRESS CATALOG CARD NUMBER 71–136309
STANDARD BOOK NUMBER 87049–118–0

INTRODUCTION

THE STATE OF TENNESSEE played a number of unique roles in the drama of secession, Civil War, and Reconstruction. It was the last state to secede and the first to fall under the force of Federal invasion. It was the only Confederate state not mentioned in President Lincoln's Emancipation Proclamation and the only Confederate state to free its own slaves. Tennessee alone among the seceded states had a considerable body of citizens who constantly sided with the Union; it was the first state in the American Union in which a military governor was appointed to head the state government; and it was the first seceded state to regain admission to the Union. It was additionally unique in its Reconstruction governor.

Among all the characters, political or military, carpetbagger or scalawag, white or black, who rose to prominence in the South during Reconstruction it would be hard to find one who achieved wider notoriety, spoke and wrote with greater invective, and inspired more bitter hatred than William Gannaway Brownlow, who took over the reins of government in Tennessee when Andrew Johnson, the military governor appointed by President Lincoln, left the state to assume the office of vice president of the United States. Unlike most of the Reconstruction governors, Brownlow was no newcomer to the public eye when he assumed his first political office in 1865, having been active as a clergyman, author, polemicist, and newspaper editor for forty years.

Left an orphan at an early age, Brownlow was first bound out as a carpenter's apprentice and later, though his education was irregular, admitted to the Methodist traveling ministry. He rode circuits for ten years in remote and isolated areas of the eastern Tennessee and western North Carolina highlands, improving his limited education and developing the coarse and crude style of speaking and writing that would later make him famous. Here "Parson" Brownlow began his spirited attacks upon the institutions and beliefs of other denominations, especially the Presbyterians and Baptists. While still a circuit rider Brownlow entered upon his career as political and theological pamphleteer by publishing a violent attack, in 1832, on John C. Calhoun and the "Nullification Rebellion," as he termed South Carolina's opposition to the protective tariff. Two years later there appeared from his pen *Helps to the Study of Presbyterianism or, an Unsophisticated Exposition of Calvinism, with Hopkinsian Modifications and Policy, with a View to a more easy Interpretation of the Same. To Which is Added a Brief Account of the Life and Travels of the Author, Interspersed with Anecdotes.* This was followed in 1842 by another polemical work with a similarly lengthy title, this time excoriating the Baptists in *Baptism Examined; or, The True State of the Case. To which is Prefixed, a Review of the Assaults of the Banner & Pioneer. To which is also Added an Appendix.*

Shifting from religious to political controversy in 1844, he published in that year *A Political Register, Setting forth the Principles of the Whig and Locofoco Parties in the United States, with the Life and Public Services of Henry Clay. Also an Appendix Personal to the Author.* In this work Brownlow made known his strong support of the Whig party, both through a vindication of the career of Clay and critical attacks on Jackson, Polk, Van Buren, and other Democrats. Brownlow was also a firm adherent of the Know-Nothing party and in 1856 published a defense of its principles in *Americanism Contrasted with Foreignism, Romanism, and Bogus Democracy, in the Light of Reason, History, and Scripture; in which Certain Demogogues in Tennessee, and elsewhere, are Shown up in their true Colors.*

A religious controversy in 1856 gave rise to one of the Parson's most famous works. The Rev. John R. Graves, a Baptist clergyman and editor of the *Tennessee Baptist,* had issued *The Great Iron Wheel, or Republicanism Backwards and Christianity Reversed in a Series of Letters Addressed to J. Soule, Senior Bishop of the M. E. Church South.* Bishop Joshua Soule was at that time an aged and infirm man, quite unequal to the task of engaging in a religious debate, even if he had been so inclined, so Brownlow assumed the task of replying to Graves. The resulting work, *The Great Iron Wheel Examined; or, its False Spokes Extracted, and an Exhibition of Elder Graves, its Builder*, was described later by its author as "a work of great severity, but written in reply to one of greater severity."

In 1856 Graves also dredged up some writings of Rev. Henry B. Bascom and republished these under the title *The Little Iron Wheel, a Declaration of Christian Rights and Articles. Showing the Despotism of Episcopal Methodism. By H. B. Bascom, D. D. [Late Bishop of the M. E. Church, South] With Notes of Application & Illustrations by J. R. Graves [Editor of the Tennessee Baptist]*. Bascom's articles had supported a movement against episcopacy which led to the formation of the Methodist Protestant Church in 1828, though he himself had remained in the Methodist Episcopal Church to his death in 1850. Brownlow felt called upon to reply to Graves' *Notes of Application* and so, having removed the false spokes from the *Great Iron Wheel*, he now proceeded to spin the *Little Iron Wheel* in a work entitled *The "Little Iron Wheel" Enlarged: or, Elder Graves, its Builder, Daguerreotyped, by way of an Appendix. To which are added Some Personal Explanations*. In both of his replies to Graves, Brownlow wrote with the same vicious satire and sarcasm that had characterized his other polemical works. A typical example of this approach was his announcement that in one instance Graves had perpetrated twenty-five falsehoods in one chapter of twelve pages, being over two lies to the page. Graves for the most part treated Brownlow with silent contempt, stopping only to declare him "notorious and scurrilous" and a "foul libeller" and stating further that he had not read Brownlow's attacks and had no intention of doing so.

In 1858 the Parson shared with the Rev. Abram Pryne authorship of another controversial work, *Ought American Slavery to be Perpetuated? A Debate Held at Philadelphia September, 1858*. A further illustration (if one were required) of the Parson's skill in satire, ridicule, and sarcasm, this book also reveals his ante-bellum views on slavery which, though no less intense, were very different from those which he later held and expressed on that subject. The meeting with Pryne grew out of an elaborate challenge issued by Brownlow to the friends of freedom in the North to debate the merits of slavery. After satisfying himself that Pryne, a Congregational minister and editor of an anti-slavery paper in upstate New York, was "in good standing with his church" and not a "gentleman of color," Brownlow agreed to a meeting in Philadelphia. Here he argued pointedly and powerfully from the Bible that American slavery was "especially commanded by God through Moses, and approved through the Apostles by Christ," and that "what God ordains and Christ sanctifies should command the respect and toleration of even Northern abolitionists." A typical example of the Parson's reasoning along this line was his assertion that in apprehending the fleeing bondwoman Hagar, "the angel of God, on this occasion, was acting in the capacity of a United States marshall, under the then existing fugitive slave laws of the Old Testament," and arresting "a fugitive slave and forcing her to return to her lawful owner."

The last of the Parson's books was his famous *Sketches of the Rise, Progress, and Decline of Secession; with a Narrative of Personal Adventures among the Rebels*, commonly known by its binder's title, *Parson Brownlow's Book*. Published in Philadelphia while the author was in exile from Tennessee in 1862, this work contains accounts of his life and of his adventures while confined in the Knoxville jail during the early portion of the Civil War. Throughout it is written in the most bitter language and is a vigorous indictment of the secession movement and the Confederate government. It was very popular in the North, where it was used as Union propaganda, and where the author is said to have realized more than sixty thousand dollars from its sale.

Brownlow's career as a journalist was equally revealing of his activities, opinions, and literary style. His ventures in this field include the *Whig* and the Jonesboro *Review*. The *Whig* was a peripatetic newspaper. Established first as *Brownlow's Tennessee Whig*, a typical party organ, at Elizabethton in 1839, it was moved the next year to Jonesboro where it remained until 1850 under the title of the *Jonesboro Whig and Independent Journal*. During the latter year it was again removed, this time to Knoxville, where it was published under the name of Brownlow's *Knoxville Whig and Independent Journal* until October, 1861, when it was suppressed by the Confederate authorities and its editor committed to jail and later exiled from the state. In 1863, the editor having returned with the Union army and aided by the proceeds derived from lectures and the sale of his *Book*, a grant of $1,500 from the Federal government, and the use of five army wagons to transport paper and other newspaper materials from Cincinnati, it was re-established as the *Knoxville Whig and Rebel Ventilator* and was edited by Brownlow until his inauguration as governor. After this occasion he discontinued his connection with the newspaper world, though the *Whig* continued under the editorship of his son, John Bell Brownlow, from 1865 to 1869 and was the organ in East Tennessee of the Brownlow administration.

Brownlow's other journalistic venture grew out of a theological controversy between the Parson and the Rev. Frederick A. Ross, editor of the *Calvinistic Magazine*, a review of substantial influence in East Tennessee. In order to facilitate his attacks on Ross, Brownlow established in June, 1847, the *Jonesboro Quarterly Review*, which in December of the same year was changed to a monthly publication. In bitterness and vituperation the *Review* exceeded anything that its editor had hitherto attempted. As usual he did not scruple at bringing personalities into the argument, to the extent of announcing that Ross was the son of a Negress and even printing a woodcut of this "dusky matron" in one issue of the magazine.

Brownlow was intemperate in both his public utterances and his writings. His caustic attacks while a circuit rider upon the members of rival denominations led to his being sued more than once for both libel and slander and made it necessary for the Holston Conference, without much success, to admonish him to alter his course in the future. As an editor he wielded a fierce and bitter pen, and because of this he was constantly involved in altercations. In Jonesboro, a long and vitriolic controversy with a rival editor, Landon C. Haynes, resulted in a street fight in which Haynes drew a revolver and shot Brownlow through the leg. On another occasion, while returning home from a church conference the Parson was attacked from behind by an assailant with a hickory club which fractured his skull, rendered him unconscious for several weeks, and doubtless shortened his life.

Matters were little improved when the *Whig* was removed to Knoxville where its editor's mottoes, "Cry aloud and spare not" and "Independent in all things, neutral in nothing," gave rise to many unpleasant situations. Here Brownlow's chief opponent was the Knoxville *Register*, an old Whig newspaper owned and controlled by some of the city's most influential men, who resented the encroachment of another organ of the same party. For years, day after day, both papers teemed with the fiercest denunciations. Finally, Brownlow succeeded in making his newspaper the official organ of the Whig party in East Tennessee, but about the same time the *Register* became a Democratic paper, a transformation which did not remedy the situation and resulted in a continuation of the conflict until the suppression of the *Whig* in 1861. The *Whig*, however, prospered in spite of opposition and persecution. Although it carried little news, it was tremendously popular among a large class of readers because of the spicy and biting views of the editor. By the opening of the Civil War it had reached a weekly circulation of ten thousand copies.

Personally and in private life Brownlow is said to have been less cynical and disagreeable than his extravagance of writing and public utterances would lead one to expect. His friend and biographer, Oliver P. Temple, described him as a man "warm-hearted, genial, and delightful . . . . far beyond most men, mild, gentle, and good natured." It must be remembered, however, that the enemies made by the Parson's public actions far exceeded in number the friends made by his amiability and patience in the family circle.

Physically, Brownlow was a remarkable specimen of splendid manhood until, in later years, disease weakened his constitution. Following his confinement in the Knoxville jail he had suffered acutely from quinzy and palsy, both of which sapped his vitality and darkened his vision at times. In 1862, nevertheless, he described himself as a man about six feet high, having "weighed as heavy as one hundred and sixty-five pounds," and with "as fine a constitution as any man may desire." He acknowledged "very few gray hairs" on his head and asserted that, "although hard-favored than otherwise," he would pass for a man of forty years. He claimed "as strong a voice as any man in East Tennessee," where he had resided for the last thirty years and had "taken part in all of the religious and political controversies" of his day and time. "I am known," he said,

throughout the length and breadth of the land as the "Fighting Parson"; while I may say without incurring the charge of egotism, that no man is more peaceable, as my neighbors will testify. . . . I have never been arraigned in the church for any immorality. I never played a card. I never was a profane swearer. I never drank a dram of liquor, until within a few years, when it was taken for medicine. I never attended a horse-race, and never witnessed their running, save on the fairgrounds of my own county. I never courted but one woman; and her I married.

This was the man who was installed as the chief executive of Tennessee in 1865, a position in which he has been described as "the wrong man in the wrong place at the wrong time." Austere in his habits and almost fanatical in his love for the Union, he was determined to restore the state to the control of the truly loyal citizens and to bend his efforts toward punishing and impoverishing those who had aided and participated in the rebellion. Believing that the former Confederates were a group of degenerate, dishonest, and corrupt monsters, undeserving of respect or confidence, he induced his pliant legislature to disfranchise a majority of the state's citizens and to admit the newly emancipated slaves to the ballot-box. In a state torn by war and devastation and anxious to return to peace-time status, Brownlow delayed this process by echoing his wartime proposal of "Grape for the Rebel masses and hemp for their leaders" and by organizing his own militia which he used to harass and terrorize those areas of the state and elements of the population which opposed him. To a state already bankrupt he added a crushing debt by sponsoring huge financial grants to railroads, some of which were by their own admission already in bankruptcy. Although he ruled for almost four years with an iron rod, his administration was preeminently destructive rather than constructive, with the result that the chaos and disorder created by his violent partisanship led to the disruption of his own party shortly after he left the state to serve a six-year term in the United States Senate, to which he had been elected by a subservient legislature.

In the Senate the Parson's career was anticlimactic and undistinguished. His physical condition was now so weak that he was not able to stand up when the oath of office was administered, and continuing illness made it necessary to carry him from his near-by boarding house to sessions in the Senate chamber. The condition of his voice was such that he made few speeches; most of what he had to say was committed to writing and read by the Senate clerk. Severe illness prevented his being present at any of the second session of the last Congress of his term, and he did not stand for re-election.

Back in Knoxville, where his *Whig* had now passed into alien hands, he still must needs have a paper by that name. Entering into a partnership with William Rule, he secured a half interest in the *Weekly Whig and Chronicle*, though the first part of the title was now completely out of date. For two years he lingered on a helpless paralytic, unable to speak above a hoarse whisper or to write, though he could still think vigorously and enjoy as much as ever the aroma of printer's ink. Death reached him at the age of seventy-two. In E. M. Coulter's words, "He was a product of his times, but his times produced none other like him."

The character of the "Fighting Parson" may be best appraised and the main events of his life reconstructed from a study of his own published works. Preeminent among these would be his widely publicized *Book* which, following his "Tour of the North" in 1862, he wrote in New Jersey at the suggestion of and on an advance furnished by George W. Childs, an enterprising publisher in Philadelphia. In lurid detail this work portrays the author's experiences with the Rebels as well as the sufferings of other Union men in East Tennessee before that area was redeemed by the Federal forces in 1863. The *Book* serves as a vivid reminder of the strong passions that were aroused in the Southern borderlands by the brutality of real civil war and is cited by a recent commentator as offering "an unusual journey into the sources of significant attitudes of the succeeding Reconstruction era."

Typically, for such an active controversialist, Brownlow published a number of pamphlets. Four of these were printed versions of lectures delivered by the Parson during his "Tour of the North" in 1862. Their contents may be readily inferred from their titles, like that of the Philadelphia pamphlet, *Brownlow, the Patriot and Martyr, showing his Faith and Works, as Reported by Himself*. This and other lectures—printed in *Portrait and Biography of Parson Brownlow* (Indianapolis, 1862), *Suffering of Union Men* (New York, 1862), and *Irreligious Character of the Rebellion* (New York, 1862)—to which an admission fee of fifty cents was usually charged, were immensely profitable to their author. The one at Indianapolis, for example, netted him the sum of $1,700. Another Brownlow pamphlet, *A Sermon on Slavery*, was preached first in Temperance Hall in Knoxville in June, 1856, and delivered again, with some additions, the next year before a meeting of the Southern Commercial Convention in Knoxville. As in his debate with Pryne, the Parson displayed so convincingly his complete Southern orthodoxy on the subject of slavery that delegates from Alabama and other Southern states called upon him to print the sermon for distribution throughout the slaveholding South.

The best single source for Brownlow's public career is his own newspaper, published successively at Elizabethton, Jonesboro, and Knoxville under titles varying from time to time but always containing the word *Whig*. A weekly paper of large circulation, it was noted for its violent partisanship and rabid Union sentiment. The editor's personal file is now held by the Library of Congress and is all the more valuable for many pencilled notes on the margins in the handwriting of the editor's son John Bell Brownlow.

The Parson's Jonesboro *Quarterly Review* (1847) and *Monthly Review* (1848), devoted chiefly to religious polemics and personal controversies, were later bound in one volume of which there are copies in the Library of Congress and in the Lawson Mc-Ghee Library at Knoxville.

One of the earliest works about the Parson, as distinguished from his own writings, was an account of his exploits jumbled into an entertaining but highly fictitious brochure by Major W. D. Reynolds, "late acting adjutant of the Western Army," entitled *Miss Martha Brownlow; or the Heroine of Tennessee. A Truthful and Graphic Account of the many Perils and Privations endured by Miss Martha Brownlow, the Lovely and Accomplished Daughter of the Celebrated Parson Brownlow, during her Residence with her Father in Knoxville*, published about 1862 in Philadelphia, and reissued the next year in the German language as *Miss Maude Brownlow oder Die Helden von Tennessee*. The measure of Major Reynolds' accuracy may be inferred from the fact that Miss Brownlow appears as Martha in one edition and as Maude in the second, though her real name was Sarah. Many other elements in the account were highly imaginative, and the whole, designed for circulation in the North, assumed a level of intelligence among Northerners far lower than must have been the fact.

The first biography of Brownlow that made any pretense of accuracy was an 85-page sketch included by Judge Oliver P. Temple in his *Notable Men of Tennessee from 1833 to 1875: Their Times and Their Contemporaries*, compiled and arranged by his daughter Mary B. Temple and published in 1912 (New York: The Cosmopolitan Press), though written much earlier. Judge Temple was a contemporary of the Parson, and his sketch, though friendly to its subject, is not unduly biased in its treatment. Brownlow is mentioned briefly in James W. Fertig, *The Secession and Reconstruction of Tennessee*, a University of Chicago doctoral dissertation (University of Chicago Press, 1898), and also in John R. Neal, *Disunion and Restoration in Tennessee*, a Columbia University dissertation (New York: The Knickerbocker Press, 1899). He is treated more recently and in considerably greater detail in James W. Patton, *Unionism and Reconstruction in Tennessee*, originally prepared as a doctoral dissertation at the University of North Carolina (Chapel Hill: University of North Carolina

Press, 1934; reprinted by Peter Smith, Gloucester, Massachusetts, 1966), and in an article "The Senatorial Career of William G. Brownlow" by James W. Patton in the *Tennessee Historical Magazine* (Series II, Vol. I [April, 1931], 153–164). Patton's treatment falls within the general framework established by the older or so-called Dunning school of Reconstruction historians whose interpretation of the period, though admitted to be fair-minded and thorough, has been censured in recent years for being implicitly pro-Confederate and predisposed toward a dim view of "the adventurers, social climbers, and black and white laborers who wielded power for what must have seemed retrospectively a brief and unpleasant hour" (Bernard A. Weisberger, "The Dark and Bloody Ground of Reconstruction Historiography," *Journal of Southern History*, XXV [November, 1959], 427–447).

The only full-length biography of the Parson that has appeared up to the present is Ellis Merton Coulter's *William G. Brownlow, Fighting Parson of the Southern Highlands*, published in 1937 by the University of North Carolina Press and herewith reissued by the University of Tennessee Press. Long experienced in the teaching and writing of Southern history at the University of Georgia, Professor Coulter was well qualified for limning the career of the fiery Parson. Using with care and discrimination the Parson's own publications along with a great variety of other sources he was able to develop a portrait clear and distinct in its outlines, vivid and picturesque in its coloring, produced with a sympathetic understanding of the subject, yet without any tendency toward eulogy. In addition, by skillful use of his sources, Professor Coulter has woven around the career of the Parson the threads of the religious, economic, and political history of his time and area. This latter feature gives the work especial importance in the historiography of Reconstruction in a Southern state.

The principal drawback encountered by Professor Coulter in the preparation of his work was failure to uncover any significant mass of Brownlow manuscripts. That such a collection once existed is a known fact but that it exists today is unlikely. A hearsay explanation is that the Parson's widow allowed stamp and autograph collectors to rummage through and dissipate the contents of the office in which his records were stored.

Two manuscript accounts by contemporaries of the Parson are in existence but until recently have not been accessible to researchers. One of these is a friendly biography written by Samuel M. Arnell, a radical associate of Brownlow. Entitled "The Southern Unionist," this item is in the Special Collections of the University of Tennessee Library, together with a typed copy edited by the writer's son Samuel M. Arnell, Jr. The Arnell family is at present unwilling to permit the publication of the biography. A manuscript diary, 1857–1868, kept by William G. McAdoo, Sr., long in the possession of McAdoo's descendants, is now in the Library of Congress and on microfilm in the University of Tennessee Library. Since McAdoo was a Democrat who was denounced by Brownlow as one of the "most intense Southern patriots" and "guilty of treachery and insincerity," it would hardly be expected that his appraisal of the Parson would be especially cordial.

While it would be interesting to know what Brownlow's correspondence would reveal, its loss may be a hindrance more apparent than real. As Professor Coulter observes, "one of Brownlow's peculiarities was his inability to hide from the public his thoughts, even the innermost. He exposed himself as completely in his books, pamphlets, and newspapers as in his private correspondence," and these records are so open, evident, and widespread "that no one can lock them up."

Since its original publication more than thirty years ago Professor Coulter's portrayal of Brownlow and his regime has not been challenged or materially altered. Neither the "revisionists" nor those historians who stir the dark waters of "Black Reconstruction" have made Tennessee the special object of their attention. Thomas B. Alexander's *Political Reconstruction in Tennessee* (Nashville: Vanderbilt University Press, 1950) emphasized the persistence of Whig-Democratic rivalry as the central theme of Tennessee Reconstruction, but his appraisal of Brownlow is essentially the same as that of Coulter. Brownlow is similarly appraised in references to him in Alexander's *Thomas A. R. Nelson of East Tennessee* (Nashville: Tennessee Historical Commission, 1956) and in the same author's introduction to a recent reprint of *Parson Brownlow's Book* (New York: Da Capo Press, 1968).

Important source material on the Brownlow administration has been made available by Robert H. White in *Messages of the Governors of Tennessee, Volume Five, 1857–1869* (Nashville: Tennessee Historical Commission, 1959), 401–702, preceded by a ten-page introduction by White in agreement with Coulter. The Coulter interpretation of Brownlow and Tennessee Reconstruction is also followed by Stanley J. Folmsbee, Robert E. Corlew, and Enoch L. Mitchell in their two-volume *History of Tennessee* (New York: Lewis Publishing Company, 1960) and in the same authors' one-volume condensation of this work, *Tennessee, A Short History* (Knoxville: The University of Tennessee Press, 1969). In the same tenor are numerous references to Brownlow in Alrutheus A. Taylor, *The Negro in Tennessee, 1865–1880* (Washington, D. C.: The Associated Publishers, Inc., 1941).

As would be expected, there are references to Brownlow in various biographies and other works on Andrew Johnson, some published before and some since Coulter's volume appeared. Significant among these are Robert W. Winston, *Andrew Johnson, Plebeian and Patriot* (New York: Henry Holt and Company, 1928); Lloyd P. Stryker, *Andrew Johnson, A Study in Courage* (New York: The MacMillan Company, 1929); George Fort Milton, *The Age of Hate: Andrew Johnson and the Radicals* (New York: Coward-McCann, Inc., 1930); Eric L. McKitrick, *Andrew Johnson and Reconstruction* (Chicago: University of Chicago Press, 1960); and LeRoy P. Graf and Ralph W. Haskins, eds., *The Papers of Andrew Johnson, Volume I, 1822–1851* (Knoxville: The University of Tennessee Press, 1967). None of these works, however, adds anything new, either of facts or interpretation, to Coulter's *Brownlow*.

Brownlow figures prominently in William B. Hesseltine, "Methodism and Reconstruction in East Tennessee," East Tennessee Historical Society's *Publications*, III (1931), 42–61, and in Verton M. Queener, "William G. Brownlow as an Editor," *ibid.*, IV (1932), 67–82. More recent articles treating specific segments of the Parson's career include Thomas B. Alexander, "Strange Bedfellows: The Interlocking Careers of T. A. R. Nelson, Andrew Johnson, and W. G. (Parson) Brownlow" (East Tennessee Historical Society's *Publications*, XXIV [1952], 68–91), containing brief biographical sketches of each of these three and emphasizing the significance of personality in the history of nineteenth-century Tennessee; LeRoy P. Graf, ed., "Parson Brownlow's Fears: A Letter about the Dangerous, Desperate, Democrats" (*ibid.*, XXV [1953], 111–114), a letter from the Parson to John Eaton, Jr., in September, 1871, alleging that the Democrats were planning to carry the Solid South by force and intimidation and New York by fraud in the election of 1872; and James W. Bellamy, "The Political Career of Landon Carter Haynes" (*ibid.*, XXVIII [1956], 102–126), dealing briefly with the Haynes-Brownlow feud. Other fairly recent articles in which Brownlow appears more or less prominently include Eugene G. Feistman, "Radical Disfranchisement and the Restoration of Tennessee, 1865–1866" (*Tennessee Historical Quarterly*, XII [June, 1953], 135–151); R. Burt Lattimore, "A Survey of William G. Brownlow's Criticisms of the Mormons, 1841–1857" (*ibid.*, XXVII [Fall, 1968], 249–256), describing the Parson's vitriolic attacks on the Church of Latter Day Saints in the Jonesboro *Whig*; and Ralph W. Haskins, "Internecine Strife in Tennessee: Andrew Johnson Versus Parson Brownlow" (*ibid.*, XXIV [Winter, 1965], 321–340), tracing the relations, usually hostile, between Brownlow and Johnson from their first recorded meeting in 1839 to about 1858 and dealing particularly with Brownlow's virulent attacks on and descriptions of Johnson during this period.

Nevertheless, Coulter continues to be the chief portrayer and interpreter of the Fighting Parson and his hectic career, thus bearing out a prediction made at the time of its original publication that this treatment of "Tennessee's most inimitable historical character will remain of enduring value to the casual reader as well as to the student of history" (Stanley J. Folmsbee in the *Journal of Southern History*, III [August, 1937], 376).

Additional evidence of enduring interest in the fiery Parson and his career was expressed when, on October 11, 1969, along with

George Roulstone, C. P. J. Mooney, Edward Ward Carmack, William Rule, Adolph S. Ochs, and four others, William Gannaway Brownlow, Knoxville *Whig* publisher, governor, and United States senator, was one of ten Tennessee editors selected for the new Tennessee Newspaper Hall of Fame in the University of Tennessee Communications and Extension Building at Knoxville.

JAMES W. PATTON

University of North Carolina
August, 1970

PREFACE

This book, first published by the University of North Carolina Press in 1937, went out of print in 1955. Continuing interest in Parson Brownlow has led the University of Tennessee Press to bring out a new edition. It is not difficult to understand why the reading public, present and future, should like to meet the Parson, for he was a unique character in American history. He was intensely human, so much so that he could scarcely restrain his emotions or language in resisting those whom he judged to be wrong and evil, whether in religion, politics, or patriotism. His language was so picturesque and vehement that the reader is carried away with it without regard to his own agreement or disagreement.

Brownlow reached low levels in his propaganda to convert mountaineers to Methodism, but in his opposition to secession and the Confederacy he reached even lower, to threaten wholesale slaughter of the traitors when he should attain power. And after returning from his self-imposed exile to become governor of Tennessee during the Reconstruction, his violent language against former Confederates and their sympathizers drove many of them out of the state. Yet Brownlow was never as dangerous as his unrestrained language would indicate. Personally he was friendly in individual contacts, and in his family relations he was ideal.

Preacher, journalist, politician, Brownlow was in fact a great actor. His stage was first East Tennessee and the adjacent bits of states; later he made it the whole country. He was not as bad as his words; actors are never so. He did not actually thirst for the blood of his enemies. Though he was quick to protect himself in single combat, he had no intention of slaughtering his Tennessee foes as he wildly threatened at times. He liked to frighten those with whom he disagreed. He had a gentle private nature, but it was only logical that he should impress his public character upon his times; and the picture he produced was not a pleasing one. He created a vast disturbance, but he produced nothing lasting. Others in history whose accomplishments were no more permanent and whose careers were considerably less exciting are much better known. Yet the fact that Parson Brownlow lived and that he lived vehemently can be no less interesting.

Professor Patton in his Introduction has so well presented Brownlow in his whole career, in his writings, and in the subsequent judgments of historians who have had occasion to refer to him, that nothing more need be said here except to note that, in all their writings, the "revisionist historians" have not found it desirable or possible to "revise" the Parson as set forth in this biography.

E. M. C.

CONTENTS

ILLUSTRATIONS

WILLIAM G. BROWNLOW

CHAPTER I

CRUSADING IN THE SOUTHERN HIGHLANDS

To ADMIT that one sprang from the second families of Virginia marks a strange trait. Indeed, it may well be argued that if the admission were publicly made and without provocation, it points to positive idiosyncrasies. So much undoubtedly can be proved on William Gannaway Brownlow, known to his time and to history as the Fighting Parson. Like Abraham Lincoln, his ancestry was the short and simple annals of the poor, but unlike Lincoln he made a virtue out of telling it.

Brownlow's father was Joseph A. Brownlow, who was born in Rockbridge County, Virginia in 1781. He spent his life drifting down the great valleys of Southern Appalachia, and by 1816, when he died, he had reached East Tennessee. Brownlow's mother was Catherine Gannaway, also a Virginian. This couple had proceeded southwestward as far as a farm in Wythe County, when their first child was born. It was on the 29th day of August, 1805, and the child was a boy. They named him William, to do honor to one of his father's brothers, and they added Gannaway out of respect for his mother's family. Two brothers and two sisters followed in rather close succession, to be his playmates. At the age of thirty-five his father died, a victim of the hard life of the frontiersman, and his mother, with feelings too tender for so dire a fate, grieved much for her departed husband, and followed him within less than three months. At the age of eleven Andrew Johnson, later to loom large on the Brownlow horizon, had lost only his father; Brownlow at the same age had lost both father and mother. Though an orphan he grew strong and by the time he became the Fighting Parson he seems to have discovered how to transform vehemence into strength, for he outlived all of his brothers and sisters by almost two decades.[1]

[1] For the early life and ancestry of Brownlow see, W. G. Brownlow, *Sketches of the Rise, Progress, and Decline of Secession; with a Narrative of Personal*

Brownlow was born in that mountainous region below Mason and Dixon's Line, which might well be called Southern Appalachia. It is one great physiographic unit, embracing more than 100,000 square miles, and extending southward 500 miles and more as far as northern Georgia and Alabama. Ignoring the mighty decrees of nature, man, with his adventitious political divisions, cut it up and parcelled it out among no less than eight states; but the natural coherence of the people of Southern Appalachia has stood out boldly in every great crisis which has confronted them. Nature built this region on a plan clear and simple. On the west is the bold Cumberland escarpment, and on the east is the Blue Ridge, which in North Carolina and Tennessee goes under the name of the Unakas and the Great Smoky Mountains. Between lies the Great Appalachian Valley, which is in fact various valleys running northeast and southwest. This region, instead of being inaccessible, and hostile to man's esthetic tastes and his economic struggles, is kindly disposed to both. The beauty of the smoothly formed green ridges and the great towering peaks, and the fertility of the broad river valleys attracted people no less in the early pioneer days than at present.

Into these beautiful valleys came the Scotch-Irish before the Revolutionary War,[2] and so eager were they and other early settlers to see and to seize what was further on that, without knowing it, they passed on out of the Old Dominion and as early as 1769 reached the Watauga and Holston valleys in the King's

Adventures among the Rebels, pp. 15-17 (This book is best known under the binder's title, *Parson Brownlow's Book* and is thus referred to hereafter); *Portrait and Biography of Parson Brownlow, the Tennessee Patriot, Together with his Last Editorial in the Knoxville Whig; also, his recent Speeches, Rehearsing his Experience with Secession, and his Prison Life*, p. 27, (referred to hereafter as *Portrait and Biography*); W. G. Brownlow, *Helps to the Study of Presbyterianism or, an Unsophisticated Exposition of Calvinism, with Hopkinsian Modifications and Policy, with a View to a more easy Interpretation of the Same. To Which is Added a Brief Account of the Life and Travels of the Author, Interspersed with Anecdotes*, pp. 242-43 (referred to hereafter as *Helps to the Study of Presbyterianism*. The personal narrative part of this book has been republished in S. G. Heiskell, *Andrew Jackson and Early Tennessee History*, III, 227-72); R. N. Price, *Holston Methodism*, III, 315-18; Oliver P. Temple, *Notable Men of Tennessee from 1833 to 1875*, p. 318; and *American Annual Cyclopaedia, 1877*, p. 79.

[2] Many Germans drifted into the Shenandoah Valley.

colony of North Carolina. With characteristic frontier initiative they set up a government of their own, writing out on American soil for the first time a fundamental charter, and calling it the Watauga Association. They fought the King at the battle of Kings Mountain and later when affairs in state and nation were not going to suit them, they showed further initiative and daring by declaring themselves the independent State of Franklin.

The spell of the frontier led people of every estate in life to drift westward, and as they trudged along, the Great Southern Highlands laid first claim on them and levied its toll. In its strategic position it stood to win some of the best as well as the worst. It had fertile valleys which satisfied the most fastidious, and it possessed barriers, which stopped the weaklings and shiftless and afforded them homes which no other would accept. So it was that some seeing the fertile lands, stopped through choice; others suffering the breakdown of a wagon wheel, remained by accident; and still others too poor and too weak to proceed farther, settled down through hard necessity.

In Southern Appalachia were developing such families as the Breckinridges, the Prestons, and the Clays who were to move out about the beginning of the nineteenth century and attach their names indelibly to other parts of the country. On the edges of this region were born the Jeffersons and the Calhouns. Originating on the outside Andrew Jackson entered it, remained for a time, and then moved on; Andrew Johnson came to stay; David Crockett and Sam Houston were born in the heart of Southern Appalachia, and both moved westward to cast their lots with Texas. Admiral David G. Farragut came from this region, and it was not by accident that he supported the Union in the Civil War. And in the latter part of the century Bob Taylor, born in East Tennessee, fiddled himself into the hearts of his fellow-citizens and into the office of governor of the state. Later his brother Alf won the same office, though through the power of the opposite party, the Republicans. And downward into the twentieth century Southern Appalachia has not ceased to attract attention. It remained for a little town in

East Tennessee to draw upon itself the eyes of the world as it
sought to prove that a great Englishman was wrong if not sacrilegious when he formulated his theory of evolution.

In such a region Brownlow found himself at the age of eleven,
an orphan. He was not of the rich valley people who tilled farms
of plantation proportions, though both the Brownlows and the
Gannaways had been sufficiently well-to-do to own a few slaves.
It is also evident that there was at that time a class of people
in the out-of-the-way places who had an economic standing
lower than the Brownlows. Manifestly a boy of eleven could
do little toward feeding and clothing a family of four younger
brothers and sisters, so these five orphans were scattered among
their relatives. Billy Brownlow was sent to his Uncle John
Gannaway, and for the next seven years he worked on a farm
and earned his keep by the sweat of his brow. As the hard life
of a farmer did not appeal to him, at the age of eighteen he got
his uncle's permission to leave, and went to Abingdon, in Washington County. Here he apprenticed himself to another uncle,
George Winniford, a house-carpenter and a planter, and for
three years worked at the business of sawing planks, and building them into houses. But he was soon convinced that he was
not destined to go through life doing such things, and so decided
to get an education and become a man of some importance.

In 1825 a camp-meeting was reported in progress at Sul-
phur Springs, twenty-five miles from Abingdon. Brownlow went
over to join the crowd, and soon found himself converted, and
then for the first time in his life was "enabled to shout aloud the
wonders of redeeming love." As he recalled the occasion a few
years later, "All my anxieties were then at an end—all my hopes
were realized—my happiness was complete."[3] A sudden change
had now come over him. He quit being a carpenter, and hurried
away from Abingdon back up into Wythe County, there to have
his rude educational tools welded by William Horne into finer in-
struments. This year ended his formal schooling, but it height-
ened his insatiable desire to read and study almost every book
he could lay his hands on.

---

[3] Brownlow, *Helps to the Study of Presbyterianism*, pp. 243-44; *Knoxville
Whig*, September 9, 1868.

Camp-meeting ecstasy as pictured by an ante-bellum artist. From *Brother Mason, the Circuit Rider; or, Ten Years a Methodist Preacher.*

As Brownlow read, he also observed. He was soon convinced that the quickest way to become a great man in his little world in Southern Appalachia was to join in the great religious boom then in progress. Not much education was needed, but a large amount of religious fervor, excitability, and pugnacity would go a long way, and if a ready tongue and a quick wit were added, the combination would be complete. As Brownlow had all these qualities in excellent proportions, he decided to join in the movement. According to the law of probabilities, he should have become a volunteer in the Presbyterian forces, for these crusaders were the first to visit the back country of Virginia, in the Scotch-Irish migrations of colonial times. The Brownlow family was Scotch-Irish and naturally was Presbyterian, but the Gannaways were Methodists and it was they who had the last word on religious matters with Billy Brownlow before he became a man. And then, too, the Methodist ways of doing things suited Brownlow much better. Finally, it was a Methodist meeting which had turned him to the Lord. So Brownlow decided to join the Methodist movement and become a leader in the front ranks. As the Holston Conference was scheduled to meet in Abingdon in the fall of 1826, he planned to attend and to apply for admission into the travelling ministry. Bishop Joshua Soule presided this year, and it was he who admitted Brownlow, assigning him to the Black Mountain Circuit, in North Carolina, an outpost on the eastern slopes of Appalachia.

What sort of task confronted this new parson in the wilderness? What had the forces of organized religion done for Southern Appalachia and what had been their manner of doing it? These questions must of need be settled. It brings no profit to any one to be able to say truly which might have been the first denomination to be represented in any given portion of the great Southern Highlands by some wandering preacher, perhaps, self-appointed; but it is of much importance as far as history goes to be able to say which denomination first came in considerable force and tended to hold the upper hand. This strategic position fell to the Presbyterians, as before intimated, but they were soon being hard-pressed by the Methodists and

Baptists. The Presbyterians were in Abingdon some years before the American Revolution broke out, for Charles Cummings went there in 1772 to serve two congregations already organized. On down into East Tennessee they drifted; when Francis Asbury passed through that region in 1802 he found them well organized. The Presbyterians were the religious aristocrats in this frontier country. They believed in education and carried out that belief by setting up academies and colleges. In 1783 Samuel Doak set up Martin's Academy at Salem. A dozen years later this was transformed into Washington College. Greeneville College was provided for in 1794, and the year 1819 saw the beginnings of Southern and Western Theological Seminary, which later became Maryville College.[4]

A few stray religious enthusiasts who called themselves Baptists seem to have made their appearance in East Tennessee, long before this name was applied to the region, even as early as the Watauga settlement. The Indians demolished one of their establishments before the Revolutionary War, but the Baptists were back again by 1781, this time at Buffalo Ridge. Thereafter one Baptist association followed another in a steady progression, bearing such names as Holston, Nolichucky, Powell's Valley, Sweetwater, Sequatchee, and Ocoee.[5]

Methodist men of God were in the back country almost as soon as a settlement would spring up; their activities began in Southwest Virginia before 1783, for it was in this year that the Holston Circuit was set up. The first Conference ever to be held west of the mountains took place in East Tennessee in May, 1788, at a place called Half-Acres; and it was the ubiquitous Asbury who presided. Later he passed through this region often in his wilderness travels, and now and then Lorenzo Dow, "the crazy

---

[4] J. E. Alexander, *A Brief History of the Synod of Tennessee from 1817 to 1887*, pp. 5, 11, 64-81; C. B. Coale, *The Life and Adventures of William Waters, the Famous Hunter and Trapper of White Top Mountain, embracing Early History of Southwestern Virginia, Sufferings of the Pioneers, etc. etc.* pp. 246-58; W. T. Hale and D. L. Merritt, *A History of Tennessee and Tennesseeans*, p. 223; *Journal of Rev. Francis Asbury*, III, 87; L. S. Merriam, *Higher Education in Tennessee*, p. 63.

[5] David Benedict, *A General History of the Baptist Denomination in America and other Parts of the World.*

preacher," came this way. Soon the Methodists were setting up their circuits throughout all Southern Appalachia. As for schools and colleges, the followers of John Wesley were not quite sure that such man-made institutions might not afford easy ways for wasting money. And at this time the feeling was not completely dispelled from among them that a Methodist preacher needed no more education than that with which the Lord had endowed him. Yet in 1831 they founded Holston Seminary at New Market, in East Tennessee, and falling into the habits of the times, they soon changed it into a manual training school. In 1836 the Holston Conference succeeded in founding a college which they had been contemplating for four years. At first they decided to locate it at Strawberry Plains, in East Tennessee, but their final decision was to go to Washington County, in Southwest Virginia. This institution developed into Emory and Henry College.[6]

Carrying religion to the frontier was beset with almost as many dangers and inconveniences as dogged the steps of the Crusaders in the Holy Land. The Methodist circuit-rider was in the forefront; the Baptist itinerant was not far behind; the Presbyterians, while generally early on the field, enjoyed more security back of the lines. The frontier preacher, though little educated, was tremendously serious; indeed, his zeal often went in inverse proportion to his learning. Hunting souls was to some adventuresome frontiersmen much the same as hunting bears might be to others. There was much the same sort of sport for both, although the soul hunter might not always recognize it. Each made a living, and neither grew wealthy. The Methodist circuit-rider was allowed about $80 a year if he could find means for getting it, and in computing this amount, gifts of food and raiment and fees for marrying couples were included. He was urged to remain single as long as he was on the circuit, and if he felt he must marry he was urged to "locate," in order to supplement his income from other means than preaching. Old Peter

---

[6] J. B. McFerrin, *History of Methodism in Tennessee;* W. W. Sweet, *The Rise of Methodism in the West,* p. 15; *Journal of Francis Asbury,* II, 33; Coale, *op. cit.,* pp. 205-8, 246-58; Brownlow, *Helps to the Study of Presbyterianism,* pp. 284-85.

Cartwright, who knew well the business of circuit-riding, observed, "But the Lord provided; and, strange as it may appear to the present generation, we got along without starving, or going naked."[7]

The circuit-rider's equipment generally consisted of a horse, a bridle, a saddle, and saddle-bags. Among the contents of his saddle-bags were a Bible, and perhaps occasionally a copy of Milton's works. The latter was valuable for descriptions of hell-fire; the former must be a constant companion, for the Bible should be continuously studied in order that the sinner might be the more easily refuted. And furthermore a frontier preacher would be forever disgraced among his fellows if he were ever caught off guard to the extent that he could not preach a sermon at the shortest notice on any given passage in the Bible. Ezek. 1:16 reads, "The appearance of the wheels and their work *was* like unto the colour of a beryl: and they four had one likeness: and their appearance and their work *was* as it were a wheel in the middle of a wheel." This difficult passage led a Presbyterian preacher to construct a sermon which he called "A Wheel Within a Wheel," and which he liked so well that he had it printed in the *Calvanistic Magazine*, an East Tennessee publication.[8] Once a Methodist bishop exhibited his learning by beginning his sermon in this wise, "My beloved hearers, I shall in the first place speak to you of the things which you know; second, of what I know, and you do not know; third, of the things that neither of us know."[9]

The frontier man of God was a hard rider, a hard preacher, and a hard liver. One who knew the Methodist itinerancy in its greatest vigor declared that

it had no ruffles or lawn sleeves that it cared to soil, no love-locks that it feared to disorder, no buckles it was loath to tarnish. It lodged roughly, and it fared scantily. It tramped up muddy ridges,

---

[7] W. P. Strickland, ed., *Autobiography of Peter Cartwright, the Backwoods Preacher,* pp. 521-22; William Henry Milburn, *Ten Years of Preacher Life; Chapters from an Autobiography,* pp. 347-88.

[8] Vol. III, No. 7 (July, 1829), pp. 199-213. This magazine was started in January, 1827, in Rogersville, in East Tennessee, by James Gallaher, Frederick A. Ross, and David Nelson. See also Milburn, *op. cit.,* pp. 365-66.

[9] *Ibid.,* p. 368.

it swam or forded rivers to the waist; it slept on leaves or raw deer-skin, and pillowed its head on saddle-bags; it bivouacked among wolves or Indians; now it suffered from ticks or mosquitoes —it was attacked by dogs, it was hooted, and it was pelted—*but it throve.*[10]

He threaded his way through the wilderness with a Bible in one hand and a sword in the other. He might have had imperfect notions of the universe outside of Southern Appalachia, but he was seriously going about the task which he knew it was his duty to perform. His language was fiery and direct, for he knew he had a great issue to settle every time he preached. He had the conviction that there were souls in his audience which if not saved then would go down to eternal damnation before he should return. An East Tennessee religious publication excitedly declared, "With unspeakable distress we have heard of the alarming prevalence and wide-spread ravages of moral death in one of the western counties of Virginia." A runner had but recently arrived and told "with streaming eyes of the ruin which appears to hang over the people."[11]

The earliest preachers of course found no meeting-houses, so they preached under some large tree or on the doorstep of some willing convert. Bishop Asbury came through East Tennessee in the fall of 1802 and reported that he "had sacrament and love feast in the woods."[12] The lack of meeting-houses and the strange religious outburst that swept over the whole western frontier at the break of the nineteenth century, led to the camp-meetings which were held out in the midst of the forest. The Great Revival seems to have had its earliest and most intense manifestations beyond the mountains out in Kentucky, but some of the strangest outbursts first appeared in East Tennessee. People for miles around went to these meetings in almost unbelievable numbers for where else could they go and what else was there to draw them together, unless it were the tricks of a politician? Bishop Asbury attended a camp-meeting in 1802 near Jonesboro. It

[10] Wm. W. Wightman, *Life of William Capers, D.D., one of the Bishops of the Methodist Episcopal Church South; including an Autobiography,* pp. 471-72.

[11] *Calvinistic Magazine,* vol. I, no. 1 (January, 1827), p. 29.

[12] *Journal of Francis Asbury,* III, 87.

lasted for four days and drew a modest crowd of about 1,500 people. According to his account, "We had a shaking, and some souls felt convicting and converting grace."[13] But it remained for "crazy Dow," who debouched from Buncombe County, in North Carolina, down the French Broad River, the next year, to discover and report on happenings strange even to the early frontier preacher. He had heard "about a singularity called the *jerks* or *jerking exercise*, which appeared first near Knoxville in August last, to the great alarm of the people. . . ." At first he considered the report "vague and false," but "at length, like the Queen of Sheba" he set out to see for himself. He was soon in the midst of things and saw remarkable sights. The afflicted threw their heads to and fro hurriedly, at the same time jerking furiously in every limb. At one of the camp-meetings, he saw jerking-saplings, "where the people had laid hold of them and jerked so powerfully that they had kicked up the earth as a horse stamping flies." Peter Cartwright knew much about jerking. He had had as many as five hundred people at one time jerking in his congregations. According to him the bonnets, hats, and combs of the women would fly off, and so violently did their heads snap back and forth that "their long hair cracked almost as loudly as a wagoner's whip." The Lord smote the people of this wilderness in other strange fashions. People ran hurriedly to and fro on the camp grounds and in the tabernacle under the trees; some lay prostrate in beds of straw; others with flays hurried out into the forests and whipped the trees as if they were chasing and chastising the devil; some went through the motions of playing the fiddle or sewing; and some went into the holy dance. Dow visited a camp-meeting across the line in Virginia where he heard a great pandemonium of the wicked break out, as they were smitten by the Lord. One preacher had used up his strength in exhorting the multitude and then another "began to exhort, when there commenced a trembling among the wicked; one, a second, and a third fell from their seats and the cry for mercy became general . . . and for eleven hours there was no cessation of the loud cries." The Quakers in

---

[13] *Ibid.*, p. 86.

East Tennessee did not seem to engage in these antics, but Dow found a sect of them "who do not feel free to wear colored clothes."[14]

These holy demonstrations gradually began to degenerate, in the eyes of some of the preachers, into gigantic frolics and horse-play performances, and the whole system of camp-meetings soon came in for condemnation. Lorenzo Dow declared that he had heard a preacher produce "ten passages of Scripture to prove that dancing was once a religious exercise, but corrupted at Aaron's calf, and from thence young people got it for amusement." But the camp-meeting was destined to outlast all its critics, even into the dawn of the twentieth century. It became one of the fixed institutions in Southern Appalachia, serving not only the religious group but also the irreligious element. The announcement of a camp-meeting brought glee to the hearts of all the bullies, drunkards, pickpockets, horse-traders, horse-thieves, and whiskey-traffickers throughout all the surrounding country. To preserve order was no easy task, but in the performance of this function, some of the best preachers developed into some of the most proficient fighters. Virile old Peter Cartwright, in his western vineyard, stood equally ready to instill the fear of God into his hearers through a sermon or by wielding a club. Once with a club he knocked a rowdy off his horse, seized him, took him before a justice of the peace and had him fined $50. On another occasion he seized the whiskey supply of a bunch of disturbers and drove them off the campground with a barrage of stones. When in the midst of his sermon a woman disturbed the meeting by kicking her converted daughters, he tripped her up and threw her sprawling among the congregation, continuing his discourse as if nothing had happened. Now and then he worked such strategems on the hood-

---

[14] T. W. Humes, *The Loyal Mountaineers of Tennessee*, pp. 339-41; *Perambulations of Cosmopolite; or Travels and Labors of Lorenzo Dow in Europe and America*, pp. 132-33; *The Dealings of God, Man, and the Devil; as Exemplified in the Life, Experience, and Travels of Lorenzo Dow, in a Period of over Half a Century; together with his Polemic and Miscellaneous Writings. Complete. To which is added the Vicissitudes of Life, by Peggy Dow*, I, 27, 85 (referred to hereafter as *Dealings of God, Man, and the Devil*). Abel Stevens, *History of the Methodist Episcopal Church of the United States of America*, IV, 433.

CRUSADING IN THE SOUTHERN HIGHLANDS

lums as playing on the vanity of their leader by appointing him peace officer and thereby turning him against his own gang, and by centering his heavenly artillery on the gang leader and subduing him. Parson Cartwright's creed was "to love everybody, but to fear no one," and he added, "I did not permit myself to believe any man could whip me till it was tried." A gentle Baptist itinerant in the Big Sandy Valley of Eastern Kentucky, by the use of his fiddle, tamed the spirit of the rowdies that might otherwise have disturbed him.[15]

To say that these fiery champions of the Lord should fight only gangsters would leave unnoticed some of their greatest battles. In this great arena of Southern Appalachia there were three bands of gladiators—the Methodists, the Baptists, and the Presbyterians—contesting for the souls of the people. Fights waxed as hot among these three groups as ever they did between preacher and rowdy. The general tendency was for the two Calvinistic groups, the Baptists and the Presbyterians, to join the fray against the Methodists. This union of forces was encouraged by the fact that the Methodists appeared to each of the other denominations to be the most dangerous rival. Methodism was a frontier religion, made so by the chief characteristics of its doctrines and by the nature of the frontiersmen. Among the cardinal principles of Methodism were free will, free grace, and individual responsibility. These ideas worked in definite harmony with frontier democracy. Such Calvinistic doctrines as predestination and foreordination could have little appeal to a headstrong son of the frontier, who wanted and would have his own way, in this world if not hereafter. So, contentions and disputes grew up in which there was none too lowly to participate and none too high. At the very time Brownlow became a parson, a war against Methodism was raging, with Nathan Bangs and John Emory boldly fighting the battles for John Wesley. Although one of the most historic fights against Methodists in Southern Appalachia was carried on by a Presbyterian, the Baptists developed the more intense rivalry with the

[15] Milburn, *op. cit.*, pp. 383-84; W. R. Jillson, *The Big Sandy Valley. A Regional History Prior to the Year 1850*, pp. 105-6; Strickland, *op. cit.*, p. 133.

Methodists and engaged in the greater number of battles.

Jacob Young, a Methodist preacher, experienced much trouble in organizing a circuit until he was able to dispel the feeling of the people that he was a Baptist. On one occasion, as darkness was fast approaching, he spied a cabin in the midst of the forest. He approached and asked the woman in the doorway whether he might spend the night. She was on the point of turning him away as a roving Baptist, when he explained that he was a Methodist. Thereupon she exclaimed, "La me! has a Methodist preacher come at last? Yes, brother, you shall stay all night."[16] The point of difference between the Methodists and Baptists that produced the greatest amount of disputing was the question of baptism. So many revivals had been held in the Clinch Circuit and the people had been preached to so much that they had become "very superstitious in their notions—looking for miracles and things out of the common order. They expected for God to tell them everything that they ought to do." According to the Reverend Mr. Young,

A class-leader became dissatisfied with the baptism he received when he was an infant, and began to think he ought to be baptized by immersion; he talked to the preachers and to the brethren, but concluded he would lay it before the Lord. One morning he arose early and went upon the mountain, and continued in prayer until late in the afternoon. But before sundown, the family heard him crying at the top of his voice, and he came down from the mountain, in full speed, crying, "Baptism, baptism, baptism, by immersion!" He thought he had received the revelation right from heaven; others thought so too, and away they went and were immersed—then they felt that all was well.[17]

Often Methodist and Baptist ministers interrupted each other in their meetings and now and then meetings were broken up by the indignant enemy. On one occasion a Baptist cried out in a Methodist service, "Sir, you have preached lies this day,

---

[16] *Autobiography of a Pioneer: or, the Nativity, Experience, Travels, and Ministerial Labors of Rev. Jacob Young with Incidents, Observations, and Reflections,* p. 83.

[17] *Ibid.,* pp. 126-27.

and I can prove it from the word of God."[18] The congregation dispersed in riotous disorder. But the Methodists were not above taking the offensive. A Baptist, after bitterly castigating a Methodist, called upon anyone in his audience to deny the truth of his charges. Peter Cartwright arose and assailed him so mercilessly that he fled from the house. Then, according to Cartwright's account, "I ordered him to stop, and told him, if he did not, I would shoot him in the back for a tory; he got out at the door. He was taken so at surprise, and charged on so suddenly, that he forgot his hat, and he peeped around the door-chink at me. I blazed away at him till he dodged back, and started off, bare-headed, for home, talking to himself by the way."[19] Parson Cartwright was greatly annoyed by the proselyting Baptists who came across his trail, and he solemnly laid this charge against them:

It was the order of the day (though I am sorry to say it), that we were constantly followed by a certain set of proselyting Baptist preachers. These new and wicked settlements [in the upper Cumberland River region] were seldom visited by these Baptist preachers until the Methodist preachers entered them; then, when a revival was gotten up, or the work of God revived, these Baptist preachers came rushing in and they generally sung their sermons; and when they struck the *long roll*, or their sing-song mode of preaching, in substance it was "water! water! You must follow your blessed Lord down into the water!" . . . indeed, they made so much ado about baptism by immersion, that the uninformed would suppose that heaven was an island, and there was no way to get there but by *diving* or *swimming*.[20]

The Presbyterians, less given to roving up and down the wilderness, carried on their warfare in the more dignified printed page. So they were answered likewise. Cartwright, equally versatile as a pamphleteer or a verbal antagonist, hurled against them such compositions as these, "A Useful Discovery: or I

---

[18] *Ibid.,* p. 80.
[19] Strickland, *op. cit.,* p. 136. This incident took place in the Cumberland River region in 1813.
[20] *Ibid.,* pp. 133-34.

Never Saw the Like Before," "The Dagon of Calvinism," and "The History of the Devil," and "Crazy Dow" entered the pamphleteer's arena against them with his "Chain."[21]

The ministers of Southern Appalachia had all the frailties of the rough frontiersmen among whom they worked. They suffered all the hardships that befell frontiersmen, but they bore them with joy for in their unshaken faith they knew they were performing the task the Lord had set for them. Had they not been combative in disposition they would never have secured a hearing or a following. People went to their meetings to be entertained, and many came away converted. When civilizing influences had softened the hard forces of nature and had tamed the savage disposition of man, the preachers, no longer having rivers to swim and rowdies to whip, intensified the warfare among themselves. Mankind is endowed with an irreducible minimum of piety which always promotes true religion, but churches have never depended on this fact alone.[22] As time went on, education and social standing were beginning to develop into religious assets, but stirring up prejudice and antagonism against the other sects was long to be a powerful weapon wielded by the preacher-warriors in Southern Appalachia.

---

[21] W. S. Hooper, ed., *Fifty Years as a Presiding Elder by Rev. Peter Cartwright*, pp. 92 ff.

[22] Controversy was nothing new in the development and spread of religious sects. It has played so consistent a part in history that it might well be considered the normal. Methodism was ushered into America in the midst of a dispute between George Whitefield and John Wesley. New England was being torn asunder by her bitter religious contentions, while Southern Appalachia was yet the peaceful home of the Cherokees.

CHAPTER II

A NEW PARSON RIDES THE CIRCUIT

BISHOP JOSHUA SOULE sent young Brownlow to one of the roughest and most inaccessible parts of all Southern Appalachia. The Holston Conference, in which Brownlow was to carry on his circuit-riding for the next ten years, was laid out with no regard at all for state lines; it embraced parts of Virginia, North Carolina, South Carolina, Georgia, and Tennessee, and the Parson on horseback carried his message into every one of these states before he was finally allowed to locate. The Conference was composed of five districts, Abingdon, French Broad, Knoxville, Hiwassee and Asheville, and the districts were made up of varying numbers of circuits. In that part of the Conference where the long ridges prevailed, the circuit was more likely than not to be made up of a single valley, as the Clinch Circuit, which at one time was simply the Powell River Valley, 150 miles long and 25 miles wide. But the Black Mountain Circuit, in the Asheville District, where Brownlow was sent, lay far over in North Carolina on the eastern slopes of the Blue Ridge where the mountains were jumbled and piled so high that they formed the roof of eastern North America.

According to the custom, he was taken on trial, and indeed if he should succeed in cultivating the Lord's vineyard in such a region as this, he should soon well deserve the full connection that each circuit-rider expected after two years. Into this region in the fall of 1826 came the twenty-one-year-old Parson, stretching upwards to the extent of about six feet, with sharp features, glaring eyes, and a determination written in his countenance that might mean defiance, fright, or fanaticism. If Joshua Soule had hoped to scare him out of the Methodist ministry by starting him off in such a place as the Black Mountain Circuit, the Bishop was much mistaken. The look in his face that some might have interpreted as fright was in fact the quintessence of defiance and fanaticism. He seems never to have developed fear of anything throughout his long life. Yet there was hidden in his being a romantic love for nature in her most heroic moods. Instead of running from these rough mountains and swift torrents, he thought they were exquisitely beautiful. He signalized the day following his first Christmas as a circuit-rider by nearly freezing to death on Cane River. As for his vineyard, "There are few places in the world which can vie with the counties of Buncombe and Burke, in beauty and novelty of scenery—the extended hill-side fields, rich ridges, beautiful springs, mountain coves, high conical peaks, and astonishing verdure covering the soil, set off to the best advantage, the lofty Black Mountain." He was also greatly attracted by Table Rock, a great jumping-off place into the Piedmont region, which extended through Burke County to the eastward.[1]

If there was romanticism in the Parson which his countenance did not show, there was a vast amount of fanatical zeal that showed in every lineament. The Baptists soon brought this characteristic into play. He had never come into contact with this sect before entering the Black Mountain region, but here he soon ran afoul of them, for they resented his activities and opposed him with much bitterness. He found them exceedingly bigoted and narrow and possessed of the certain feeling that they were the only ones who held a claim on "the bounty of the skies." He ran into one of their meetings where they were engaged in the religious observance of foot-washing and he observed, "never did I, before or since, see as many big dirty feet, washed in one large pewter basin full of water!"[2]

The next year he was moved back toward Tennessee to the French Broad Circuit, still in the Asheville District, but before the year was out he was sent to the Maryville Circuit in East Tennessee for three months, and then transferred again back into Buncombe County. While out in the Maryville region he had his first skirmish with the Presbyterians, who were very

---

[1] Brownlow, *Helps to the Study of Presbyterianism*, p. 245; *Autobiography of a Pioneer*, pp. 106-27.

[2] Brownlow, *Helps to the Study of Presbyterianism*, p. 244.

strong in that vicinity. He complained of being continuously pursued by a little Calvinistic upstart who made no end of pestering him about such subjects as moral inability and the impossibility of falling from grace. He attended a meeting, where a Presbyterian was trying to describe the comical dress of a Methodist preacher. With a great bluster Brownlow stood up and asked the audience to look for themselves. This unexpected move threw the meeting into an uproar. By such acts Brownlow was becoming known and getting talked about far and wide. While in Knoxville one day he ran up on a Presbyterian minister enjoying much fun in a movement he had launched to raise money for having Brownlow's picture painted. This promoter asked Brownlow for a subscription, whereupon the Parson quickly replied that he would contribute if it were set up "as a pattern for minister-making." By this time Brownlow had discovered that his ugliness, which he never denied, served only to spread his name and reputation farther. This year he also had his brushes with the Baptists again, and when he heard them ridiculing and reviling the Methodists he rose up in their meetings and denounced and confused them. He declared the Baptist ministers were very quarrelsome even among themselves, that they often fought over a division of the money in the collection plate.

Amidst all his contentions with the Calvinists, he found time to admire the beauty of nature and to try his powers of description upon it. How beautiful it was in the summer! "But O, the huge, enormous mountains! the steep and dizzy precipices; the pendant horrors of the craggy promontories—how wild and awful they look of a rainy evening!"[3]

At length another year rolled by and Brownlow prepared to attend the Annual Conference, which met this year at Jonesboro, across the line in East Tennessee; and Bishop Joshua Soule was to preside again. In his mind he revolved this leave-taking of his beloved mountains, "Adieu to those scenes, till the last loud trump of God shall sound; and until eruptions, earthquakes, comets, and lightnings, disgorge their blazing maga-

---

[3] *Ibid.,* pp. 246-48.

zines!" Soule seems to have approved of his underling's contest with the Presbyterians and the Baptists, for the Parson noted with much pleasure that the Bishop in a sermon at the Conference "certainly tore the very hindsite off of Calvinism!" This year the Parson was sent on his way into southeast Tennessee to the Washington Circuit in the Washington District. In this region he let his zeal for disputing run riot to such an extent that he soon found himself in the midst of a slander suit, which he, however, succeeded in getting dismissed. Here he also made another discovery. For the first time he now ran into a sect called the Cumberland Presbyterians, a group who had broken away from the regular Presbyterian Church out in Kentucky in 1810 because they believed the latter required too much education for those seeking to enter the ministry.[4] He found their chief activities to be proselyting from the other churches and preaching long sermons. He declared, "I do not recollect to have ever heard more than *one* who closed till he was completely out of *strength, words,* and *ideas!*" He also observed that he did not believe in long sermons and that no sermon should be longer than an hour, for "of all the deaths that ever any people died, there is none so distressing as that of being preached to death!"[5] This observation he soon forgot.

The Parson seems to have had a great deal of curiosity in his make-up. Down in southeastern Tennessee he was in the former home of the Cherokee Indians, and not far removed from their abode at that time. He decided to make them a visit to see how they looked, how they lived, and what their religion was like. At this time Georgia was having trouble with her unwelcome redmen, so Brownlow decided to carry out his visiting in Alabama. Since he had an uncle living near Muscle Shoals, on the Tennessee River, he first went there and then traveled through the Cherokee nation. He found those Indians who were not savages to be good Methodists, and he heard an excellent prayer delivered by Turtlefields, one of their preachers.[6]

---

[4] For an account of the rise of this sect see Lewis and R. H. Collins, *History of Kentucky*, I, 433-36.

[5] Brownlow, *Helps to the Study of Presbyterianism*, pp. 249-51.

[6] *Ibid.*, pp. 251-52.

In 1829 the Holston Conference met in Abingdon, Virginia. Though he remained in the same district as formerly, Brownlow was transferred to the Athens Circuit. While on this circuit, the Parson succeeded so well in his work that his enemies named a dog for him. He also got himself involved in a newspaper controversy.[7]

Brownlow as a crusader seemed to suit the Methodists, for in 1829 he was admitted into full connection, and the next year he was given elder's orders. This year the Annual Conference met at Ebenezer in Greene County, Tennessee, attended by the two bishops, William M'Kendree and Joshua Soule. The latter presided, and sent Brownlow this year to the Tellico Circuit in the Hiwassee region of Tennessee. Here the Parson ran into an eddy of that disturbance which was sweeping over the country under the name of Anti-Masonic movement. He heard a great deal of talk about Masonry, but since he was not quite able to gain from the outside a knowledge of just what it was, he decided to exercise a bit of self-restraint and not preach a sermon against it. But here and elsewhere he was to run into a species of quacks, which he felt quite sure he did understand, and he thundered out against them with all his vehemence. They were the so-called steam doctors, who carried around a concoction which they gave for all ailments.[8]

The Parson traveled over Southern Appalachia more or less according to the laws of a cyclone. He had a daily motion inside the circuit and a great circular forward movement, on which he advanced each year by the aid of Bishop Soule. He began in the eastern confines of the Holston Conference in North Carolina and receded westward down the French Broad River into East Tennessee and then southwest into the southeast corner of Tennessee, only to be pushed back eastward toward the place of his beginning. At the 1831 Conference he was sent to the Franklin Circuit, which lay around about the three-state corner, where North Carolina, South Carolina, and Georgia touched one another. This year he made three tours through the southeastern ramparts of the Southern Highlands,

---

[7] *Ibid.*, pp. 252-54.
[8] *Ibid.*, pp. 256, 281-82.

the "Taxaway Mountains" as he chose to denominate them, and he later marvelled that he did not lose his life.

He found this region infested with Baptists and he adjudged them as pestiferous as ever. They were always shouting "water! . . . as if the Saviour of mankind were a *pennywinkle*, and could only be found hanging to a sand-stone, in the bottom of some water course!" One of them, named Humphrey Posey, he endured as long as he could, and he finally took the offensive and accused Posey of selling Bibles which he was being paid to give away free. Parson Posey denied the charges and indicted Brownlow for libel. Brownlow had been rather bold to act as he did in this Baptist community, and he should have expected the decision which the court handed down. The case was tried at Franklin, in Macon County, North Carolina. According to Brownlow the judge was "corrupt and drunken," and even worse, a Baptist, so he fined Brownlow $5 and the costs. The Parson felt able to pay the $5 and he reckoned the costs to be negligible, so he went about his business of preaching, worrying none about the court's decision. But one Sunday morning while he was in the midst of a meeting, "a corrupt and inexperienced deputy sheriff," with a bill of exhorbitant costs, run up by a great horde of Baptist witnesses who had been summoned without Brownlow's knowledge, levied upon all the Parson's available worldly possessions and seized them—"an elegant dun mare, saddle, bridle, saddle-bags, and umbrella." This trick rankled deep in Brownlow's soul, and he never forgot it. He declared this trial and the subsequent proceedings to be an outrageous travesty on justice, the like of which had never disgraced the annals of mankind since the trial of William Penn at Old Bailey, excepting possibly the persecutions of John Wesley at Savannah, and of Lorenzo Dow at Charleston.[9]

Twenty years later the Parson took an inventory of the "wicked crew" who had done this deed to him, and to his great delight he found just what he expected: The judge had died "in a drunken fit of debauch"; Parson Posey had before his

---

[9] *Ibid.*, pp. 257, 259, 261, 269-72; J. P. Arthur, *Western North Carolina, A History;* MSS Archives of Macon County, Franklin, N. C.

earthly departure, turned into "a wretched and raving maniac"; one of the jurors "died, drunk in the woods"; another was serving a sentence in the penitentiary for store-breaking; another had fled the country to escape prosecution for forgery; and still another guilty of perjury was in hiding to escape just punishment. As for the remainder of these corrupt jurors, he had not heard from them for a time, "but the probability is, the Devil has those of them, who have departed this life, while the living ones are likely in some state prison!" Thus, had the Lord finally vindicated the name of one of His chief circuit-riding parsons.[10]

But unjust trials and court decisions could never stop Parson Brownlow or dampen his ardor for carrying Methodism to the people. The year 1833 became historic on account of a strange manifestation of nature so unusual that the tradition concerning it has lasted down to the present generation, even among the unlettered in the most out-of-the-way places. This was "the year the stars fell." This beautiful display of comets produced great excitement in the Southern Highlands and led the more curious to seek explanations. Some of the Baptists soon guessed that this had been a sign placed in the heavens to indicate the downfall of the Methodists, but one Hopkinsian lady had what she considered a more plausible explanation. She had heard that Parson Brownlow had died, and in some way had squeezed into heaven, and on his entry he had created such a disturbance that he was put out. But this ejection in being accomplished had jarred loose from their moorings all the stars which came tumbling headlong to earth.[11]

The Annual Conference in 1832 was held in Evensham, Virginia, presided over by Bishop John Emory. The Bishop shifted Brownlow slightly to the southeast to the Tugaloo Circuit, which lay mostly in Pickens District, South Carolina, but partly in Georgia. The Parson was soon convinced that he could do very little good here since the whole region was "overrun with Baptists." Nevertheless he was determined to try. He swam the

---

[10] *Knoxville Whig and Independent Journal,* July 5, 1851.
[11] Brownlow, *Helps to the Study of Presbyterianism,* pp. 276-77.

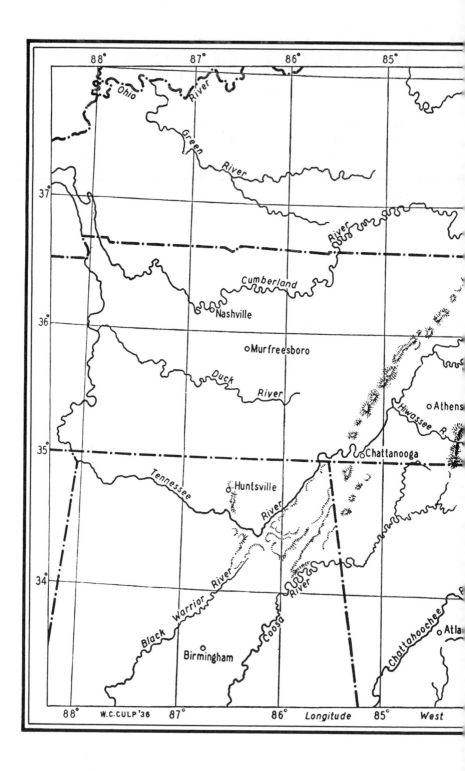

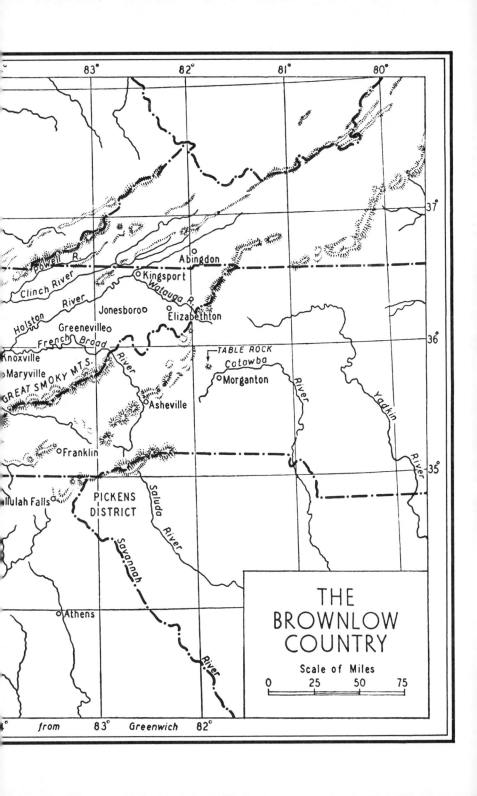

83°   82°   81°   80°

37°

Powell R.
Abingdon
Clinch River
Kingsport
Watauga R.
River
Holston
Jonesboro
Elizabethton
Greeneville
French Broad
36°
River
Knoxville
TABLE ROCK
Catawba
Maryville
GREAT SMOKY MTS.
Morganton
River
Asheville
Yadkin
River
Franklin
35°
Tallulah Falls
PICKENS
DISTRICT
Saluda River
Savannah
Athens
River

THE
BROWNLOW
COUNTRY

Scale of Miles
0   25   50   75

from   83°   Greenwich   82°

Tugaloo River four times in "the dead of winter" and preached
more than once with his wet clothes frozen stiff about him.
Once he was nearly swept over the shoals and "was in a squirrel's
jump of the good world." But over in the Georgia part of his
kingdom he saw something which delighted his nature-loving
soul; it was the "Telulee Falls."[12] Never had he "witnessed a
scene which struck my mind with such profound awe, and so
completely filled me with admiration of the infinite skill of the
great Architect of nature." It was the general report that they
were more grand than Niagara. He could scarcely describe the
effect they had upon him, but it seemed to him after looking at
them for a while that he felt a desire to reach the eternal world
to see the Maker of such a wonderful work of nature.[13]

While on the Tugaloo Circuit in Pickens and Anderson districts, Brownlow came as near the lowlands of the slaveholding
planters as he had ever before approached; he was on the verge
of running out of his beloved mountains. He would naturally
look with misgiving upon these aristocrats, but the time of his
arrival was most unpropitious for the planters. They were in
the midst of their Nullification Movement, and Brownlow immediately turned away with loathing detestation. He was a
Unionist; he had ridden the circuit in five states and had not
got out of the Holston Conference of the Methodist Church in
doing it. He loved all these states equally well, scarcely knowing
or caring when he passed from one into another. If South Carolina should successfully defy the United States Government
she might break up the Union and the Holston Conference with
it. He bitterly opposed this heresy, and years later declared
that the movement had been engineered by the descendants of
the Tories of the Revolution. He charged that more Tories
had lived in South Carolina "than in all the other States put
together." The Parson was not surprised to find that all the
Presbyterians and Baptists were Nullifiers and that they were
boldly announcing that Christ was a Nullifier. The insignia

---

[12] Nature was, indeed, in a grand mood at Tallulah Falls; but twentieth century Georgians, having more shriveled souls than the Parson, destroyed this
beautiful cataract, turning its wasted power into electricity.

[13] Brownlow, *Helps to the Study of Presbyterianism*, pp. 268-69.

of the Nullifiers was a blue cockade. To help along the cause the Parson aided some Unionists in pinning these cockades on the tails of the worthless curs of the neighborhood that they might carry high Nullification. Starved out by the Nullifiers, Brownlow was glad to retreat back into the Union-loving mountain region, but before going, according to his word, he took a parting shot at them in a pamphlet, for which, he claimed, they tried to hang him.[14]

The government of the Methodist Church provided for the governmental meetings known as "conferences"—(1) a quarterly conference in each district, (2) an annual conference in each regional division, which embraces a number of districts and which as a region is called a conference, and (3) a quadrennial conference embracing all the regional divisions, or conferences, in the whole United States. These meetings gave the ministers a chance to show themselves to their fellows, they gave more tone and respectability to the backwoods circuit riders, and they afforded a chance for the play of ambition for future preferment. It fell within Brownlow's easy reach to attend the quarterly and annual conferences, and through the very nature of his irrepressible self he became well-known at these meetings within the annual Holston Conference, and succeeded in getting this group to appoint him a delegate to the General Conference to meet in Philadelphia in 1832. Here was a glorious opportunity to see what the big world outside of Southern Appalachia looked like. The Conference no doubt thought that if Brownlow should ever become properly tamed he might develop into a mighty man in Methodism, whose influence would extend far beyond the Holston Conference. In doing this elongated mountaineer of only twenty-seven years so high an honor they sought indirectly to tame him, but at the same time they were direct and frank with him. They mildly condemned him for his caustic style of writing in the newspaper controversies he got into and for his wild and unbridled manner of opposing

---

[14] *Ibid.*, pp. 265-66; *Parson Brownlow's Book*, pp. 21-23. I have never been able to discover a copy of this pamphlet or to see a reference to it except in Brownlow's claim. According to the Parson his pamphlet contained 70 pages and was entitled, *Suffering of Union Men*. See *Portrait and Biography*, p. 44.

the other denominations. This condemnation was not made greater than the Parson could bear, for his very condemners were guilty more or less of the same offenses.[15]

In the spring of 1832 the Parson quit for a time his riding around in circles and set out on a bee line for Philadelphia, more than six hundred miles away. He started early enough to stop on the way, to see the sights. His first great objective was Washington. He spent a week at his country's capital, viewing the sprawling muddy town, and listening to the oratory of congressmen. Being quite an important man himself, he decided to pay a visit to Andrew Jackson, in the White House. Two Tennesseeans so far away from home ought to be mutually glad to see each other. Brownlow seemed to be duly impressed with the height of Jackson, and he thought perhaps for that reason that he was "a very fine looking old man"—but he left with the feeling that he could not quite approve of the President. The Parson, being a Whig in the making, had never voted for Jackson, so perforce he could never approve of such a person. Having turned his thumbs down on the first citizen of the land, Brownlow continued his journey on to Baltimore where he again busied himself looking at the sights. He was attracted by the penitentiary, and on seeing so many people who could not run away, he immediately asked permission to preach to them. He slyly contrived to get the report carried back to his enemies in Tennessee that he was in the penitentiary in Baltimore—a fate they had long been predicting and hoping for.

At last he arrived in Philadelphia where he spent the whole month of May. He likely found more sights here than at any other place he had visited, and without a doubt he himself was a sight for many of his more urbane brothers in Methodism. When not sitting with his own Conference or viewing other objects of interest, he slipped over to the Presbyterian Assembly, which happened to be meeting in the same city. Of course, nothing good could come from Presbyterians nor would looking at them and listening to them afford anything more than amuse-

---

[15] Price, *op. cit.,* III, 316, 318; *Journals of the General Conference of the Methodist Episcopal Church,* I, 362.

ment. He heard wrangles among them "which would, for intemperance of language and wholesale abuse of private character, absolutely disgrace the lowest porter house, or ale cellar, in the lowest place in the lowest town or city in the lowest country in the world." The Parson took an extremely inconspicuous part in his own Conference. There is no record in the minutes of his having introduced a motion or seconded one or even spoken a word. He was appointed on no committees. Perhaps Bishop Soule, who presided much of the time, had suppressed Brownlow —or could he possibly have been awed by this august body? His only accomplishment in the Conference, which he ever mentioned, and later regretted, was his aid in getting James O. Andrew elected bishop.[16]

After the Parson had seen Washington, Baltimore, and Philadelphia, it might well be guessed that his circuit-riding days would soon come to an end; and, indeed, he was destined to ride only three more circuits—the Dandridge, around the confluence of the Holston and French Broad rivers; the Scott, in Southwest Virginia; and the Elizabethton, in the extreme northeastern tip of Tennessee.[17]

Brownlow was coming to believe that he was important enough to be written about; his name had been heralded all over Southern Appalachia and even to far-away Philadelphia. He imagined that people must want to know more about himself, so in the absence of any biographers, he decided that he would write his own biography, though his scope of life had yet been less than thirty years. He entitled his work, *A Narrative of the Life, Travels, and Circumstances Incident Thereto, of William G. Brownlow.*[18] True enough this autobiography was an appendix to a larger work which he called *Helps to the Study of Presby-*

---

[16] Brownlow, *Helps to the Study of Presbyterianism*, pp. 262-64; *Irreligious Character of the Rebellion. An Address by Parson Brownlow. Delivered before the Young Men's Christian Association, at Cooper Institute, New York, May 19, 1862*, p. 28; *Journals of the General Conference of the Methodist Episcopal Church*, I, 362-423.

[17] For the record of Brownlow's itineracy see *Minutes of the Annual Conferences of the Methodist Episcopal Church for the Years 1829-1839*, I, 518, 519, 550; ibid., II, 12, 13, 52, 90, 133, 181, 234, 300, 366, 430. See also Brownlow, *Helps to the Study of Presbyterianism*, pp. 275-89.

[18] This work embraced 53 pages.

terianism or, an Unsophisticated Exposition of Calvinism, with Hopkinsian Modifications and Policy, with a View to a More Easy Interpretation of the Same. To Which is Added a Brief Account of the Author, Interspersed with Anecdotes. This work was printed for him by Frederick S. Heiskell, at Knoxville in 1834. The Parson was very frank with himself in his *Life.* Never having heard of psychoanalysis, he made no attempt to put himself through that process, but he was willing to state his case in the best manner of which he was capable. He listed the principal objections that had been urged against him as: his inconsistency of character, a quarrelsome nature, his style as a writer, talents as a preacher, and manners as a man, and a dislike by great numbers of people. He vigorously defended himself against every charge. As to his quarrelsome disposition, "I pretend not to be a candidate for the honors of martyrdom, yet, I should feel that I had gone down to my grave disgraced, did I not incur the censure and abuse of bloated bigotry, and priestly corruption." And, whether people liked him or not, he cared little: "I never professed to have a great deal of polish about me, nor do I desire to be polite." With a sort of a wounded feeling, he added, "I never thought I was a great man—I never desire to be what the world calls a great man." The Parson may have misread himself a slight bit here; his whole subsequent career was proof that he had a craving for power over people but perhaps, not so much for adulation as for vengeance.[19]

For a long time his wrath had been piling up against the Presbyterians. He had been dealing with the other wing of the Calvinistic forces, the Baptists, in a rough and tumble method; but the Presbyterians had been writing things against his religion, and he would now show them that there was at least one Methodist who could also write, and who would write without restraint if need be. One activity which he especially disliked was a publication called the *Calvinistic Magazine,* edited by James Gallaher, Frederick A. Ross, and David Nelson, who hurled this missile at the Methodist Church from their stronghold

---

[19] Brownlow, *Helps to the Study of Presbyterianism,* pp. 290-94.

in Rogersville, East Tennessee, in the midst of the Brownlow country. As they entered upon this undertaking the very first year the Parson began riding the circuit, doubtless he considered it a direct thrust at him and his work. They began their first number with the prayer of a crusader and closed it with a declaration of war against all who denied the doctrines of the Presbyterian Church. Warfare it would be, between truth and falsehood.

We are commanded to hold a controversy with the sinfulness of our hearts, and it is equally obligatory to contend against error wherever we find it. Written discussions, upon religious subjects, are never to be deprecated, for error has never progressed so rapidly, as when the watchmen upon the walls of Zion, remain silent and inactive. It will be said, controversy produces unchristian feelings, and that it brings before the public, the differences of those who worship the same Lord and follow the same Saviour. The first objection is strong, only, against those who attempt to find truth without asking for the holy aid of the Spirit of truth. The second objection is plausible, but deceitful, because, falsehood, in moral opinion, is sin, whether it is seen in the belief of an infidel or a christian. No man can reject the doctrines taught by Christ and his apostles and be guiltless.[20]

They quoted with approval the dictum of a contemporary, "The fact is, whatever progress the cause of truth and holiness has made in the world, has been made by controversy."[21]

This magazine carried on an offensive against the Methodists by ridicule and by all the other weapons it could command. In a skit entitled, "A Dialogue Between a Methodist and a Calvinist," the follower of John Wesley was demolished with ridicule and contempt.[22] Through four numbers in 1828 this magazine reviled and mocked the Methodists in "Dialogues on Church Government Between a Citizen and a Methodist Circuit-Rider."[23] The trinity of Presbyterian divines who edited this

---

[20] P. 31. The *Calvinistic Magazine* came out monthly.
[21] *Calvinistic Magazine,* vol. II, no. 10 (October, 1928), p. 298.
[22] Vol. I, no. 5 (May, 1827), pp. 145-49.
[23] Vol. II, nos. 4-7 (April-July, 1828).

magazine published the following as a typical verse in a Methodist songbook:

"The Devil, Calvin, and Tom Paine,
May hate the Methodists in vain;
Their doctrines shall be downward hurl'd—
The Methodists shall take the world."[24]

The wonder is that the Fighting Parson, as he was later to be called,[25] showed so much self-restraint and desisted so long from entering the fray. The Presbyterians had long been pestering him, and just to prove how contentious they were, he wrote for the *Newmarket Telegraph*, a Tennessee newspaper, an article proving there was a God; and according to the Parson, a Presbyterian immediately denied that eternal truth.[26] But now, in the year 1834, he resolved to buckle on the armor of the Lord and go out to do battle with the infidel Presbyterians and all other Calvinists. He had written his book, and in a style that many people might not like. As for his "exuberance and redundancy of language," he gladly admitted that they might "be justly considered one, among the many other *winning ways* I have to make folks hate me." He, too, believed in religious controversy—"had it not been for *controversy*, Romish Priests would now be feeding us with *Latin masses* and a *wafer god!*"[27]

Brownlow selected some of the principal Calvinistic doctrines and savagely attacked them. The ones to which he gave his particular attention were: that God decrees whatever comes to pass, that there is unconditional election and reprobation, that Christ died only for the elect, that there is irresistible grace to bring in the elect, and that it is impossible to fall from grace. To show how absurd and even sacrilegious these doctrines were, the Parson called attention to these two facts: that if God decrees all things, then he produces murders, lying, and sins of all kinds; and that if people are already saved or damned from the beginning, what good is there in preaching or carrying on missionary

---

[24] Vol. III, no. 12 (December, 1829), p. 383.
[25] George D. Prentice is said to have given Brownlow this title. *Putnam's Magazine,* vol. III, no. 16 (April, 1869), p. 528.
[26] Brownlow, *Helps to the Study of Presbyterianism,* p. 279.
[27] *Ibid.,* pp. xii, viii.

work?[28] If it be foreordained that certain people are to be saved, why baptize them; "they will be saved if they never see water, and die drunk in the bargain!"[29] In order to escape these hard and irresistible conclusions, many of the Presbyterians had run off into what came to be called Hopkinsianism, a name given to the doctrines promulgated by Samuel Hopkins, of Newport, Rhode Island, in order to soften and side-step some of the more severe tenets of Calvinism.[30]

But Brownlow was particularly interested in showing what a terrible threat the Presbyterian Church organization carried against the liberties and political institutions of the United States. He called attention to the fact that the Presbyterians and the New England Congregationalists were all of a feather in their general doctrines and ambitions, that during the War of 1812 New England had been pro-British and her ministers had preached disloyal sermons, and what was most ominous of all, that at one time New England had had a virtual union of church and state which bond the Presbyterians were now secretly praying to be restored throughout the nation. He greatly feared this Presbyterian plot, for if it succeeded they would soon be burning people as heretics. They were already referring to the regions where the Methodists were strongest as "great moral wastes." In his opinion, "There is indeed no bigotry so intolerable as religious bigotry, nor any hatred so unrelenting as religious hatred." He sounded the warning: "Let the Presbyterians once enslave us, as they are aiming to do, and we may whine, and scold, and murmur, and wince, and threaten, and beseech them to condescend, graciously to have mercy on us, but it will all be to no purpose."[31]

The Parson had not allied himself with the Jeffersonian school in politics and he had generally not looked to Thomas Jefferson for his ideas but he was in perfect agreement with the

---

[28] *Ibid.*, pp. 208-9.
[29] W. G. Brownlow, *The Great Iron Wheel Examined; or, Its False Spokes Extracted, and An Exhibition of Elder Graves, its Builder, in a Series of Chapters*, p. 173.
[30] *Ibid.*, p. 216. For the nature of this doctrine, see Nathan Bangs, *A History of the Methodist Episcopal Church*, III, 11-29.
[31] Brownlow, *Helps to the Study of Presbyterianism*, pp. vii, 94, 113-65, 167-76.

Sage of Monticello on the subject of Presbyterianism. He was delighted to find this paragraph in a letter Jefferson had written to William Short in 1820, and he quoted it with approval: "The Presbyterian clergy are the loudest; the most intolerant of all sects, the most tyrannical and ambitious; ready at the word of the lawgiver, if such a word could be now obtained, to put the torch to the pile, and to rekindle in this virgin hemisphere the flames in which their oracle Calvin consumed the poor Servetus. . . ."[32]

But Brownlow was not depending on Thomas Jefferson or on any other person for his proof of how wicked the Presbyterians were or of their insidious attempt to unite church and state, with themselves at the helm. A great many societies and organizations had been springing up with ostensible religious uplift programs, but the wary Parson knew too well that if one should dig deep enough it would soon be evident that Presbyterians were in charge of all of them, and that these organizations were gigantic tentacles to draw the people unaware into one great Presbyterian consolidation. There was the American Sunday School Union, generally referred to by Brownlow as the A. S. S. Union, which, according to reports, was non-denominational, but which Brownlow knew was controlled by the Presbyterians for the sneaking purpose of entering politics and winning elections. The American Tract Society was got up and controlled by the Presbyterians, though it claimed to have all the principal denominations represented in it. Brownlow knew this claim to be a subterfuge, for did not the Methodists have a tract society of their own? The American Bible Society was controlled by the Presbyterians. It claimed to be giving away Bibles, but Brownlow knew that the Presbyterians and their Calvinistic co-conspirators, the Baptists, were actually selling these Bibles and growing rich from plundering the poverty-stricken seekers after religion. He had charged as much against Parson Posey at Franklin, North Carolina, and the only reason he had not proved his charges was because a Baptist was the

[32] *Ibid.*, p. 179. This letter may be found in T. J. Randolph, ed., *Memoir, Correspondence, and Miscellanies, from the Papers of Thomas Jefferson*, IV, 322.

judge. No true Christian could object to the American Temperance Society, but Parson Brownlow predicted that the Presbyterians would soon control it, for they were "a set of infatuated fanatics." As for the Baptists, they were actually against temperance, but he explained that situation on the ground that they were "about a century behind the march of mind."[33]

The American Education Society was also under the domination of these self-seeking Presbyterians. Brownlow was not opposed to education, if it were not of the Calvinistic variety. "Ignorance," he declared, "never produced one item of felicity to any man; the opinions of the Roman Catholics and Baptists to the contrary notwithstanding." He believed the American Home Missionary Society was, perhaps, the most reprehensible and insidious of all these Presbyterian-controlled organizations. "And who are home missionaries?" queried the Parson. "Why, every one of these little college-bred chaps and theological scavengers, who are without regular salaries, or other means of support." He declared they went "prowling and skulking about through our country, . . . making proselytes and begging money. . . . And is not the bulk of their time spent," he asked, "in trying to invent new, and improved patent triggers, for their national gull-traps?"[34]

And as for the poor heathens in foreign lands, what person could think without a shudder of the millions worshiping stones and reptiles, of mothers casting their infants to alligators or sacrificing them on altars, of widows being burned upon the funeral pyres of their husbands, of fanatics being crushed under the wheels of vehicles bearing their idol gods? Yet the American Board of Commissioners for Foreign Missions, dominated by the Presbyterians, had made the business of saving souls so expensive that there was not enough money in all the world to finish the job. The Parson had demonstrated this truth by simple arithmetic. Under the caption, "The History and Mystery of a Certain Forty-one Dollars and Forty-four Cents," he ex-

---

[33] Brownlow, *Helps to the Study of Presbyterianism*, pp. 16-78, 86-95, 103-7.
[34] *Ibid.*, pp. 78-86, 95-98.

posed the secret of how the Presbyterians had raised this amount of money from a congregation with the promise that it should go to missions but with the result that the Calvinists kept it.[35]

By 1836, Parson Brownlow had served an even decade in the Methodist itineracy, and had worked harder and been more zealous and vociferous in promoting Methodism than any other circuit-rider in the Holston Conference. He had fought the Baptists, the Presbyterians, and the devil in the fastnesses of the mountains, in the courts of law, and in newspapers, pamphlets, and the printed book. He was now thirty-one, and might well begin to think about marrying. But if he should marry he must quit the circuit, for no circuit-rider could support a family from his earnings. Moreover the Church frowned on the itinerant marrying, and it had no objection to all of its ministers remaining single. But on that day when the Parson looked into the eyes of Eliza O'Brien, he knew he had met the first and only girl he was ever to love. He immediately laid siege to her with all the powers he could command, and according to Eliza, herself, "he was so earnest, persistent, and eloquent in his wooing, there was no resisting him." She also considered him a great man, for he had talent, he was more talked about than other preachers in the conference, and he always drew the largest crowds when he preached. The wedding took place on September 11, 1836, and what could be more appropriate for celebrating such an event than a camp-meeting. So it happened at the Turkeytown camp-grounds, in Carter County, in the heart of the mountains of East Tennessee. He now "located"[36] and in the course of time the Parson's family grew to the number of seven children—two boys, and five girls.[37]

---

[35] Ibid., pp. 98-103, 194-201.

[36] "The difference between travelling and local preachers and ministers, consists chiefly in the fact that the former give themselves wholly to the work of the ministry, while the latter pursue some secular calling in connection with the sacred office—the former might properly be called regular ministers, and the latter secular ministers." P. D. Gorrie, Episcopal Methodism, as It was, and is, p. 294.

[37] Price, op. cit., III, 315, 346; Temple, op. cit., p. 318; Parson Brownlow's Book, p. 18. Eliza O'Brien was born at Kingsport, Tennessee, September 25, 1819. When Brownlow retired from the circuit, the Holston Conference numbered about 18,000 white communicants and about 2,000 colored. Minutes of the Annual Conference of the Methodist Episcopal Church for the Years 1829-1839, II, 13.

CHAPTER III

PERSONAL JOURNALISM

PARSON BROWNLOW possessed not only a ready tongue, but also a quick pen, and while riding the circuit he had made much use of both. So now when he was about to settle down to preach, he found it advantageous to use the latter more. Methodist preachers who had located, still found that they were not considered worthy of their hire, since it was necessary to supplement the church allowance by any gainful employment they could find. The Parson soon decided to capitalize his pen, and what could be more lucrative than a newspaper, and, indeed, what could give the Parson a better outlet for what he thought? He now prepared to occupy himself with a business which was to grip him for almost all his remaining life. He would always be known as the Parson, and he never gave up his license to preach, but he should never again allow his usefulness to be hemmed in by the limits of a location or the confines of any circuit. He was not compromising with his conscience, for he could preach the Lord through his newspaper as well as from a pulpit.

It happened that he settled in Elizabethton, the seat of justice in Carter County, in the beautiful Watauga Valley of extreme northeastern Tennessee. So here, in this town of about 200 people, he began his first newspaper venture. Being a Whig, he called his journal the *Whig*, but expecting to become the mightiest journalist in Tennessee if not in the nation, he prefixed the distinguishing term *Tennessee*. As a concession to local pride, he used on the inside pages the running head *The Elizabethton Whig*. The first issue appeared on Thursday, May 16, 1839, with the slogan prominently displayed, "Life, Liberty and the Pursuit of Happiness." The Parson was a great believer in mottoes and in their use. He kept a large supply on hand, and selected from them a new one now and then, to keep step with his changing moods. By the time the issue of July 4 was due, pugnacity and patriotism had come so to control him that he threw away his less positive motto, and ran up the streamer of defiance, "Cry aloud and spare not."

The cost of the paper was to be two copies for five dollars a year, and the Parson would not be too fastidious as to what he would accept in payment: "Indeed, we had like to have said, that a well-executed counterfeit, on a solvent Bank would do, but we forbear, lest the 'democracy of numbers' should handle the proposition to our prejudice!" The purpose and policy of the paper, announced at the beginning, were to support Whig principles and to advocate the nomination and election of Henry Clay for president. The sub-treasury system and presidential despotism were the twin demons which the editor set out to attack; the times were serious, liberty was on the wane with the country ruled by the Democrats. Brownlow so far mistook his own mind and heart as to announce in the first issue that "religious controversies, village squabbles, neighborhood broils, and family feuds" would find no place in his paper. But the signs were unmistakable that he would be a fighter and that he would make the coves and valleys, the mountain tops and the plains, of all East, Middle, and West Tennessee resound with the din of battle. He was impatient to start: ". . . Let us get the *blast* on, as we have been several days *heating*, and we will cast our 'sayings and doings' before you, as fast, as hot, and thick, as ever darts flew in the Trojan War!"

It was an evil day for this little mountain town when Brownlow came here to live. It would have been as unnatural for the Fighting Parson to lead a quiet life as it would have been for him to turn Baptist. He soon had the village torn with strife. It was unfortunate from Brownlow's standpoint that here on the banks of the Watauga in 1816, Landon Carter Haynes, another self-willed man, was born. He had gone to Washington College and had graduated there the year Brownlow finished his circuit-riding. Now back again dividing his time between Jonesboro and his home town, he soon became convinced that he could never agree with the parson-journalist, as they differed from each other both in politics and in religion. Furthermore, Haynes considered himself a gentleman of ancient lineage who should try to keep away as much as possible from an interloper like Brownlow, who had perhaps crept out of a hollow log, and was now attempting to become a great man.[1] Others had come to agree with Haynes that Brownlow was an insufferable trouble-maker and a pest, and so it came about that someone whom Brownlow could never discover and history has never revealed attempted either to assassinate Brownlow or merely to scare him out of town.

On March 2, 1840, the Circuit Court was holding a session in Elizabethton, and as was the custom, there was a crowd in town and some rowdyism prevailed. On the evening of this day, between eight and nine o'clock, the Parson was sitting at a table in his home before a candle, writing. Suddenly a shot rang out, and two bullets whizzed by his head, one burying itself in the chimney-piece and the other, in the ceiling. The Parson immediately sprang to the door and, following the attacker across the garden, shot at him as he leaped through a gap in the garden fence. Brownlow had expected to be attacked but he thought "an attempt would be made to *mob* me—not to shoot me in this way." In preparing to repel the assault Brownlow secured the reënforcement of his friend, James W. Nelson, who now joined the Parson in his pursuit of the enemy, snapping his pistol at the culprit three times. But Nelson in his haste to follow had lost the cap from his pistol, and his onset was futile. Brownlow now openly charged Haynes with this attempted assassination. He secured a number of affidavits from his friends which seemed to cast suspicion on Haynes and a few years later he published them in his newspaper. The Parson's final verdict was that Haynes likely did not do the shooting but that he had had some hand in the sorry business. Haynes seemed little troubled by

---

[1] Haynes was born in Elizabethton, Tennessee in 1816 and died in Memphis in 1875. He studied law and became prominent in Tennessee politics. When the Confederacy was set up he became a Confederate Senator and continued to serve throughout the life of the government. He was a brilliant orator. Bob Taylor, the Tennessee governor of "Fiddle and Bow" fame was a nephew of Haynes.

Brownlow's charges, holding that the Parson was "the infamous perpetrator of an attempt at his own mock assassination." Brownlow had trumped up the whole story in an attempt to destroy Haynes or to win pity—"that he might once again command the commiseration and sympathies of the people."[2]

Whatever the truth concerning "the attempted assassination," it is an uncontested fact that the Parson was not scared out of town when he moved away from Elizabethton exactly a year after setting up his *Whig*, for he went to Jonesboro, in the adjoining County of Washington, where Haynes was entering into the business of a newspaper editor. He would here have better opportunities to come to close quarters with his enemy both fistically and journalistically. And he would be in a larger town. He now called his paper simply *The Whig*, adding *Jonesboro* about a year later. On the inside pages he gave the more lengthy title, *The Jonesboro Tennessee Whig*.[3] Having learned during his first year that running a newspaper would not likely be a peaceable business, he began his second volume with the threatening motto, "Unawed by power, unbribed by gain, the people shall be heard, and their rights vindicated." But he did not confine his warlike attitude to mottoes, for he made the plain statement, "The 'Whig' will be courteous and respectful to all who *behave themselves*, and who when speaking of it, or its editor, or patrons, keep within the bounds of moderation. Toward those who act otherwise, this paper will conduct itself as heretofore, *only more so*." In fact the Parson would be perfectly frank and admit that a perusal of the *Whig* would

perhaps, conduct any candid and dispassionate mind to the conclusion, that, in point of severity, and wholesale abuse of individuals, our paper is without a parallel in the history of the Ameri-

---

[2] W. G. Brownlow, *A Political Register, Setting Forth the Principles of the Whig and Locofoco Parties in the United States, with the Life and Public Services of Henry Clay. Also an Appendix Personal to the Author; and a General Index*, pp. 332-39 (Referred to hereafter as *Political Register*); *Jonesboro Whig*, February 8, 1843.

[3] Brownlow used both Jonesboro and Jonesborough indiscriminately. I use the former spelling, except in quoting or where it is otherwise necessary to depart from it.

can Press. The existence of this truth, in connection with this bold confession, however, finds an apology, in the fact, that it has been peculiarly our misfortune to have to encounter a disciplined corps, of the most obdurate sinners, and unprincipled scoundrels, that ever annoyed any community.[4]

Brownlow's stay in Jonesboro was to be tempestuous. In fact his very entrance into the village was signalized by a bloody fight. Haynes was the editor of the *Jonesboro Sentinel,* and he looked with no pleasure on competition in the newspaper business, especially from such a person as he considered Brownlow to be. Haynes being a gentleman, and being aware of it, cast some slurring remarks in his paper on the ancestry of the Parson. Brownlow interpreting this move as an insult to the memory of his mother, who had been dead a quarter of a century, prepared for battle. On May 14, 1840, the two met on the streets of Jonesboro, and a bloody fray ensued. Brownlow, who went armed with a pistol and a sword cane, sought to determine whether Haynes possessed a pistol, but the latter cleverly deceived the Parson. Not wanting to take advantage of an unarmed person, Brownlow seized Haynes and began beating him with his cane and then throwing his left arm around Haynes' neck he held his head down and began pounding him with his pistol butt. The exact order in which the fight proceeded seems never to have become straightened out by the various witnesses, but at some stage of the combat Haynes produced a pistol and shot the Parson through the thigh. Neither was injured seriously, but from then on Brownlow carried on a savage warfare in his *Whig* against the editor of the *Sentinel,* referring to him as the "prince of villains, hypocrites, and political prostitutes." He followed after Haynes to the minutest personalities, charging him with joining the Presbyterians in 1841 and the next year with getting converted at a camp-meeting and joining the Methodists, and lastly with getting a license to preach and then being deprived of his license two months later for "slander and falsehood." The Parson charged him with not only being a

---

[4] *Jonesboro Whig,* May 14, 1840.

turncoat in religion but a traitor to the Whigs, whom he had deserted for the Democrats in 1839.[5]

The next encounter that was of sufficient importance for the Parson to chronicle prominently in his *Whig* took place in the late summer of 1842 at a camp-meeting. This time his enemies with clubs executed an attack upon him from the rear. He wheeled around quickly, warding off some of the worst blows, and at the same time whipped out a derringer pistol which he fired point-blank at his chief assailant. Only the cap exploded; otherwise he would certainly have killed his attacker. The Parson admitted in the *Whig* that his enemies had given him a rather bad beating, but he still had much to be thankful for, for "out of the nine blows and wounds, I received, they failed to hit me on the *right* arm, the hand I use when I write out the history of rogues, perjured villains, stealers of TOLLS, of HOGS, and of all other *like* measures."[6]

It happened that Brownlow's conception of what should go into a newspaper fitted excellently into the situation, for he always had a great supply of just the things he wanted. He reveled in a fight, and he filled his paper with vituperation, abuse, and denunciation of his personal enemies close by, of his religious enemies not much farther away, and of his political enemies everywhere whom he knew to be scoundrels either because they were Democrats like Andrew Jackson or because they were turncoats and traitors like John Tyler. With Brownlow, journalism was peculiarly personal, for he, himself, was in the very midst of much of his news. He was fearless, and he had a highly developed feeling of personal rights. Hence he was quick to sense an insult and utterly reckless in following it up. In this manner he made a large amount of news for the *Whig*.

There can be no doubt that Brownlow's enemies gave him ample provocation, but his methods of retaliation were bound to aggravate rather than cure any controversy. In 1843 a quarrel broke out with J. M. Smith, who according to Brownlow, was "an infamous old blackguard, though a member of the

[5] *Ibid.*, May 20, 1840; Brownlow, *Political Register,* pp. 339-43; Price, *op. cit.,* III, 348 and V, 112.

[6] *Jonesboro Whig,* August 24, 1842; Price, *op. cit.,* III, 349.

Church to which I belong." It was, perhaps, true that the quarrel was started by the Parson's enemies for the purpose of provoking him to do something to such an excess that his Church would take away from him his license to preach. Knowing that Brownlow loved his Church and clung to his ministership as tenaciously as a child to a toy, they would thus attack him at a place where a victory would mean the most. Those who were not of the Brownlow camp, however, seemed to think there might have been another reason for Smith's charges. The Parson had sometime previously published what appeared to him to be a bit of news of the highest value and propriety, that Smith's son had broken into a store, stolen money, and then fled to the far West. Smith specifically charged that Brownlow, while attending the Whig Convention in Nashville in 1840, had stolen some jewelry and that an enraged mob had seized him, escorted him to the nearest cedar tree to which they tied him, and that they then proceeded to whip him until he turned over the stolen jewelry.[7]

This news, whether true or not, was highly important in the eyes of many newspaper editors—from Georgia to Massachusetts—for journalist Brownlow's fame had gone far. Four newspapers immediately published the good news. They were the *Jonesboro Sentinel*, the *Abingdon Virginian*, the *Boston Olive Branch*, and the *Sandersville* (Georgia) *Telescope*. Pounced upon here by two sets of enemies, Brownlow decided to deal with the editors first. To begin with, these four "infamous papers" were "conducted by convicted liars, expelled Methodist Preachers, thieves and debauchees." For his near neighbor the *Jonesboro Sentinel* he had the most vitriolic hate:

It is the most reckless sheet in the State; and those who are acquainted with its history, will agree with us, that it has, from first to last, been edited by more *broke down Preachers*, and lewd, lying, irresponsible men, than any other single sheet in existence. And yet, in point of depravity, a want of honor, and a total disregard for truth, its present Editor is a head and shoulders taller than any ruffian who has yet controlled its filthy columns.

---

[7] *Jonesboro Whig*, December 27, 1843; Brownlow, *Political Register*, pp. 323-24.

And the Parson hereby published him "to the world, with the evidence, as guilty of almost every crime known to the criminal laws of the country." As for the other three newspapers—the editor of the *Abingdon Virginian* was a renegade from the Methodist Church, who had spent a term in prison and who had "lived in adultery with a notorious woman, to the annoyance of a decent wife"; the editor of the *Boston Olive Branch* had been expelled from the Methodist Church for seduction; and the editor of the *Sandersville Telescope* was so depraved that the Parson hesitated to use language to describe him.[8]

Following out his old plan of defense the Parson secured from his Nashville acquaintances a bundle of recommendations, showing great surprise that anybody could ever have thought of such absurd charges as were presented by Smith. Armed with these documents he appeared before a meeting of the congregation, proved his innocence, and had Smith thrown out of the Church for lying. Smith defended himself by saying that if he could not prove the jewelry-stealing and whipping charges against Brownlow, he could prove other things just as bad, and he appealed from this decision to the Quarterly Conference. This conference met on December 5, 1843, and affirmed the decision of the first trial. Thus was the Parson vindicated and much news made for the *Jonesboro Whig*.[9]

Brownlow's newspaper ethics were very much more meagre than the average in a generation when editors' codes of honor were extremely short. When he began his paper, he promised to conduct it far above the plane of feuds and broils, but these promises he immediately forgot, never to be recalled again except as quickly to be broken. Scarcely two years had passed before his beloved Methodist Church in Quarterly Conference was trying him for printing violent and harsh things against the brethren. But there was never much danger of Brownlow not being able to control a quarterly conference. He was acquitted by a vote of 20 to 3. Quite often thereafter he was pestered by his enemies in these quarterly conference trials, but it had not

[8] *Jonesboro Whig,* December 27, 1843; Brownlow, *Political Register,* pp. 214, 323-24.
[9] *Jonesboro Whig,* December 27, 1843; Brownlow, *Political Register,* p. 325.

been to no purpose that he had ridden the circuit for ten years.[10]

In 1844, the Parson made a strange announcement in the *Whig*. On December 11th, he declared that he would print no further personalities in his newspaper. This sudden relapse into gentleness toward the enemy was not the result of the approaching Christmas times; it was because he needed the space for other purposes—and he would also make it plain that no one had advised him to take this course. But however honest he was in this announcement, he should have known the utter impossibility of his abiding by it—the leopard could not change its spots nor the Ethiopian the color of his skin. On New Year's Day, less than three weeks after this promise, Brownlow launched a savage attack against his most detested enemy, beginning, "Liar Culprit [Landon Carter] Haynes. This thrice convicted private and public debauchee and hypocrite . . .," and so on. Brownlow became so intolerable in the eyes of certain Jonesboro citizens that they contemplated treating him and his newspaper establishment after the fashion of the enraged Kentuckians, in Lexington, who had recently dealt with their insufferable Cassius Marcellus Clay and his anti-slavery *True American*, by sacking the newspaper office and shipping the type into another state.[11]

It has been sufficiently evident that Brownlow's mental acumen, nervous tension, and physical prowess existed in a highly developed degree; and as far as that part of the world which might desire to know may ever find out, all these qualities came through natural development. But in 1848, he suffered a clubbing, which throughout the remainder of his life left his health not only physically impaired, as he thought, but which also probably affected him mentally. Certainly, as time went on, he became more reckless as his power increased; perhaps, it was not due entirely to his natural bent—his assailant's club left permanent marks and impressions on his skull. The Parson's party had had little to do with the making of the Mexican War and had done even less by willing service in carrying it on, but

---

[10] *Jonesboro Whig*, September 1, 1841.

[11] *Ibid.*, September 17, 1845.

this situation did not blind him to the fact that if he could discover anyone whom he thought to be a deserter, he would thereby make some timely news for his *Whig*. In 1848, he developed such suspicions concerning a Jonesboro citizen and published the fact. The fellow retaliated in a true deserter fashion by waylaying the Parson in the darkness and striking him down with a hickory club. This put the Parson to bed for two weeks, and while thus helplessly confined, the miscreant pelted his house at midnight with a barrage of rocks.[12]

The report got abroad that the Parson had been killed in the encounter, and from the tone of the *Clarksville Jeffersonian*, the news was received among the newspaper editors generally with joy and relief. It said, "A gentleman who arrived here last night from East Tennessee, reports that the notorious parson Brownlow, was shot dead a few days since, by a soldier he had abused in his paper. Whether the report is true or not, it is very certain that he long since deserved this fate at the hands of hundreds he has vilely slandered."[13]

Amidst all his physical encounters and his journalistic scalpings at the hands of his fellow-editors, the Parson never forgot the work which he had originally set out to do and which had given him his title. He would never forget the Lord and the service he owed Him, neither would he ever forget that the terrible Baptists and Presbyterians should be exterminated. Therefore, the *Whig* devoted a considerable amount of space to religious contention, his first love. Baptism and the correct methods of administering it, would always be news as far as the *Whig* could judge, and the intelligence of the Methodists adding converts to their faith called for jubilation signs such as screaming eagles. The *Whig* carried the following block of news, sur-

---

[12] *The Jonesboro Monthly Review,* vol. II, no. 12, pp. 376-80; Price, *op. cit.,* III, 349. Browlow talked and wrote much about the war. He had a four-hour speech which he often delivered in which he condemned President Polk for having appointed Catholic army chaplains, and yet he called upon the people to enlist even though it was a Democratic war. He, himself, joined a company called the "Protestant Invincibles," but it never marched. See V. M. Queener, "William G. Brownlow as an Editor," *East Tennessee Historical Society Publications,* IV January, 1932), 78.

[13] *Knoxville Whig and Independent Journal,* May 19, 1849.

mounted by an eagle carrying in its mouth a streaming ribbon with the word *victory* written upon it: "We have just heard . . . of the perfect triumph of the Redeemer's Kingdom, at Stone Dam, in Greene County, over 'the world, the flesh and the devil'." One hundred converts were added to the Church.[14] As an aid in his fight against the Presbyterians, he set up a special magazine devoted almost entirely to one of their chief local representatives, Frederick A. Ross. He called this publication *The Jonesboro Quarterly Review*, and claimed that it was a religious review. The first issue appeared in 1847; the next year he made it into a monthly so that he might the better exterminate his great religious enemy Ross.[15]

Editor Brownlow did not give over his newspaper entirely to personal encounters, neighborhood broils, and religious disputations; he kept himself well informed on national politics, developing prejudices as keen and using language as cutting as in any of his other activities. When the Whigs in 1840, using expediency at the expense of principle, had nominated John Tyler as a running mate for "Old Tippecanoe" Harrison, they should have known they were foolishly laying up troubles for the future. The death of President Harrison one month after his inauguration, elevated Tyler to the presidency. Whig troubles began immediately, and the national administration was soon torn to pieces over the issues of the day. Brownlow, following the lead of his hero Henry Clay, soon opened up the vials of his wrath against traitor Tyler. Thus was he speaking of the President of the United States not more than six months after his accession: "*The Long-eared Virginia Ass*, who occupies the Presidential chair, has vetoed the bill incorporating the 'Fiscal Corporation of the United States,' otherwise a *National Bank*."[16]

Brownlow could never desert the Whig Party, but he felt that he should do some independent thinking. He would never be restrained even by the Whigs, especially when John Tyler was trying to run the party, so in 1842 he compromised with the

[14] *Jonesboro Whig*, September 28, 1842.
[15] This publication will be discussed further in Chapter IV.
[16] *Jonesboro Whig*, September 22, 1841.

name *Whig* in his newspaper title by adding *"and Independent Journal."* About this time he adopted a few new slogans, running them at conspicuous places in his paper. He padded a former motto and presented it thus, "Cry aloud—spare not; show my people their transgressions, and the house of Jacob their sins—Scripture." At the head of his editorial column he placed the banner, "Be just and fear not."

The Parson had ridden the circuit throughout the Southern Highlands for ten years, then he had become an editor and in two little mountain towns had conducted a newspaper for ten years in an amazing fashion. This brought him down to 1849 and to a stage in life when he thought another change was necessary. He was not leaving the newspaper business; he would merely leave Jonesboro. He loved the mountains and would never desert them, but Jonesboro was too far up the creek. He decided to move down to Knoxville, on the Holston River, made so deep by the waters of the French Broad that steamers could navigate it. Here was the metropolis of the Southern Highlands, a town of almost 4,000 population, the center of Highland culture and education. Brownlow had been growing in importance in the world, his *Whig* had been quoted throughout the nation, it should not hereafter be necessary to search the map for the town in which it was being published. It was with dread that many of the élite of Knoxville and the newspaper editors heard of Brownlow's coming, and well might they have been disturbed, for here he was to spend the rest of his days, and for the next quarter of a century so to order his coming and his going as to make his name a by-word throughout the nation.

On April 19, 1849, the *Jonesboro Whig* ran through the printer's press for the last time. Exactly one month later there appeared on the streets of Knoxville Brownlow's *Knoxville Whig and Independent Journal;* and immediately a newspaper war began whose devastating effects soon made themselves felt in almost every detail of the city's life. He continued to bespeak his mind in his little mottoes. To his Jonesboro slogans he added "Willing to praise but not afraid to blame"; and by 1853 he

announced another article of faith, "Independent in all things
—Neutral in nothing." At this time the Whig Party was showing signs of disintegration, and the Parson was, no doubt, in
this sentiment making easy the road for his escape from the
catastrophe. Stephen A. Douglas, the "Little Giant" from Illinois, put through his Kansas-Nebraska bill in 1854, and thereby demolished the party that had sheltered Brownlow from his
youth. As the Know Nothings were now appearing on the horizon, the Fighting Parson cleared the decks of all outworn mottoes, and preparatory to joining them in an assault upon the
foreign enemy and the Catholics, ran up to the masthead the
banner, "Put none on guard but Americans."

But Brownlow had enemies in Knoxville long before he had
discovered the foreign foe, and he began fighting them on almost
the very day he arrived. Many citizens had deeply resented
Brownlow's removal to Knoxville, and the more bold ones determined to take the initiative and drive him out before he
could secure a foothold. Even Whigs and Methodists joined
in the campaign, and eight years after his entry into Knoxville
he openly admitted that he had not got the sympathy and support that he considered his due.[17] The two principal newspapers,
the *Register* and the *Sentinel*, Whig and Democratic respectively, welcomed him with a fusillade of indictments new and old.
There was undoubtedly some lack of sportsmanship in this, for
knowing that they could never hope to attain the publicity and
circulation that came through vituperative language and wholesale abuse, which Brownlow could so effectively employ, they
feared his competition. The personal abuse that filled up these
three papers came near wrecking the respectability of the Knoxville press. There was no possibility of the *Register* and the
Sentinel coping with Brownlow in the utter devastation that
could be wrought through the use of words; so before he had
been in Knoxville scarcely six months there was a cry to adjourn
personalities. But the Fighting Parson refused to enter into

---

[17] *Knoxville Whig,* July 18, 1857 (This short form is used in footnotes throughout this book.)

such an agreement. He claimed that he had not started the fight, and that if it was to be stopped the enemy must first quit attacking him.[18]

On December 15, 1849, the *Whig* appeared on a small sheet of four columns, printed on only one side; the regular issue consisted of four pages, with seven columns to the page. The Parson in explaining this abbreviated edition, declared that a mob had attempted to destroy his printing office and presses, and that he was able to snatch from defending himself time sufficient only for the four columns. His enemies and rivals declared that this was only another typical Brownlow trick, that no attack had been made on his printing plant and that none had ever been contemplated. The Parson was merely looking for sympathy.[19]

The old charges of stealing jewelry and being flogged for it in Nashville in 1840 were revived against Brownlow, and the Knoxville press was filled with personal indictments and abuse *ad nauseam*. Landon C. Haynes was soon back in the fight with each abusing the other and charging him with crime. Brownlow again accused Haynes of shooting at him in Jonesboro a decade previously, and Haynes declared that his assassination had been plotted by Brownlow through the latter's brother, and that Brownlow's brother had admitted it. In 1851, Brownlow declared that for the past two years his enemies had been contriving his destruction in every way imaginable, by assassination, by wrecking his paper, and by tampering with his labor force. At times, single-handed and even when sick, he had defended himself against the whole horde—but he explained his preservation by covertly charging cowardice against them: "They could not find us while they were enraged, and had no disposition to kill when they got in a good humor."[20]

Another enemy whom the Parson long and bitterly hated, threatened, and fought was William S. Swan, who with John Mitchell, the exiled "Irish Patriot," had set up in Knoxville a

---

[18] *Knoxville Whig*, June, 1849, December 22, 1849, July 5, 1851. Brownlow's most bitter newspaper enemy in Knoxville was Miller McKee, the editor of the *Register*.

[19] *Knoxville Whig*, December 15, 29, 1849.

[20] *Ibid.*, July 5, 1851.

newspaper called the *Southern Citizen*. For reasons good and sufficient in the Parson's eyes, he appeared before Judge Swan's home, and armed with a six-shooter, paced back and forth denouncing him.[21] There was considerable rejoicing in the camps of the enemy when someone discovered a lottery advertisement in the Parson's paper and procured an indictment against him. Unknown to the Parson there was an old Tennessee law against the publication of such material, but before a conclusion had been reached in the proceedings, the legislature repealed the law, the indictment was dismissed, and he escaped his enemies again. He declared that the *Register* was responsible for this persecution.[22]

That the standards of journalism were no higher could certainly be laid largely at the Parson's door, yet he was not solely responsible. The enemy editors were not deterred by standards when they thought they might get an advantage over him. It unfortunately happened that one of the Parson's sons, in school at Emory and Henry College, in Southwest Virginia, in a fight with a schoolmate, killed him. The young student was indicted and held under a $1,000 bail for trial. Such happenings were legitimate news, however devastating to the feelings of kinsmen their publication might be. Enemy editors here had an excellent opportunity to make some stinging thrusts at the self-righteous Parson. That they did so can hardly be doubted for very soon Brownlow was calling them liars, thieves, and assassins of character. But he was soon able to rejoice again, for his son was acquitted.[23]

With all his other exaggerated characteristics, Brownlow had a vast store of determination and stubbornness. He was absolutely abnormal in his utter lack of fear, either physical or mental. It is, perhaps, no great compliment to his generation to say that these attributes made it impossible for a person to fail. Certain it was that Brownlow soon became the greatest journalistic force in Knoxville, and he drew constant attention to his *Whig* throughout the South, and as a matter of fact was

[21] Temple, *op. cit.*, pp. 273-76; Price, *op. cit.*, III, 350.
[22] *Knoxville Whig*, December 1, 1849; Temple, *op. cit.*, p. 276.
[23] *Knoxville Whig*, March 3, April 21, 1860.

4

by no means unknown in the North. Brownlow's *Knoxville Whig and Independent Journal* had one of the largest circulations of any newspaper in the Southern States. When he went to Knoxville in 1849 he had about 2,000 subscribers; in 1861, he had 10,700. His utter abandon in style made the paper readable; readability brought large circulation; ten thousand subscribers made it an effective advertising medium, and all these things conspired together to produce an income for the Parson of $10,000 yearly.[24] In 1859 he reached out for that class of people who read little either because they thought it was a waste of time or because their low intelligence gave them little inclination; he set up the *Tri-Weekly Whig*, issuing the first number on January 4.

Editor Brownlow, when he first entered the newspaper business in Elizabethton, had facetiously offered to accept a "well-executed counterfeit" in payment for subscriptions; when he had graduated up to Knoxville he was still willing to accept iron, flour, wood, and other miscellaneous goods. In promoting his paper, he was not afraid to indulge in self-praise. He declared that the *Whig* was "superior as an Advertising medium to any other paper"; he also admitted that "we make up the best newspaper in circulation, in these ends of the earth."[25] His ideas of honesty were so highly developed that he could not with equanimity see people subscribe for his paper and never pay for it. These "equivocal gentry" he soon lost patience with, and then he began publishing the names of those who owed him, under the title of "Black Knights." Now and then his patience with them became so exhausted that he threatened to sue them for debt.[26]

As has appeared, the Parson's style was amazing, and much of his journalistic success was due to this fact. He had an extravagance of expression and a sharp cutting diatribe which reckoned little the limits of good taste and tact. His language had a wild earthy flavor which it might be thought only the most rugged and inaccessible parts of the Southern Highlands

[24] Price, *op. cit.*, III, 320.
[25] *Knoxville Whig*, May 19, 1849, July 21, 1855.
[26] *Jonesboro Whig*, December 1, 1841, March 23, 1842, November 24, 1847.

could have produced, a language as impervious to outside polish and associations as his will was unbending in the face of the enemy. The primitive frontier in which the Parson grew up receded, but his style of language remained immutable. The frontier soon outgrew the barbarity of physical gouging, but the Parson never gave up his literary gouging. He was so impetuous and fiery that he overstepped his rugged honesty without always knowing it. He often contradicted himself and frequently dealt in inconsistencies. He was as unrestrained in his language as the mechanism of warfare was on the battlefield, and no doubt, when he realized his contradictions, he argued with his conscience that everything was fair in a fight. He was often sued for libel, but he generally slipped through the meshes of the law either by reasoning cleverly or by playing on the sympathy of the jury.[27]

In all the vehemence and indignation that the Parson could so easily express, there was some reason to think that there was present a slight element of the comic-opera—and that the Parson himself dimly realized it at times. For he had a sense of humor which his ponderous pugnacity, indomitable will, and self-righteous intolerance could never quite smother out. Like Abraham Lincoln he was not afraid to admit that he was ugly, and he was even willing to joke about it. Brownlow received a letter purporting to come from Esopian Hall, Devil's Fork of Little Red River, Arkansas, which carried the salutation "Deformed Sir" and which notified him that he had been unanimously elected to membership in the Ugly Club of the Hard Favored Fraternity. In answer the Parson denied that he was eligible, for "We are a rather good looking man than otherwise, and especially when we have our Sunday clothes on." In recommending the work of a friend who made daguerreotypes, the Parson declared "He has copied our *beautiful* face, to a gnat's heel."[28]

He had various little idiosyncracies and tricks of style which he constantly used to draw attention to his paper. A catch-

---

[27] *Ibid.*, September 30, 1846; *Knoxville Whig*, March 6, 1858.
[28] *Jonesboro Whig*, November 24, 1847.

phrase which he frequently used was "Stick a pin down here."
When in vigorous pursuit of the enemy he would often say,
"We are after them with a sharp stick, and no mistake." A
favorite characteristic of his in a diatribe was to begin each
paragraph with the expression, "Keep it before the people."

The great sectional struggle beat down upon the country,
setting up a vast disturbance, and the Parson was soon left hopelessly behind the times. Brownlow's *Knoxville Whig and Independent Journal* made its last appearance on October 24, 1861,
and everybody except the Parson marvelled that the Confederate authorities had permitted it to continue so long. But this
story is one of politics more than of journalism. War came and
swept the Parson out of his Highlands, but the receding tide
left him where it had found him. And the first thing he did on
his return was to set up his newspaper again, but that was in
another age and it must bide its time.

CHAPTER IV

RELIGIOUS WARFARE RENEWED

WHEN PARSON BROWNLOW turned journalist, he had no intentions of giving up his interest in the promotion of Methodism and least of all did he expect to forego that great pleasure of religious disputation. As has heretofore appeared, he gave over a considerable portion of his *Whig*, whether at Elizabethton, at Jonesboro, or at Knoxville, to quarrels with the enemy churches and to news of the Methodists. For certain periods he dedicated a special column or corner of his paper to some particular religious leader who happened to be his greatest enemy at the time. As the Baptists and Presbyterians were his chief antagonists, it turned out that a representative from each of these denominations began a combat with the Methodists and before the contest was over, each was forced to do battle against the Parson. The two clerical gladiators who crossed swords with Brownlow and who led him into the two most bitter religious contests he ever waged were Frederick A. Ross and J. R. Graves, Presbyterian and Baptist respectively. Warfare with Ross broke out first.

The Presbyterians were the best educated church on the frontier and perhaps it was for this reason that this denomination was devastated with more internal quarrels of a cataclysmic nature than were the other chief religious groups. Early in the century it lost its New Light wing and then soon thereafter the Cumberland Presbyterians split off. Next came the Campbellite or Christian Church, which did not follow a direct schism in the Presbyterian Church but which a former Presbyterian minister largely organized, and which thereby militated considerably against the Presbyterians. And then by 1840 the rock on which the old Church sat was split in twain, and out of it came the Old School and the New School. So it appears that to quarrel was a natural proclivity of the Presbyterians, and when they found no family matter to dispute over, they began to attack the barbarian Methodists. In 1829, they started publishing *The Pedobaptist* in Danville, Kentucky, and every month religious disputation ran through its columns, especially on the subject of infant baptism, which they strongly upheld. The next year *The Presbyterian Advocate* sprang up in Lexington and carried on a very particular quarrel with the Methodists. The Campbellites were born in controversy and grew up making quarrels. Their *Millenial Harbinger* was started in 1830 at Bethany, Virginia by their chief leader Alexander Campbell. But not all the Presbyterians thrived on controversy; in Columbia, South Carolina in 1847 they started the *Southern Presbyterian Review*, a quarterly, which was dignified and scholarly and which bespoke a directive power and a clientèle of culture. Of like dignity was a publication begun in 1855 and edited by Stuart Robinson and Thomas E. Peck of Baltimore, called *The Presbyterian Critic*.

But in East Tennessee people lived more vigorously than in any other part of the South, and they fought more desperately, both religiously and otherwise. Whether the champion represented the Presbyterians or Baptists or Methodists, he would likely become so reckless before the fight was over that he would find himself disowned by certain ones of his own brethren who lived in less belligerent regions. The Presbyterian terror who roused Brownlow to a greater boldness and rashness than any other religionist ever succeeded in doing was Frederick Augustus Ross. Ross was born at Cobham, Maryland, on Christmas day, in 1796. His father was a wealthy landowner, and on his death the son came to East Tennessee to look after some of the property. Here he became a gay irreligious dandy, building a handsome home at Rotherwood, near Kingsport, where his lavish entertainment became famous. Now and then he went to church either out of curiosity or for company, and by accident he was converted by the Presbyterians in 1823. Two years later he became an evangelist and made his home at Kingsport, where he preached for the next quarter of a century.[1]

---

[1] Alexander, *op. cit.,* pp. 120-22.

As has been previously noted, he was one of three who began the *Calvinistic Magazine* at Rogersville, two years after he began preaching. He dedicated the first number to controversy and soon had declared war on the Methodists, because this denomination was charging the Presbyterians with a plot to unite church and state. The Holston Conference had retaliated by setting up the *Messenger*. The *Calvinistic Magazine* ran for five years and then gave up the fight, having defeated the Methodists according to Ross. About this time the Eleven Years' War broke out inside the Presbyterian Church. This resulted in the Old School and New School divisions, and while this civil war was in progress, the enemy outside the gates were allowed to rest. But in January, 1846, the *Calvinistic Magazine* was revived on the grounds that the Methodists had renewed hostilities, especially in their *Episcopalian*, published at Knoxville. Ross was aided by Isaac Anderson, James King, and James McChain, and the publication was now issued from Abingdon, Virginia.[2]

Ross started a major offensive immediately. In 1846, besides reviving the *Calvinistic Magazine*, he wrote a book which was published in Philadelphia, entitled *The Doctrine of the Direct Witness of the Spirit, as Taught by the Rev. John Wesley, Shown to be Unscriptural, False, Fanatical, and of Mischievous Tendency*. A great amount of disputing went on over the simple doctrinal point that God's spirit and the individual's spirit bear witness to the latter that he is a child of God. These foolish zealots attempted to tear each other to pieces over impractical metaphysical distinctions while needy neighbors might freeze in the winter or die of starvation—but thus did they gratify their pugnacity and fight the battles of the Lord.[3]

Having announced his offensive with this piece of heavy artillery, Ross laid down a barrage with lighter guns. In the eleventh number of the first volume of his *Calvinistic Magazine*

---

[2] *Calvinistic Magazine* (new series), vol. II, no. 1 (January, 1847), pp. 21-46. This publication later became the *Presbyterian Witness,* a weekly paper published at Knoxville. The last issue of the *Magazine* was vol. V, no. 12 (December, 1850).

[3] Brownlow, *The Great Iron Wheel Examined,* pp. 112-40.

he began a series of articles which he called "The Great Iron Wheel" and which continued intermittently through eight numbers, lasting from November, 1846 to April, 1850. These articles made up a consistent and sustained attack on Methodism, from almost every imaginable angle but emphatically on the despotism of the Methodist form of church government. It was a great iron wheel which would run down and crush the liberties of America. He declared the Methodist Church was, therefore, a menace to the country and ought to be put down by the sword. Furthermore, Methodists voted only for candidates for public office who were followers of John Wesley. Methodists could not be patriots for they were largely descended from the Tories of the American Revolution, made so by the teachings of John Wesley, the greatest of English Tories.[4]

Having been Tories in the Revolution, they were now naturally of the lower classes, "the wool hats and coperas-breeches gentry," who in camp-meetings whipped up the unsuspecting hearers to such a pitch of madness that they joined the Methodist Church. They had their "amen corners" and their "anxious seats," and they went through the barbaric custom of "shouting" like red Indians. All of this great excitement and display was worked up not only to secure new members but also to make the old ones forget that they had lost their liberties. In fact, according to Ross, camp-meetings were highly vulgar and often downright immoral.[5]

Not only was the Methodist Church tyrannical in government and unattractive in membership, but its doctrines were worse. Wesley, its high priest and founder, believed in witches, spooks, signs, and omens, and naturally all Methodists believed likewise. Methodism was a "debauched pietism, in which the imagination has run wild, and passion, bodily sympathy, and mysticism are supreme, while true moral character is subordinate and degraded."[6] The Methodist band and class-meetings were so

---

[4] *Calvinistic Magazine*, vol. III, no. 2 (February, 1848), p. 62; no. 12 (December, 1848), p. 361; *Jonesboro Monthly Review*, vol. II, no. 1, p. 15.

[5] *Calvinistic Magazine*, vol. II, no. 1 (January, 1828), pp. 9-12; Price, *op cit.*, IV, 24.

[6] *Calvinistic Magazine* for August, 1846, quoted in Brownlow, *Great Iron Wheel Examined*, p. 139.

coarse and vulgar, that Ross declared he found it necessary to print in Latin the questions asked. The Reverend Mr. Ross in the early part of the fight declared that he had routed the Methodists and subdued their proud spirit—that they "walk softly, in flannel socks, before Presbyterians in Abingdon, Jonesboro, Greeneville, Rogersville, Kingsport, Athens and Knoxville!"[7]

Ross not only wrote against the Methodists, but he preached against them also. He had a special address known as the "Turnpike Sermon" which he dedicated to the Methodists and used against them on numerous occasions. The followers of Wesley might have excused the Presbyterians of blame for the wild and intemperate charges made by Ross had not certain of the synods endorsed this warrior and his "Iron Wheel." [8]

Some Methodists would ignore Ross, but others believed to do so would be to admit his calumnies and to acquiesce in their endorsement by organized groups of the Presbyterian Church. Francis Hodgson immediately set about writing a book in answer, which he called *The Great Iron Wheel Reviewed: or, A Defense of the Methodist E. Church Against the Caluminous Assaults of Rev. F. A. Ross and Rev. A. Converse, D.D.* Ross and his henchmen could now be considered answered, book for book, but the pounding effects of periodicals like the *Calvinistic Magazine* must be met and returned. The Methodist *Episcopalian* in Knoxville carried on, and after its demise, its successor the *Holston Christian Advocate* struck many licks. Down in Georgia, Russel Reneau fortified one of the hills at Rome, set up the *Armenian Magazine*, in January, 1848, and answered Ross blow for blow.

But where was the Fighting Parson? It would be unthinkable to have such an attractive religious war going on with the Parson absent. No one in East Tennessee, in the Southern Highlands, or in all America could surpass the Parson in the extreme abandon with which he could use sharp cutting words and vulgar

---

[7] Quoted in *Jonesboro Quarterly Review*, vol. I, no. 1 (June, 1847), p. 24.

[8] Among those endorsing Ross was the Athens Synod, in southeast Tennessee. Brownlow, *Great Iron Wheel Examined*, p. 104; *Jonesboro Quarterly Review*, vol. I, no. 4 (October, 1847).

phrases and innuendos. Some of the Methodists were already trying to answer Ross but not according to the Parson's style or ability, and others who were to come later in the fight were never able to equal him. On May 12, 1847, Brownlow announced in the *Jonesboro Whig* that he was preparing to declare war on Ross for his attacks on the Methodist Church, and he claimed that this degenerate Presbyterian deserved capital punishment "for his wanton assaults on the dead body of JOHN WESLEY." The Parson was going to set up the *Jonesboro Quarterly Review* and he announced that "if he does not make Mr. Ross sick of his wicked and uncalled for assaults upon the Methodists, and his friends sorry for him, in one short year, he will agree to quit all controversy, in all time to come."

The first issue appeared in June, 1847, and though the Parson held it up as a religious publication, he also let it be known that this periodical was designed definitely against Frederick A. Ross. He was entering a rough and ugly war with Ross, and he would not consciously swerve away by any attempts to be nice and polite. In fact the Methodists already had a publication which was answering Ross in that fashion, but it could not use Brownlow's methods, for it went into the homes of refined people who "would be disgraced, were it to lay hold of Ross and his extremely vulgar charges, and hold them up to the public gaze." Hence the necessity of the Parson's *Review* to deal out justice to a man "whose insolence, insults, and unmitigated villainy ought no longer to be tolerated." Some of his friends had suggested that it be a monthly but he disagreed, for "*one* such publication every three months, will be as much as mortal man can bear!"[9] But once in the heat of battle the Parson changed his mind, and quickly bringing his first volume to an end within less than six months, he began the *Jonesboro Monthly Review* in December, 1847. He bound the first volume and made a repulsive caricature of Ross the frontispiece, stating that he was preserving the review in this fashion for posterity "when I am dead and gone," that they might know the charges he had brought against Ross.

---

[9] *Jonesboro Quarterly Review,* vol. I, no. 1 (June, 1847), pp. 4, 39.

In beginning the monthly, he promised that it "shall be less *smutty* than our Quarterly has been, having disposed of the *obscene* items necessary to be noticed." Yet, he promised, it would be severe. Ross had announced that he had enough ammunition to continue the war another twelve months against the Methodists. Brownlow replied that he had enough munitions "for a *twelve years war*, and promised, to serve 'during the war,' making new and extraordinary disclosures every month!" He reported in early 1848 that he had already 1,200 subscribers.[10]

Through his *Review*, quarterly and monthly, the Parson printed such scurrilous charges in such open and direct language as would have led in another age to prosecution of the editor and denial of the publication's rights to the mails. The Parson issued this declaration of war in the first number, "War he would have, and now that war exists by his own acts alone—he shall have it to his heart's content. No misteries [*sic*], no secret plots, no private relations, or domestic delicacies connected with his past and present history, which shall not be brought to light, before we are done with him."[11] Some of the Methodists had made the mistake of treating Ross as a "dignified Christian minister"; Brownlow would make no such mistake: "I take the slanderer by the throat, and drag him forth from his hiding-place, and shake him naked over hell, in all his deformity!"[12]

Ross was "a low-bred, false-hearted, adulterous, and unprincipled free negro";[13] he was a "ruffian by birth and instinct — a practical amalgamator—and habitual adulterer—a loathesome blackguard—a notorious libeller—a common liar—the son of an old Revolutionary Tory—the degraded offspring of a Negro wench. . . ."[14] "His admirers shall know, that there are better men in *Hell* than he is! He shall be shown up—*he shall*."[15]

If the Reverend Mr. Ross wanted to deny these charges, let him prosecute the Parson in the courts for libel, for Brownlow

---

[10] *Ibid.*, no. 4 (October, 1847), p. 175; *Jonesboro Monthly Review,* vol. II, no. 2, p. 123; *Jonesboro Whig,* November 24, 1847.

[11] *Jonesboro Quarterly Review,* vol. I, no. 1 (June, 1847), p. 5.

[12] Brownlow, *Great Iron Wheel Examined,* p. 108.

[13] *Ibid.*, p. 131.

[14] *Jonesboro Monthly Review,* vol. II, no. 1, p. 67.

[15] *Jonesboro Quarterly Review,* vol. I, no. 1 (June, 1847), p. 39.

gave warning he would "rake, pound and pummel" him.

Brownlow pressed his charges regarding the ancestry of Ross, both as to Tory and African antecedents, and he often referred to him as "Frederick Africanus Ross." He charged that David Ross had begat Frederick through a Negro slave belonging to Governor John Page of Virginia, and that he had secretly bought her and set her free; but this did not make F. A. Ross a free man. He quoted the Virginia law concerning Negro preachers, called forth by Nat Turner's Insurrection in 1832, and declared that if the law were enforced Ross would receive thirty-nine lashes for preaching. The Parson now and then slackened his fire sufficiently to deal in the supposedly more gentle art of poetry:

> "Lay it on him, Billy Brownlow,
> He gives you *cause* enough,
> You've got 'de nigger' down low,
> And treat him mighty rough."[16]

The Parson having touched the depths of scurrility in his war against Ross, then resorted to a method of attack which he had employed before and would use again; he set out in pursuit of Ross' kin. A brother had cut open a pair of saddlebags and "stole therefrom six thousand dollars"; his father, besides being a Scotch Tory, had "died as he had lived, a debauched old thief"; a niece had run away with a married man and the two were then "living together as man and wife"; a nephew had left his wife and child, eloped with a base woman, and was then living in the far West; another brother had committed suicide; and his son had at a camp-meeting been guilty of immodesty so gross that the Parson would not fully describe it. This charge led the son to threaten to shoot the Parson on sight. In retaliation the Parson devoted two pages of his *Quarterly* to young Davy Ross, and while disclaiming any intention of pushing the combat with either father or son, he announced the warning,

---

[16] *Ibid.,* no. 2 (July, 1847), pp. 73-76; no. 3 (September, 1847), p. 100; *Jonesboro Monthly Review,* vol. II, no. 1, pp. 44, 47; Brownlow, *Great Iron Wheel Examined,* pp. 146-51. He even charged Ross with consorting with the hired girl. *Jonesboro Quarterly Review,* vol. I, no. 2 (July, 1847), pp. 58-61.

"Let either of them, or any of the breed, *dare* move toward us, with a view to assault us!"[17]

Thus again did the Parson fight the battles of his Lord and of his Church. But this deluded crusader, perhaps, deserves more pity than blame, for he lived in an age which produced many other such figures who tried to be just as earnest as the Parson but who were less able and therefore not so successful. To those Methodists of his own generation who thought that he had lost his balance and that he had passed beyond the stages of good taste, he replied, "What! write lovingly about one who calls us all hypocrites—usurpers of man's rights—robbers of men's privileges and prosperity—*tyrants* in government—persecutors of the innocent—*slanderers* of others—*popes—friars —inquisitors—adulterers—slaves—vassals—dupes—fools!* As soon would heaven form an alliance with hell, as for Methodists to have Christian fellowship for those who have thus accused them!"[18]

Parson Brownlow not only thundered out defiance against Ross in his *Review*, and not only set aside in the *Jonesboro Whig* an "F. A. Ross Corner," but he took to the dusty road, and like Peter the Hermit, preached a crusade against this calumniator of Methodism. He devoted much of the summer of 1847 to this sacred duty of carrying the war up and down the Southern Highlands from Knoxville to Abingdon, Virginia. Each day he spoke "three long hours and upwards," taking off "the mortal covering of the darkest subject ever discussed"; and he announced that all "who consider it *Sabbath breaking* to attend, are respectfully, but *earnestly* urged to remain at home, and read the '*Calvinistic Magazine*'."[19] At Abingdon he talked to more than 1,000 people "for more than four dreadful hours,"[20] and in an outburst of zeal nothing short of fanatical, he travelled in the course of four days 100 miles, talking at the top of his voice for a sum total of sixteen hours and forty min-

[17] *Jonesboro Quarterly Review,* vol. I, no. 1 (June, 1847), pp. 11, 19; no. 3 (September, 1847), p. 103.

[18] *Ibid.,* no. 3 (September, 1847), p. 99.

[19] *Ibid.,* no. 1 (June, 1847), p. 40.

[20] *Jonesboro Whig,* July 5, 1848.

utes.[21] In October, 1847, he announced three engagements to talk against Ross, each of which was to last four hours, promising "If in good health, and good trim, as I now am, I propose, with God's help, to make the wool fly!"[22] The Parson, who delighted to use statistics in most unusual circumstances, reckoned that during the course of two years he had talked for thirty-three solid days to at least 50,000 people. But his message had gone even further for he had printed it in the *Review*, which had 3,000 subscribers.[23] No churchman in all America had likely exerted himself more within an equal length of time, and the Lord had smiled on all this work, for "during all that time I have been but once interrupted by rain (at Greeneville, Tenn.,), and never have had so much as a bad cold to prevent my speaking."[24] Down in the highlands of Georgia, the *Armenian Magazine* looked on and applauded. It declared, "Ross in a wonderful oblivion of memory overlooked the fact that Brownlow was in Tennessee and was a dangerous customer."[25]

So sure was the Parson of his ability to overwhelm Ross in a word to word combat that he issued a challenge to him to a joint speech-making tour. These were the specific charges the Parson would debate:

1. I shall charge you with *wilful and malicious lying*, in various instances, and prove you guilty. 2. I shall charge you with *personal dishonesty*, and give chapter and verse. 3. I will charge and prove home upon you, *corrupt forgery*. 4. I will charge upon you the awful crime of *adultery*, and give the proof. 5. I shall charge that none other than Tory blood courses through your veins, and as such you cannot be friendly to a Republican form of Government. 6. I shall charge that but for the worst species of immorality, you never would have been in existence, and that you are the last man in the world who ought to complain of a want of respectability among others!

And lastly he would prove that the Athens Synod of the Pres-

[21] *Jonesboro Quarterly Review,* vol. I, no. 3 (September, 1847), p. 142.

[22] *Ibid.,* no. 4 (October, 1847), p. 176.

[23] Brownlow, *Great Iron Wheel Examined,* p. 102.

[24] *Ibid.,* p. 161.

[25] Vol. I, no. 5 (March, 1849), p. 203.

byterian Church in passing resolutions of approval of Ross' work was made up either of liars or ignoramuses. So innocent was the Parson of all knowledge of the standards of good taste that he seriously concluded his challenge with the statement, "I will say nothing during the day, offensive to any Lady who may be present."[26] Ross, though his sense of propriety was somewhat below the highest standards of his day, was not so foolish as to put his head in the lion's mouth, by going out and engaging in a rough and tumble bout with the terrible Parson.

Brownlow was by no means alone in his speech-making against Ross, nor did he hold the championship in a single endurance record. President Charles Collins, of Emory and Henry College, preached to an audience for seven hours without intermission, and then after allowing the multitude a short breathing spell, turned them over to Brownlow for an unstated time.[27]

So easily did the Parson find it to attack Ross personally that he largely forgot all about doctrinal disputation; and likely he thought he had fought the battle of the Lord sufficiently when he had destroyed the reputation and character of the enemy. In answer to Ross' charge that Wesley believed in spooks, Brownlow declared that people generally believed in witchcraft in those earlier days, but he averred the Presbyterians still believed in it. He declared that Ashbel Green, a distinguished Presbyterian clergyman, "reflected upon the subject of *necromancy* and *sorcery* until he finally concluded that he was a veritable *teapot*, and so declared himself from the pulpit. He would place one hand on his hip, so as to form the *handle*—the other arm he would elevate to an angle of 45 degrees, and declare it to be the *spout*. The opposite leg from the spout he would give a *tilt*, and make an effort to pour out the tea!"[28] Brownlow also knew another Presbyterian who sent to heaven by a dying man "a whole batch of *local news* from *Blount County*—as if the inhabitants of heaven cared more about Blount than any other county in the Lord's moral vineyard!"[29] And Ross and many other Pres-

---

[26] *Jonesboro Monthly Review*, vol. II, no. 5, pp. 191-92.

[27] Price, *op. cit.*, IV, 121-22.

[28] Brownlow, *Great Iron Wheel Examined*, p. 156.

[29] *Ibid.*, p. 157.

byterians believed in divining-rods which they used in attempts to find stolen money and silver mines. In fact Brownlow declared that Ross had recently set up in a Presbyterian Church festival in Jonesboro a fortune-telling wax doll which would predict the future for fifty cents. The Parson did not know what the doll had told Ross but he believed it must have whispered, *"Frederick Augustus! in 1847 and '48, Brownlow is to get after you with a sharp stick, and such another time you never had in this life!"* And as for James McChain, another Presbyterian and an editor of the *Calvinistic Magazine*, "I confess to you frankly, that I know nothing about the man, only that he is a WEAK BROTHER, having scarcely sense enough to practice the enchanted frauds of the marvellous believers in witchcraft."[30]

Brownlow felt that he had already sufficiently dealt with Presbyterian doctrines in his book *Helps to the Study of Presbyterianism*, which he had written while he was still riding the circuit. But he dedicated a verse in his *Review* to Presbyterian ministers:

"Vile Preachers!—Demons blush to tell,
    In twice two thousand places;
Have taught poor souls the road to *Hell*,
    Escorted by Calvinian graces!"[31]

The Parson loved his God, his Church, and his country, and he and the church-going Southern Highlanders generally irrespective of creed stood up boldly for this trinity, each expressing that love in his own particular way. Their solicitude for the first two has been amply demonstrated; their regard for the last they almost instinctively expressed in their use of the word *Tory*. To call a person a Tory or the descendant of a Tory was to touch almost the lowest depths of abuse. Hence the glee with which the Presbyterians and Baptists charged Toryism against John Wesley. The Methodists, having great difficulty in defending Wesley, switched the argument as quickly as possible to the generally expressed charge that all Methodists were

[30] *Ibid.*, p. 159.
[31] *Jonesboro Monthly Review*, vol. II, no. 2, p. 173.

Tories, and here they let no one outdo them in testifying to their love for their country. Brownlow was quick now, as well as in 1861, to boast of his patriotic ancestry. His father and his father's five brothers had fought in the War of 1812, and his Gannaway uncles had also been soldiers.

The great American eagle screamed loudest in his native haunts; the farther it was in the Highlands, the louder it screamed. It is, perhaps, no exaggeration to say that there were Highlanders who were either so ignorant or so patriotic as to believe that their Revolutionary forefathers had not only defeated Great Britain but that they had destroyed the British nation. When John Mitchell, the Irish patriot, banished to Van Diemem's Land by the British, made his escape and came to East Tennessee to live, some of the natives from far up the creek marvelled at the mention of the British government as still being in existence. One of them expressed his surprise with the remark, "I thought we had whipped that consarn out long ago."[32]

The active fighting in the Brownlow-Ross War ended in 1849, when the Parson moved to Knoxville. He ceased firing in April with the last number of the *Jonesboro Monthly Review*. He declared that he had won the victory, for soon thereafter Ross left East Tennessee and settled in Alabama. The Parson boasted that he had driven him out, and very likely there was much truth in this claim, for whether Brownlow's accusations against Ross were true or not, he had heaped such unrestrained abuse upon him that any person with sensibilities would rather flee them than involve himself in a defense.[33]

---

[32] Humes, *op. cit.,* p. 29.

[33] Ross made his home in Huntsville and there died in 1882. He long remained an active figure. In 1857 he published a book called *Slavery Ordained of God,* giving the familiar argument that slavery was a divine institution, and bitterly condemning the North and its customs. In a speech at the General Assembly of the Presbyterian Church held in Buffalo, in 1853 he said, "I have little to say of spirit-rappers, women's rights, conventionalists, Bloomers, cruel husbands, or hen-pecked. But, if we may believe your own serious as well as caricature writers, you have things up here of which we down South know very little indeed. Sir, we have no young Bloomers, with hat to one side, cigar in mouth, and cane tapping the boot, striding up to a mincing young gentleman with long curls, attenuated waist, and soft velvet face—the boy-lady to say, "May I see you home, sir?' and the lady-boy to reply, 'I thank ye—no; Pa will send the car-

But no sooner was Brownlow out of one war than he was plunging himself into another. This was a battle of books more than of pamphlets and periodicals. As has been previously mentioned, religious disputes and clerical debates were characteristic of the development of sectarianism in America from colonial days. In some cases disputation went on orally in joint encounters and the speeches were published later in book form; in others, it was a contest of book against book. Back in 1829 a contest took place which is well described in the title of the book that was published as a record: *Debate on the Evidences of Christianity; Containing an Examination of the 'Social System' and of all the Systems of Scriptures of Ancient and Modern Times, Held in the City of Cincinnati, Ohio, From the 13th to the 21st of April, 1829 between Robert Owen of New Lanarck, Scotland, and Alexander Campbell, of Bethany, Virginia.*[34] In 1834, Campbell engaged in another bout which was recorded in the book, *A Debate between Rev. A. Campbell and Rev. N. L. Rice on the Action, Subject, Design and Administration of Christian Baptism; also on the Character of Scriptural Influence in Conversion and Sanctification and on the Expediency and Tendency of Ecclesiastical Creeds, as Terms of Union and Communion: Held in Lexington, Ky., from the Fifteenth of November to the Second of December, 1843, a Period of Eighteen Days. Reported by Marcus T. C. Gould, Stenographer, Assisted by A. Euclid Drapier, Stenographer and Amenuensis.*

Book war and sectarian debating continued unabated during the 1850's. In 1850, Alexander McCain wrote a book entitled *A Defense of the Truth, as Set Forth in the "History and Mystery of Methodist Episcopacy," Being a Reply to John Emory's "Defense of our Fathers."* In 1857, a debate took place in the Baptist Church at Ghent, Kentucky, which lasted for three days. This debate, reported by George C. Steadman, "Phonographer," and published at Louisville the next year under the

---

riage'." *Ibid.*, p. 20. He was instrumental in starting the trouble which resulted in the organization of the United Synod of the Presbyterian Church in the United States of America.

[34] It was published at Bethany by Campbell, in two volumes.

title, *Debate on Some of the Distinctive Differences between the Reformers and the Baptists, Conducted by Rev. Benjamin Franklin and Elder T. J. Fisher.* In 1855, Jeremiah B. Jeter wrote *Campbellism Examined* and two years later Moses E. Laird replied in *A Review of Rev. J. B. Jeter's Book Entitled "Campbellism Examined."* Sectarian promotion also ran through a glorified fiction period with such books as *Thodosia Ernest or Heroine of Faith* and *Theodosia Ernest, or Ten Days Travel in Search of the Church.* These two books were described as "the most charming works ever published in America," but they did not charm William P. Harrison, who combatted them with his *Theophilus Walton; or, The Majesty of Truth.* In 1856, loyal Baptists were being urged to buy R. B. C. Howell's *The Influence of Baptists in the Formation of the Government of Virginia,* J. M. Pendleton's *Three Reasons Why I am a Baptist* and *An Old Landmark Reset,* and J. F. South's *Objections to Methodism.* A Baptist journal, set up in Louisville in 1852 and edited by John L. Waller, which fought the Methodists as well as the Presbyterians, was the *Christian Repository. A Religious and Literary Monthly.*

Parson Brownlow, beset by a journalistic war in Knoxville, might have withstood the various book-attacks being made on Methodism had it not been for the activities of J. R. Graves, who assumed the position of commander-in-chief of the Baptist warriors in Southern Appalachia. Graves was born in Vermont in 1820, of French Huguenot and German ancestry. He went to Ohio where he taught school for a time; then he drifted down to Kentucky to continue teaching, and there was ordained a Baptist preacher. In 1845, he moved to Nashville, preached in the Second Baptist Church, and edited the *Tennessee Baptist.* Aided by J. M. Pendleton he set up ten years later the *Southern Baptist Review and Eclectic.* These activities highly displeased the Parson, but the *casus belli* of the Brownlow-Graves War was a book which Graves wrote in 1856 and which he called *The Great Iron Wheel; or, Republicanism Backwards and Christianity Reversed.* In the same year Graves also furbished and published *The Little Iron Wheel, A Declaration of Christian Rights, And Articles Showing the Despotism of Episcopal Methodism by H. B. Bascom, D.D.*[35]

How the Parson pictured the duplicity of his religious and political enemy, J. R. Graves. From Brownlow's *The Great Iron Wheel Examined.*

It was *The Great Iron Wheel* which infuriated Brownlow. The contents of this work, previous to publication in book form, had appeared in the *Tennessee Baptist* in a series of forty letters addressed to Bishop Soule, senior bishop of the Methodist Church, South. But most of the material that went into these articles and that later made up the book had been first used by Frederick A. Ross in his *Calvinistic Magazine* in a series of eight articles as previously stated, and this fact maddened the Parson still further. Graves declared that he had written this book to ward off the attacks that the Methodists had been making against the Baptists in a deluge of books and tracts. He dedicated it "To Every American who loves our free institu-

---

[35] As indicated, this book had been written by Bascom, a Methodist who was dissatisfied with Methodism and later joined the Episcopal Church. Graves added *Notes of Applications and Illustration.*

tions and scorns to be degraded or enslaved in Church or State. . . ."

The Methodist Church organization was an acute danger to the country. It was a great despotism which tyrannized its membership and threatened the stability of civil government. It was like a great iron wheel which had wheels within wheels. The bishops were the great outer rim which made a revolution every four years. There were twenty-eight conference wheels revolving around annually. To these were attached one hundred presiding elder wheels which moved 1,200 quarterly conference wheels revolving once every three months. Governed by these were 4,000 travelling preacher wheels revolving monthly and setting in motion 30,000 class leader wheels which whirled round weekly. These controlled between 700,000 and 800,000 member wheels which went spinning around every day like whirling dervishes.[36]

He also "assaulted the dead body of John Wesley," and took up the familiar points of sectarian contention—all of which can best be discussed in connection with the Parson's answers. Here it is pertinent to inquire what Graves' standing was among Southern Baptists and what reception his *Great Iron Wheel* received.

This militant Baptist was one of the most powerful leaders in his church and was looked upon by multitudes of his co-religionists as "an eloquent speaker and a very handsome writer" and as their greatest hope on earth. Joseph E. Brown, governor of Georgia from 1857 to 1865, declared that Graves had done more for the Baptist Church than any fifty men living,[37] yet it would be foolish to say that every Baptist agreed with him or supported his methods. The world is not ordered in such a fashion. Brownlow declared that Graves was a "sort of *Hindoo leader* of the warlike wing of his Church," and that the better Baptists disowned him and his *Tennessee Baptist*, but the Parson's statement here is subject to a heavy discount since he

---

[36] J. R. Graves, *The Great Iron Wheel; or, Republicanism Backwards and Christianity Reserved*, pp. 159-60.

[37] J. H. Borum, *Biographical Sketches of Tennessee Baptist Ministers*, p. 288.

was in the midst of an argument.[38] Yet this much is true, that
a little later Graves' pugnacity got him into trouble with his
own Baptists and that as a result the Nashville church deprived
him of its fellowship.[39] He went off on an extreme angle of the
Baptist religion, which was called Landmarkism, and in support
of it he wrote a book called *Landmarkism—What is it?*[40]

As for *The Great Iron Wheel*, it received the endorsement and
acclaim of Baptists throughout the country, North and South.
It was endorsed by a great many Baptist associations, and some
of them, like the State Line Baptist Association, included in
their endorsement Graves' *Tennessee Baptist*.[41] The Baptist
Publishing Society of North Carolina adopted it for sale and
circulation through its agency, and the *North Carolina Biblical
Recorder* in its fight against the Methodists used many texts
from *The Great Iron Wheel*.[42] North Carolina Baptists were par-
ticularly loud in their praise and zealous in their promotion of
this book. When the *Richmond Christian Advocate* declared *The
Great Iron Wheel* to be false, foul, and slanderous, the Baptist
Publication Society challenged Leroy M. Lee, the editor of the
Advocate to debate the question with Graves in Raleigh.[43] On
Lee's refusal they challenged Charles F. Deems, of the North
Carolina Conference, but he also refused the "degrading propo-
sition." Next they sought to bring out Dr. Smith, president of
Randolph-Macon College, but he also declined to turn clerical
gladiator.[44]

The book had an immense sale and every day, according to
Graves, its acclaim was becoming "more general, warmer and
louder." The sale of it during the first twenty months after its

---

[38] Brownlow, *Great Iron Wheel Examined*, p. 22.

[39] P. H. Mell, Jr., *Life of Patrick Hues Mell*, pp. 108-24.

[40] J. J. Burnett, *Sketches of Tennessee's Pioneer Baptist Preachers*, pp. 184-
98; B. F. Riley, *A History of the Baptists in the Southern States East of the
Mississippi*, pp. 177-78.

[41] J. R. Graves, *The Little Iron Wheel, A Declaration of Christian Rights, and
Articles Showing the Despotism of Episcopal Methodism by H. B. Bascom,
D.D.*, pp. 244-307; Brownlow, *Great Iron Wheel Examined*, p. 292.

[42] *Ibid.*, p. 298.

[43] *Biblical Recorder*, August 9, 1855 quoted in Brownlow, *Great Iron Wheel
Examined*, pp. 256-57.   [44] *Ibid.*, pp. 259-61.

publication had averaged a thousand copies a month, and at no time had the supply equalled the demand. It was claimed that over 100,000 copies were ultimately sold. Graves boasted of many people being converted from Methodism by it, but he never stated the number of dollars it had turned toward him.[45]

Just as Brownlow had come to the rescue of the Methodists in his *Review* when Ross and his Presbyterians had attacked them, it was naturally to be expected that he would join the issue with Graves and his Baptists in their latest onset against the followers of Wesley. Again must the Parson buckle on the armor of the Lord and go out to do battle. He had written already five books of a controversial nature and he had hoped that it would not be necessary to write a sixth, but the enemy had forced it upon him.[46] Amidst many other duties, he set to work and wrote *The Great Iron Wheel Examined; or, Its False Spokes Extracted, and an Exhibition of Elder Graves, its Builder, in a Series of Chapters.* He lost little time, for it appeared the same year in which Graves' book was published, 1856. It was printed in Nashville. He made a hostile demonstration in the dedication and then for 331 pages he fought Graves and the Baptists with fire and sword, not neglecting to make some of his worst assaults on Ross, who had afforded Graves so much ammunition. In this spirit he began:

TO

Every honest and impartial reader,
who loves Truth and despises Falsehood, whether perpetrated by a Priest or
a Levite, for the sake of Fame, or money-
making: To every Protestant Christian, who,
to whatever sect or denomination he may be attached, is unwilling to see a sister Church pulled
down by a collection of tales, fabrications, and blackguard insinuations, which a decent man should be ashamed
to listen to, and utterly too disgraceful for a Minister of
the Gospel to repeat and publish, this work is confidently

---

[45] Graves, *Little Iron Wheel,* p. 287.
[46] Brownlow, *Great Iron Wheel Examined,* p. xii.

DEDICATED BY ITS AUTHOR:

Who here, most respectfully, as a Local Preacher of the
Methodist Episcopal Church, South, apologizes to the
Christian public for the seeming severity of this
work, in some parts, on the ground that he has
performed the painful task of refuting a series
of the most scurrilous falsehoods, and a collection of the lowest abuse of the age!

He felt equal to the task and sufficiently informed on true
religion for he had during the past twenty years read the whole
Bible fifteen times and the New Testament twenty times.[47] As
was his custom in dealing with his enemies, he first disposed of
Graves' character, charging among the crimes he had committed, slander for which he had been fined $7,500.[48] And further-
more, at a service he held at Bowling Green, Kentucky, Graves'
abuse of other sects had been so low and "his conduct so degrading, that a Baptist lady remarked that if any one would hold
him, she would *cowhide him!*" He had actually been horsewhip-
ped on the streets of Nashville.[49]

The Parson had been viciously inclined toward the Baptists,
since the days when he first rode the circuit and had come into
collision with Humphrey Posey. He charged most of the Baptist preachers with being illiterate and opposed to learning,
claiming that they objected to "the use of any and all books
except the Bible," that they "publicly boast that they have no
'*edecation*' or '*human larnin*'," and that they "announce to an
audience such texts of Scripture as God *reveals* to them for
special purposes and occasions, either after their arrival at the
place of worship, or on their way thither!"[50] With impatience
the Parson exclaimed, "When will this denomination learn wisdom. When will the hide-bound clerical dolts of that order, ac-
quaint themselves with the Scriptures."[51]

---

[47] *Ibid.*, p. 207.
[48] *Ibid.*, pp. 263-77.
[49] *Ibid.*, pp. 70, 264.
[50] *Ibid.*, p. 191.
[51] *Jonesboro Whig*, May 18, 1842.

Baptist preachers were not only innocent of common learning, but a third or a half of Baptists were superstitious, often giving "no other evidence of a genuine conversion to God than that of *a dream*, the *hearing of a voice*, the *sight of a ghost*, or the visitation of an *angel*, or of *God himself!*"[52] Brownlow declared that a woman had been received by the Baptists in Carter County, Tennessee on the testimony that she had "walked out into the woods, where she met *Christ* and the *apostles*, in open daylight, under a large tree, singing a *Baptist* song!"[53]

As a blanket indictment, the Parson charged the Baptists "with selfishness, bigotry, intolerance, and a shameful want of Christian liberality."[54] They assumed to be the only true Church and the only way to Heaven, and as an example of their "combined bigotry and despotism," he cited a recent meeting at Sinking Creek, in Carter County, which was typical of the Baptists in the South and West. At the meeting described, the preacher after informing the Methodists and Presbyterians, who had been invited to be present, why they should not be allowed to commune, announced that *"all who were in good standing in their own Churches might occupy the front seats, and see the Lord's people partake of his shed blood and broken body."*[55] There were even some Baptists, known as Close Baptists, who prescribed other Baptists on various points.

Having disposed of the character of both Graves and the Baptists generally Brownlow began the defense of his Church against Graves' charges. After rescuing Wesley's good name from both his Savannah experiences and his subsequent career in England, he repelled the charges against the form of the Methodist Church government. As for the Baptists, they had no government, being "without form and void," or, indeed, the most that might be said was that they had "a sort of *Indian Council-ground form of government."* Against the charges that the Methodists were not Christians because they had been founded by a man, and that they were too young to be a Church and that

---

[52] Brownlow, *Great Iron Wheel Examined,* p. 96.

[53] *Ibid.,* p. 98.

[54] *Ibid.,* p. 181.

[55] *Ibid.,* p. 182.

they were dying out, the Parson hurled a table of statistics showing how fast the Methodists had been growing and he abused the Baptists as being "sectarian bigots," "*pig-pen orators* and *whiskey-shop saints.*"[56]

The Parson found so many falsehoods in Graves' book that he scarcely knew where to begin answering them. With his flair for statistics, he announced that Graves had perpetrated twenty-five falsehoods in one chapter of twelve pages, being over two lies to a page.[57] But the greatest subject for sectarian dispute in all the land was baptism. There was scarcely any one, no matter how lowly, who did not hold his immutable views on this subject and argue learnedly about it. The word *Baptizo* had as great currency in the Southern Highlands as it had had in ancient Greece; it was analyzed, parsed, declined, and conjugated from "Dan to Bersheba."[58] This was the great rock on which the Baptist Church rested, and to budge an inch was blasphemy. Of course, the Baptists held that immersion was the only way

---

[56] *Ibid.*, pp. 27-90.

[57] *Ibid.*, pp. 243-44.

[58] For the Parson's discussion of it see *ibid.*, pp. 224-31. The Parson used this story to illustrate the importance the Baptists put on baptism; he also thought it would illustrate Baptist bigotry: "I am here reminded of two *dreams* by two preachers, the one a Baptist, the other a Methodist. They had been holding a protracted meeting together, which lasted for days, and which resulted in the conversion of a number of souls to God. The two preachers now agreed to open the doors of their respective churches, and gather in the fruits of their labors. It was agreed that the Baptist brother should lead the way. He stated to the audience generally, and to the young converts in particular, that he had had a remarkable dream, in which he had died and gone to hell! His Satanic Majesty received him very politely, and proposed to escort him through all the apartments of the infernal regions before assigning to him his position. He travelled extensively through the dark dominions, and met with quite a number of Methodists, Episcopalians, Presbyterians, and Catholics, but did not see one Baptist in all the infernal regions—their compliance with the ordinance of *baptism* having carried them all safe to God's habitation!

"The Methodist minister followed. He too had dreamed a remarkable but similar dream! He had died and gone to hell as he stated to the audience; and, like his Baptist brother, the Devil had conducted him through all ·his dark dominions. He saw 'lots and squares' of Methodists, Presbyterians, Episcopalians, and Catholics, but not a single Baptist. He inquired of the Devil, with anxious solicitude, if there were no Baptists there? His Satanic Majesty seized him by the arm, turned him suddenly around, and said, 'Come out here!' The Devil raised a large trap-door and pointed to a multitude, grappling in 'a lower deep,' and exclaimed, 'These, sir, are all Baptists holding *close communion!*'" *Ibid.*, p. 217.

to Heaven, and according to Parson Brownlow they held that
people "could no more get to heaven without being *immersed by
a Baptist preacher*, than they could arrest the sun in his course,
or check the impetuous cataract of Niagara in its onward and
terrible progress!"[59]

The Parson objected to immersion for many reasons. In the
first place he was opposed to the method, for it propelled the
convert into the Church backwards. Most Christians entered
the Church "face foremost," but "Our Baptist brethren are
almost alone in their vulgarity in *backing into the Church of
God!*"[60] And they held even immersion was not efficacious unless
performed by a Baptist preacher who must not be friendly to
missions or friendly to any minister who was friendly to missions.[61] But the Parson especially objected to immersion because
of its vulgarity and to prove it to be thus he published an illustration of "Elder B. Changing Clothes Before the Ladies, After
Immersion!"[62] The process of immersion, he described thus:

The usual custom throughout the South and West is to bandage
the forehead of a delicate and beautiful female, and tie a handkerchief round her waist, as a sort of *handle* for an awkward Baptist
preacher to fasten upon; and thus she is led into the water, step
by step, in the presence of a mixed multitude, who are making their
vulgar remarks and criticizing her steps as she *fights down her
clothes,* which rise to the top of the water, and float around her
delicate and exposed limbs! She is taken by the preacher, who
fastens one hand in her *belt,* and the other on the back of her head;
and after planting his big feet firm upon the bottom of the stream,
and *squaring himself* as though he were about to knock a beef in the
head, he plunges her into the water![63]

Immersion was not only very cumbersome to perform but it
was also contrary to the Bible John's form of baptism was not
Christ's; it was merely "one of those divers washings in use
among the Jews." And even at that it was not immersion, for

---

[59] *Ibid.,* p. 183.
[60] *Ibid.,* pp. 202-3.
[61] *Ibid.,* p. 305.
[62] *Ibid.,* opposite p. 241. For the Parson's description see *ibid.,* p. 241.
[63] *Ibid.,* p. 214.

One of the Parson's graphic arguments against the Baptists. The Baptist pastor "after immersing several persons, came out of the water and changed his clothes in the presence of the multitude, as indicated by this engraving, and all in the presence of males and females. He was a very tall man, knockkneed and rawboned—anything but handsome when dressed." From Brownlow's *The Great Iron Wheel Examined*.

reasons that Brownlow ingeniously worked out. Again did he enter the realm of mathematics and now work out a statistical commentary on the Bible. Through a sifting process he determined that there were in the Holy Land "just three millions of human beings" whom John baptized. Estimating the length of John's ministry at nine months (and that he continued longer "cannot be proven from the Bible, by all the Baptist preachers and writers in existence," though the Parson would grant ten months), and allowing six hours a day given over to baptizing, the total number of hours that John devoted to this rite would be 1,300. The inexorable mathematical conclusion would be that John baptized 2,000 to the hour, thirty to the minute, or one every two seconds. Now common sense proved that he could not have *immersed* them at this rate. It was therefore inescapable that John *sprinkled* them—and likely with a sprig of hyssop, since that was an old Jewish custom.[64] Should further proof be demanded against the use of immersion by John, the Parson would cite all skeptics to the physical characteristics of the Jordon River. The banks of this stream were so steep and the current so swift that no person could hope to enter its waters and not be drowned.[65]

Again, the Parson analyzed the great Biblical baptizing on the Day of Pentecost, and proved that immersion could not have been used. He estimated that the Twelve Apostles baptized 3,000 on that day, but not until they had preached to the multitudes long enough to leave no more than five hours to be devoted to baptizing. Dividing these 3,000 equally among the Twelve, the Parson reckoned that each Apostle would be forced to baptize fifty to the hour. To immerse at this rate would tax beyond the breaking point the physical endurance of anyone. Furthermore, the nearest stream was the Brook Kedron, which at this time of the year was almost dry. Manifestly no person could be immersed in such a stream; for not only was there little water in it, but what little existed was polluted. At the very thoughts of immersing a person there, the Parson's anger welled

---

[64] *Ibid.*, pp. 206-11.
[65] *Ibid.*, pp. 231-32.

up: "If one of the apostles had taken a wife or daughter of ours, and *plunged* her into this filthy brook, he would not have immersed another female soon again."[66] The Baptists placed much emphasis on the case of Philip and the eunuch, but both went down into the water, and if "going down into the water" meant immersion, then Phillip immersed himself at the same time he baptized the eunuch. Absurd, the Parson concluded.[67]

Pictorial proof that sprinkling was the form of baptism in Biblical times. This representation, said to be the centre-piece in the dome of the baptistery in the Ravenna Cathedral, was used as an argument by James L. Chapman, a Tennessee Methodist minister, in his book *Baptism, with Reference to its Import, Modes, History, Proper Use, and Duty of Parents to Baptized Children.* Here John the Baptist is sprinkling water upon the head of Christ, while the mythological figure representing the River Jordan views the act.

To Brownlow's way of thinking, immersion was impractical and foolish from any point of view. It was not only spiritually

---

[66] *Ibid.*, pp. 234-35.   [67] *Ibid.*, p. 235.

wrong, but it was physically dangerous—and surely the Lord would not have doomed to damnation the 8,000,000 people living in the Polar Regions.[68] If immersion were correct, how could it be done? The inescapable conclusion was that sprinkling was the proper method of baptism: "And we defy every Baptist on earth to produce explicit proof from the Scriptures of any persons ever having been immersed in the primitive Church."[69] The Parson also battled against the Baptists to save the infants from eternal damnation.[70]

Graves had attacked the Methodist Church for its schism in 1844, and attributed the cause to the form of Church government and to the ambitions of a corrupt and designing ministry. The Parson was as good a Southerner as he was a Methodist, and forgetful of Nullification days, he called on John C. Calhoun as his champion. And he would inform Graves that it "was a glorious act on the part of the Methodist Church, and a proud day in her history," when she broke with the abolitionist North.[71] Brownlow declared that the separation of Southern Methodists from Northern Methodists was "both inevitable and desirable," and he expected all other denominations in the South to break with the North.[72] Graves should be looked upon with suspicion by a true Southerner, for he was born "north of Mason and Dixon's Line," and he had written his *Iron Wheel*, of 570 pages, and had not said "one word AGAINST ABOLITIONISM, or one word in favor of SOUTHERN SLAVERY." He should be "forced to define his position at once, or leave the South in hot haste." The Parson saw a dark future:

We are on the eve of unconjecturable events, and every Southern man ought to show his hand. . . . A struggle of unequalled fury is swiftly approaching us; and if the ties of our cherished Union come out of it unrent, they are made of sterner stuff than the history of the past would seem to warrant! The bonds of the Union have resisted political agitation, but can they withstand religious

[68] *Ibid.*, pp. 238-41.
[69] *Ibid.*, p. 238.
[70] *Ibid.*, pp. 221-23.
[71] *Ibid.*, p. 283.
[72] *Jonesboro Whig*, May 28, 1845.

fury? Abolitionism has travelled from political dominion to religious conviction, and has infected the whole mind and heart of the North. Under its palsying touch, some of the strongest cords that held the Union together have snapped: others are now assailed, and I fear will give way![73]

The Parson identified Methodist independence with Southern nationalism and pledged himself to support both with equal vehemence.

Having examined *The Great Iron Wheel* and removed its false spokes, the Parson believed he had performed his major task, but there still remained *The Little Iron Wheel,* which the Parson felt he could not ignore. So he proceeded to spin *The Little Iron Wheel* in a book he entitled, The *"Little Iron Wheel" Enlarged; or, Elder Graves, its Builder, Daguerreotyped, by Way of an Appendix. To Which are Added Some Personal Explanations;* and so the war was continued over familiar ground.[74] Graves, for the most part, treated the Parson with silent contempt, stopping only to declare him "notorious and scurrilous" and a "foul libeller." He stated that he had not read Brownlow's attacks and had no intention of doing so.[75]

Undoubtedly all Methodists, Baptists, and Presbyterians were not as crude, impetuous, and contentious as were Brownlow, Graves, and Ross, but great numbers supported these three clerical gladiators and others like them who for their churches fought and gouged fairly and foully. The Southern Highlanders were pugnacious, manly, and brave; they enjoyed a fight religious or otherwise. The churches would not have been so foolish as to refrain from using one of the handiest devices for securing members, even if it had not naturally suggested itself. Many a Highlander could never have been induced to enter a church or attend a religious gathering if he were not assured ahead of time that there would be a great deal of excitement. Coming in unsuspectingly he might be made a member through guile. The public debate on religious questions was used to

---

[73] Brownlow, *Great Iron Wheel Examined,* pp. 285-86.

[74] This book was published by Brownlow in 1857 at Nashville.

[75] Graves, *Little Iron Wheel,* pp. 244, 248. Graves also had a quarrel with Alexander Campbell.

gather in those who either could not read or did not care to make the effort, while the book war either brought in or strengthened the faith of those who were better educated. Graves sold more than 100,000 copies of his *Great Iron Wheel,* to be read and passed around among the Baptists; Brownlow claimed to have sold a like number of his *Great Iron Wheel Examined,* which delighted the hearts of at least an equal number of Methodists.[76]

It would, therefore, be a vain argument to say that those who served and received their religion in this manner were in numbers negligible. The pugnacious proselyting church members were respectable in numbers even if they might not be in religious character. And they did not act as individuals; conferences, synods, and assemblies stood back of their respective warriors and endorsed their methods. Graves said, "Look at the distracted state of christendom! . . . Methodists and Baptists engaged in an exterminating warfare. Presbyterians and Methodists in East and West Tennessee unchurching and unchristianizing each other, and pronouncing each other's peculiar doctrinal teaching dangerous to the souls of men."[77] In East Tennessee the Methodists and Baptists were about equal in numbers, while the Presbyterians were a weak third. Primitive ideas lasted a long time in the Southern Highlands. As late as 1845 the Holston Conference declared that instrumental music in churches was "preventive of the worship of God in spirit and in truth."[78] At the same time this group of Methodists resolved that they would support "prudently conducted institutions of learning" yet they would disapprove and would "oppose any means tending to or savoring of the establishment of a theological institute or seminary."[79]

In Southern Appalachia there were valley lands as beautiful and as fertile "as ever the sun shone on," and inhabitants as cultured and as learned as could be found elsewhere in the South.

---

[76] These religious contentions were not peculiar to the Highlands. The plantation South played a minor part and in addition developed quarrels of its own, though on a somewhat different basis. Into them entered such names as Thomas Cooper, Horace Holley, and James H. Thornwell.

[77] Graves, *Great Iron Wheel,* p. 16.

[78] Price, *op. cit.,* IV, 21.

[79] *Ibid.* The ban on theological institutions was removed by 1858.

These people were Presbyterians, Methodists, and Baptists like their less fortunate neighbors farther back in the mountains. They were a minority in numbers, yet their influence was great. Though they could not prevent these devastating religious wars, they could disapprove of them and hope that the day would come when religious denominations would not choose such methods by which to promote their growth. They founded and supported colleges and hoped that education and culture would direct into the souls of the people all the religion they were capable of truly absorbing. Parson Brownlow in the midst of his war with Ross stopped long enough to make the damaging admission:

There are many kind-hearted Methodists in the country who are opposed to all of this angry controversy, and who oppose it from correct motives. Their kindness feeds on *reflection* rather than *impulse*: they know that Christians cannot add to their graces by this busy, bustling spirit of controversy—this struggle to be seen and heard. They recollect that Elijah found not the Lord in the *tempest*, but in the quiet and calm—"*Be still, and know that I am God.*"[80]

Another Methodist objected to joint religious debates, declaring, "As feats of intellectual gladiatorship, they attract a gaping crowd of those who admire the pugnacious combatants, or who care nothing for them or the subject they are to fight about, and who are only a little less interested than they would be in 'seeing the elephant' and 'stirring up the monkeys' in a menagerie."[81]

Without reference to how sincerely they embraced their religion or how efficacious it was, it can be said that a majority of the Southern Highlanders joined a church.[82] It can also be

---

[80] Brownlow, *Great Iron Wheel Examined*, p. 145.

[81] *Ibid.*, pp. 259-60, quoting from the *Richmond Christian Advocate*.

[82] The United States census for 1850 and for 1860 did not attempt to give statistics on church membership. The most the marshals who took the census tried to do was to estimate the number of accommodations in the churches and school-houses, according to denominations. Virginia, whose population was in 1860, 1,596,318 had church accommodations for 1,067,840; Tennessee, with 1,109,801 population, had accommodations for 728,661; North Carolina, with 992,622 population, had accommodations for 811,423; and Georgia, with 1,057,286,

said that this fact was the result of a vast deal of hard preaching, hard fighting, and hard praying. If success was to be measured by the standard of numbers, then did Southern Appalachia well deserve the title of being a vineyard of the Lord.

---

had accommodations for 763,812. *Eighth Census of the United States, 1860, Mortality and Miscellaneous Statistics,* pp. 497-502.

CHAPTER V

BLACK SLAVES AND MOUNTAIN WHITES

THE FIRST Southern Highlanders came into being through a sifting process which produced both the strong and the weak, and in the struggle for existence a person might pass from one class to the other, but the two classes continued, even as it must always be in a normal society. There was no reason calling for the weaklings to increase their proportion over their more fortunate neighbors to any greater extent in the Southern Highlands than in the Southern Lowlands and Piedmont regions. Southern Appalachia was never so densely populated that many of its inhabitants were forced through the scarcity of land to live on the steep slopes of its rugged mountains.[1] Those who chose to live in the out-of-way places made their decision because they were natural lovers of solitudes, or else because they were so shiftless that hard circumstances washed them there with little resistance on their part. The isolated Elizabethan mountaineers developed in no greater proportions than did the "poor white trash" in the piney woods and wire grass country. There was no part of the South that did not have its unfortunates, and at no period and in no region was it all the one or the other. To denominate all mountaineers as illiterate ne'er-do-wells would be as absurd as to claim that all lowlanders were cultured aristocrats.

Making a living is ever a conscious thought with all normal people, but how much it shall take and the manner in which it shall be done vary widely. Southern Highlanders differed not with this philosophy of life. For some a small field and a rude cabin were sufficient, and the number of hogs kept could be made to vary inversely with the number of bear hunts the fall might

---

[1] Even in the year 1936 there are great stretches of the Southern Highlands which have never known the mountaineer's cabin.

produce. This class of people lived rudely but well. They were not in the business of producing anything for sale, although they were never without something to sell. They never knew the meaning of financial depressions and of the hunger and poverty that the industrial revolution brought to their twentieth century descendants in Elizabethton, in Kingsport, in Bristol. But highlanders were just as ambitious as lowlanders; they were just as desirous of becoming great as were the people in any other part of the country. They would turn their hand to whatever business their region best promoted. The river valleys of the Tennessee, the French Broad, the Powell, and the Clinch and many less spacious levels, called coves, which the mountains so obligingly provided, afforded agricultural land of the greatest fertility. Here farms sprang up and some of them grew to such sizes that they came to be none other than Southern plantations.

Agriculture came in with such vigor that it was forced to do homage to that handmaid of ante-bellum Southern agrarianism, slavery. In 1860 there were thirty counties which made up what was called East Tennessee, and in every one of them slavery gained a lodgment. With the exception of Scott County where the proportion of slaveholding families to non-slaveholding was one to fifty-seven, the East Tennessee counties ranged in the proportion of slaveholders to non-slaveholders from one to twenty-one, to one to five. Two-thirds of these counties had a tenth or more of their population holding slaves. For the whole South the average was about a third. The number of slaves per county ranged from 59 in Scott County to 2,370 in Knox County. Exactly two-thirds of these counties had more than 500 slaves each, and an even dozen had more than a thousand. While most of the slaveholders owned less than fifteen slaves, about 170 owned twenty slaves or more, and one planter in Jefferson County owned more than 200. These East Tennessee farmers and planters raised corn, wheat, rye, oats and other grains. They also raised hay, cattle, and swine, and horses and mules.

There was also a sort of industrialism growing up, which was not allied to planters nor necessarily friendly to agricultural philosophy. A great deal of flour and meal was manufactured, amounting in each of seven counties to more than $100,000 annually. In 1860 the value of this product in Knox County was $263,000. Lumber, leather, liquor, and cotton goods were also produced in varying quantities, and in 1860 Hamilton County packed $130,000 worth of pork and beef. Mining interests were beginning to be developed, with Marion County taking out of the ground in 1860 coal to the value of $408,000, and Polk County producing copper worth $404,000. Little cities like Knoxville were growing into industrial centers of some importance.[2]

In the earlier days East Tennessee had been self-sufficient, shut-off, and contented, but as this region began to produce something to sell, it became more interested in the way out. Nature had provided two main roads—up the valleys toward Roanoke, Lynchburg, and Richmond, and down the valley toward Chattanooga, Atlanta, Birmingham, and Nashville. Minor ways lay northwestward through Cumberland Gap and eastward up the French Broad to Asheville. However, in the case of the latter two ways, it was necessary to cross the two great mountain systems which flanked the Tennessee valleys. But the people beyond the Gap were the competitors of the East Tennesseeans in selling their products to the planters, so the Cumberland Gap became a pass into and through East Tennessee to the southward. The road up the French Broad led to Asheville without great difficulty, but the markets that would buy what East Tennesseeans wanted to sell lay far on beyond to the southward, and between was a mountainous country yet to be crossed. So strongly did the magnet of trade draw to Columbia, Charleston, and Augusta, that the great six-horse wagons dragged themselves through this mountain highway, sliding down through Saluda Gap into Greenville District, South Carolina. The first easy way to market was down the Holston and into the Tennessee River to Chattanooga, but soon the Tennessee unobligingly broke navigation at the Muscle Shoals,

[2] *Eighth Census, 1860, Manufacturers,* pp. 560-79; *ibid., Agriculture,* pp. 132-39.

and then later illogically wandered northward, finally emptying
into the Ohio River, five hundred miles away from East Tennessee's markets. A canal around the shoals would allow unim-
peded navigation across the whole stretch of Alabama, but the
project never produced anything more valuable than the plans.

The markets that stood gaping for East Tennessee flour,
meal, salt, iron, pork, horses, mules, sheep, and hay lay to the
south and southeast, in Georgia and South Carolina. These
great plantation markets by right belonged to East Tennessee,
for they were close by. Yet they lay beyond a great wall of
mountains which was not so accommodating as even to allow a
water course to trickle through. But in the early 1820's, a reso-
lute East Tennesseean determined to take a cargo to the low-
land markets of Alabama, mountain walls and Muscle Shoals
notwithstanding. He built himself a keel boat on the Holston,
loaded it down with flour and whiskey, and embarked on a remarkable Odyssey. He floated down the Holston, past the mouth
of the French Broad and on into the Tennessee until he reached
the Hiwassee. Here he turned his boat southeastward up this
stream and poled it until he reached the Ocoee. He belabored
his boat up this stream almost to the Georgia boundary, when
being unable to proceed further he dragged both boat and
cargo across the height of land to the headwaters of the Cona-
sauga. Down this river he floated into the Oostanoula, Coosa,
and Alabama, and finally deposited his cargo in Montgomery.[3]

It was easy enough to see that East Tennessee would have
great difficulty in reaching her markets as long as navigating
rivers and canals was the national mode of travel. And so it
was that new hope sprang up in East Tennessee when news
reached there that a railroad was a practical invention and that
it could be built where people would never dream of trying to
put canals. Knoxville, which had long been the wagon center
of East Tennessee,[4] now aspired to be the railroad center. An
enthusiastic meeting held here in 1831 humbled the mountains
and determined that a railroad should be built across them to

---

[3] *Niles' Register*, XX, 63, 64 (March 24, 1821).
[4] In 1825 it was estimated that the number of wagons entering Knoxville
averaged 975 annually. *Niles' Register*, XXIX, 263 (December 24, 1825).

Charleston, South Carolina.[5] The next year, Asheville, North Carolina, which expected to be on this new railroad, was the scene of another enthusiastic meeting.[6] This idea of a railroad through the heart of the Southern Highlands soon came to be developed into a grand conception which fired the imagination of Calhoun, Hayne, and many other Southerners. This road would not stop at Knoxville, but should speed its conquering way into the heart of the Ohio Valley—to Cincinnati. Not only would the Southern Highlands be annexed to the South Atlantic, but the wealth of the Middle West would flow southward, and with it would come an alliance so powerful that the South could defy all New England and the East, commercially as well as politically.[7]

The whole country had now become excited over railroads, and nowhere was there greater enthusiasm than in the Southern Highlands and in the Southeast. On July 4, 1836, more than 400 delegates from nine states met in the Methodist Church in Knoxville to promote the Charleston and Cincinnati project. Without waiting for the slower parts of the country to awaken, the East Tennesseeans organized during this year the Hiwassee Railroad Company, and in the course of the next few years, before being overtaken by bankruptcy, they spent more than a million dollars in their fruitless efforts to pierce the mountains. The twentieth century reminder of this former ambition to go through the mountains rather than around them is a short line of track from Knoxville to Maryville, which still bears the ambitious title, Knoxville and Augusta Railroad. The attempt to join by a railroad the Lowlands and the Highlands was revived in 1848. This time a flank attack would be made on the mountains. Under the name of the East Tennessee and Georgia Railroad, this project was begun at Dalton, Georgia, in 1850

---

[5] *Ibid.*, XL, 307 (July 2, 1831).

[6] U. B. Phillips, *A History of Transportation in the Eastern Cotton Belt to 1860*, pp. 170, 171.

[7] This was the famous Charleston and Cincinnati Railroad, which as such was never built. See *ibid.*, pp. 168-220. For a discussion of this project which grew up after the Civil War and which resulted in the Cincinnati Southern Railway from Cincinnati to Chattanooga, see E. M. Coulter, *The Cincinnati Southern Railroad and the Struggle for Southern Commerce.*

and by the end of the following year it had been pushed north-ward to Athens, Tennessee. It continued northeastward, cross-ing the Tennessee River in 1852 and reaching Knoxville in 1855. In 1859 a branch was built from Cleveland, Tennessee to Chat-tanooga, to connect with roads to Nashville and Louisville and with the Western and Atlantic, which had been built by the state of Georgia from Atlanta to the latter city, and had been completed in 1851. By 1860 the Virginia and East Tennessee Railroad had been pushed through Lynchburg and on to Rich-mond. At this time East Tennessee found herself well connected with all the principal cities of the United States through this strategic line which passed from Chattanooga to Bristol.[8]

East Tennessee was never plantation country and never would have become so, but by 1860 it was fast making preparations to tie itself to the planter class by the tough thongs of a lucrative trade. Though entirely different from the Lower South in topog-raphy and largely in occupation, it was not an enemy territory alien in sympathy. On the all-absorbing Southern institution, it was harmonious with the rest of the South. It had been exposed very early to influences hostile to slavery, but it had listened no more attentively and had reacted no more favorably than many other regions of the South not in the mountains.

It was characteristic of the pioneer preachers, irrespective of denomination, to oppose slavery, coupling with it the other great sin, whiskey-drinking. These impecunious wanderers, having no worldly possessions, saw few slaves in their earthly kingdom, but those few they did see likely belonged to people who considered themselves too high in the scale of life to notice, except to spurn, the frontier preacher. Coupled with this wholly human personal feeling against slaveholders and therefore against slavery, were specific teachings of some of the denomi-nations. The Quakers were as well-known for their anti-slavery sentiment as for any other doctrine. Methodists, Presbyterians, and Baptists were likewise in varying degrees opposed to slav-ery. As the Presbyterians became more wealthy and educated they soon forgot their hostility, and left the Methodists to get

[8] Phillips, *op. cit.,* pp. 372-76, 382-85.

away as best they could from the teachings of John Wesley and the pronouncements his Church had made.

Wesley had declared that slavery was a "complicated villainy," and that man-buying was no more respectable than man-stealing. The earliest Methodist saints, such as Thomas Coke and Francis Asbury, imbibed their anti-slavery feelings from Wesley, and when in 1784 in Baltimore they set up the Methodist Church in America, they forbade all members of the Church to own slaves, except in states where manumission was prohibited by law. But they had climbed onto too high a plane; within less than six months the rule was indefinitely suspended. As far as slavery was concerned the Methodists were now in a state of nature until 1796, when they marched toward high ground again by forbidding all Church officials to own slaves or any Methodist to buy or sell slaves "Unjustly, inhumanly, or covetously." They soon suffered a relapse and in 1808 they repealed all rules which attempted to regulate a private member's dealings with slavery. The Methodist Church was now becoming wealthy enough in the South and respectable enough, to feel an interest in the destiny of its surroundings, and so Bishop Asbury came to the conclusion that it were much better to work for the salvation of the slave's soul and the alleviation of the harshness of his position rather than to attempt further to have him set free. In 1840 the Church abandoned the subject of slavery entirely, by repealing the rule against officials owning slaves. But at the next conference in 1844 the storm broke, and the Church split into two permanent bodies on the subject of slavery. Southern Methodists now like other denominations in the South became a church for the land of slavery, a land that was consciously developing a nationality.[9]

East Tennessee very early became the scene of vigorous attempts to organize manumission societies, and some of the earliest anti-slavery leaders who came to be best known made their start here. Samuel Doak came into the Holston River Valley before the end of the Revolution and for the next generation

[9] Milburn, *op. cit.*, pp. 347-88; *Journal of Francis Asbury*, III, 290; J. N. Norwood, *The Schism in the Methodist Episcopal Church*, pp. 9-22.

educated the people against slavery both from the pulpit and in Washington Academy and Tusculum Academy, which he founded. A pupil who showed the results of this teaching, fifty years later in far-away Texas, was Sam Houston. By 1814 the Quakers had organized the Manumission Society of Tennessee and had begun their appeal to all, but especially to the religious denominations, to help spread the movement. In 1816 this society held a meeting in Greene County, and over the names of Thomas Doak, Elihu Embree, and others, it sent out an appeal for the gradual emancipation of the slaves.[10]

East Tennessee became the cradle of the emancipation press. In Jonesboro in 1816 the *Manumission Intelligencer* sprang up, soon to be followed by the *Emancipator*, edited by Elihu Embree. When Embree died his place was taken by Benjamin Lundy, who set up his *Genius of Universal Emancipation*, first begun in Ohio and later moved to Greeneville. But with all the writing by newspaper editors and all the preaching by Quakers, Methodists, Baptists, and Presbyterians, the manumission movement made little progress in Southern Appalachia. Before slaves were brought in, the Highlanders could not become greatly excited over something about which they had no first-hand information, and when the valley farms began to be developed sufficiently to make slaves desirable, the manumission movement became correspondingly undesirable. Abstractions never took up a great amount of the time Southern Highlanders had at their disposal. Although Lundy's program was innocuous as compared with the later abolition movement conducted by William Lloyd Garrison, yet it appeared vicious enough to lead East Tennesseeans to threaten Lundy in various ways. "Often the bullies," declared Lundy, "vapoured around me with bludgeons, in such a manner, that the sparing of my life might seem to have been providential." In 1824 Lundy moved out with his *Genius of Universal Emancipation* and continued it in Baltimore.[11]

---

[10] *Niles' Register*, XIV, 321 (July 4, 1818).

[11] *The Life, Travels and Opinions of Benjamin Lundy, Including his Journey to Texas and Mexico; with a Sketch of Contemporary Events and a Notice of*

It has heretofore been amply demonstrated that Parson Brownlow was interested in all the religious and journalistic activities in the Highlands, and it might well be inferred that he would spring into the midst of any movement which he might succor or belabor and in which he might whip up excitement. The Parson did not necessarily predicate his position on conformity with the prevailing sentiment; he was entirely too eccentric, independent, and honest for such slavishness. So it does not logically follow that to explain East Tennessee is to explain the Parson. Yet in the matter of internal improvements and of slavery, it is true that Brownlow coincided with his surroundings and that he had no little part in directing and supporting sentiment in East Tennessee on these two subjects. In his newspaper he gave a great deal of space to railroads, and he applied to the abolitionists some of his most devastating invective.

The question might well be asked, How did Brownlow look upon aristocrats, both in his midst and on the slave plantations? It expresses much to say that he did not hate them and never hurled his terrible bolts at them. Through grim circumstances he had been forced to believe in hard labor; the aristocrats frowned upon manual labor as something for the slave to do. The Parson with good feeling told them how mistaken they were in upholding such a system of philosophy.[12] Andrew Johnson had a personal feeling against aristocrats because he had begun life among them as a poor white, and he held them responsible for his hard lot. Brownlow had grown up among his own kind, and when he came into contact with aristocrats he had become a man of some importance. In fact Brownlow was not sure that he would not like to be an aristocrat, if he could only learn the formula. The most that the Parson had to say about aristocrats was to make some good-natured fun at their expense.

He was well acquainted with the planter aristocrats and with their ways, for he travelled widely throughout the South as politician, preacher, moral lecturer, or delegate to any kind of a meeting to which he could get the appointment. He was an in-

---

the Revolution in Hayti, pp. 20-21; William Birney, James G. Birney and his Times, pp. 74-78; Humes, op. cit., pp. 32-33.

   [12] Knoxville Whig, June 19, 1852.

veterate wanderer, and most of his travels were in the South. In 1848 he turned up at Madison, Georgia in the heart of planter aristocracy, with no other reason than to attend the meeting of the Georgia Conference there.[13] In 1854 he set out on a lecture trip which took him down through the Lowlands from Charleston to Savannah and up through the heart of Georgia. He showed no distaste for the planters, though at times they showed a dislike for him. On this trip he visited the little intellectual and aristocratic center of Athens, Georgia, and spoke in the town hall on temperance. The élite of the town came out to listen, "attracted more through curiosity than anything else" and expecting to hear something "original and racy." Their expectations were fully gratified, for the Parson soon dipped into low and vulgar allusions and set the aristocratic ladies to leaving the meeting or blushing behind their fans in the most approved fashion.[14]

If no other evidence existed, the fact that the Parson attended some of the meetings of the Southern commercial conventions would be sufficient to show that he was climbing up among the planter aristocrats and was attempting to become respectable among them. By appearing at such meetings he was tending to identify himself with that longing in the South to develop Southern nationalism and Southern unity and to speed the day when the destiny of the South would be fully realized, under aristocratic leadership. He attended the convention which met in Charleston in 1854, and although he did not dominate the meeting like he would a Methodist conference, still he slipped in a speech whenever possible and in other ways made the convention realize that he was present. In 1857 the Southern Commercial Convention met in Brownlow's home city, Knoxville, and, of course, the Parson was there. He announced his presence early in the session when he opposed a movement to keep out the "Black Republican" and Yankee newspaper reporters, by declaring that he would be in favor of admitting a reporter from his Satanic majesty if one should appear. Other East Tennessee

---

[13] *Jonesboro Monthly Review*, vol. II, no. 2, p. 107.

[14] *The Southern Banner*, April 27, 1854. For a trip into Alabama in 1858 see *Knoxville Whig*, February 13, 1858.

leaders such as Horace Maynard and Oliver P. Temple, were here also identifying themselves with Southern extremism. This Knoxville convention was so outstanding in the threatening attitude which many speakers took toward the Union that the Parson later admitted that these conventions were becoming too dangerous to please him.[15]

But what were the Parson's definite views on slavery, this institution which made possible the great planter class? Having been born with a seeming prejudice against Negroes he naturally considered their proper position to be one of slavery as long as they remained in his sight. His earliest views were strictly in keeping with those of Henry Clay, whom he had chosen as his guide for all earthly affairs. While he was still riding the circuit, the question came up, and he admitted that to solve the problem would take a better mind than his "or those possessed by these emancipating preachers, who are continually bawling out *set your negroes free.*"[16] As his own Methodists held a halting record on the slavery question, he was unable to attack other churches for opposing slavery, but he could at least say that the American Colonization Society would be an excellent organization, if it could be kept free from the Presbyterians. As a true disciple of Henry Clay's he favored colonizing all freed Negroes in Liberia or elsewhere outside the United States. He was opposed to free Negroes remaining in America, and when in 1840 it appeared that the testimony of a free Negro had been accepted in a trial in the navy, Brownlow made a bitter attack on President Van Buren for allowing such an outrage.[17]

In line with the development of the slavery argument in the South, Brownlow declared that the free Negroes in both North and South were more miserable and destitute than the slaves. By the 1850's he stood as a strong friend of slavery, and in defending it he would go as far as the boldest—"even dying in

---

[15] *DeBow's Review*, XVI, 633, XVII, 99, XXIII, 304; *Ought American Slavery to be Perpetuated? A Debate between Rev. W. G. Brownlow and Rev. A. Pryne, held at Philadelphia, September, 1858*, p. 32; Herbert Wender, *Southern Commercial Conventions, 1837-1859*, pp. 185-206.

[16] Brownlow, *Helps to the Study of Presbyterianism*, p. 110.

[17] *Ibid.*, pp. 107-11; *Parson Brownlow's Book*, p. 25; Brownlow, *A Political Register*, pp. 184-90.

the last ditch!" Slavery was wholly scriptural throughout, divinely planned by the Lord, and clearly intended by Him to "exist even to the end of time."[18]

Nothing aroused the Parson to a greater heat of passion than to have the institution attacked by Northerners, whom he variously denominated "fiery bigots," "vagabond philanthropists," and "vile Abolitionists."[19] Back in 1839 he announced in his *Whig:* "A young upstart from Philadelphia, who figures with as many ALIASES as the Emperor of Russia has titles" visited East Tennessee for the purpose of getting converts to abolition, but not a soul would hear him.[20] *Uncle Tom's Cabin,* the Parson considered the greatest outrage ever perpetrated in book form, and as for Mrs. Stowe, "We are sorry to say that she is certainly a *deliberate liar,* and it is the greater pitty [*sic*], as she is the daughter of a Clergyman, and has been better raised!"[21] Later on when the Parson saw her picture he passed the further comment on her: "She is as ugly as Original sin—an abomination in the eyes of civilized people. A tall, course, vulgar-looking woman—stoop-shouldered with a long yellow neck, and a long peaked nose—through which she speaks."[22]

The Parson was maddened to the extent of being willing to accept any wager of battle the Abolitionists might throw down. In 1853, in the most advanced fire-eating fashion he declared, " 'A bloody revolution' is the only alternative the Abolitionists of the North intend to present to the South. As a Southern man, we accept the proposition for 'a bloody revolution,' and we are ready to go into it, whenever the ball opens."[23]

Having thundered out against the Northern Abolitionists for twenty years in his newspaper, Brownlow in 1856 decided to preach a formal sermon against them.[24] On June 8th he spoke

---

[18] Brownlow, *Great Iron Wheel Examined,* pp. 314–21.

[19] W. G. Brownlow, *Americanism Contrasted with Foreignism, Romanism, and Bogus Democracy, in the Light of Reason, History and Scripture; in which Certain Demagogues in Tennessee, and Elsewhere, are shown up in their True Colors,* p. 197.

[20] *Elizabethton Whig,* September 19, 1839.

[21] *Knoxville Whig,* February 5, 1853.

[22] *Ibid.,* August 13, 1853.

[23] *Ibid.,* August 6, 1853.

[24] Of course, he had much to say about slavery, in his sermons heretofore.

in Temperance Hall in Knoxville for an hour and fifteen minutes on slavery, showing the great part that institution had played in history, how Abraham had had more slaves than any cotton-planter in South Carolina or Mississippi, how it was through slavery that King Solomon built his Temple, how the Egyptians built the Pyramids, and how the great civilizations of Greece and Rome had been reared and maintained. It was nothing to their credit that Northerners did not own slaves, for "their virtuous and pious minds were chiefly exercised in slave-stealing and slave-selling." As for the pious Abolitionists, they preached against slavery on Sunday, "and on the next day, in a purely business transaction, behind a counter, or in the settlement of an account, cheat a Southern slave out of the *pewter* that ornaments the head of his cane!" "Nay," cried out the Parson, "the *villainous piety* of some leads them to contribute *Sharpe's Rifles* and *Holy Bibles*, to send the *uncircumcised Philistines* of New England into Kansas and Nebraska, to shoot down the Christian owners of slaves, and then to perform religious ceremonies over their dead bodies!"[25]

Having improved upon this sermon and made some additions, the next year he displayed his complete Southern orthodoxy before the meeting of the Southern Commercial Convention then being held in Knoxville, by delivering it in Temperance Hall before the assembled delegates and others. At this time he took the opportunity to renew his warfare against Elder Graves and to vindicate his beloved Methodist Church South from the slanders of the Reverend Presbyterian. His chief quarrel with Graves now sprang out of the latter's statement that the Presbyterians in a recent schism in the New School wing were the first religious denomination to allign itself definitely in support of slavery. Brownlow, after castigating Graves, reminded him that the Methodist Church South had wedded slavery back in 1844.[26] So pleased were the Southern Commercial Convention delegates with this sermon that ten of them from Alabama and eighteen from various other Southern states called upon Brownlow to

[25] Brownlow, *Americanism Contrasted with Foreignism,* pp. 195-201.

[26] W. G. Brownlow, *A Sermon on Slavery; A Vindication of the Methodist Church South: Her Position Stated,* pp. 22-31.

print the sermon in pamphlet form to be scattered throughout the slaveholding South. They also respectfully begged the Parson to repeat his "Lecture" in all the principal cities and towns. Brownlow, greatly pleased by the reception he had received from these planter aristocrats, agreed to comply with both kind invitations.[27]

The Parson's blood was now tingling for the fray with the Abolitionists. His slavery sermon appeared to him to be irresistible. He would not waste it on East Tennesseeans and other Southerners, who were already favorable to slavery; rather would he challenge the combined hordes of all the North to come out and fight. He would especially like to cross swords with Theodore Parker or Henry Ward Beecher, and he was not afraid to have the combat on Boston Commons amidst a ten acre lot full of people. The reputation of the Parson was too well known in the North for his challenge to be immediately accepted or even considered. The first "black hope" of the North to come out was Frederick Douglass, whom the Parson spurned as an untouchable. It would be an immeasurable disgrace to debate with a Negro. But the Parson was in earnest in his desire to debate any white Abolitionist and he hoped one would appear. Late in the spring of 1858 a radical Garrisonian emerged from his retreat at McGrawville, New York, and informed the Parson that he would debate the question of slavery with him. This champion for the North identified himself as Abraham Pryne, a Congregational clergyman, and the editor of an anti-slavery paper, the *Central Reformer*. Should Brownlow like to know more he was referred to Joshua R. Giddings, Gerritt Smith, or Mark Hopkins. Pryne stipulated that the debate must be held somewhere in the state of New York, and that he must have four weeks notice.[28]

The Parson was eager to begin the fight, and he got his heart's content, for hostilities began even before the terms of the debate had been settled. Pryne not getting an immediate answer to his acceptance of the Parson's challenge addressed him

---

[27] *Ibid.*, p. 2.
[28] *Ought American Slavery to be Perpetuated*, pp. 5, 6, 129, 281.

7

again with the hope "that after your blustering announcement that you would meet the entire North on this question, you will not back out from the first debate offered you."[29] Brownlow came back with a ready answer: He had not replied sooner because when Pryne's letter arrived he was 1,000 miles away "on a tour of observation among the negroes, and sugar and cotton plantations of Mississippi, Arkansas, Louisiana, and Alabama." Having already been insulted by the Negro, Frederick Douglass, the Parson was wary of Northerners whom he did not personally know. "There are two points of information I wish from you," he wrote, "before I respond to your challenge. First, what church are you connected with? Next, are you a white man, or a gentleman of color?" Not to be trapped by a Negro or an atheist, Brownlow on the same day wrote Giddings, asking the same two questions about Pryne. Giddings informed him that Pryne was a Congregationalist, but he did not mention his color. This aroused Brownlow's suspicions, and again he demanded of Pryne his color, stating that since there was a Negro college in McGrawville, he suspected that Pryne was its president. Pryne now replied that he was "not a very white man," but that there was no Negro blood in his veins.[30]

Now that Pryne's color was established, Brownlow would consider the terms of the debate. He did not want to debate in the state of New York, but he would be satisfied with Philadelphia. Pryne acceded, agreeing to debate anywhere from Augusta, Maine to Chicago. As to the nature of the question and its statement, Brownlow wanted great latitude, for he had determined to take advantage of this occasion not only to defend slavery and all things Southern but to carry out a terrific assault against the North and all of its ways. He declared, "I will be the judge of what is to the point, and will not be ruled out of order, or off of the subject, by any moderators, or judges of the debate." He would begin the debate and let Pryne close it, and it might continue through as many installments as Brownlow might desire. Each should speak an hour, and neither should

---

[29] *Ibid.*, p. 6.
[30] *Ibid.*, pp. 6-9.

continue more than an hour and a half. There should be no
interruptions, and however much Pryne might need the help
of others he must fight alone, but Brownlow would not object
to him surrounding himself "with all the anti-Slavery leaders
at the North, and with counselling them, and being prompted
by them at intervals; and when we are through, if any one of
them shall think you have not done me or the South justice, I
will renew the contest with him." Brownlow wanted it understood that he was not entering this debate for the purpose of
making money. Therefore, it ought to be "a free fight"; but he
could not afford to be at greater expense than his fare to Philadelphia and return and his lodging while there. Consequently,
if the hall should not be free, then an admission price must be
charged. Pryne was sure that it would be wholly permissible
to charge an admission fee, for in fact that was the custom in
the North. Although Brownlow would not debate with a Negro,
he would not object to having Negroes listening to him debate.
So it was agreed that all without regard to color should be admitted, if they presented the required tickets. The debate should
be held in early September. Now that the terms were fixed and
the date set, the Parson warned Pryne "to be fully ready, as I
purpose to give you battle after a style you have not been accustomed to. . . ."[31]

During the summer the Parson marshalled his facts at spare
moments, and on September 3, he arrived in Philadelphia—
but not ready for the fight: He had ammunition sufficient to
annihilate the North, but he was unable to fire it at the enemy.
He had lost his voice. He suggested to Pryne that the debate be
postponed, explaining, "By speaking both too long and too
loud, and by over-heating myself in a controversy during the
last summer, I have brought upon myself bronchitis, rendering
it impossible for me to speak, or even converse, without an effort somewhat painful." With a feeling akin to humility he
admitted that this was the first time he had found himself without a strong and powerful voice for thirty years. Pryne de-
murred: The hall had been engaged and the audience was ready;

---

[31] *Ibid.*, pp. 9-14.

no one must be disappointed. Brownlow had never been a coward and rather than have the appearance of being one now, he hired a reader to perform for him. But the great joy of appearing before an audience in exciting debate he was now forced to forego, and although those who listened to his speeches heard language unusual to their ears, they missed the greatest attraction which the joint debate had promised.[32]

This forensic disputation was held in the National Guard Hall, and beginning on September 7, it lasted through five successive evenings, attracting considerable attention among the Philadelphians. On the first evening there were about 400 present, and according to the *Pennsylvanian,* the audience throughout the five days was a "mixture of whites and blacks— Southern students, Quakers, Black Republicans, and negro barbers and bootblacks, and the Abolitionists outnumbered the decent portion three to one."[33] Despite the fact that this debate was much like giving the play with Hamlet left out, the Parson's arguments seem to have drawn much attention. One Philadelphia paper declared that his speech was received "with especial favor,"[34] and another reported that it "abounded in racy denunciation, keen hits, and amusing and felicitous turns of expression" and "the audience applauded immensely."[35]

As the two participants were fanatical in their zeal on opposite sides of the same subject, there was no reason for a polished debate, neither logical argument nor nice personal considerations. Perhaps the audience might have been disappointed and less appreciative had the debate turned out otherwise. The Parson very early complained of being interrupted by people in the audience crying out, "Time expired." He charged the guilty ones with being "ruffians and insolent free negroes," who were Pryne's chief supporters, for "Southern men, unlike Abolitionists, are men of good breeding!"[36] According to Brownlow's estimate the audience was in the proportion of five to one

---

[32] *Ibid.,* pp. 15-16.
[33] September 13, 1858.
[34] *North American and United States Gazette,* September 8, 1858.
[35] *Pennsylvanian,* September 8, 1858.
[36] *Ought American Slavery to be Perpetuated,* p. 140.

against him, and he explained it by declaring that Pryne had "a horde of free negroes and fugitive slaves here all the time clapping for him, and *hissing* me."[37] In closing the debate Brownlow said, "For the general decorum and most exemplary behavior of the decent portion of the audience, I return my sincere thanks. To the opposite class, largely in the majority, my competitor will no doubt make suitable acknowledgments!"[38] Brownlow also found the newspapers of the city prejudiced against him. They gave to Pryne's speeches much more space than to his own—and he openly confronted them with charges of this favoritism.[39] Pryne accused Brownlow of running over his time in almost every one of his speeches. Smarting under some of Brownlow's thrusts, he declared that he had stooped lower than he had anticipated when he agreed to debate the Parson. He took especial offense at this question which Brownlow asked him: "Would he be willing to see his daughter married to the son of such distinguished *buck negroes* as Sam. Ward or Fred. Douglass?" He answered that he would not stoop to such tactics as the Parson employed, but he would say that his daughter should never marry a Southern slaveholder.[40]

At times during the debate Brownlow assumed that he had demoralized Pryne and had thrown him into a disorganized retreat. He challenged him to repeat the debate throughout the North and South—especially would he have it repeated in the South. Pryne snarled back at the Parson and refused, for Southerners "meet reason with brickbats and pistols, and settle questions of ethics and logic with *gutta percha* canes, even on the floor of the Senate. . . ."[41]

Personalities added excitement to the debate, but most of the time was consumed with arguments, new and old, Southern and Garrisonian, in which the slaves sometimes got lost amidst the display of bitter sectionalism. At the outset Brownlow announced that slavery had been found to be in existence at the

[37] *Ibid.*, p. 215.
[38] *Ibid.*, p. 278.
[39] *Ibid.*, p. 277.
[40] *Ibid.*, pp. 171-72, 216, 221.
[41] *Ibid.*, pp. 282-83.

dawn of history and that it would also be found at the setting thereof. He had traced slavery "up the stream of time to God's awful mysteries which enshroud the origin of society!"[42] Abolitionists should know that "if their great-grand-children live to see 'American Slavery' eradicated from the States South, where it now is, by the sanction of law and the provisions of our Constitution, as well as with the approbation of God himself, they will live until their heads are as grey as a Norwegian rat."[43] Indeed, he would go further: "When the angel Gabriel sounds the last loud trump of God, and calls the nations of the earth to judgment—then, and not before, will slavery be abolished south of Mason and Dixon's line!"[44]

He found slavery Biblical throughout, and no Christian could deny that slavery had been ordained by God. He exhibited dozens of passages from the Bible to prove his point. He declared that Abraham owned "more slaves than any cotton-planter in South Carolina, Georgia, Alabama, or Mississippi; or any tobacco or sugar planter in Virginia or Louisiana."[45] God not only established slavery but he ordained fugitive slave laws for its enforcement. The proof he found in Genesis 16:9, which reads, "And the angel of the Lord said unto her, Return to thy mistress, and submit thyself under her hands." This passage referred to Hagar's flight from Sarai. At the peril of having his audience charge that he was crazy, Brownlow declared that he would solemnly say "that the Angel of God, on this occasion, was acting in the capacity of a *United States Marshal* under the then existing fugitive slave laws of the Old Testament, and arresting a *fugitive slave.* . . ."[46] Christ had seen slavery of the worst kind on all sides, yet he had never preached against it, neither had St. Paul. In fact St. Paul had opposed the abolitionists of his day.[47]

Slavery was a great Christianizing influence. In Africa the black savages worshiped "stones, insects, and reptiles." In their

[42] *Ibid.*, p. 202.
[43] *Ibid.*, p. 270.
[44] *Ibid.*, pp. 217-18.
[45] *Ibid.*, p. 20.
[46] *Ibid.*, pp. 79-80.
[47] *Ibid.*, pp. 212, 255.

barbarism they were "fierce, cruel, cowardly and treacherous," ignorant and lascivious, constantly fighting among themselves, burning each other at the stake, and actually devouring each other. American slavery had rescued them from this terrible existence and had placed them in the salubrious South where they ate the bread of contentment and where every Sunday hundreds of thousands heard the Gospel preached.[48] Slavery "has brought five times more negroes into the fold of the Church than all the missionary operations of the world combined. Slavery has tamed, civilized, *Christianized*, if you please, the brutal negroes brought to our shores, by New England *kidnappers*...."[49] The slaveholders, even those who were not members of any church, had encouraged the Christianization of their slaves. As a result there were in the South 466,000 slaves who were members of churches. The Parson had found slave churches in all the principal cities of the South, and he had preached to many slave congregations. In Mobile he had recently seen a slave congregation of 700 members, who owned a church building costing $7,000. In his own home town of Knoxville, there were two slave Sunday Schools.[50]

The Abolitionists had attempted vast damage to God's Kingdom among the slaves. They had forced the Methodist Church to divide into a Northern and a Southern branch, for "we cannot affiliate with men who fight under the dark and piratical flag of Abolitionism, and whose infernal altars smoke with the vile incense of Northern fanaticism!"[51] The Southern Methodist Church was then doing "more for the souls and bodies of the negro race; than all the Wendell Phillipses, Josh Giddingses, Horace Greelys, Ward Beechers, Loyd [*sic*] Garrisons, Theodore Parkers, Madam Stowes, and other freedom-shriekers, now out of the infernal regions!"[52] No Abolitionists merited a place in Heaven, and if the Parson should ever discover any of them there he would be forced to conclude that "they have entered

---

[48] *Ibid.*, pp. 98-99.
[49] *Ibid.*, p. 101.
[50] *Ibid.*, pp. 99-100, 166.
[51] *Ibid.*, p. 41.
[52] *Ibid.*, p. 39.

that world of joy, by practicing a gross fraud upon the door-keeper!"[53]

The Abolitionists were continually shouting freedom for the slaves, as if such a condition would be helpful. The free Negroes already in existence were horribly treated in the North, and those in the South found no possible position in which to live, economical or otherwise. With few exceptions the slaves were kindly treated by their masters. "Cruelty, starvation, and naked-ness," declared Brownlow, "does not exist in the South, but in the disordered imaginations of Abolition preachers, travellers, and slanderers, who pass hurriedly through the South, getting up materials for book-making."[54] In fact, "In our cotton-grow-ing States, our hardest task-masters are *Northern* men, by birth and education!"[55] The Parson was convinced that if given their freedom, one-half of the slaves in East Tennessee would refuse it.[56] Furthermore, the Negroes were an inferior race, and only ignorant and bigoted Abolitionists argued otherwise. Psycholo-gists had determined that Africans at maturity did not have brains equal to Caucasians at birth, and other scientists had found that a dark skin was a mark of degeneracy.[57]

So excellent an institution was slavery that the United States was under obligation to civilization and to Christianity to carry it to other parts of the world. The Parson would not waste time in minor filibustering expeditions to Cuba and to Central Amer-ica. Rather he would become an imperialist in the grandest pro-portions. He would seize Africa and develop it—a vision which the imperialists of Europe did not catch for almost a quarter of a century. Africa was vast and rich, and the Negroes there had forfeited any further claim to it. "Let us seize upon the vast territory of Africa," pleaded the Parson, "cultivate its rich soil, and force its millions of indolent, degraded, and starving natives, to labor, and thereby elevate themselves to the dignity of

[53] *Ibid.*, p. 41.
[54] *Ibid.*, p. 80.
[55] *Ibid.*, p. 94.
[56] *Ibid.*, p. 98.
[57] *Ibid.*, pp. 213-14. The discovery had been made that a certain tribe of Jews who had inbred became darker.

men made in the image of God!" Such a move would accomplish more in Christianizing the Negroes than all the efforts of all the missionaries America could send. According to the Parson "God looks to the people of the United States to develop the resources of Africa, and I honestly believe he requires us to do that work"[58]

Brownlow found the Abolitionists detestable from every angle. "What an unmitigated generation of hypocrites! They *stole* and sold into *perpetual bondage*, a race of human beings it was not profitable to keep, and for whom they now, like so many graceless pirates, refuse all warranty. And what few American ships are in the trade now, at the peril of piracy, are New England ships." He believed these craft were "owned and manned by the hypocritical freedom-shriekers of the Northern States, who desire to recover the several sums of money they have contributed, under excitement, to aid the cause of 'bleeding Kansas.' "[59]

The Abolitionists were despicable cowards. Pryne had said that the slave-owners slept with pistols under their pillows through fear of a slave uprising. At least the slaves would fight, declared the Parson, which was more than the Abolitionists would do. "If none but *blue-bellied* Yankees and unmitigated Northern Abolitionists come down upon us, we shall sleep with nothing more terrific under our pillows than *spike-gimblets*!"[60] Pryne was almost as radical as John Brown, and he bespoke it before John Brown had acted his part in the drama. Pryne declared, "I would far rather contribute Sharp's rifles, pistols, and bayonets —in order that the negro might be defended in possessing his freedom on our own soil, and living among us, where he has a right to live."[61] Brownlow charged that such agitation would break up the Union, for the South could not exist in such a situation. Pryne gave the answer characteristic of the extreme Abolitionists: "What if the agitation should drive the Southern

---

[58] *Ibid.*, pp. 252-54.
[59] *Ibid.*, pp. 33-34.
[60] *Ibid.*, p. 109.
[61] *Ibid.*, p. 191.

States out of the Union? Who cares? Not I." If forced to a choice between Union and abolition, he would choose the latter.[62]

Brownlow sincerely loved the Union and he had always glorified it. He, therefore, hated the Abolitionists the more for imperilling it. He believed that they were actually bent on breaking it up. But he would not be tricked by them, for he understood their low purposes. He gave the warning: "But we of the South intend to fight you *in* the Union, not *out* of it! And when your *blue-bellied Yankees* come South, with 'Sharp's rifles and Holy Bibles,' to seize upon our slaves, let me say to you, that they will not find themselves in *Kansas!*"[63] Brownlow assumed the Union position in the debate, and commented on the fact that Pryne had said nothing in favor of the glorious government. In his concluding speech, for the special benefit of Pryne, the Parson dedicated to the Union this apostrophe:

Who can estimate the value of the American Union? Proud, happy, thrice happy America!" the home of the oppressed! the asylum of the emigrant; where the citizen of every clime, and the child of every creed, roams free and untrammelled as the wild winds of heaven! Baptized at the fount of Liberty, in fire and blood, cold must be the heart that thrills not at the name of the American Union![64]

Pryne sought to hold the debate as close as possible to a strict discussion of slavery. He side-stepped somewhat the Parson's Biblical arguments, and was soon off into a metaphysical dissection of the Constitution of the United States to show that slavery was not protected by that document. Pryne declared that the Declaration of Independence had abolished slavery, and it was only natural for him to continue with this species of logic to prove that the Constitution of all American law rested on the Declaration. And even if the Declaration of Independence had not by inference abolished slavery through the Constitution, there was the fact that the Constitution directly abolished it, for according to the preamble a more perfect union was to be

---

[62] *Ibid.,* p. 230.
[63] *Ibid.,* p. 271.
[64] *Ibid.,* p. 272.

set up and justice was to be guaranteed. But how, inquired Pryne, can these things be with slavery—especially if the Abolitionists declared that they would break up the Union if slavery were not abolished?[65]

It would have been difficult for a Southerner and a Northerner in the 1850's to hold a debate over slavery without running off into a great deal of sectional arguments. Brownlow seized the initiative by devoting a whole evening to proving how criminal and undesirable Northerners were. He examined the latest reports of the penitentiaries in most of the Southern States and determined that most of the felons there incarcerated were of Northern birth, and by a similar examination of the reports of Northern penitentiaries he found that few of the criminals had been born in the South, "unless it be a villainous negro the Abolitionists have stolen from us, and then sent to prison to get rid of him!" He also discovered that the North had more bank failures, more deserters from the United States Army, and more mulattoes, while the South had a greater per capita wealth. Northerners were drifting into "Free Lovers, Free Soilers, Abolitionists, Spiritualists, Trance Mediums, Bible Repudiators, and representatives of every crazy other *ism* known to the annals of Bedlam." To Brownlow they were an extremely unattractive people, who outraged completely the old conservative principles of morality and homely virtues which still held sway in the South.[66]

Pryne searched Helper's *Impending Crisis* for information to prove that the South was far behind the North in wealth and progress of every kind. Just as Brownlow held that slavery was the secret of the South's superiority over the North, Pryne now held the same institution responsible for the very reverse. In answer to Brownlow's charges of criminality against Northerners, Pryne declared that the South's 250,000 slaveholders were the greatest criminals of the age. He determined that the South was $12,000,000,000 poorer on account of slavery, at which he exclaimed,

---

[65] *Ibid.*, pp. 67-72.
[66] *Ibid.*, pp. 142-70.

What a sum to sink into the fathomless maw of such a monster crime! all for the purpose of allowing 250,000 slaveholders to lord it over their negroes, keep race-horses, and vary the amusements of gambling, fighting, and drinking, by an occasional dash into politics, to play the game of Southern statesmanship, and, when weary of that, to astonish the waiters and attachées of Northern hotels by blustering about Northern watering-places.[67]

Before the debate had been finished Brownlow developed into almost a perfect champion of the Southern position in the sectional dispute. An aristocrat with a thousand slaves could not have stated his own attitude better. Brownlow referred to John C. Calhoun as "that great and towering intellect, and tried patriot, . . . who literally died in *Southern harness*, battling for the rights of the South, under the Constitution."[68] He sang the familiar praises of Southern wealth and Southern might, with as flawless notes as J. D. B. De Bow or a hundred other Southern patriots would have used. The South could take care of herself—she was "throughout her whole extent, by the act of God, in contact with the commercial world."[69] "At any time, upon short notice, the South can raise, equip, and maintain in the field a larger force than any power on earth can send against her," the Parson proudly stated.[70] The South had both wealth and rights, "And these rights," he declared, "we intend to enjoy, or to a man we will die, strung along Mason and Dixon's line, with our faces looking North!"[71] He then put forth his best effort on this panegyric of the South:

Yes, gentlemen, ours is the land of chivalry, the land of the muse, the abode of statesmen, the home of oratory, the dwelling-place of the historian, and of the hero; the scenes of classic recollections and of hallowed associations lie south of Mason and Dixon's Line; and when the South is prostrated (which God in his mercy never intends), the genius of the world will weep amid the ruins of the only true Republic ever known to civilized man![72]

Having finished his task, self-imposed, of going five hundred miles to defend at his own expense and with great vehemence the very soul of the South of which he was not a part, the

---

[67] *Ibid.*, pp. 173-95.   [68] *Ibid.*, p. 40.   [69] *Ibid.*, pp. 259-63.
[70] *Ibid.*, p. 265.   [71] *Ibid.*, p. 263.   [72] *Ibid.*, p. 271.

Parson returned to his Tennessee home to await, unknown to him, the next great contest which was to be the greatest of his life and of his country. Brownlow was neither a planter nor an aristocrat, yet he had all of their prejudices personified only awaiting their unloosening by the Abolitionists. Slavery played no basic part in the economic life of the Southern Highlanders, but it was absolutely fundamental in their mental complex. Two more bitter personal and political enemies never lived in East Tennessee than Brownlow and Andrew Johnson, yet these two were one on the question of slavery. Slavery was the great common denominator among the Southern Highlanders. Johnson declared that he would help carry on a war to exterminate the Negroes if the North forcibly freed them. He stated what the Southern Highlander as well as the Southern Lowlander felt, when he said "If you liberate the Negro, what will be the next step? . . . What will we do with two million Negroes in our midst? . . . Blood, rape and rapine will be our portion. You can't get rid of the Negro except by holding him in slavery."[73] Slavery solved the race question, and so if there must be Negroes in his midst the Southern mountaineer was just as eager to maintain slavery for protection as the Southern planter was for profit.[74] And there was no inconsistency in being for the Union and for slavery at the same time, for only through the maintenance of the Union, did it appear in the eyes of many people, that slavery could be continued.[75] But if it should ever happen that the slaves were freed, then they must either be exterminated, as Andrew Johnson would have it, or they must be deported, a plan which many of the mountaineers thought to be the best solution.[76]

[73] R. W. Winston, *Andrew Johnson, Plebeian and Patriot*, pp. 118-19, 134.
[74] For an admirable exposition of this thesis see U. B. Phillips, "The Central Theme of Southern History," *American Historical Review*, vol. XXXIV, no. 1 (October, 1928), pp. 30-43.
[75] *Relief for East Tennessee. Address of Hon. N. G. Taylor*, pp. 27-28.
[76] It must be kept in mind that there was a difference between disliking Negroes and disliking slavery. The ante-bellum Highlander felt that if there must be Negroes around, they should be slaves. Henry Clay, the patron saint of Brownlow and of his East Tennessee followers, felt the same way; and Hinton Rowan Helper, who knew that slavery was a great curse to the South, would rather see the Negroes exterminated than have them remain in the South free. The aversion of mountaineers to Negroes continues down to the present day, and in some sections of the Southern Highlands Negroes are not tolerated.

CHAPTER VI

ANTE-BELLUM POLITICS

IN INTRODUCING himself to the North in 1862, the eccentric Parson stated that he had always been, and still was, "quite a politician," though he had never been either an office-seeker or an office-holder. It would have been an eccentricity beyond credulity had he not embraced the proud opportunities for disputation and combat offered him by American politics, and in the face of facts to the contrary, it must be recorded against the Fighting Parson that his memory served him very ill when he rather boastfully said, "I have never been an office-seeker nor an office-holder." True enough, he never made office-seeking a continuous occupation, and without a doubt, he had never been able to induce people to vote for him in sufficient numbers to gain an election, but the annals of ante-bellum politics have it that after having fought for other people for a decade and more he then sought spoils for himself, and that he failed.

As the Parson had a mind that ran on various tracks at the same time, there was no reason why he should not be selecting a political party about as early as he should join a church. He did not make a study of theology before selecting his religious denomination, neither did he enter into the mysteries of government before aligning himself with a political group. He hit upon both rather accidentally, and in doing so he may have had an experience different from most Americans. Yet he used no less reason, for it requires no more mental effort to gain a position by inheritance than to acquire one by accident. It is the common practice to find reasons for an act already done rather than to seek beforehand what it is best to do.

The Parson grew into political competency amidst shouts of "Bargain and corruption," "Put the rascals out," "Hurrah for Old Hickory Jackson," and other expressions of equal de-

cisiveness. It would seem that the leader of such a fight would
have immediately endeared himself to a person of Brownlow's
characteristics, but perhaps it must remain one of the minor,
if not insignificant, mysteries of history why the Parson turned
so vehemently against Andrew Jackson. It might be best to leave
it as merely another reason why the Parson was eccentric. It
happens that Brownlow reached his majority in time to vote
first in the presidential election of 1828, and that he cast his
ballot for John Quincy Adams. The reasons which he recalled
thirty-four years later were that Adams "was a learned statesman, of pure moral and private character, and because I regarded him as a FEDERALIST, representing my political
opinions."[1] Perhaps likes repel and unlikes attract in the
mental realm as they do in the physical world. Whatever the
cause, the Parson hated Old Hickory with stinging bitterness
and did not cease attacking him in his grave.

Those who opposed Jackson and his species of democracy
gradually drifted together and called themselves Whigs. They
all knew what they disliked, but they found great difficulty in
agreeing on anything to like. As Brownlow was a good hater,
he naturally belonged to this group. With the passing of time
the Whigs accumulated a stock in trade which they labelled
with their trade-mark, composed of such principles as federal
aid to internal improvements, a protective tariff, a strong central bank, and a strengthening of the national government with,
at the same time, a debasing of the presidency. True to human
nature, the Parson set to work in his newspaper, which he always
called the *Whig*, to defend these Whig doctrines, for good
reasons if he could discover them, or for no reason at all. He
favored federal aid to internal improvements because it would
help East Tennessee to reach a market, and perhaps if Whiggery in this region had any reasoned cause for existing it must
have been due to this Whig principle. He fought valiantly for
the recharter of the Second United States Bank, because Jackson had opposed it and Clay had championed it. The common
man's knowledge of the Bank did not extend beyond the limits

---

[1] *Parson Brownlow's Book*, p. 19.

of his prejudices, but he knew it was something about which it was easy to raise a fight, so it was one of the principal issues between the Democrats and Whigs in Tennessee. Brownlow was sure that the foreign stockholders did not control the Bank as the Democrats had argued, and when President Tyler vetoed the Fiscal Corporation bill, Brownlow called him a "corrupt traitor."[2]

Whether Brownlow knew why he joined the Whig Party or not, he spent the next twenty years informing himself and the country on the reasons why people should be Whigs. He wasted his first vote on John Quincy Adams in 1828; his vote for Clay in 1832 failed to bring victory; in 1836 he supported the forlorn hope of the Whigs in the South by voting for Hugh White. It began to seem that Brownlow had chosen to go through life voting for people who could never be elected. But as the next presidential election approached there were high expectations in the Whig Party, for it seemed that the old adage was about to come true, that it is an ill wind that blows no one good. The Panic of 1837 must certainly sweep Van Buren and his Democrats out of office, and plant the Whigs in power. The Whigs now pushed aside Brownlow's ideal, Clay, and put up William Henry Harrison, because Clay had tried for the presidency twice and had failed and furthermore he had not fought in the battle of Tippecanoe. This action outraged Brownlow somewhat less than it did his ideal, and soon in the midst of coonskins, log cabins, and casks of hard cider he was the most enthusiastic Whig in America. He later declared, "I sung louder, jumped higher, and fell flatter and harder than anybody else in the whole state of Tennessee. I wrote upon log cabins, and waved coon-skins and water-gourds high and low."[3]

The inauguration of the first Whig president was for the Whigs as great an occasion as was the inauguration of Jackson for the common man. True enough it was a smaller army that invaded Washington, but among those who beat down upon the city was Brownlow. After attending the inauguration, he in-

[2] Brownlow, *Political Register,* pp. 29-49, 55-57.
[3] *Portrait and Biography,* p. 29.

dulged his mania for travelling by visiting New York City. But rejoicing was soon turned into gloom, for Harrison was scarcely well placed in office when he died. Brownlow grieved after the fashion of having lost a close friend. And he added a rising anger to his grief when it became evident that John Tyler, who now became president, would continue to be what he had always been — an old-fashioned Democrat who could not endure Jacksonianism.

To win an office and then to be cheated out of it first by the Grim Reaper and then by a Traitor was too great a strain on Brownlow's complacency. He heaped some of his choicest abuse on John Tyler, and wrote a book against Jackson and the Democrats. He called his book *A Political Register Setting Forth the Principles of the Whig and Locofoco Parties in the United States, with the Life and Public Service of Henry Clay.* The Parson as usual could not desist from including something about himself, so he added to the title *Also an Appendix Personal to the Author, and a General Index.* He wrote the book mostly in 1843, and he published it in his *Jonesboro Whig* office the next year, in time to make it the opening gun in the campaign of 1844. That it might in part live up to its title of being a political register, he inserted some statistics on the area of the states and the votes in previous elections and lists of the presidents and some of their cabinet members. But the main purpose was to give "the phantom of Jacksonian democracy a skinning."

The Parson now had ample provocation for entering the fight with all the peculiar weapons he could command. The Whigs must regain what an unkind fate had taken away from them in 1841, and what could be more inspiring for Brownlow and most others in the party than marching again under the banner of Henry Clay! So enthusiastic did the Parson become that he decided the next year to add to the furor by himself running for Congress. But first he made haste to assault the reputation of Andrew Jackson, before death, which was fast approaching, could carry Old Hickory out of reach. Without hesitation he pronounced the "elevation to the Presidency of this wicked man and vulgar Hero" to be "the greatest curse that

8

ever befell this great and growing Republic."[4] Furthermore, "I calculate that the victory of the eighth of January [the battle of New Orleans] cost five hundred of millions of dollars, besides the small expense of entailing upon the country a set of drivellers whose folly has taken away all dignity from distress, and made even calamity ridiculous."[5] So malignant was the Parson's detestation of Jackson that he followed him to the grave with his abuse. In this wise did he inform the readers of the *Jonesboro Whig* that Jackson was dead, "After a life of eighty long years spent in the indulgence of the most bitter and vindictive passions, which disgrace human nature, and distract the human mind the existence of ANDREW JACKSON terminated" near Nashville. "We would not, if we could, turn aside the veil of the future, to show his deluded followers and blind admirers, what awaits him!"[6]

Brownlow had the Whig contempt for Democrats greatly exaggerated. To him they were a "notorious band of political robbers," who went under various names in different parts of the country. In New York, they were the "Locofocos"; in New England they were known as "Pig-Ringers" and "Subterraneans"; "Butt-enders" was their name in Maryland; they were "Wring necks" in Maine; in South Carolina they went under the name of "State Rights Republican Nullifiers"; the decent people in Ohio called them "The Entire Swine Party"; in Virginia they were the "Republican Abstractionists"; in the Middle West they were called the "Relief Law Party"; and intelligent Tennesseeans called them "Barn-Burners," "Wool-Stealers," and "Counterfeiters."[7]

The Democrats were so slippery and ubiquitous that they reminded the Parson of the stanza,

> They wire in and wire out,
> And leave a body still in doubt.
> Whether the snake that made the track;
> Was going South or coming back.[8]

---

[4] Brownlow, *Political Register*, p. 9.
[5] *Ibid.*, p. 63.
[6] June 18, 1845.
[7] Brownlow, *Political Register*, pp. 13, 125.   [8] *Ibid.*, p. 129.

All Democrats were bad; John Cataline Calhoun was the Parson's way of referring to the great South Carolinian; all were disgusting, even eating with Negroes and going to their dances. In the eyes of the Parson, the whole world was sick, and the Democrats were the cause. "Every government in the civilized world is at present tottering," he declared, and mob violence had broken out in most of the states of the American Union and in the great cities.[9] Now was the time for action, when a man like Henry Clay was leading. Should the people sit and see the country go to ruin, asked Brownlow, "while the political quacks of the country, like the Madagascar Bat fan us to sleep with the wide spread wings of 'free trade and sailors rights,' at the same time literally sucking us to death."[10] Wages were low, prices were ruinous, people were starving, and the Democrats had brought it all about by the low tariff. The only remedy that would restore prosperity was Clay's American System. Not only had the Democrats given the country hard times, but they had also piled up a huge national debt.[11]

There was just one point on which Brownlow found himself standing with the Democrats; he favored the national bankruptcy law which the Whigs had recently repealed. He had no desire to take advantage of such a law to escape his debts, most of which had come by his going on surety bonds for his friends, in doing which he was following Biblical precedent. He declared that the fifteenth chapter of Deuteronomy contained the ancient Jewish bankruptcy law and differed from the late law of Congress only in phraseology. He also found another bankruptcy law recorded in the Lord's Prayer.[12]

The Texas question, on which the election of 1844 really turned, seemed to bother the Parson very little. Perhaps he was wise enough to see Clay's predicament as the latter became more involved in explaining his position, and, therefore, he decided not to make Clay's labors harder by enlarging the discussion. In fact, Brownlow's unbounded idolatry of Clay became

---

[9] *Ibid*, pp. 9, 173; *Jonesboro Whig*, Decemebr 4, 1844.
[10] Brownlow, *Political Register*, p. 120.
[11] *Ibid.*, pp. 50, 58-66.
[12] Brownlow, *Political Register*, pp. 146-48.

as intense as ever his hatred waxed against his most detested enemy. The "bargain and corruption" charges which pestered Clay throughout his life enraged Brownlow. He declared that he had the proof of their falsity and that anyone who should read it and not be convinced "we hesitate not to pronounce a VILLAIN, in the most extensive meaning of the epithet."[13] Two years before the election Brownlow began the movement for Clay, proclaiming, "For the Presidency, in 1844, we have declared for HENRY CLAY *vs.* THE WORLD."[14] The next year he paid tribute to his hero by writing his life which made up 81 pages in his so-called *Political Register.* He attended the Whig National Convention in Baltimore and helped to nominate his "Harry." In the campaign he rode the circuit for Clay with as much fervor as he ever displayed when he rode it for the Lord. He was in Raleigh, North Carolina, when Clay made his famous speech there, and he imitated his hero by speaking also. This speech the Raleigh *Standard* declared to be "smutty, ultra, insulting and blasphemous."[15]

There was almost unbounded hope and expectation among the greater part of the Whigs that Clay would be successful, so when the sad intelligence of his defeat reached Brownlow, he wept. According to his son, John Bell Brownlow, the Parson was never known through his long life to have given way to his emotions in such a fashion except once, when a near relative had died. The Parson sobbed, "Heaven spare our friends the bitter pang we feel in announcing this *horrible* intelligence," and with all the reverence at his command he printed in his *Whig* a live coon upside down—so unexpected was the defeat that he had never dreamed he would need a dead coon with which to illustrate the election news.[16]

Brownlow had made much use of Whig coons in his journalistic activities, but never before had he been inclined to feel that the old coon had died. Only a few years previously in announcing a Whig victory in Tennessee politics, he represented

---

[13] *Ibid.,* p. 315.

[14] *Jonesboro Whig,* May 18, 1842.

[15] *Ibid.,* February 28, May 1, 1844; Brownlow, *Political Register,* p. 205.

[16] *Jonesboro Whig,* November 20, 1844.

the Whig coon destroying the Democratic rooster, adding the explanation, "The Coon in Tennessee, has covered himself with glory, and a portion of that imperishable renown, he is about to impart to the *Dominecker* of Locofocoism."[17] The Parson naturally took much interest in state politics, and when in 1842 after the Whigs had captured the legislature, thirteen Democratic senators by obstructive tactics prevented the election of the United States senator, he bitterly attacked them and published their names under the heading, "Thirteen Black Knights."[18]

The defeat of Clay for the presidency was immeasurably a greater calamity to Brownlow than his own failure of election to Congress the next year. In his own campaign he obtained what was after all dearest to his heart, for he had an opportunity to assault throughout East Tennessee the character and reputation of his bitterest political enemy, Andrew Johnson. That Johnson was a Democrat was sufficient in Brownlow's eyes to brand him a traitor to the best interests of his country. That he was a rival for the leadership of East Tennesseeans was further provocation. Before the campaign was over, employing the sort of abuse that he liked best to administer, Brownlow declared Johnson to be an atheist, a coward, and a bastard.[19] But as Johnson was more reasoned in his political methods and was more ambitious for political preferment, he won in 1845 and many times thereafter. A personal and political feud already bitter was now made devastating, and disaster to either one or to both was prevented only by Brownlow and Johnson never speaking to each other again until the Civil War.

There was yet another chance for Clay, Brownlow thought. So a year before the party should make the nomination, he began running in his *Whig* the name of Clay for president and "Old Rough and Ready" Taylor for vice-president.[20] But the manipulators in the Whig Party were not taking orders or advice from Brownlow; they nominated Taylor for president and

---

[17] Brownlow, *Political Register,* p. 203.
[18] *Ibid.,* pp. 138-45.
[19] Winston, *op. cit.,* pp. 42, 50, 63-65. Johnson won by about 1,300 majority.
[20] For instance, *Jonesboro Whig,* May 26, 1847.

Millard Fillmore for vice-president. Clay felt the sting of traitorous friends almost as keenly as he did in 1840, while Brownlow
was angered beyond repair. With sorrow and revenge he took
down the name of Clay, but he refused to raise the Taylor
banner. If he could not support Clay, he would support no one.
On November 1, he informed the people what he proposed
to do. He would vote for the regular Whig electors and he would
do something just as constitutional as what the Whig National
Convention had done: He would instruct the electors to vote for
Clay for president and John Morehead of North Carolina for
vice-president, by writing their names on his ballot. He had now
respected his conscience, but his reason seemed to tell him that
in so doing he might be throwing away his vote. So thorough a
Whig was the Parson that he advised no other Whig to vote
in this method, and in addition he promised to convert two Democrats to regular Whiggery.[21]

Satanic luck seemed always to follow the Whigs when they
succeeded in capturing the presidency. President Taylor did
not survive his inauguration long. He was succeeded by Fillmore,
who lived long enough to win the approval of the Parson. The
troublesome problems growing out of the Mexican War were
leading many Southerners to talk of disunion. Brownlow agreed
with them on the slavery question, but he let it be known that
he would follow no one out of the Union. Naturally he opposed
the Nashville Convention of 1850, and if for no other reason
than Clay's part in it he supported the so-called Compromise
of 1850. The next year he showed his love for the Union by
sarcastically referring to South Carolina's enthusiastic observance of the Fourth of July as likely being due to her threat
that this would be the last Fourth which would find her in the
"meshes of this accursed Confederacy."[22]

Brownlow like Clay was beginning to despair of the Whig
Party ever making the proper nomination for the presidency.
It had never named the Great Commoner when the Whigs could
win, and at other times it had merely sacrificed him. The Parson

---

[21] *Ibid.*, August 30, November 1, 1848. Brownlow attended the inauguration,
met Taylor, and marked him down as lacking vehemence.

[22] *Knoxville Whig*, July 5, 1851.

looked upon the haggard countenance of Clay and feared that he would not live to be proposed again, in 1852. In June of this year, the famous Kentuckian died, and Brownlow lost the only man he had ever idealized and loyally followed. He declared that "the territories of the dead on the continent of America, never were honored with richer spoils."[23] The Parson's feelings toward Clay show that he could love an ideal as tenderly as he could bitterly hate an enemy.

With Clay gone, Brownlow decided upon Fillmore as his choice for the presidency, but again the Whig National Convention disappointed and displeased the Parson by nominating Winfield Scott. He especially opposed this choice because he claimed Scott was a Northern candidate put forth by sixty-six Abolitionists and that his election would mean the overthrow of slavery and the beginning of sectional strife. But Brownlow had no strong convictions on giving Fillmore a second term; he was still longing for Clay. He later said that he "would have willingly voted for Clay's last pair of pantaloons, stuffed with straw!" He never forgot Clay. While in New York City during the Civil War, he facetiously declared that he intended to have a national convention called to nominate the last suit of clothes worn by Clay.[24]

The Whig National Convention might want Winfield Scott and William A. Graham, of North Carolina, for president and vice-president, but the Parson preferred Daniel Webster and Charles J. Jenkins, of Georgia. But the grim old joker, Death, came in on the 24th of October and robbed the Parson of Webster. Not to be outdone even by Fate, the Parson together with tens of thousands of other Americans, voted for the great Massachusetts leader in his grave.[25]

---

[23] *Ibid.,* July 3, 1852.

[24] *Portrait and Biography,* p. 69; *Knoxville Whig,* October 23, 1852. The chief reason for Brownlow's preferring Fillmore rests on the fact that at the very end of his term, Fillmore appointed the Parson on a commission to improve navigation on the river between Knoxville and Chattanooga. When Pierce became president, he filled the commission with Democrats, and according to the Parson, nothing was accomplished and no one received any pay. See V. M. Queener, *op. cit.,* p. 74.

[25] *Ought American Slavery to be Perpetuated,* p. 42; *Knoxville Whig,* October 23, 1852.

During the late 1840's and the early 1850's, Brownlow busied himself with the temperance movement, but not to the extent of deserting the Whigs and joining it as a political party. The temperance leaders generally took control of the Fourth of July celebrations with the hope of gaining converts through guile, but on such occasions the amount of liquor was almost certain to destroy the effects of all temperance propaganda. Speaking of the celebration in 1848 at Jonesboro, Brownlow declared that there was *"liquor* enough in our houses to *counteract* the influence of any Temperance address that can be made here."[26] He wrote voluminously for temperance and made many speeches for it, but he never accepted money for his services. For a time he was one of the editors of the *Sons of Temperance*, a semi-monthly published in Knoxville.[27]

Andrew Johnson's continued political activities in Tennessee appeared to the Parson to be particularly pernicious, both to him personally and to the state. After serving in Congress for ten years, Johnson became governor of Tennessee in 1853 and again in 1855. As these successes were entirely too regular to please Brownlow, he never ceased attacking Johnson. It was an outrage that Tennessee could not elect a religious man to be her ruler, and it was equally disastrous that she must have an Abolitionist. Brownlow claimed that Johnson had voted for the Wilmot Proviso, and as further proof of his anti-slavery proclivities, he cited Johnson's attempt to have the Negroes left out of the count in determining population for state purposes. This, Brownlow held, was a direct thrust at the large slave-holders, and represented an attempt to array class against class.[28]

In 1855 the Whigs made a desperate attempt to defeat Johnson for the governorship. They nominated Meredith P. Gentry to bring success, but Gentry soon turned out to be too dignified in his campaign methods to please Brownlow. The Parson headed a committee which went to Gentry to inform him that East Tennessee was not accustomed to gloved methods in political

---

[26] *Jonesboro Whig,* July 5, 1848; *Knoxville Whig,* July 5, 1851.

[27] *Ibid.,* December 28, 1850; February 21, March 29, 1852.

[28] Brownlow, *Americanism Contrasted with Foreignism,* pp. 22-24.

campaigns. They demanded that Johnson be dragged out into the open and that all of his terrible sins both private and public be exposed. Gentry's refusal to make such a campaign did not lessen Brownlow's insistence.[29]

To Brownlow the campaign against Johnson was perpetual; the mere fact that he had been reëlected in 1855 only intensified the fight that must be continued against him. So vitriolic had been Brownlow's attacks on Johnson that a mob surrounded the Parson's home in Knoxville after the election, jeering and groaning against him, and singing songs for his benefit.[30] That an atheist even if he were governor of Tennessee, should issue a Thanksgiving Proclamation recounting the mercies of the Lord and calling for more seemed to Brownlow an intolerable usurpation of power. There must be a rebuttal to such impudence, so he inserted in his *Knoxville Whig* a long prayer against Johnson, begging the Lord to forgive Tennessee for her great sin in electing him governor. He called upon the churches to use this prayer in their services.[31] The Parson felt quite sure that in a contest with Johnson for the affections of the Lord he could easily win.

He both prayed and preached against Johnson and used every occasion to villify him. On October 9, 1856, he spoke to an immense crowd in the public square in Nashville, almost under the window of the Governor, and assaulted Johnson in the most pronounced fashion. He declared, "I therefore pronounce your Governor, here upon his own dunghill, an UNMITIGATED LIAR AND CALUMNIATOR, and a VILLAINOUS COWARD." Continuing he said, "He is a member of a numerous family of Johnsons, in North Carolina, who are generally THIEVES and LIARS; and though he is the best one of the family I have ever met with, I unhesitatingly affirm, tonight, that there are better men than Andrew Johnson in our Penitentiary."[32] More than a dozen years previously he had pub-

[29] Temple, *op. cit.*, p. 287.

[30] Brownlow, *Americanism Contrasted with Foreignism*, p. 66.

[31] December 1, 1855; Brownlow, *Americanism Contrasted with Foreignism*, p. 75.

[32] *Ibid.*, pp. 66, 71.

lished in the *Jonesboro Whig* Johnson's pedigree, accompanied by a cut of a man hanging on the gallows, who ought to have been Andrew Johnson but who happened to be a first cousin.[33]

Johnson was an atheist, according to the Parson, and he was wise enough to belong to a political party which was fast becoming the tool of the Pope of all the Roman Catholics. Back in the 1830's Brownlow saw on the horizon a small cloud no larger than a man's hand, but to him it looked threatening. It was the cloud of Catholicism, against which the people must quickly be warned. In 1834 in his *Helps to the Study of Presbyterianism* he had raised storm signals, and five years later when he set up his *Whig* at Elizabethton he raised them still higher. He ran a series of articles during 1839 and 1840 warning the people against Catholics. Again in his *Political Register*, in 1843, he called upon the people to give heed.[34]

The great danger to America was to be seen in this Democratic alliance with the Pope. Had not Martin Van Buren, as Secretary of State, in 1830, written a letter to the Pope in which he had called him "Holy Father"?[35] The Catholics were fast dominating all Europe and now they were seeking through the Democratic Party to seize America. Should we aid those "feeding us and our children, upon *latin masses* and *wafer gods?*"[36] The Democrats were already carrying crosses in their processions. They were preaching that Christianity and Democracy were the same; they would unite church and state. Not only were the Democrats embracing the un-American Catholics, they were also absorbing such other monstrosities as the Mormons and the Millerites. And there were certain Democratic "clerical stump-orators" who were so blind as not to see all these things.[37] The Parson was not afraid to speak out, even to interrupt a prayer if necessary, as actually happened in the campaign of 1840. "Old Father Aiken," a Democratic Methodist, entered into an agreement with Brownlow at a camp-meeting

---

[33] March 29, 1842.

[34] Brownlow, *Political Register*, pp. 75-119.

[35] *Ibid.*, pp. 75, 109-10.

[36] *Ibid.*, pp. 75-119.

[37] *Tennessee Whig*, September 19, 26, 1839; *Jonesboro Whig*, December 14, 1842.

that the former should pray and the latter preach. In the midst of his prayer, "Old Father Aiken" suddenly overcome by his love for the Democratic Party cried out "Lord, deliver us from Whiggery!" Brownlow quickly interrupted, "God forbid," whereupon "Old Father Aiken" left praying long enough to exclaim, "Billy, keep still when I am praying."[38]

All down through the 1840's and 1850's Brownlow was issuing warnings against the Catholics and calling attention to their alliance with the Democrats. In 1846 he offered a reward of $20 to anyone who would tell him how much President Polk and his officeholders had given to the new Catholic Church in Washington. He would give an additional $10 if it fell under $1,000.[39] In 1856 there was to be another presidential election. The small cloud no bigger than a man's hand which the Parson had spied a quarter of a century earlier, had now almost overcast the sky. There could be no doubt that if the growing numbers of Catholics in this country portended evil, then the Parson's cloud was positively threatening. In 1830 there had been only 600,000; twenty years later the number had jumped to 3,500,-000;[40] and by 1856 there were likely 4,000,000. The influx of the Irish and Germans had contributed much to this growth. To Brownlow's way of thinking, foreigners were bad enough, but to be Catholics in addition was intolerable. Something must be done about it. As the old Whig Party had been disrupted in 1854 by the Kansas-Nebraska Law, there was now an excellent chance to organize a new party out of the old Whigs and turn it against the foreigners and Catholics. In the 1830's the Native American Party had been organized for this very purpose, but it had died out by the end of the 1840's, and in 1850 its germ of life passed over into the Order of the Star Spangled Banner. This new order soon developed into the so-called Know-Nothing Party, and it was into this secret group that many of the old Whigs entered. As the Democrats decried this proscription of the newcomers, Brownlow might truthfully say that Catholic Irishmen were voting the Democratic ticket.

---

[38] L. P. Stryker, *Andrew Johnson*, p. 10.
[39] *Knoxville Whig*, July 1, 1846.
[40] W. W. Sweet, *The Story of Religions in America*, p. 395.

While the country was organizing a party against the Catholics the Parson was writing a book against them. In 1856 he brought it out and called it *Americanism Contrasted with Foreignism, Romanism, and Bogus Democracy, in the Light of Reason, History, and Scripture; in which Certain Demagogues of Tennessee, and Elsewhere, are Shown up in their true Colors.* He dedicated his book to the Young Men of America and called upon them to save the country from the greatest dangers that had beset civil and religious liberties in America since the Revolution. No argument was ever complete with the Parson until he had summed up the figures against the enemy. Now would he expose the Catholics through the simple rules of arithmetic. He determined from history that the Catholics had killed 68,-000,000 human beings "for no other offense than that of being *Protestants*." If one were to "average each person slain at four gallons of blood, . . . it makes TWO HUNDRED AND SEVENTY-TWO MILLIONS OF GALLONS!—enough to overflow the banks of the Mississippi, and destroy all the cotton and sugar plantations in Mississippi and Louisiana!"[41]

The methods by which this blood-letting had been carried on, the Parson illustrated by various cuts throughout the book, with such titles as "Roman Cruelties of the Inquisition—The Rack," "Burning of Bradford, Ridley, Latimer, Philpot, and Others; and the Holy Bible!" "Horrible Cruelties Inflicted by the Catholics on the Protestants in Ireland, in 1641," and "Horrible Cruelties by Catholics." These scenes represented the kind of people the Democrats were embracing, and he was sorry to see otherwise good Methodist ministers following along. He declared that the title of Augustus B. Longstreet, a Democratic Methodist minister, now president of the University of Mississippi, should read "Professor of Methodism, Romanism, and Locofocism."[42]

By the end of 1854 Brownlow was promoting the Know-Nothings with all of his might. It mattered not to him that Catholics and foreigners were almost non-existent in East Ten-

[41] Brownlow, *Americanism Contrasted with Foreignism*, pp. 56-57.
[42] *Ibid.*, pp. 25-36.

nessee. As long as there were any in the United States, and as long as he was convinced that the charges made against them were true, he would have them crushed. He set aside a column in his *Whig* for his new party and transformed his Whig coon into a Know-Nothing coon.[43] He became a member of the National Council and attended the National Convention of the Know-Nothings in Philadelphia in 1856.[44] Two weeks after the Whig defeat in 1852, Brownlow ran up the name of Fillmore for the nomination in 1856.[45] With the break-up of the Whigs and the rise of the Know-Nothings, he switched over to John Bell, of Tennessee, for president, but by the beginning of 1856 he had switched back to Fillmore. At this time he wrote Bell that he was for Fillmore first and then for Bell.[46] When the convention met, Brownlow for once saw his choice for nominations confirmed. Fillmore was nominated for president and Andrew Jackson Donelson for vice-president.[47] Indeed had the Parson travelled a long distance when, in order to support to the fullest a namesake of Andrew Jackson, he should heap full praise on "Old Hickory" and discover that he had had Know-Nothing principles in their pristine vigor.[48] Many Southerners joined the Know-Nothings in an attempt to lay the Banquo ghost of slavery, and others like Brownlow joined because they could never degrade their pride to the level of becoming Democrats, and too, because the Know-Nothings offered some objects on which it was easy to muster up a full-sized amount of native hatred. But the Know-Nothings were forced in the North to divide the opposition to the Democrats with a new crusading party called the Republicans. As a result Brownlow saw Fillmore defeated, but he rejoiced at the victory of Buchanan over the Black Republican candidate John C. Frémont.

Politics offered quite a problem for Brownlow for the next four years, but there were a few points that he always kept straight. He knew that he continued to love the Union and that

---

[43] *Knoxville Whig,* December 2, 1854.
[44] Brownlow, *Americanism Contrasted with Foreignism,* pp. 14, 86.
[45] *Knoxville Whig,* November 13, 1852, January 20, 1855.
[46] John Bell MSS. Letter dated January 15, 1856.
[47] *Knoxville Whig,* January 26, March 15, 1856.   [48] *Ibid.*

he hated as much as ever the Democrats and the Abolitionists. With the shrivelling up of the Know-Nothing movement, there was the question as to where he should go next, but he knew it would not be to the Democrats. In 1859 he said, "With the Democratic party, we never can act, even in a conflict between them and the Devil. We would as soon be engaged in importing the plague from the East, as in promoting the principles and policy of the party calling themselves DEMOCRATS."[49] According to Brownlow the Democratic Party was still the refuge of the "unwashed and uncombed Foreigners," who were all Abolitionists.[50]

His hatred of the Democrats did not mean that he considered himself less Southern or that he liked the North better. John Brown's crazy scheme enflamed Brownlow as completely as if he had been the owner of a plantation of ten thousand acres and a thousand slaves. He declared that Brown was a vile creature and that Pryne, whom Brownlow had debated a few years previously in Philadelphia, was even worse. He wrote an open letter to Pryne in which he said, "Had you, as a 'Preacher of Righteousness' exhorted the old scoundrel, and his villainous boys, to repentance and faith, they might have become religious, instead of dying in this disgraceful act of rebellion and going to Hell, as they doubtless have done. Shame on you, you vile hypocrite."[51] Thereafter for a season Brownlow pelted Pryne with a series of open letters. He believed activities like John Brown raids were the conscious efforts of people in the North to break up the Union. He felt that Northern people were mostly alike and should be looked upon with suspicion. In 1853, when a Mr. Wheeler of Vermont was elected president of the University of East Tennessee, Brownlow declared that the patrons of the University did not want their sons placed under a man "who has encountered the snows and chills of SIXTY winters, in the notorious Free Soil State of *Vermont*."[52]

"Bleeding Kansas," Brooks' assault on Sumner, and riots

---

[49] *Knoxville Tri-Weekly Whig,* August 4, 1859.
[50] *Ibid.,* February 24, 1859.
[51] *Ibid.,* October 27, 1859.
[52] *Knoxville Whig,* July 30, 1853.

over attempts to rescue runaway slaves tore the North and the South still further apart. The principal churches had long ago parted company between their Northern and Southern membership. The Whig Party had disappeared, and the sectional Republican Party had arisen to contest the control of the nation. What a gloomy outlook for those who loved the Union so thoroughly as did Brownlow! Any one who would deliberately endanger the Union further was worse than a traitor. And so when the Democrats took up the months of April, May, and June of 1860 to split into two parties, Brownlow concluded that the perpetrators of this deed deserved a fate worse than eternal damnation. Douglas, of the Northern wing, was no appealing figure to the Parson, and Breckinridge, of the Southern wing, was even much less so. Brownlow supported John Bell and Edward Everett. He went to the National Convention of that group of people who said they stood for the Constitution and the Union, and he saw these two men nominated.[53] He now had a party to support as well as three to condemn, for the Republicans under Abraham Lincoln were as bad as the Democrats.

But there seemed to be some question in the mind of a certain Jordan Clark, of Arkansas, as to whether the Parson might not soon come out and join the Democrats. At least he thought there might be no harm in dropping the Parson a note to inquire if the rumor were true and when the happy event would be announced. For this inquisitiveness and his pains Jordan Clark got addressed to himself one of Parson Brownlow's most celebrated phillipics. Brownlow wrote him on August 6, 1860:

I have your letter of the 30th ult., and hasten to let you know the *precise time* when I expect to come out and formally announce that I have joined the Democratic party. When the sun shines at midnight and the moon at mid-day; when man forgets to be selfish, or Democrats lose their inclination to steal; when nature stops her onward march to rest, or all the water-courses in America flow up stream; when flowers lose their odor, and trees shed no leaves; when birds talk, and beasts of burden laugh; when damned spirits swap hell for heaven with the angels of light, and pay them the boot

[53] *Ibid.*, May 26, 1860.

in mean whiskey; when impossibilities are in fashion, and no proposition is too absurd to be believed,—you may credit the report that I have joined the Democrats!

I join the Democrats! Never, so long as there are sects in churches, weeds in gardens, fleas in hog-pens, dirt in victuals, disputes in families, wars with nations, water in the ocean, bad men in America, or base women in France! No, Jordan Clark, you may hope, you may congratulate, you may reason, you may sneer, but that cannot be. The thrones of the Old World, the courts of the universe, the governments of the world, may all fall and crumble into ruin,— the New World may commit the national suicide of dissolving this Union,—but all this, and more, must occur before I join the Democracy!

I join the Democracy! Jordan Clark, you know not what you say. When I join the Democracy, the Pope of Rome will join the Methodist Church. When Jordan Clark, of Arkansas, is President of the Republic of Great Britain by the universal suffrage of a contented people, when Queen Victoria consents to be divorced from Prince Albert by a county court in Kansas; when Congress obliges, by law, James Buchanan to marry a European princess; when the Pope leases the Capitol at Washington for his city residence; when Alexander of Russia and Napoleon of France are elected Senators in Congress from New Mexico; when good men cease to go to heaven, or bad men to hell; when this world is turned upside down; when proof is afforded, both clear and unquestionable, that there is no God; when men turn to ants, and ants to elephants,—I will change my political faith and come out on the side of Democracy!

Supposing that this full and frank letter will enable you to fix upon *the period* when I will come out a full-grown Democrat, and to communicate the same to all whom it may concern in Arkansas,

I have the honor to be, &c.,

W. G. BROWNLOW.[54]

Brownlow was no more positive that he would never be a Democrat than he was that preachers should keep out of politics. He severely condemned P. P. Neely, an Alabama Methodist preacher, for taking part in the campaign of 1860 and

---

[54] *Parson Brownlow's Book,* pp. 62-64.

for calling upon the people not to submit to the inauguration of the Black Republican Lincoln if he should be elected.[55] Others besides Brownlow had similar feelings, and the *Banner of Peace* was set up by the Cumberland Presbyterians in Nashville in 1860 for the purpose of promoting peace. This paper solemnly asked, "How can a man get down from a successful political harangue on Saturday, and enter the holy desk to preach a meek and lowly Saviour on Sabbath?"[56] But people forgot then as they have often done since that churches will always enter politics, promote wars and support them to the extent and to the degree that their membership are convinced of the righteousness of their causes. Churches are man-made institutions managed by men to promote their longings to find and worship the Supreme Being, but in supporting these things it often seems necessary to deal with human affairs no less than divine.

Parson Brownlow was somewhat of a chameleon. He could pose as a preacher when it was to his interests to do so, but at other times he could choose from a variety of occupations what he would be. In 1860 it was more convenient not to be a preacher. Yet he dealt in the paraphernalia of preachers and used it in politics. Hearing that the Episcopal Church had composed a special prayer to be used in South Carolina he decided to interpose against it one for all the local preachers in East Tennessee to use "in all their public ministrations." He prayed for those who were seeking to preserve the Union and frowned upon "those traitors, political gamblers, and selfish demagogues who are seeking to build up a miserable Southern Confederacy, and under it to inaugurate a new reading of the Ten Commandments, so as to teach that the chief end of Man is Nigger!" The rest of this prayer was characterized by such words and expressions as "Southern mad-caps and Northern fanatics," "fire-eaters," "mean whiskey," "corrupt Democracy and its profligate leaders," and "wicked leaders of Abolitionism." This prayer he published in his *Knoxville Whig* in January of 1860.[57]

---

[55] *Ibid.*, pp. 75-80.
[56] August 16, 1860.
[57] *Parson Brownlow's Book*, pp. 28-30.

9

As the campaign of 1860 became more heated, Brownlow was maneuvered into an extreme position by his strong will and his characteristic methods of carrying on a fight. He had visited too much among planter aristocrats and extreme Southerners to have any latent antipathy to them, yet before November of 1860 he was thundering out abuse against them as terrible as any he had ever used against the Abolitionists. But his opposition to both was born of the same reason; each was bent on a program which would destroy the Union.[58]

Brownlow made the direct charge that the Southern Democratic leaders had plotted secession, that they had broken up the Convention at Charleston deliberately as a step in the plot, and that they had nominated John C. Breckinridge for no other reason. He declared, "The leaders of the Democratic party who procured his nomination by a *rebellious faction* at Baltimore, took that method of accomplishing a long-cherished object,— the dissolution of this Union and the 'precipitating of the Cotton States in a revolution.' "[59] They had no intention or desire to elect Breckinridge, for he was not even a slaveholder. In fact he had an anti-slavery record, contended Brownlow. Their whole purpose was to see Lincoln elected and then secede, as they had been openly threatening. "TO MAKE THAT CONTINGENCY CERTAIN, THEY ARE RUNNING BRECKINRIDGE," charged Brownlow. If the Democrats wanted a slaveholder as president, why should they not vote for John Bell, who owned 83 slaves in his own name—and his wife owned 83 more. Brownlow declared that he intended to stand by the Union and that if a Southern Confederacy were organized he would rebel against it. Nay, he would do more, "I will sustain Lincoln if he will go to work to put down the great Southern mob that leads off in such a rebellion!" These sentiments and others he expressed in a speech before the Bell and Everett Club of Knoxville in October, 1860. Nearing the close, he declared:

These are my sentiments, and these are my purposes; and I am no Abolitionist, but a Southern man. I expect to stand by this

[58] *Portrait and Biography*, p. 30.
[59] *Parson Brownlow's Book*, p. 191.

Union, and battle to sustain it, though Whiggery and Democracy, Slavery and Abolitionism, Southern rights and Northern wrongs, are all blown to the devil! I will never join in the outcry against the American Union in order to build up a corrupt Democratic party in the South, and to create offices in a new Government for an unprincipled pack of broken-down politicians, who have justly rendered themselves odious by stealing the public money. I may stand alone in the South; but I believe thousands and tens of thousands will stand by me, and, if need be, perish with me in the same cause.[60]

The Parson had not been afraid of the Nullifiers in South Carolina in 1832 when he was riding the circuit there; with equal vigor would he oppose the Nullifiers of 1860. Nullifiers throughout all history had come to grief. Adam and Eve had nullified God's law in Eden, and they had been thrown out; Cain nullified God's will, and he was branded in the forehead as a traitorous murderer; the Jews nullified holy law, and they perished in the siege of Jerusalem; Sodom and Gomorrah nullified it, and they were consumed with fire and brimstone; the King of the Egyptians nullified the will of God, and he and his army were drowned in the Red Sea; and if South Carolina had kept up her nullification in 1832, "Old Hickory Jackson would have drowned them in the harbor of Charleston."[61]

There could be no doubt that Brownlow was pursuing a course which would make trouble for himself. There was always freedom of speech in the South, at least for Southerners, but there were limits beyond which the Southern leaders could not be attacked without replying. Brownlow's nervous excitability and his exaggerated style had long made him an object of merriment or contempt among Southern leaders, although they did not consider him important enough or serious enough to be resented. And so in this campaign he was noticed chiefly by the lesser leaders of the South. Only once did he have a brush with a Southern fire-eater of the first magnitude, and in dramatic effect it stood out boldly. In the heat of the campaign William L. Yancey appeared in Knoxville to advocate the election of Breckinridge.

[60] *Ibid.*, p. 206.   [61] *Ibid.*, p. 73; *Knoxville Whig*, October 13, 1860.

After the speech had passed the three-hour mark, a voice from the audience cried out, "Hurrah for Bell!"; another shouted, "What will you do if Lincoln is elected?" In order to deal effectively with the disturbers Yancey invited them to the platform. After quizzing one of the audience who answered the invitation, Yancey learned that the heckler was merely acting for a committee of five headed by Brownlow. He now invited this group to the platform. Brownlow, with "a cocked Derringer" in his pocket acted as spokesman. With what Yancey considered insufferable impudence, the Parson boldly said, "I propose, when the Secessionists go to Washington to dethrone Lincoln, to seize a bayonet and form an army to resist such an attack and they shall walk over my dead body on the way." Yancey with great seriousness turned to the audience and replied, "If my state resists I will go with her and if I meet this gentleman marshaled with his bayonet to oppose us, I will plunge mine to the hilt through and through his heart, feel no compunctions for the act, but thank God my country has been freed from such a foe."[62]

Such encounters as this greatly excited the South, but they riveted Brownlow's control over his pugnacious East Tennesseeans. John W. Palmer, a South Carolina subscriber to the *Knoxville Whig*, wrote Brownlow that "your remarks to Yancey convince me fully you are a traitor to the South and to your country." He informed Brownlow that if he found him in the ranks of the Abolitionists, "I will kill you the first man." He promised that if Brownlow were ever caught in South Carolina he should have thirty-nine lashes on his bare back and "a coat of tar and feathers afterwards to heal up the stripes." He closed: "If my time is not out, stop my paper, anyhow. I make you a present of all you owe me, believing you would steal it if I did not." Brownlow answered, enclosing twenty-four cents in stamps, which he said was the amount still due. He was glad to be rid of

---

[62] J. W. Du Bose, *The Life and Times of William Lowndes Yancey*, pp. 494-96; *Suffering of Union Men, An Address by Parson Brownlow (Rev. W. G. Brownlow, D.D.) Delivered Before the Citizens of New York, at the Academy of Music, May 15, 1862*, pp. 23-24; Humes, *op. cit.*, pp. 81-84; *Parson Brownlow's Book*, p. 67.

the South Carolinian and all of his disunion friends. The *Knoxville Whig* still had 12,000 subscribers, which was a greater number than any other paper in the state. As for the thirty-nine lashes, if Palmer would leave his mob behind, Brownlow would be willing to meet him at any time and place he should designate. He then proceeded to read a lecture to the South Carolinian on patriotism.[63]

The election came, and those in the South who had feared the victory of Lincoln sorrowed and those who had silently hoped for it secretly rejoiced. The former knew not what to do; the latter knew that they would secede and set up a Southern nation.

---

[63] *Parson Brownlow's Book,* pp. 65-74; *Knoxville Whig,* October 13, 1860.

CHAPTER VII

SECESSION

WITHOUT A DOUBT, the majority of Tennesseeans under ordinary circumstances were unwilling to break up the Union, and in 1860 they considered the times not sufficiently out of joint to constitute a provoking situation. They cast their electoral vote for John Bell, giving him 69,000 popular ballots; while about 65,000 Tennesseeans recorded their preference for Breckinridge. As an added warning that Tennessee would have no seceding on her part, 11,000 citizens stood out for Stephen A. Douglas, the "Little Giant" from Illinois. By this vote 80,000 Tennesseeans seemed to indicate a preference for the continuation of the Union, and it can by no means be said that the 65,000 who voted for Breckinridge were recording a preference for disunion.

Thus in the early stages of the secession movement Brownlow found himself with the overwhelming majority of Tennesseeans. He was an original Union man with his Unionism dating back to Nullification days. For forty years he had gloried in his country's greatness, he had bragged about her, and had flung against his enemies as one of his ugliest thrusts the charge of being Tories. The Parson felt doubly important when he thought of his American citizenship, for the great mass of people in this world had not been blessed with this distinction. Like many other Americans, he felt this honor to be a definite personal possession. He declared "Our Government is the greatest and the best the world has ever seen."[1] So, to jeopardize his country's integrity or to take him out of it through the secession of his state was to rob him of one of the great consolations of being alive.

---

[1] *Knoxville Whig*, October 13, 1860, quoted in *Parson Brownlow's Book*, p. 67.

He had been arguing against secession long before the election of 1860 and he did not cease his opposition until as governor of the state six years later he saw it restored to the Union. Neither before the election of Lincoln nor afterwards was he able to find one good argument for secession. He was for the Union equally as much because he was a Southerner as he was because he was an American. He was convinced that there could be no peaceable dissolution of the Union; secession meant war and war of the most terrible character. Almost a month before Lincoln's election, he said, "The man who calculates upon *peaceable* dissolution of the Union is either a madman or a fool."[2] In the war that would surely follow secession he saw the people "drafted as soldiers, and forced to abandon our peaceful homes, never to see them more, to perish by exposure, or hunger, or disease, on long and dreary marches, or to fall by the hands of our countrymen, in a war that never ought to have been waged."[3] And, moreover, it would not be a short war; "this is to be the most fearful war that ever raged in the civilized world."[4] And what was worse, Tennessee and the border states would become the great battlefields and the source of vast numbers of soldiers who would be driven into the maelstrom of war to fight the battles of the lords of the "Cotton South." Tennesseeans would be "forced to leave their wives and children to toil and suffer, while they fight for the purse-proud aristocrats of the Cotton States, whose pecuniary abilities will enable them to hire substitutes!"[5]

The Parson knew that the South was not a unit in its thinking and in its needs and desires. He knew that what the cotton barons wanted would not of necessity be advantageous to his East Tennesseeans. Many Southerners had been gradually during the past decade and more coming to the belief that the South could never attain her destiny until she should become an independent nation. She had the potentialities for becoming the richest and most powerful nation on earth. All she needed was

[2] *Knoxville Whig*, October 13, 1860, quoted in *Parson Brownlow's Book*, p. 68.
[3] *Knoxville Whig*, December 22, 1860, quoted in *Parson Brownlow's Book*, p. 51.
[4] *Knoxville Whig*, April 27, 1861.
[5] *Ibid.*, December 22, 1860, quoted in *Parson Brownlow's Book*, pp. 49-50.

freedom from the grasping and parasitic North, and then, indeed, would she come into her destiny. Brownlow knew that such a Southern Republic would be dominated by leaders and interests foreign to the upper South, so he registered a solemn determination to oppose all schemes for Southern nationality.

He lost patience with the Southern leaders who were precipitating secession for not being able to see that they were playing the game of the Abolitionists—they were allowing themselves to be driven out of their own house. The Abolitionists were the mutineers and the revolutionists—why allow them to take control? Brownlow would fight them to the last—to hand over the country to the Abolitionists and withdraw was exactly what these revolutionists wanted. The Parson was too bold and tenacious a fighter to engage in such an unwise course. He remembered well the disunion sentiments expressed by the arch-Abolitionist Parson Pryne, whom he had debated a few years previously in Philadelphia. The detested Northern Abolitionists might drive out of the Union the senseless Southern leaders, but he refused to be dispossessed of his heritage, his glorious Union. He would allow no Abolitionists to deprive him of the right to be called an American, and neither would he submit to being dragged away from that title by silly Southerners, who were so foolish as not to see what the Abolitionists were doing. The Parson called upon the people to stay in the Union and help fight the Abolitionists where there was some chance of winning. "Secession," he declared, "is no remedy for any evils in our Government, real or imaginary, past, present, or to come."[6]

It was because he was so ardently in favor of slavery that he so vigorously upheld the Union. The Abolitionists wanted to drive the South out of the Union in order to demolish the institution of slavery. As soon as the South should set up a government of its own, the old fragment of the Union would abolish slavery there, and then Canada would in effect be brought to the very front door of the South, and slavery would then fast disappear. And it would not be entirely due to the fact that many slaves might run away to the land of freedom. Conditions

---

[6] *Knoxville Whig,* December 8, 1860, quoted in *Parson Brownlow's Book,* p. 43.

among the slaves who might choose to remain in the South or
who might not be so lucky as to escape would become chaotic
and the institution would become untenable. Then the Negro
would attain a degree of freedom which would bring up that
deep and fundamental fear in the South of the rise of a race
question. And this fear was no less present among those who
never owned slaves than among the greatest planters. The Negro
free might indeed become a greater menace to the social, economic, and political position of the non-slaveholders than to
the lord of a thousand black serfs.

Brownlow, who was just as anxious as the most loyal Confederate soldier to preserve slavery, thought that the institution
could be best maintained by remaining in the Union and fighting for the rights that amply guaranteed it and protected it
under the Federal Constitution. And this was the position assumed by the East Tennessee Unionists. Brownlow was throughout the secession struggles as strongly determined in his support
of slavery as was the most advanced secession slaveholder. He
declared in the presidential campaign that if Lincoln should
advocate interference even with the interstate slave trade and
if Congress should pass hostile legislation and the Supreme
Court should uphold it, then "I would take the ground that
the time for Revolution has come,—that all the Southern States
should go into it; AND I WOULD GO WITH THEM."[7] Not
until the war had changed the whole aspect of slavery did the
Parson weaken in his wholehearted support of it. Two months
after the Southern Confederacy had hoisted the flag of a new
nation, he was as loyal to its position on slavery as if he had
been its president. Mindful of his former battles with Abolitionists, he continued to declare that God had placed slavery upon
the earth for a good purpose. "And, however much the bonds
of the slaves of the South may provoke the wrath of the ultra
Abolitionists of the North, the Redeemer of the world smiles
alike upon the devout master and the pious slave!" He looked
upon slaveholders as God's chosen people, declaring "that all
the finer feelings of humanity may be cherished in the bosoms of

---

[7] *Knoxville Whig,* October 13, 1860, quoted in *Parson Brownlow's Book,* p. 69.

slave-owners"[8] He quoted with approval in 1862 what he had said thirty years previously, that those who fed and clothed their slaves well "and instruct them in religion, are better friends to them than those who set them at liberty."[9]

In fact so thoroughly did Brownlow defend slavery and so completely did he consider it to be of the essence of the South that he made it the principal position from which he would not retreat—the ground he would hold even to the point of revolting against the Union. In May, 1861, he declared that when he was convinced that Lincoln "contemplated the *subjugation* of the South or the *abolishing* of slavery, there would not be a Union man among us in twenty-four hours. Come what might, sink or swim, survive or perish, we would fight you to the death, and we would unite our fortunes and destinies with even these demoralized seceded States, for whose leaders and laws we have no sort of respect."[10] Lincoln's past record on the slavery question led the Parson to believe that the new President would not interfere with slavery in the states. He knew that Lincoln was not an Abolitionist and that he had no great respect for Abolitionists.

Brownlow was convinced that the election of Lincoln was no proper cause for seceding. In fact, he denied the right of secession under any provocation whatsoever. When conditions should become unbearable, then the proper method would be through revolution. But the time for revolution had by no means arrived with the coming in of the Rail-splitter. He admitted that Lincoln was a sectional president, elected without a single vote in the Southern States, but the Parson queried whether the Constitution required a person to receive Southern votes in order to be validly elected. Lincoln could not carry out the program of the Abolitionists even should he desire to do so. His oath of office would prevent it. "And who will say that he intends taking that oath with treason in his heart and perjury on his tongue?" To break up the Union merely on the supposition that Lincoln would

[8] *Knoxville Whig*, May 18, 1861, quoted in *Parson Brownlow's Book*, pp. 108-9.

[9] *Parson Brownlow's Book*, pp. 24-25.

[10] *Knoxville Whig*, May 18, 1861, quoted in *Parson Brownlow's Book*, pp. 110-11.

do illegal acts "would be wicked, treacherous, unjustifiable, unprecedented, and without the shadow of an excuse." The South should wait for the overt act; then there would be time aplenty. If the Black Republicans should succeed in violating the Constitution, then in 1864 conservative men both north and south would join together and put the government on a more solid basis than it had been within the past quarter of a century.

But Lincoln could do no harm even if he should try. He was only the President. The House, the Senate, and the Supreme Court must all agree before any act of importance could be done; and Lincoln and his party controlled not one of these important bodies. The South should not complain of its opportunities in the past for running the government. Out of the seventy-two years of the country's existence, it had held the presidency forty-eight years to the North's twenty-four. And the Parson might have added that out of those twenty-four years, the South controlled the Northern-born presidents most of the time. Despite the company in which Brownlow found Lincoln, he was inclined to favor the President-elect because the latter had been a great admirer of Henry Clay, and held much the same position on slavery as Clay held.[11]

Brownlow found a great deal to condemn in the attitude the Southern leaders had taken throughout the secession movement. He did not believe that secession had sprung from the desires of the mass of the people. On the contrary he repeatedly stated that the whole conspiracy had been hatched in the dead of night by fourteen senators from seven Southern states. He and other Tennesseeans felt that the ground for this conspiracy had been prepared consciously and unconsciously over a period of years by a few people—some wily, some deluded, and some stupid. The editor of the *Banner of Peace*, a Tennessee newspaper established to carry out the purpose announced in its name, declared that those responsible for the troubled condition of the country could easily be grouped into three classes: first, newspaper editors; secondly, demagogues in politics; and third-

---

[11] *Knoxville Whig*, November 17, 1860, quoted in *Parson Brownlow's Book*, pp. 30-37.

ly, political preachers. He asked, "Who does not see that if the press was generous, just, honest, and pure; if we had a race of statesmen; and if we had no political preachers, our country today would have been one broad land of contented, prosperous, and happy brothers."[12]

If the Southern leaders had felt sure of their cause, why, queried the Parson, did they rush into secession in the dark and without consulting with all the Southern States. The border states had been ignored by the cotton states leaders, who hoped to cross the Rubicon and commit the rest of the South so completely that it would be forced to follow. They had refused to call a general convention of all the slave states for that was not the way of conspirators. These Southern leaders would forcibly deprive the people of their greatest heritage. They would drag out of the Union Florida, Louisiana, and Texas, territories for which the United States had paid, according to the Parson's ready mathematical calculations, $617,822,928. Such actions could not be considered "in any other light than that of *dishonesty* and *treason*, meriting the scorn and contempt of the civilized world."[13]

The Parson had never liked South Carolinians since they had driven him out in Nullification days. It was only natural to expect them to be the first ones to attempt to break up the Union. Addressing one of them shortly before South Carolina seceded, he said, "You may leave the vessel,—you may go out in the rickety boats of your little State, and hoist your miserable *cabbage-leaf* of a Palmetto flag; but, depend upon it, men and brethren, you will be dashed to pieces on the rocks!"[14] The great mass of South Carolinians had been Tories in the Revolution, he declared, and as proof he called the roll of Tory South Carolinians through 206 names. R. Barnwell Rhett, one of the South Carolina fire-eaters, had grown up under the name of Smith, but because of his Tory ancestry and because of high crimes

---

[12] December 13, 1860.

[13] *Knoxville Whig*, March 23, 1861, quoted in *Parson Brownlow's Book*, pp. 233-35.

[14] *Knoxville Whig*, December 8, 1860, quoted in *Parson Brownlow's Book*, pp. 43-44.

he himself had committed, he induced the legislature to change
his name to Rhett. Indeed, declared Brownlow, "there have
been more names changed in South Carolina, by Act of General
Assembly, than in any State in the Union!" South Carolina still
had many of the royal trappings, reminiscent of the days when
she was ruled over by a king. He sounded the warning:

> These are not the people to head a Confederacy for Tennessee-
> ans to fall into. Their notions of royalty, and their contempt for
> the common people, will never suit Tennesseeans. . . . Let Tennessee
> once go into this *Empire of Cotton States*, and all poor men will
> at once become the *free negroes of the Empire!* We are down upon
> the whole scheme.[15]

Secession ordinances, declared the Parson, were "covenants
with death and agreements with hell." Southern senators were
in Congress receiving nine dollars a day "for proclaiming
treason, rank and damning,—for which they ought to be hung,
and would be if the laws of the land were enforced." If Tennessee should madly plunge into secession, still he would fight
on against "fanaticism at the North" and "demagogues and
traitors at the South," and for doing so he fully expected to be
hung. Thus mused the Parson in January, 1861.[16]

In early February, the Confederate States of America was
born in Montgomery, Alabama, and the Parson launched forth
on more bitter and blighting denunciations of the new government and of all who had had a part in its making. He now
became savage in his defiance:

> I would as soon be engaged in importing the plague from the
> East, as in helping to build up a Southern Confederacy upon the
> ruins of the American Constitution. I expect to be abused for my
> defence of the Union. "Tray, Blanche, and Sweetheart" will all
> bark at me. The kennel is now unloosed: all the pack—from the
> deep-mouthed bloodhound of South Carolina and Florida to the
> growling cur of Georgia—are baying at me. If I were to stop to

---

[15] *Knoxville Whig*, January 12, 1861, quoted in *Parson Brownlow's Book*,
p. 88.
[16] *Knoxville Whig*, January 19, 1861, quoted in *Parson Brownlow's Book*,
pp. 89-95.

throw stones at all the snarling puppies that yelp at my heels in South Carolina and elsewhere, I should have little time to do any thing else.[17]

The Parson was not disappointed in his prediction that he would be bitterly set upon and condemned for his course, and he might well have guessed that some of the most threatening missiles would be hurled at him from South Carolina. One of the citizens of the Palmetto State wrote the Parson to tell him that he was "the greatest liar out of hell, and one of the most infamous scoundrels living between heaven and earth" and adding "that nothing would afford us as much pleasure as to see you in Abbeville, where we could treat you to a coat of tar and feathers." The Parson answered that he expected the "vials of contumely, reproach, and defamation will be poured upon me by a hireling press of a corrupt and plundering Southern Confederacy, by the insolvent bullies, hardened liars, and vulgar cut-throats whose only ambition is to serve as tools under an arrogant and hateful pack of aristocratic leaders." He informed the South Carolinian "that our Constitution is not built upon such a sandy foundation as to be shaken and demolished without the rotten pillar of reputed South Carolina orthodoxy to support it." He concluded his defiant answer: "Finally, sir, when you put forth your batch of villainous falsehoods, through the *brawling Jacobin journals* of a demoralized Southern Confederacy, have the *candor* and *charity* to accompany them with this reply, and I will remain the defiant opponent of a wilful and despicable South Carolina rascal!"[18]

South Carolinians were not the only ones to feel aggrieved at the Parson's course. A flood of denunciation and threats poured upon him from throughout the South. A Georgian, writing with more pity than anger for the Parson, informed him, "From all appearances, you have turned from a *private* and *respected citizen* to a *contentious, quarrelsome* politician,—from a Southern-Rights man to a friend of the North. . . ." A Mississippian

---

[17] *Knoxville Whig*, February 16, 1861, quoted in *Parson Brownlow's Book*, pp. 99-100.

[18] *Knoxville Whig*, February 16, 1861, quoted in *Parson Brownlow's Book*, pp. 96, 98, 99, 103-4.

threatened him as follows if he should turn against the South:
"Now, Parson, if you adopt this policy, what do you think will
be the consequence? You will certainly be hung, as all dogs
should be, until you are 'dead, dead.' Your crime will be treason
of the deepest dye." He declared the Parson was a "money-
making Yankee; and, if you will give me time, I will look into
your nativity. When Tennessee secedes, I will head a company
of Tennesseeans and Mississippians and proceed to hang you
by law, or by force if need be. The South can look upon you in
no other light than as a traitor and a Tory, and the twin brother
of *Andrew Johnson.* Remember, and beware, you shall be hung
in the year 1861, unless you conclude to live the life of an exile."
In his answer the Parson declared that instead of being a
Yankee, he was a native of Virginia, "and, although I am now
fifty-five years of age, I walk erect, have but few gray hairs, and
look to be younger than any whiskey-drinking, tobacco-chewing,
profane-swearing Secessionist in any of the Cotton States, of
forty years." As for being hanged he asked for ten days' notice
"and I will muster men enough in the county where I reside, to
hang the last rascal among you, and then use your carcasses
for wolf-bait!"[19]

It was incomprehensible to many Southerners that Brownlow
could submit to Lincoln and defend the Union without being a
Republican. To the charge that he belonged to that political
faith he pithily answered, "Any man saying—whether of high
or low degree—that I am an Abolitionist or a Black Republican,
is a LIAR and a SCOUNDREL."[20]

So easy was it to set the Parson loose on a withering flow of
invective, so original as to become amusing, that now and then
he was baited for the entertainment that would come in his reply.
So the report was spread that General Gideon J. Pillow, who
was organizing a Confederate regiment, was counting on the
Parson to become his chaplain. This was an insult the Parson
could not refrain from answering in the most resentful language. "When I shall have made up my mind to go to hell," he

---

[19] *Knoxville Whig,* January 19, 1861, quoted in *Parson Brownlow's Book,*
pp. 89-95.

[20] *Knoxville Whig,* May 25, 1861, quoted in *Parson Brownlow's Book,* p. 58.

replied, "I will cut my throat, and go *direct*, and not travel round by way of the Southern Confederacy."[21]

In assessing the blame for the secession movement, the Parson laid a huge proportion of it at the doors of the churches, and so completely had he become steeped in his Unionism that he was not afraid to charge his erstwhile beloved Methodist Church with deserving the lion's share of it. He declared that the clergy, high and low, without regard to denomination, "have raised the howl of Secession, and it falls like an Indian war-cry upon our citizens from their prostituted pulpits every Sabbath."[22] These "reverend traitors to God and their country" went about delivering "inflammatory stump-speeches." "The South is now full of these reverend traitors," he declared, "and every branch of the Christian Church is cursed with their labors."[23] In Nashville, in 1862, he said, "Here, as in all parts of the South, the worst class of men are *preachers*. They have done more to bring about the deplorable state of things existing in the country than any other class of men."[24] And a little later he said, "The worst class of men who make tracks upon Southern soil are Methodist, Presbyterian, Baptist, and Episcopal clergymen, and at the head of these for mischief are the Southern Methodists."[25]

It was becoming a practice among the Secession preachers "to take the hides off Union men by holding them up before their congregations in prayer." The Parson thought that the parties assailed ought to be "allowed *a division of time*, in laying the other side before the Lord." He charged a Presbyterian minister in Knoxville with attacking Horace Maynard in a prayer in which he begged the Lord "that his traitorous feet might never again press the soil of Tennessee." Another Presbyterian in the same city implored the Lord to raise the blockade of the South and fervently prayed for Him "to strike Lincoln's ships with lightning and scatter them to the four winds of

---

[21] Frank Moore, ed., *The Rebellion Record*, I, 60.

[22] *Knoxville Whig*, May 18, 1861, quoted in *Parson Brownlow's Book*, p. 111-12.

[23] *Knoxville Whig*, July 6, 1861, quoted in *Parson Brownlow's Book*, p. 146.

[24] *Parson Brownlow's Book*, p. 392.

[25] *Ibid.*, p. 189.

heaven!" In one of these blockade prayer-meetings this pastor "assisted by several old *clericals,* made a desperate effort to raise the blockade!" This was the same preacher, according to the Parson "who boasted in his pulpit that Jesus Christ was a *Southerner,* born on Southern soil, and so were His apostles, except Judas, whom he denominated a *Northern* man! Speaking of the Bible, he said he would sooner have a Bible printed and bound in hell, than one printed and bound north of Mason & Dixon's line!"[26]

So far did the distempers of the times affect Brownlow that he began to advocate destroying the chief foundations of the past thirty-five years of his existence. He would depart from denominationalism, which had made possible so many joyous fights for him in the past, and have a union of all the churches. He argued:

We have—among us—brought disgrace upon the church, destroyed confidence in the ministry, disbanded our congregations, and broken up the social and religious ties that formerly bound us together. It is useless for us to meet in our churches on the Sabbath, put on long, pious faces, offer up long prayers, hand round the bread and wine, and then pass out in society and vilify each other as a set of pickpockets, liars, and traitors, and keep up this holy and patriotic warfare until we meet again the next Sabbath. The fool, the wayfaring man, and the untutored African can see that we are wicked, and on the high-road to the devil! Let us break up our hypocritical organizations called churches, and out of a half-dozen of them make up one new one, whose pastor and members shall neither preach, exhort, nor pray anything connected with party politics.[27]

But the Parson was not so blind in his support of the Union as not to see that the Northern preachers were just as guilty of departing from Christianity as were the Southerners. He declared that "the curse of the country has been that, for years, north of Mason & Dixon's line, you have kept pulpits open to the abuse of Southern slavery and of the Southern people."[28]

---

[26] *Ibid.,* pp. 141-43. [27] *Ibid.,* pp. 144-45.
[28] *Knoxville Whig,* May 18, 1861, quoted in *Parson Brownlow's Book,* p. 111.

10

Brownlow had not been alone in Tennessee in his opposition to secession; only in the devastating language with which he opposed it was he unique. John Bell in the early stages of the movement stood by the Union, then he halted in the twilight zone of neutrality, and finally he deserted for the Confederacy. Andrew Johnson in the United States Senate poured out his condemnation of the Southern secessionists, as one Southerner after another departed with maledictions upon this Tennessee renegade. But he won the applause of Brownlow, who had not spoken to him for twenty years.[29] Other East Tennesseeans held true to the Union and backed up Brownlow and Johnson —T. A. R. Nelson, Horace Maynard, Nat Taylor, and many more.

But the South was aflame; Tennessee would not fiddle while Rome burned. The withdrawal of South Carolina set going a wave of secession which swept all of the Gulf states except Texas out of the Union before the close of January, 1861. Governor Isham G. Harris, whom Brownlow denominated "Eye Sham," seized with the contagion, called immediately after South Carolina's secession an extra session of the legislature to determine what Tennessee should do in the crisis. He recommended that a Sovereign Convention be provided for. The legislature met on the 7th of January and on the 19th it called upon the people to vote on the 9th of the following February whether they would have a Sovereign Convention and at the same time to elect delegates to that convention.

Brownlow, fearing that this was the first step which would plunge Tennessee into secession and ruin, called upon the people to force all candidates who should seek election to the Sovereign Convention to declare their position unequivocally. He declared, "It will not be Whig and Democrat, Bell and Breckinridge, or Douglas, but *Union or Disunion*."[30] And immediately he intensified his campaign against the Southern secessionists, filling his *Knoxville Whig* with warnings against the

---

[29] George Fort Milton, *The Age of Hate, Andrew Johnson and the Radicals*, p. 103.

[30] *Knoxville Whig*, December 22, 1860, quoted in *Parson Brownlow's Book*, p. 49.

evils to come and with denunciations of the Southern conspirators, as has heretofore appeared. In the election for the Convention, Tennessee clearly declared that she did not consider the election of Lincoln sufficient excuse for seceding, or, indeed, for even considering the matter at all. More than 91,000 votes were cast for Union delegates, whereas a few less than 25,000 voted for the Disunion delegates. All three of the grand divisions of the state, East, Middle, and West Tennessee, overwhelmingly voted for the Union. But there was less unanimity of feeling on the propriety of calling together a convention. Many who were for the Union felt that there could be no harm in discussing the distempers of the times, but Brownlow declared that as every convention that had been called had passed secession ordinances, the safest way would be to reject the Convention. So it was that Tennessee after electing Union men in a vast majority, nevertheless refused to trust those same Union men. The majority against the Convention was almost 12,000. Only the cotton-growing West Tennesseeans gave a majority for the Convention. East Tennessee voted it down by more than 25,000 majority, and even the stock-raising gentlemen farmers of Middle Tennessee declared against it by a majority of 1,382. Only two counties in East Tennessee voted for the Convention.[31]

Then Fort Sumter was fired upon, Lincoln called for troops, and the lid was blown off Pandora's box. In answer to Lincoln's call for troops, Governor Harris defiantly replied, "Tennessee will not furnish a man for purposes of coercion, but 50,000, if necessary, for the defense of our rights, and those of our Southern brothers." He immediately issued a call for a special session of the legislature to meet on April 25, an ominous move. Union-loving Tennesseeans were frightened; John Bell and others issued an address to the people deploring the bitter choice that was now held out—either to secede from the Union or to aid in the despicable business of coercing the South. Mindful of what was going on in the hearts of their neighbor Kentuckians, they

---

[31] *The American Annual Cyclopaedia*, 1861, pp. 677-78; *Parson Brownlow's Book*, pp. 220-23; J. W. Fertig, *The Secession and Reconstruction of Tennessee*, p. 19.

counselled neutrality as against the insanity that was sweeping all before it in both North and South.

But there was no staying the fate that awaited. The legislature met, and listened to the recommendations of Governor Harris that Tennessee declare her independence and consider a Union with the Confederate States of America. A month back was now ancient history, so swiftly had events been moving. There was no time to call a Sovereign Convention, a procedure, which under much less provocation, the state had recently rejected. To save time, the legislature should do these things, and then submit its work to a vote of the people. One after another of the neutrality men saw the impossibility of their position and fell in with Governor Harris. Acting with swift precision the legislature on May 1 directed the Governor to enter into a military league with the Confederacy, so that preparations might immediately be made to hold the northern frontier against the invaders. On the 7th the Governor reported that a league had been formed with the Confederacy and awaited ratification. The legislature accepted it immediately. The previous day it had paved the way for this action by adopting a Declaration of Independence and an Ordinance dissolving its relations with the Federal Government. They wasted no time arguing over the abstractions of secession; they chose the road hallowed throughout history. They asserted the right of revolution. On June 8, the people should vote whether they would accept the Declaration and the Ordinance and also whether they would join the Confederacy.

In the meantime the state began organizing for war. By the time the day for the voting had arrived, the state had provided for raising 55,000 troops and the borrowing of $5,000,000. Democracy does not operate most efficiently amidst the alarms of war, and undoubtedly the din of military preparations carried many Tennesseans out of the Union in their voting and riveted others to the Union or deterred them from voting at all. To friend and foe of Union alike, by the time the month of June had dawned, the state seemed to have already been committed to a policy from which there appeared no turning back.

The voting was general over the state and when the ballots were canvassed and announced on June 24 it was found that a majority, of 57,675 had favored independence and about the same majority, a union with the Confederacy. So, on June 24, Governor Harris proclaimed the new position of Tennessee, the last of the states to leave the Union.[32]

Parson Brownlow had been thundering out denunciations on all sides while the disjointed times had been fast sweeping Tennessee out of the Union. His influence was great but with all the other Union leaders of Tennessee he was unable to hold the state in the final plunge. The vote for the three divisions of the state in the June 8 election follows:

	Disunion	Union
East Tennessee	14,780	32,923
Middle Tennessee	58,265	8,198
West Tennessee	29,127	6,117
Military Camps	2,741	0

Thus alone of the state's divisions did East Tennessee hold true to the Union, and this was largely due to Brownlow, Andrew Johnson, T. A. R. Nelson, Horace Maynard, and other Unionists in the eastern part of the state. Six of the East Tennessee counties voted for independence and union with the Confederacy and thereby repudiated the Parson's counsel and leadership. The East Tennessee secessionists, according to a Unionist, were the "rich and persons of best social position."[33] The majority in the state the Parson rather wildly declared had been dragooned into disunion by Southern bayonets.[34]

In August Tennessee would elect a governor. The Parson began thinking about it in March, while Tennessee was yet peacefully in the Union. He had visions of becoming the state's governor and guiding it for the next two years through the perils that were besetting the nation. His campaign for this

---

[32] *American Annual Cyclopaedia*, 1861, pp. 678-83; Fertig, *op. cit.*, pp. 19 ff.; Temple, *op. cit.*, pp. 326-27; Edward McPherson, *The Political History of the United States of America during the Great Rebellion*, p. 5.

[33] Humes, *op. cit.*, p. 91.

[34] *American Annual Cyclopaedia*, 1861, p. 683; *Parson Brownlow's Book*, pp. 220-23.

honor sprang up, flourished, and died within the scope of a month. But during that time the Fighting Parson had the pleasure of carrying war into Africa. His platform was one of support of the Union and denunciation of the Southern Confederacy, and he carried out his campaign through his *Knoxville Whig* and in handbills, which he scattered over East Tennessee by the thousands. He could not take the stump, as he had been unable for the past two years to speak "loud enough to be heard ten steps."[35] He promised not to use cheap political tricks by telling about an humble origin, but his enthusiasm for himself soon led him to repeat his familiar story of having no "influential relatives," of having been left a destitute orphan when quite small, and of working at the trade of house-carpenter. His was a self-starting campaign; he would run of his own accord and not be nominated by a convention. Specifically he was "for the Union as it is, first; for a Border State Confederacy next; and for the Southern Confederacy *never*, in any contingency, or under any circumstances that may arise!" In his platform he repeated his indictment of the secession conspirators and the Southern Confederacy. On the traitors' "heads will be gathered the hissing curses of all generations, horrible as the forked-tongued snakes of Medusa." He would rather join the worst European monarchy than this *"bogus* Confederacy." People shouted *coercion.* "Coercion of a State," rejoined Brownlow, "is an adroit form of expression, coined in the school of Secession to give dignity to treason." The rebels were breaking up the Union, and he would fight them back; "Let the gates of the temple of Janus open," he exclaimed. He indorsed Lincoln's Inaugural Address "for its temperance and conservatism and for its firm nationality of sentiment." Though most of his platform was made of denunciation, he had thought somewhat on state policy. He would build two more penitentiaries, and he would sweep the secessionists out of the bank and railroad positions they held. The Parson wanted to be governor not only to checkmate the secessionists but with all candor and perhaps a touch of levity, he "would like to fill the office for two

---

[35] *Parson Brownlow's Book*, p. 242.

years, for the sake of the THREE THOUSAND DOLLARS PER ANNUM."[36]

As has been noted, the Parson's campaign did not last long. A few county meetings were got up to support him, but he did not appear to the Unionists to possess the proper temperament they would have in their candidate. He was accused of being a Lincoln hireling which displeased him and which brought forth this disclaimer: "We are no Lincoln man—we neither admire him or his councillors, nor do we approve of his policy or principles—and we have the consolation of knowing that we did all in our power to prevent his election!" But it was foolish to say that Lincoln began the war; and as for the Parson, he would never admit that "honor, patriotism, or a love of country, influenced the vile, hypocritical, corrupt, and insincere leaders who have plunged the Cotton States into this revolution."[37] So, having no great expectation of becoming governor, Brownlow soon withdrew in favor of William H. Polk. By the time of the election in August, conditions had so completely changed that Harris easily defeated Polk.

Brownlow's reaction to secession differed vastly from that of many other Southern Unionists. While the question was yet in the argumentative stage he used much the same line of reasoning employed by Alexander H. Stephens of Georgia. Stephens' speech before the Georgia legislature on November 14, 1860, and Brownlow's newspaper editorials ran parallel in a great many instances. But when secession came in Georgia, Stephens bowed to the inevitable, and like thousands of other Unionists, embraced the new order with the zeal becoming the principle of majority rule. Brownlow and most of his East Tennesseeans became defiant and determined to fight the Confederacy. But the development of the secession movement in Georgia and in Tennessee were not similar, and in that difference there is much to explain the Parson's position. In Georgia the Unionists were not strong enough to prevent the first effort from succeeding; in Tennessee the Unionists were so powerful that they prolonged

---

[36] *Knoxville Whig*, April 27, 1861; *Parson Brownlow's Book*, pp. 224-44.
[37] *Knoxville Whig*, April 27, 1861.

the fight through much bitterness and held the state in the Union so long that she became the last to leave.

The Parson's erratic temperament, however, opened up possibilities which no one could predict, and when finally Tennessee did leave the Union he had crossed the Rubicon and there was no turning back. Had Tennessee left the Union quickly, like most of the other states of the Confederacy, it would do no violence to his character to say that, following the example of Stephens, he might have cast his support to the Confederacy. A tradition has subsisted that he had in the early stages of the movement written an editorial in which, repudiating his old position, he announced his adherence to the South. An opponent hearing of the change, before the editorial had been published, seized the opportunity to charge Brownlow with inconsistency. Thereupon the Parson settled down to a position of Unionism from which he never budged.[38] George D. Prentice, with whom he later had a bitter quarrel, declared that it took all the persuasive powers of Judge Trigg and John Williamson to prevent him from joining the Confederacy.[39] During the decade directly preceding the Civil War, he had come much under the spell of the Southern planters. He had embraced slavery and had gone out valiantly to do battle against the Abolitionists. He had made frequent trips through the plantation country of the South, and he had developed an antipathy against Northerners as sharp as any to be found. He had even begun to attend the Southern commercial conventions, those nurseries of Southern nationalism. Two weeks after Lincoln's election he was making statements which might have served as easy entries into a Southern accord. On November 17 he said, "*Individually*, we are willing to go with the South, *even unto death*, but we feel bound to aid in making the South herself *go right!*"[40]

John Bell called for neutrality and then joined the Confederacy; T. A. R. Nelson travelled farther along the road of Unionism and then strayed off slightly on a by-path; perhaps

[38] Price, *op. cit.*, III, 323-24.
[39] *Southern Watchman*, May 30, 1866.
[40] *Knoxville Whig*, November 17, 1860, quoted in *Parson Brownlow's Book*, p. 34.

Parson Brownlow, just because he was not like other people, might have landed in the camps of the Confederacy. But East Tennesseeans without the valiant leadership which they had in such abundance could never have developed the will or the power to make their region so menacing a stronghold of Unionism as to provide a major problem for the Confederacy.

CHAPTER VIII

EAST TENNESSEEANS REBEL AGAINST REBELLION

THE SPECTRE of secession was a horrible nightmare to East Tennesseeans. It haunted them. Knowing that it was best to crush it before it should settle down upon the state, they did not wait until the June election to raise an outcry.

In fact, Brownlow and his East Tennessee associates in Unionism, Horace Maynard, Emerson Etheridge, T. A. R. Nelson, O. P. Temple, John Baxter, John Fleming, John Netherland, Nat Taylor, F. S. Heiskell, C. F. Trigg, W. B. Carter, and many others, old Whigs and Democrats alike, had been fighting secession since it ominously appeared on the horizon with the election of Lincoln. The troublous times brought together in spirit even two such inveterate enemies as Brownlow and Andrew Johnson, the one holding the fort of Unionism in the highlands of East Tennessee and the other in the Senate in Washington boldly denouncing secession and its leaders. Though he was in Washington, Johnson's influence in East Tennessee was great.[1] Brownlow was now to show that he could use language just as abusive in defending Johnson as he had formerly used in opposing him. He denounced a forger of Johnson's name as a "corrupt liar, low-down drunkard, irresponsible vagabond, and infamous coward."[2] When the special session of the Senate adjourned in the latter part of March, Johnson hurried back to Tennessee. He was coming to help his East Tennessee compatriots to save the state for the Union in the plebiscite to be held on June 8.

In East Tennessee there was a strong feeling, impatient and

---

[1] Winston, *op. cit.*, p. 190.
[2] *Parson Brownlow's Book*, p. 128.

bitter, that Middle and West Tennessee had forced disunion through the legislature in May and that they were preparing to work a grim joke on the people by dragooning them into voting for it on June 8. Brownlow and others having determined to prepare for the day by organizing a campaign of opposition in East Tennessee, issued a call urging every county to send delegates to a convention to be held in Knoxville on May 30. At noon on the day set, C. F. Trigg called to order in Temperance Hall between 450 and 500 delegates from twenty-six counties. Most of them were from Knox, Roane, Anderson, Greene, Sevier, and Blount counties. So vehement was the Parson that he appeared as a triumvirate all in one— he was a regular delegate from Knox, and for each of the counties of Marion and Hancock he served by proxy. He was denied the praying of a long prayer with which the convention was opened, and he was not elected president, an honor which went to T. A. R. Nelson; but he was appointed to membership on the Business Committee, and given double power through his holding proxies for Marion and Hancock counties.

This committee, composed of members from the various counties, was the all-dominating group which shaped the purpose of the convention. It immediately set to work and on the second day presented a report and twelve resolutions, setting forth the perils of the times and breathing defiance against the government of Tennessee. The convention unanimously adopted these resolutions and ordered them to be printed in Brownlow's *Knoxville Whig* (and three other newspapers) and gave Brownlow the contract to print 5,000 copies of its proceedings. The next day the convention adjourned to await the outcome of the voting on June 8. In this movement there was a distinct threat of secession from a state.[3]

East Tennessee made a determined fight to vote disunion down not only in her own section but to raise such a large majority against it that the whole state would be saved, for she

[3] *The War of the Rebellion: A Compilation of the Official Records of the Union and Confederate Armies* (hereafter cited as *Official Records*), ser. I, vol. LII, pt. 1, pp. 152-56; Humes, *op. cit.*, pp. 105-15.

remembered that in the February election on the question of holding a convention it was the East Tennessee majority that had defeated the move. But, as has previously appeared, Tennessee gave her majority vote for disunion in the June election, and the East Tennesseeans now saw serious days ahead. Bitterness was beginning to usurp the throne of reason in all parts of the commonwealth, and threats of murder were beginning to be heard. Rumor had it that Brownlow and Johnson were marked for the slaughter, and so seriously was it regarded that the Parson made a special effort to have Johnson warned of his danger. He sent one of his sons to rescue the East Tennessee Senator from a trap, and shortly thereafter, about the middle of June, the Union leaders, concluding that Johnson was in danger as long as he remained in Tennessee, spirited him out by way of the Cumberland Gap.[4] The Union cause in Tennessee was now in the hands of Brownlow and his associates. Johnson could be of greater aid in Washington; Brownlow could best do his work by remaining in Tennessee.

As soon as it was evident that disunion had prevailed in Tennessee, T. A. R. Nelson, the continuing president of the adjourned Knoxville Convention, called upon his East Tennesseeans to reassemble on June 17 in Greeneville. East Tennessee was in no mood to submit to disunion, and the second session of the Convention would decide upon what should be done next. The delegates first assembled in the Greene County courthouse, held the morning session of the second day out under the trees, and adjourned to the Greeneville College auditorium for the remaining meetings. The Convention lasted four days. Thirty East Tennessee counties were represented, but the total number of delegates was not as great as in the Knoxville session. Brownlow was one of the Knox County delegates and at the same time increased his power and importance by representing Marion County in the guise of an "alternate." Each meeting was opened with prayer, but the Parson as a politician seems to have eclipsed his clerical attainments, for he was not given the chance to call down the vengeance of the Lord upon the enemy at any time

---

[4] Winston, *op. cit.*, p. 196; Milton, *op. cit.*, p. 107.

during the Convention. The powerful Business Committee, the Directory of East Tennessee, retained the same membership which it had had at Knoxville. Brownlow thus continued to occupy a position of great importance. After three days of impassioned oratory by the convention, the Business Committee reported on the last day its "Declaration of Grievances," which was in effect a declaration of independence. It provided for three commissioners to be appointed to go before the Tennessee legislature to ask for separate statehood, and it called for an election to choose delegates to go to another convention which should meet soon at Kingsport. This report was adopted, but not without some dissent. Twenty thousand copies of the proceedings of the convention were ordered to be printed and distributed.[5]

A remarkable situation had here developed. An historic issue had come to a head in the most distressing circumstances. East Tennessee had been conscious of her separateness from the surrounding country even before the state had been formed. From the beginning of the Watauga Association, down through the fiasco of the State of Franklin and on, East Tennessee had felt a social, economic, and geographical completeness which never entirely gave up the hope for separate statehood. During the 1840's Brownlow was pursuing this idea with a vigor suggestive of a religious quarrel. In 1842 he was arguing that the time had come to cease paying tribute to Middle Tennessee. A meeting was held at Jonesboro to consider forming a new state which would be somewhat increased in size by the annexations of parts of North Carolina and Virginia. The next year a bill was introduced in the legislature for this purpose.[6] The example of the western Virginia movement was now before the eyes of the East Tennesseeans, and, indeed, on the very day the Greeneville session began, the Wheeling convention declared the independence of western Virginia from the Old Dominion. Being less advantageously situated for so bold a course and being weaker, the East Tennesseeans were contented with an appeal to the Tennessee legislature for what the western Virginians violently

---

[5] *Official Records,* ser. I, vol. LII, pt. I, pp. 168-77.
[6] *Jonesboro Whig,* December 20, 1843.

seized. Yet in the Greeneville Convention there was a strong move to declare independence, set up a provisional government, and raise an army. As it was, this convention had assumed an attitude and usurped powers that came close on the heels of treason, for its assumption of the right to order elections and otherwise to control the people of East Tennessee could not be regarded in any other light. The serious intentions of this convention were either not known to the state and Confederate authorities or they were lightly regarded, for Southern soldiers passing through Greeneville for Virginia looked upon the convention as a ridiculous performance.[7]

The committee appointed to beg statehood at the hands of the legislature quickly performed its task. But the Tennessee legislature now had much more important work to do than to commit mayhem upon itself and to cut the jugular vein of the Confederacy. The petition was disposed of in short order. East Tennessee was the most strategic region in all the South, for it was through this region that the armies in Virginia would maintain quick communication with all the South and Southwest from the Savannah to the Mississippi and beyond. That both the East Tennesseans and the Confederacy knew this fact was soon to be amply evident.

With Tennessee out of the Union and a member of the Confederacy, Brownlow now entered upon a campaign of withering denunciation so wild and abandoned that it is one of the minor miracles of history that he was permitted to continue so long. He was not the only Union leader in East Tennessee boldly to keep up the fight against the accomplished fact, but he was incomparably the most open and spectacular in his language. His strength was not in oratory and speechmaking but in the printed page of his *Knoxville Whig*. When he began his bold fight against secession soon after Lincoln's election, he began to lose many of his subscribers who were outraged by his language, but in that very picturesqueness of language he was appealing to many other people, and according to his claim he was making a net gain of two hundred subscribers a week.

---

[7] Humes, *op. cit.*, pp. 115-19; Hale and Merritt, *op. cit.*, p. 590.

Before a long-suffering government put a stop to his wild course, he had accumulated fourteen thousand subscribers and was for the first time in his life approaching the doors of wealth.[8]

Just before the plebiscite of June 8, Brownlow, in defending the right to fly a United States flag which he had hoisted over his home in February, declared that if the state should vote herself out of the Union "then we should have to come down, and bring our flag with us, bowing to the will of the majority with the best grace we could." He had been put to as much trouble in protecting his flag as in defending his principles of Unionism. His neighbors had troubled him much about his flag, and when troops began coming through Knoxville on their way to Virginia they were induced to tease the Parson. He would come out of his house, shake his fist at his tormentors, bandy words with them, and make mock bows to them. Once his twenty-three-year-old daughter Susan confronted with a revolver two would-be flag-snatchers and forced them to retreat. The tale was later embellished by saying that the two men came back with ninety reënforcements but the doughty daughter held the fort against all comers.[9] The Parson blamed the whole trouble upon his Knoxville enemies, who afraid to confront him, had induced these "strangers, under the influence of whiskey, to do a dirty and villainous work they have the meanness to do, without the courage." Against them he poured out a tirade of abuse:

If these God-forsaken scoundrels and hell-deserving assassins want satisfaction out of me for what I have said about them,—and that has been no little,—they can find me on these streets every day of my life but Sunday. I am at all times prepared to give them satisfaction. I take back nothing I have ever said against the corrupt and unprincipled villains, but reiterate all, cast it in their dastardly faces, and hurl down their lying throats their own infamous calumnies.[10]

The Parson's flag may have been furled after June 8, but

---

[8] *Parson Brownlow's Book,* p. 100; Temple, *op. cit.,* p. 276.

[9] Frank Moore, *op. cit.,* I, 109; *Portrait and Biography,* p. 50. The defense of the flag was later written into a highly imaginative propaganda pamphlet featuring the Parson's daughter. See pp. 244-45 of this book.

[10] *Knoxville Whig,* May 25, 1861, quoted in *Parson Brownlow's Book,* p. 57.

he forgot to submit to the will of the majority as he repeatedly promised he would do. No one was too high or none too low to escape his poisoned arrows. Former associates turned Confederate he especially loathed. "Men change in a night," he declared. Furthermore,

Men rise up and dress as Union men, and turn Secessionists before breakfast is over. . . . The malady is short; the disease runs its course in twenty-four hours, and the patient heads a committee to order better men than himself to leave the State in a given time. He believes every lie he hears, and swears to the truth of every lie he tells. He drinks mean whiskey, and associates with men whom the day before he would have scorned. The disease is contagious, and a clever man will contract it by drinking mean whiskey out of the same tumbler with one afflicted with it.[11]

He did not attack merely through generalities; he called names and labelled them, high and low in Confederate and state offices. General W. H. Carroll, was a "walking groggery"; at one time John H. Crozier was "a goggle-eyed little scoundrel" and at another "the most unmitigated scoundrel in Knoxville"; J. C. Ramsey, the Confederate States District Attorney, and the son of "the vain old *historian of Tennessee*," was a "*corrupt scoundrel* and most unprincipled knave"; W. G. Swan was a member of a "villainous clique"; and W. G. McAdoo was one of the "most *intense* Southern patriots" of the cowardly variety.[12] The editor of the Knoxville *Register* was "a man of bad morals, bad associations, and the tool of the worst class of men in Knoxville."[13] A month after Tennessee had become a member of the Southern Confederacy, Brownlow characterized the leaders of the new nation as the real traitors, naming Yancey, Rhett, Toombs, Pryor, Davis, Keitt, Iverson, Wise, Mason, Wigfall, Breckinridge, and Lane. He boldly declared, "If there are any men in this country who deserve the doom of traitors, it is these authors of our national calamities," and he predicted that if the

---

[11] *Knoxville Whig*, July 6, 1861, quoted in *Parson Brownlow's Book*, pp. 147-48.
[12] *Parson Brownlow's Book*, pp. 295, 304-5, 360-61.
[13] *Ibid.*, p. 215.

war lasted from three to five years they would all be fugitives in foreign countries.[14]

With reckless abandon he fell upon the head of the Confederacy:

I have been expected to state in every issue of my paper, that the mantle of Washington sits well on Jeff Davis! This would be a funny publication. The bow of Ulysses in the hands of a pigmy! The robes of the giant adorning Tom Thumb! The curls of a Hyperion on the brow of a Satyr! The Aurora Borealis of a cotton farm melting down the icy North! This would be to metamorphose a *minnow* into a WHALE![15]

The Parson received in October, 1861, a package containing about half a yard of brown cloth which he felt sure was innoculated with smallpox. "Handling it with tongs" he took it out in the yard of his printing-office and burned it, and then wrote an editorial denouncing his would-be assassin, and declaring that this "attempt at our death, by the planting of a masked battery manned by the iniquitous spirit of Secession, entitles the cowardly villain who did it, to the honor of being picketed in the deepest gorge leading to hell!"[16]

The first wave of enthusiasm for volunteering soon spent itself both North and South, when once the bloody business of war had set in. The Parson noted the slackening zeal of the Knoxville warriors who continued to fight with words only. He taunted them with as much satanic glee and irony about their holding back from the army as ever a small boy teased a playmate.[17] In fact if Brownlow had been planning a campaign of martyrdom for himself and his paper he could not have done better than to follow the course he had taken since Tennessee left the Union. He did not call directly for rebellion against the Rebellion, but he kept up a bombardment against the Confederacy which could point to no other conclusion if it were allowed

---

[14] *Knoxville Whig,* July 6, 1861, quoted in *Parson Brownlow's Book,* pp. 148-49.
[15] *Knoxville Whig,* June 29, 1861, quoted in *Parson Brownlow's Book,* p. 119.
[16] *Parson Brownlow's Book,* p. 136.
[17] *Knoxville Whig,* October 12, 1861, quoted in *Parson Brownlow's Book,* pp. 245-49.

to continue. He published in his paper time after time the accounts of Confederate tyrannies, including the arrests of people even for praying for the president of the United States. To live in the Confederacy under such conditions, he declared, "is literally to live in hell!"[18] and "Wrongs less wanton and outrageous precipitated the French Revolution."[19]

Brownlow's continuous agitation against the South had produced in East Tennessee a dangerous situation. All the elements were present for a rebellion against the Confederacy here. The Greeneville Convention, not dead but only adjourned, afforded a rallying point for the organization of a Lincoln government in the most strategic and vulnerable part of the Confederacy. Open military rebellion had not broken out yet, but political rebellion actually existed, for the East Tennesseeans refused by their actions in the August 1 election to recognize the Confederacy. Indeed, it was an intolerable situation: This was the occasion for the election of the governor, the legislature, and the delegation to the Confederate Congress. The three congressional districts in East Tennessee elected Unionists to represent them in the Congress at Washington. Horace Maynard, one of the Unionists, made his escape by way of Cumberland Gap and Kentucky and was present to claim his seat when Congress assembled in December; T. A. R. Nelson, the president of East Tennessee by virtue of his presidency of the adjourned Greeneville Convention, attempted to slip away to Washington through Southwest Virginia, but he was arrested in the early part of August near Abingdon and was pardoned by President Davis on his promise to submit as a citizen of Tennessee to the Confederate Government; and George W. Bridges, the third of the East Tennessee incorruptibles, ultimately made his way to Washington, where he took his seat only six days before the term for which he was elected expired. An anomalous situation thus existed; a part of the Confederacy had elected representatives to the law-making body of a foreign country, and those

---

[18] *Knoxville Whig*, June 29, 1861, quoted in *Parson Brownlow's Book*, p. 139.
[19] *Knoxville Whig*, October 26, 1861, quoted in *Official Records*, ser. II, vol. I, p. 914.

representatives were seated. And at the same time, this same region was represented in the Confederate Congress.[20]

If East Tennessee should slip from the control of the Confederacy, the power of this new government would be vitally impaired. In early July, General Leonidas Polk telegraphed to Richmond warning the government that no time should be lost in dealing with East Tennessee, although at that time there were 2,000 soldiers there. He declared that 10,000 ought to be sent at once, that a department ought to be created, including East Tennessee and portions of North Carolina and Georgia, and he recommended the appointment of Felix K. Zollicoffer to command it. Secretary of War Walker immediately ordered Governor Harris to send two Tennessee regiments to Jonesboro or Haynesville. By August 20 three more regiments, two from Mississippi and one from Alabama, had been ordered into East Tennessee. Disquieting reports were streaming out of this region, and it seemed a near panic was on among the Confederate authorities there. By December 9, East Tennessee had become a field of major interest for the Confederacy, engaging the energy and anxiety of the Richmond officials and requiring the presence of 11,000 infantry, cavalry, and artillery which were badly needed elsewhere. General Zollicoffer was placed in command in July and shortly thereafter he issued an order commanding his troops to cultivate the good will of the East Tennesseeans and strictly enjoining upon them "the most scrupulous regard for the personal and property rights of all the inhabitants." He also warned his soldiers to refrain from alarming or irritating those who had been Unionists but had now submitted to the authority of the Confederacy.[21]

The Parson thought as well of Zollicoffer as he could of any person who was so deluded as to join the Confederacy, but he had words of bitterness for the Confederate occupation of East Tennessee and for the soldiers who carried it out. He let it be

---

[20] Humes, *op. cit.*, pp. 126-29; Temple, *op. cit.*, p. 140; *Official Records*, ser. II, vol. I, pp. 825-27. A. J. Clements, of the Fourth Congressional District, claimed election to Washington, and was seated there January 13, 1862.

[21] *Official Records*, ser. I, vol. VII, p. 751; ser. II, vol. I, pp. 827-32.

known that the presence of soldiers in Knoxville would not cause him to change the tone of his newspaper. "I shall continue to denounce secession and all concerned in it," he declared, "though all the allied powers of hell and the Confederacy be quartered at my doors. Come what may, through weal or woe, in peace or war, no earthly power shall keep me from denouncing the enemies of my country until my tongue and pen shall be paralyzed in death. I covet no higher honor than to die in such a holy cause, and your brutal soldiery, therefore has no terrors for me."[22] He charged the Confederate soldiers with being the riff-raff of the country and claimed that not a few of them had joined the army "to get rid of their wives and children."[23] They were either a deluded or a vicious pack. "Ask one of them what rights he had lost and was so vehemently contending for," said Brownlow, "and the reply would be, the right to carry his negroes into the Territories. At the same time, the man never owned a negro in his life, and never was related, by consanguinity or affinity, to any one who did own a negro!"[24] He had a special antipathy for the soldiers from the Cotton South. He held that many of them who came through East Tennessee were "*vagabonds* and *wharft-rats* from New Orleans, Mobile, and Texas . . . brimfull of prejudice against me and my paper."[25]

With such opinions of the Southern soldiery and with such opinions boldly expressed, the Parson should not have been surprised to have the same low opinions reciprocated. Soldiers occasionally jeered at him and made life miserable for him in as many ways as they could think of. He claimed that his enemies in East Tennessee incited them against him, and that when the meanest of these deluded grey-coats arrived in Knoxville they would visit the whiskey shops and then "swarm around my printing office and dwelling-house, howl like wolves, swear oaths that would blister the lips of a sailor, blackguard my family, and threaten to demolish my house, and even to hang me."[26] Troops

[22] "Fighting Parson Brownlow of Tennessee," by J. W. B., in *Chicago Tribune*, August 25, 1895.
[23] *Parson Brownlow's Book*, p. 273.
[24] *Ibid.*, pp. 273-74.   [25] *Ibid.*, p. 277.
[26] *Ibid.*, pp. 277-78.

passed his house daily "flourishing their knives, pointing their guns at the windows, and threatening to take my life."[27]

President T. A. R. Nelson, of the Greeneville Convention and Congressman-elect to Washington, might bow his knee to President Jefferson Davis and his Confederate army, but Parson Brownlow would become more determined in his opposition, irrespective of whether the soft hand or the mailed fist were extended. With the coming of Zollicoffer to Knoxville the Confederacy had taken an extremely liberal and friendly attitude toward the people, in view of the political rebellion the Unionists had raised and especially in view of the extreme importance of East Tennessee to the strategy of the Confederacy. But the Parson and his followers had evidently assumed that liberality meant weakness, so President Davis sought to do the only logical thing left to him. He issued a proclamation calling upon all East Tennesseans to swear allegiance to the Confederacy or to depart by October, 1861.[28] This proclamation the Parson ignored, since he neither departed nor swore allegiance to the Confederacy. On November 6, the election of a president and vice president for the Confederacy was held, but so well had Brownlow trained his East Tennesseans that they ignored the whole procedure, the sheriffs not even deigning to open the polls.[29]

The irreconcilable attitude of Brownlow and other East Tennesseans was not due entirely to an unreasoning fatuity; they had cause to believe that their precarious position was being well considered in the North. One of the principal reasons why Andrew Johnson had fled in June was to provide sinews of war for East Tennessee and to set in motion an army of rescue. In Washington he would have the ear of Lincoln and of high army officers. But East Tennessee was not as accessible to Northern succor as was western Virginia, and while help was preparing, the East Tennesseans were left to their own devices.

When Tennessee passed out of the Union and into the Confederacy, there was a considerable movement of East Tennes-

---

[27] *Ibid.*, p. 279.

[28] *Official Records*, ser. I, vol. VII, p. 722; ser. II, vol. I, p. 850.

[29] *Portrait and Biography*, p. 51.

seeans through Cumberland Gap into Kentucky. Here they expected to build themselves into an avenging army, to rescue their homes when they should become strong enough. They felt a particular friendliness for Kentuckians, who had at this time adopted a position of neutrality, and through this very situation they expected not only the active support of Kentucky in their fight to recover East Tennessee but they had the promise of aid from the United States Government. William Nelson, encouraged and incited by President Lincoln, set up a training camp at Camp Dick Robinson on the edge of the eastern Kentucky mountains, defending himself with lame reasons against the charge that this was a breach of Kentucky neutrality, and here at least 2,000 Tennesseans came together during the summer and fall. They trickled through the mountain passes, principally Cumberland Gap, until the Confederate troops barred it. In early November it was reported that from 20 to 100 Tennesseans a day were emerging on the Kentucky side. They were training and arming and impatiently awaiting the day to march back to rescue their homes and expel the Confederates. Rumors were continually flying through East Tennessee that the army of rescue was on the march.[30]

There were other East Tennesseans who determined to remain in their homes and defend them. They early began secretly organizing, arming, and training; and some of them were not opposed to taking the offensive in open violence, as was demonstrated as early as the latter part of April when Unionists cut down the telegraph wires in Knox and Roane counties.[31] Almost every county in East Tennessee had its companies of Union men who were drilling in the mountain coves and out-of-the-way places, awaiting the day when they might join an army of deliverance. There was much excitement among the scattered Confederate forces, who expected to be ambushed at any time. Disturbing reports were coming in of groups of Union soldiers leaving for Kentucky to join the army shortly to enter East

---

[30] *Official Records*, ser. II, vol. I, pp. 833-37; Humes, *op. cit.*, pp. 325-27; *Parson Brownlow's Book*, p. 264.

[31] *Knoxville Whig*, April 27, 1861. Brownlow and other Union leaders deprecated such actions on the part of their followers.

Tennessee. W. G. Swan declared that these scattered Union forces had a secret system of communication and that on the shortest notice they could join forces. He declared that 1,000 recently flew to arms on an alarm which turned out to be false. Landon C. Haynes, soon to be elected to the Confederate Senate, wrote Secretary of War Walker that military rebellion was flaring up in East Tennessee, that there were 10,000 Union men armed with rifles and shotguns, and that Brownlow had declared that civil war was inevitable.[32]

There can be no doubt that East Tennessee was on the verge of an explosion, for the vast majority of the people, whipped into a fury by Brownlow and others, were inexorably opposed to submitting to Confederate rule. If they had not been cut off from Federal aid by mountains on all sides the major operations of the Civil War might have begun in the heart of the Confederacy rather than on the fringe. Bold efforts were made to run ammunition and guns into East Tennessee, and occasionally they were successful as on November 11 when the Federals in Kentucky sent in 45 pounds of rifle powder, 50 pounds of lead, and 20 boxes of rifle caps.[33] It was undoubtedly discouraging to be Unionists in East Tennessee, where the people were forced to live mostly on hopes, yet the tradition persists that the First Congressional District embracing this section of the State, sent a bigger proportion of its population into the Union army than any other district in the entire country.[34]

That East Tennessee did not become a battlefield until the latter part of 1863 was no fault of the East Tennesseeans. Plans were early being devised by the Washington authorities for seizing East Tennessee as one of the first great objectives of the Federal armies. Andrew Johnson had gone to Washington in June to lay such plans before Lincoln and the army leaders. East Tennessee's struggle for the Union was made to seem even more heroic than it actually was, and thus was a great deal of sentiment injected into the movement. Strategic reasons were well considered and found to be highly compelling. Two great

[32] *Official Records,* ser. II, vol. I, pp. 828-37; Temple, *op. cit.,* p. 104.

[33] *Official Records,* ser. II, vol. I, pp. 889-90.

[34] Price, *op. cit.,* III, 322.

army movements could be made to impinge on this region. Mc-
Clellan's operations against Richmond could be greatly helped
by creating a diversion in East Tennessee; and General Buell's
armies which were forming in Kentucky should make this region
their definite objective. Thus would the East Tennessee fugitives camping on the edges of the mountains become part of a
mighty army of deliverance. The whole conception was grand
and it appealed with vast force to the minds of Lincoln and Mc-
Clellan. Thus was sentiment, politics, and strategy mixed up in
a grand scheme.

The East Tennessee leaders were cognizant of these plans,
and this information was largely responsible for the military
units which were training and hiding throughout the regions,
awaiting the day when they would join the grand deliverance.
On November 7, 1861, General McClellan wrote General Buell:
"It therefore seems proper that you should remain on the de-
fensive on the line from Louisville to Nashville while you throw
the mass of your forces by rapid marches by Cumberland Gap
or Walker's Gap on Knoxville in order to occupy the railroad
at that point and thus enable the loyal citizens of Eastern Tennessee to rise while you at the same time cut off the railway communication between Eastern Virginia and the Mississippi."[35]
In preparation for this grand entry the East Tennessee leaders
now decided to execute a stroke at the Confederacy which they
had long had in mind and which the Confederacy had long feared.
If the idea did not originate with Parson Brownlow, it was at
least first prominently set forth by him. All the railway bridges
in East Tennessee from the Georgia line to Virginia should be
destroyed. On May 25, 1861, the Parson published in the *Knoxville Whig*, in answer to a rumor that he and other Union leaders were to be arrested and taken out of the state, this plan of
action:

Let the railroad on which Union citizens of East Tennessee are
conveyed to Montgomery in irons be eternally and hopelessly
destroyed! Let the property of the men concerned be consumed,
and let their lives pay the forfeit, and the names will be given!

---

[35] *Official Records,* ser. II, vol. I, p. 891.

Let the fires of patriotic vengeance be built upon the Union altars of the whole land, and let them go out where these conspirators live, like the fires from the Lord, that consumed Nadab and Abihu, the two sons of Aaron, for presumption less sacrilegious! If we are incarcerated at Montgomery, or executed there or even elsewhere, all the consolation we want is to know that our partisan friends have visited upon our persecutors — certain Secession leaders—a most horrible vengeance! Let it be done, East Tennesseans, though the gates of hell be forced and the heavens be made to fall![36]

The Greeneville Convention, on June 20, called attention to this weapon that East Tennessee held in her hands. Although East Tennesseeans had not interposed obstacles to soldiers passing through "our territory," and although they objected to violence to the railroads, "yet if the grievous wrongs inflicted by some of the troops are not stopped, we warn all persons concerned, including the officers of said roads, that there is a point at which a population of 300,000 people, outraged, insulted, and trampled upon, cannot be and ought not to be restrained."[37]

The Confederate authorities were thus amply warned of the possibility of this disaster happening to their communications through East Tennessee, and to ward it off they set guards at all the important railway bridges. But the guards were entirely too small to beat off a determined attack by bridge-burners; and sensing the imminent danger Landon C. Haynes on July 6 wrote Secretary of War Walker his expectation of hearing at any time that the bridges had been destroyed.[38]

Brownlow was one of the most cunning men in all the land; he was no bridge-burner. But he could arouse a state of mind in East Tennessee which would breed bridge-burners aplenty. So he was not found among those who planned and executed the bridge-burning. In September, William Blount Carter went to Washington to present the plan to the United States Government. He saw Lincoln, McClellan, and Seward and they all agreed that the bridges should be fired preparatory to the in-

---

[36] Quoted in *Parson Brownlow's Book,* p. 300.

[37] *Official Records,* ser. I, vol. LII, pt. I, p. 177.

[38] *Ibid.,* ser. II, vol. I, p. 824.

vasion of Buell's army.[39] In the latter part of September General George H. Thomas, in Kentucky, wrote General McClellan that he had seen Carter and that he was convinced that the bridges could be destroyed. It would take some money and he thought the Government should provide it. Quick preparations were now put under way. Captain David Fry was given $1,000 and ordered to enter East Tennessee to enlist the bridge-burning forces.[40]

On November 6 the Confederate presidential elections were held. Maddened by this make-believe performance, East Tennesseeans spurned the whole procedure; but two days later, on the night of the 8th, they gave their answer to the Confederate Government. Five important railway bridges blazed forth and left a trail of ashes and charred remains. This was their reply to the "bogus Confederacy," and a signal to the Union armies to march in. Two bridges had been burned on the Western and Atlantic Railroad, one on the East Tennessee and Georgia, which ran from Chattanooga to Knoxville, and two on the East Tennessee and Virginia, which ran from Knoxville to Bristol. It seemed now that the long-feared explosion had come. On November 11, Colonel W. B. Wood said "The whole country is now in a state of rebellion," and a Jonesboro resident wrote President Davis, "Civil war has broken out at length in East Tennessee." A precarious situation was reported: A thousand armed Unionists were within six miles of the Strawberry Plains bridge; 500 Unionists had left Hamilton County presumably to attack Loudon Bridge; 300 men were encamped in Sevier County; great Union concentrations were in progress in Carter and Johnson counties; an encampment was forming at Elizabethton; and so came rumors and reports from all parts of East Tennessee. It was feared that these forces were preparing to burn the remaining bridges; it was known that they expected to welcome a Federal army from Kentucky, and that they were cutting the telegraph wires as fast as they could be repaired. On November 12, Governor Harris wrote President Davis that

[39] Temple, *op. cit.*, p. 90.
[40] *Official Records*, ser. II, vol. I, pp. 889-90; *Congressional Globe*, 41st Cong., 2nd sess., I, 139; 41st Cong., 3rd sess., I, 598.

he was sending into East Tennessee immediately 10,000 troops, and at the same time he requested reënforcements from the Confederacy.[41]

Quick steps were taken. Troops were sent out in all directions to break up the Union forces and to arrest their leaders. On November 18, a force of 300 rebellious Unionists was dispersed and thirty prisoners were captured. General Zollicoffer, who had heretofore pursued a policy of kindness in East Tennessee, now realized that his confidence had been misplaced, and that the Unionist leaders were guilty of treachery. He ordered the immediate disarming of all Unionists and the seizure of the chief trouble-makers. "The leniency shown them has been unavailing," he declared. "They have acted with base duplicity and should no longer be trusted."[42]

In order to stamp out future trouble the Confederacy now felt it necessary to treat the East Tennesseeans with the suspicion and harshness that war always imposes upon those who have it within their power to hinder victory. Squads of soldiers were sent out into every district to break up Unionist gatherings, to disarm the populace, and to arrest the leaders. Squads were also sent out to enforce contracts for hogs and cattle, which Unionists had made with the Confederacy but were now slow to fulfill. On December 11, General Carroll declared martial law in Knoxville. This action greatly displeased Brownlow, who later wrote, "Every little upstart of an officer in command at a village or cross-roads would proclaim *martial law*, and require all going beyond, or coming within, his lines to show a pass, like some negro slave."[43] This campaign of pacification seems to have been carried out with too much vigor, for in the latter part of December Captain G. H. Monsarrat, commanding the post at Knoxville, wrote Judah P. Benjamin, who had now succeeded L. P. Walker as Secretary of War, that marauding bands of armed men, who claimed to be agents of the Confederate Government, were impressing men into the service, threatening them with imprisonment as Unionists unless they volunteered,

---

[41] *Official Records*, ser. II, vol. I, pp. 838-43.   [42] *Ibid.*, pp. 842-43.
[43] *Official Records*, ser. II, vol. I, p. 855; *Parson Brownlow's Book*, p. 346.

seizing their horses, and forcing the care of themselves and their horses upon the people without pay. He also charged that they "Plunder the helpless, and especially *quondam* supporters of Johnson, Maynard, and Brownlow."[44]

John Baxter, an erstwhile Unionist now acquiescing in the Confederate rule, called upon Secretary Benjamin to treat the people with more leniency, believing that as a result of such a course he would find the East Tennesseeans more amenable to Confederate supremacy. But Benjamin had determined that those who were guilty of crimes should be punished and especially should the bridge-burners be made to suffer. Great numbers of people were arrested and brought into Knoxville and Nashville which served as clearing stations. By November 26, seventy people were in jail in Knoxville, many of whom were believed to be mixed up with the bridge-burning business. Feeling that the mass of the people had been deluded by their wily leaders, Benjamin ordered all the lesser prisoners to be released upon their taking the oath to support the Confederacy, but the important agitators should be held for high treason. The bridge-burners were a class unto themselves and should be dealt with summarily. He ordered them to be tried by drum-head court martial and if found guilty to be "executed on the spot by hanging," and their bodies left dangling in the air as a warning. The trial was set for November 28, and on the 30th two were hanged. C. A. Haun, another bridge-burner, was sentenced to be executed on December 11, but before carrying out the sentence, General W. H. Carroll telegraphed to Secretary Benjamin for the President's approval, which he believed was required. Benjamin replied: "Execute the sentence of your court-martial on the bridge-burners. The law does not require any approval by the President, but he entirely approves my order to hang every bridge-burner you can catch and convict."[45]

Brownlow bitterly condemned this execution, claiming that Haun had been condemned "without any defence allowed him by a drum-head and whiskey-drinking court-martial." "They

---

[44] *Official Records*, ser. I, vol. VII, pp. 704, 803-4.
[45] *Ibid.*, p. 726; ser. II, vol. I, p. 848.

One of the Parson's "Rebel atrocities." This represents the hanging of two of the bridge-burners, Jacob Harmon and his son, Henry. From Brownlow's *Sketches of the Rise, Progress, and Decline of Secession.*

drove up a cart with a coffin in it," he said, "surrounded by a hardened set of Rebel troops, displaying their bayonets and looking and talking savagely."[46]

On December 27, Harrison Self, another convicted bridge-burner, was notified that he would be hanged at four o'clock that day. His daughter came to visit him, and Brownlow, who was present, exclaimed "My God, what a sight! What an affecting scene! May these eyes of mine, bathed in tears, never look upon the like again!" He seized a piece of paper and wrote for the girl to President Davis: "My father, Harrison Self, is sentenced to hang at four o'clock this evening, on a charge of bridge-burning. As he remains my earthly all, and all my hopes of happiness centre in him, I implore you to pardon him. ELIZABETH SELF." The girl hastened to the telegraph office and had it dispatched to Davis. Two hours before the date set for the execution General Carroll was ordered to spare his life.[47]

Thus could the Confederacy show leniency as well as vigor in dealing with its rebellious East Tennesseans. The bridge-burners had been guilty of a most hazardous undertaking which, according to the usages of war, subjected them to the extreme penalty. The Confederacy could not in a matter of such transcendent importance to its very existence do less than was done.

While the bridge-burners were being dealt stern punishment, many other East Tennesseans were being either set at liberty or sent on their way to Tuscaloosa, Alabama, where the Confederacy had decided to incarcerate many of its political prisoners. A carload of prisoners left Knoxville for Tuscaloosa on December 7, but four days later there were still 150 in the jail. By the 19th more than 400 prisoners from East Tennessee had been sent to Tuscaloosa.[48]

Some Confederates believed that too harsh a policy had been adopted toward the East Tennesseans following their abortive uprising in November, while others held that the East Tennesseans by their duplicity had left no other course open. It was

---

[46] *Parson Brownlow's Book,* pp. 312-13.
[47] *Ibid.,* pp. 326-27.
[48] *Official Records,* ser. II, vol. I, pp. 743, 759-60, 777-79, 858.

a fact which no one could dispute that a heritage of hatred for the Confederate element was burned into the hearts of the East Tennesseans, a heritage which Parson Brownlow a few years afterwards was to capitalize to the fullest extent.

The East Tennesseans were not wholly to blame for the evil days that befell them after the bridge-burning rebellion. High hopes had been held out to them by their leaders at home who in turn gathered their enthusiastic vision of the near future from the highest leaders of the nation. The army of deliverance never came, because it never set out; and it never made the attempt, because of divided counsel. Thus were the East Tennesseans, ill organized and poorly armed, left to certain conquest by the Confederates. It appeared that the Federal Government had merely led them into a trap. Any other people less obstinate and less blindly patriotic would have heard the siren notes the Confederacy wafted forth, after a few months of repression, and would have submitted.

But the East Tennesseans were never told that the army of rescue would not come, and perhaps in that fact lay their continued hope, and support of the Union. While dissensions prevailed in the high councils of the nation, the East Tennessee fugitives up in Kentucky were made almost desperate in their desires to go to the rescue of their homes and families. Andrew Johnson was in Kentucky trying to prevail on General Thomas to send the East Tennesseans back even if no other troops should go. In answer Thomas said, "If the Tennesseans are not content and must go then the risk of disaster will remain with them."[49] Thomas continued adamant even in the face of such reports as this: "The condition of affairs there is sad beyond description and if the loyal people who love and cling to the Government are not soon relieved they will be lost."[50] General Thomas refused to make the attempt or to give his permission to the East Tennesseans to try to return, for the Confederates had laid hold of Cumberland Gap, and under Zollicoffer were soon to invade the state of Kentucky from that

---

[49] *Ibid.*, ser. II, vol. I, p. 891.
[50] *Ibid.*, p. 894. S. P. Carter to G. H. Thomas, November 24, 1861.

vantage point. Yet Horace Maynard pessimistically wrote Thomas on December 8:

You are still farther from East Tennessee than when I left you nearly six weeks ago. There is shameful wrong somewhere; I have not yet satisfied myself where. That movement so far has been disgraceful to the country and to all concerned. I feel a sense of personal degradation from my own connection with it greater than any other part of my public actions. My heart bleeds for these Tennessee troops.[51]

Where was the blame for the projected, but unaccomplished, rescue of East Tennessee to be placed? Perhaps on the Cumberland Mountains first, and on General Buell secondly. The inaccessibility of East Tennessee was never more impressive than to an army seeking to enter across the Cumberland escarpment. Lincoln, who had set his heart on seizing East Tennessee, was soon arguing for a military railroad to be built from central Kentucky to Knoxville—thus would he gain entrance.[52] General McClellan urged Buell time and again to march on East Tennessee, where he would be received by warm friendship, rather than to try to seize Nashville where he would find a withering hostility. He should move to the aid of "the noble Union men of Eastern Tennessee."[53] On November 25, McClellan was still convinced that "political and strategical considerations render a prompt movement in force on Eastern Tennessee imperative." Four days later he thought "we owe it to our Union friends in Eastern Tennessee to protect them at all hazards." On into December and beyond he continued to beg Buell to direct his march to East Tennessee. Andrew Johnson and Horace Maynard added their plea on December 7: "Our people are oppressed and pursued as beasts of the forest. The Government must come to our relief."[54] On January 6, 1862 Abraham Lincoln added his voice to the chorus that went up

---

[51] *Ibid.*, p. 898.

[52] He advocated this project in his message to Congress in December, 1861. Congress discussed the subject but never acted. See J. D. Richardson, ed., *A Compilation of the Messages and Papers of the Presidents*, VI, 46.

[53] *Official Records*, ser. II, vol. I, pp. 891-96.

[54] *Ibid.*, p. 898.

to Buell on behalf of the East Tennesseeans: "My distress is that our friends in East Tennessee are being hanged and driven to dispair and even now I fear are thinking of taking rebel arms for the sake of protection. In this we lose the most valuable stake we have in the South." Lincoln would not show to Johnson and Maynard, Buell's recent dispatch giving reasons for not making the march, because "They would despair; possibly resign to go and save their families somehow or die with them."[55]

General Buell felt that an attempt on East Tennessee would be wholly impracticable and that moreover he could best help the East Tennesseeans by seizing Nashville. The country was stripped of its provisions; it would take 3,000 wagons constantly going to supply the army necessary to occupy and hold East Tennessee. He declared in a letter to General McClellan, January 13, 1862, in answer to a roseate plan someone had advocated: "The plan of any colonel whoever he is for ending the war by entering East Tennessee with his 5,000 men light—that is with pack-mules and three batteries of artillery, &c.—while the rest of the armies look on though it has some sensible patent ideas is in the aggregate simply ridiculous."[56] Buell went his way on to Nashville and left East Tennessee in the hands of the Confederates, to continue so for almost two years.

To this low estate, then, had Brownlow's teachings brought East Tennessee. But how had the Parson himself fared in these evil days from late October when the bridge-burners were in the making, down through their trials, tribulations, and execution, and into the new year of death and destruction? The answer comes next.

---

[55] *Ibid.*, p. 900.
[56] *Ibid.*, p. 901.

CHAPTER IX

IN JAIL AND OUT

IF THERE WERE any limits to the freedom of the press in the Confederacy, Brownlow had not been able to discover them. As has amply appeared heretofore, he had since the beginning of the secession troubles been pouring forth in his *Knoxville Whig* an unending and ever-mounting stream of vitriolic denunciation of the Confederacy and of all the Confederates. If he had been seeking martyrdom, it seemed he could have found no better method, but the slowness with which the Confederacy acted against him appeared to indicate that it considered his desires to be martyrdom, and that it could displease him best by letting him alone. But he had plenty of enemies in and about Knoxville who made his lot as hard as possible and they could always set soldiers to having their fun with the excitable Parson.

Nevertheless there seemed to be an end to the patience of anybody who was forced to endure his attacks, and even the Confederacy could not go on forever ignoring the dangers he was developing. With all this forebearance there might well have been mixed a fear that an uprising among East Tennesseeans would result if their chief leader should be seized. Perhaps, too, the Confederacy had put too much faith in a voluntary communication Brownlow had sent General Zollicoffer in which he pledged himself to promote among the East Tennesseeans peace and obedience to the constituted authorities of both the state and the Confederacy.[1] Although the Confederacy did not suppress Brownlow's paper, certain enemies of his impeded its circulation as much as possible. The Confederates by their forebearance were undoubtedly consciously trying not to emulate the recent ex-

---

[1] *Official Records,* ser. I, vol. VII, p. 804.

ample of the Federal Government in its suppression of the *Louisville Courier* and the *New York Day Book*.

Whether true or not, the rumor was soon afloat that Brownlow would be indicted by a Confederate court in Nashville for treasonable articles which had appeared in the *Whig*, and that he was to be arrested immediately. At last his day of martyrdom had come, or at least he would convince himself and his readers that it had, so he decided that the final edition of his paper would appear during the last week of October (1861). If the Confederates would not suppress his paper, he would suppress it himself by throwing the editor in his imagination into jail. An excellent opportunity he would now have to commiserate with himself in a last editorial, and to reproduce some of his articles which he thought must be considered his most treasonable ones. With a vivid imagination, he described the terrible future that awaited him at the hands of the Confederacy. He could likely escape it by signing a peace bond, but he would refuse; he would even decline to allow fifty of his friends to post a bond of $100,000 to secure his freedom—a procedure he was sure they would attempt. Rather he would go to jail and he was ready to start immediately. "Not only so," he declared, "but I am prepared to lie in solitary confinement until I waste away because of imprisonment or die from old age." Conscious of his innocence he would "submit to imprisonment for life or die at the end of a rope before I will make any humiliating concessions to any power on earth." Then forgetful of all that he had said or done for the past six months, he paradoxically declared, "I have discouraged rebellion publicly and privately. I have not assumed a hostile attitude toward the civil or military authorities of this new government." He knew why he was about to be arrested: The Confederacy wanted "to dry up, break down, silence and destroy" the last Union paper in all the Confederacy —the only paper that would tell the truth. He then continued to praise his tenacity of principles, likening himself in his imaginary jail to John Rodgers at the stake, and intimating that his heroic resignation even suggested that occasion in Biblical times when the "infuriated mob cried out, 'Crucify him! Crucify him!'"

He was proud of his position and of his principles and he would leave them to his children as "a legacy far more valuable than a princely fortune." Louis XVI had been beheaded for crimes less heinous than those committed by the Confederacy. With thoughts of Lexington and Bunker Hill, he exchanged "with proud satisfaction, the editorial chair and the sweet endearments of home for a cell in the prison or the lot of an exile."[2]

Thereupon the Parson began his vigil to await the coming of his arresters, feeling doubtless that if the previous editions of his paper had not warranted this expectation, this last one would bring down vengeance upon him. The mountain had now labored, but not even a mouse came forth. The Confederacy most savagely left him alone, and there was none so high nor none so low as to molest him except the ever-present soldiers who now and then tormented him by cocking their pistols and pointing their bayonets at him, and making grimaces at him.

But Brownlow had bitter personal enemies in Knoxville, and although the Confederate authorities at Richmond were showing no disposition to arrest him, a private citizen might take vengeance upon him. And as the bitterness between Unionist and Confederate increased, it was not too much to expect governmental officials at Knoxville to secure his indictment and arrest. In fact, unknown to Brownlow, John C. Ramsey, the Confederate District Attorney for Tennessee, had planned to proceed against him during the early part of November, but was unable to do so on account of the failure of the court to meet.[3] In this situation of uncertainty, Brownlow contemplated at one time making an attempt to slip out through the Cumberlands and make his way to Camp Dick Robinson, in Kentucky, but he found the mountain passes guarded too well.[4]

As it was quite likely that he might become the center of a dangerous disturbance at any time, without his own choosing, he was prevailed upon by his friends to leave Knoxville. He

---

[2] A copy of this editorial may be found in *Official Records,* ser. II, vol. I, pp. 912-14 and in *Parson Brownlow's Book,* pp. 249-55.

[3] *Official Records* ser. I, vol. VII, p. 744, J. C. Ramsey to J. P. Benjamin, December 7, 1861.

[4] Temple, *op. cit.,* p. 308.

would not flee to secure his own safety, for his extreme pugnacity had erased from his mind the fear of any man; but his presence in Knoxville might involve the security of his family, and this latter possibility led him on November 4 to mount a horse and with James Cumming, a seventy-seven year old preacher, as a companion, to ride away to the eastward into Blount and Sevier counties, the greatest hotbeds of Unionism in East Tennessee. Additional reasons he found in the opportunities that would be afforded him to collect debts due him for his defunct *Whig* and to attend the court in Maryville. On reaching Maryville, he stopped at the home of Parson W. T. Dowell, and soon the town showed hurried activities beyond anything called forth by the meeting of a court. Brownlow became the center of Unionist activities, and it was later reported that he had predicted the capture of Knoxville soon by the oncoming Federal army. There were undoubtedly great expectations in East Tennessee, for a few days later, on November 6, the railway bridges were burned. Immediately Brownlow was suspected of plotting the bridge-burning, and for a time no report could be so lowly in its origin as not to be believed. One such report which was dignified sufficiently to be sent in to the Confederate District Attorney, J. C. Ramsey, came from the hired girl of a Maryville family who had got it from the hired girl in the Dowell family, as the two met one day at the spring. The former, who belonged to the Sesler family, innocently remarked after she had heard of the bridge-burning, "La me! Phoebe Smith told me at the spring last Wednesday that the bridges were to be burned Friday night, but I didn't believe it." It turned out that Phoebe Smith had been peeping through the keyhole and listening, and she had seen and heard the two parsons talking about bridge-burning.[5]

Brownlow knew human nature well enough to realize that it was time for him to retreat into the fastnesses of the mountains to escape the wrath that would come down upon him. In company with other Unionists who feared Confederate vengeance, he set out for the Great Smokies and entered their defiles "quite

---

[5] *Official Records*, ser. I, vol. VII, pp. 775-77, J. G. Wallace to J. C. Ramsey, December 18, 1861; ser. II, vol. I, p. 902.

beyond the precincts of civilization." They camped on high ridges and in deep gorges "where no vehicle had ever penetrated." They were fed by friends from Wear's Cove, "and in the meantime one of our party killed a fat bear, which supplied us with meat." These refugees wandered back into Wear's Cove in Sevier County and then southward across high ranges into Tucaleechee Cove, in Blount County.[6] As there was constant danger of so large a party being trapped by Confederate scouts, they broke up into groups of two's. The two parsons, Brownlow and Dowell, rode to the home of a friend within six miles of Knoxville and there entered into secret communication with friends in the city.[7]

Brownlow was now in an uncomfortable position, for although his hiding-place was not then known to the Confederate authorities there was little doubt that he could be found if the scouting parties should make a determined effort to seek him. In fact his enemies declared that the soldiers could have easily found him.[8] He knew that he was suspected of bridge-burning, and he should have known that the circumstantial evidence was strongly against him. It was, therefore, wise in him, while many of his associates and acquaintances were being arrested for this crime, to establish his own innocence. On November 22, from his hiding-place he addressed a letter to General W. H. Carroll, and had his friend John Williams deliver it. After describing the circumstances of his recent flight from Knoxville and his reasons for leaving, he declared his complete innocence of the bridge-burning business. "As regards bridge-burning," he declared, "I never had any intimation of any such purpose from any quarter at any time and when I heard of the burning of the bridges on the Saturday night after it occurred I was utterly astonished. I condemn the act most unqualifiedly and regard it as an ill-timed measure calculated to bring no good to any one or any party but much harm to innocent men and to the public.

---

[6] *The Independent*, May 22, 1862; *Parson Brownlow's Book*, pp. 279-82.

[7] The Parson's hiding place was in what is today one of the most inaccessible parts of the Great Smoky Mountains National Park.

[8] The *Knoxville Register*, December 13, 1861 said, "He could have been picked up in three days at any time during his absence by a deputation of ten soldiers." Quoted in *Official Records*, ser. II, vol. I, p. 925.

A scene from the Great Smokies of East Tennessee. It was in a region of this sort that the Parson in 1861 took refuge from the Confederates. Copyrighted by Thompsons, Inc., Knoxville, and used by permission.

"The Southern Loyalists' Convention at Philadelphia—'Parson Brownlow' passing through the Ranks of the Northern Delegation, in Independence Square." "The old man, so weak that at intervals he was compelled to stop and rest, passed down the entire line, greeted by all with shouts of enthusiastic welcome." From *Harper's Weekly*, September 22, 1866 (vol. X, no. 508, p. 593).

Had a knowledge of any purpose to burn the bridges been communicated to me," he continued, "I should have felt bound in all honor and good conscience to disclose the fact to the chief officers of the roads." And he significantly added, "I am ready and willing at any time to stand trial upon these or other points before any civil tribunal; but I protest against being turned over to any infuriated mob of armed men filled with prejudice by my bitterest enemies."[9]

Brownlow was at great pains to establish his innocence of the bridge-burning charges. He with his two preacher friends, James Cumming and W. T. Dowell, issued a statement and swore to it before Solomon Farmer, a justice of the peace of Blount County, denying the hired-girl story about the bridge-burning conference in Maryville and affirming that none of them had communicated with the fugitives in Kentucky at any time during the whole summer or fall. They swore that they had never heard of the bridge-burning plot and that if they had "we should have protested against it as an outrage."[10] A few months later, when Brownlow was safe among his friends, he said of the bridge-burning, "I was not concerned in the matter, and can't say who did it. I thought to myself that the affair had been most beautifully planned and executed, and enjoyed it considerably in my quiet way."[11]

There now developed a conspiracy of circumstances which were likely very materially shaped by Brownlow himself, and which tended to throw the Confederacy into an uncomfortable position, much to the advantage of the Parson. He began to carry on with General Carroll, in Knoxville, negotiations for surrendering himself, and at the same time some of his friends, perhaps largely unknown to him, began conversations with President Davis and Secretary of War Benjamin in Richmond. There was not a complete interchange of information among the army in Knoxville, the civil authorities in East Tennessee, and the Confederate Government in Richmond, with the result that

---

[9] *Ibid.*, pp. 902-3. In *Parson Brownlow's Book*, pp. 282-83 the letter is neither fully nor correctly quoted.

[10] *Official Records,* ser. II, vol. I, p. 905, December 2, 1861.

[11] *Portrait and Biography*, p. 53.

it appeared that Brownlow was promised one thing by one authority and something else by another. Since it had seemed in Brownlow's letter to Carroll that his chief desire was to secure protection from the Confederate soldiers, and very likely cleverly to escape the trial by court-martial for bridge-burning which the other suspects were to suffer, Carroll replied on November 28 that he would use his full force to protect all citizens loyal to the Confederacy and that Brownlow could be assured that he would meet with no personal violence in returning home. He also added, "If you can establish what you say in your letter of the 22d instant you shall have every opportunity to do so before the civil tribunal if necessary provided you have committed no act that will make it necessary for the military law to take cognizance."[12] It will be seen that this letter did not preclude the possibility of the Parson's arrest by the military authorities, but it did definitely guarantee him against personal violence. He seemed to be promised the right to a civil trial on the bridge-burning charges, which was a great victory for him unless Carroll was as clever as the Parson in adding this saving phrase, "provided you have committed no act that will make it necessary for the military law to take cognizance."

In answer Brownlow wrote Carroll on December 4 a letter in which he enclosed two documents, viz: the affidavit denying the hired-girl story and a long withering denunciation of his chief enemies, whom he called by name. He began his denunciatory document by praising his two preacher companions-in-exile, Cumming and Dowell, as a matter of contrast for what should follow. Thereupon he assaulted the Confederacy, charging that it was "a bogus Government, that originated in fraud and falsehood, perjury and theft." He then came to the main point in his letter: "I cannot feel safe in returning, for I am not sure that your letter offers protection to me." He had that feeling because Carroll had said that loyal Confederate citizens would be protected, and the Parson hereby disclaimed any loyalty for the Confederacy for he recognized only the United States Government. He was not bearing arms against the Con-

---

[12] *Official Records,* ser. II, vol. I, pp. 903-4.

federacy; he was a neutral who wanted to be left alone "to the quiet enjoyment of opinions I honestly entertain and cannot conscientiously surrender." Having thus declared his military neutrality, he launched forth upon a verbal barrage with which he hoped to annihilate his enemies. John H. Crozier was "a corrupt demagogue, a selfish liar, and an unmitigated coward," who hated the Parson because he had been driven into private life by him. J. C. Ramsey was a kinsman of Crozier's and "but a few degrees removed from an idiot." W. H. Sneed was "corpulent" and "swaggering," and "a giant in his own estimation." "His eyelashes are nearly scorched off by alcoholic fire; and nature, to keep up appearances, in a fit of desperation is substituting in their stead a binding of red, which looks like two little rainbows hanging upon a storm, such as he often passes through in the domestic circle!" He had recently been defeated in an election and "Since then he has been travelling in search of his rights, and swears that he will follow them on to the other side of sundown!" The Parson expected this whole pack to take to their heels as soon as the vanguard of the Federal army arrived. "I may not be living," he declared, "when a Federal army enters East Tennessee, but if I am living next spring, I expect to enjoy the luxury." Having thus bespoke his mind he in approved Patrick Henry fashion added, "If this be treason, make the most of it!"[13]

Thus did Brownlow reject General Carroll's terms of surrender, but Carroll did not know it for the friend intrusted with the delivery of this letter withheld it on the intelligence of an important decision by the Confederate Government. The negotiations in Richmond which had been going on at the same time, and largely unknown to the Parson, had brought results. In fact even before Brownlow had first written General Carroll relative to coming into Knoxville to stand a civil trial, friends of the Parson had been besieging Secretary Benjamin in Richmond to grant him a passport to leave the Confederacy. On November 20, Benjamin had written General George B. Crittenden, stationed at Cumberland Gap, that he understood that

---

[13] *Parson Brownlow's Book,* pp. 284-92.

Brownlow, fearing violence, had hidden himself but that he was willing to leave Tennessee. The Confederate War Secretary said he could not give him a formal passport though he "would greatly prefer to see him on the other side of our lines as an avowed enemy," and he would not object if Crittenden would allow him to escape.[14] But Crittenden did not receive this letter until other important transactions had taken place. Apparently Benjamin had not prejudged Brownlow as sufficiently guilty of bridge-burning even to arrest him should he by leaving, thereby help to compose East Tennessee.

John Baxter, who in the early days of the secession movement had been one of the outstanding leaders of Unionism in East Tennessee, and who had later on accepted the Confederacy in good faith, was in Richmond in November attempting to guide the Confederacy to a true policy in dealing with East Tennessee. On November 29, he had a conference with President Davis and Secretary Benjamin in which he advocated a lenient policy toward East Tennesseeans, and incidentally requested, if it were not against public policy, that a passport be given to Brownlow. Baxter had not been asked by Brownlow to act, and in fact the Parson did not know that the request had been made. Mrs. Brownlow and friends of the Parson, who felt that they knew what was best for him in his situation more truly than he did himself, begged Baxter to get the passport.[15] Evidently Benjamin and Carroll had had little correspondence with each other concerning Brownlow. On November 26, Carroll informed the War Secretary that he had seized the Parson's printing establishment and converted it into a shop for altering arms and that he had promised his son indemnity from the government. He was sure that Brownlow himself was out aiding and abetting the enemies of the Confederacy. Two days later Carroll informed Benjamin that Brownlow had promised to surrender if he were guaranteed against personal violence,[16]

---

[14] *Official Records,* ser. I, vol. VII, p. 806.

[15] *Ibid.,* pp. 799-800, Baxter to Benjamin, December 28, 1861; ser. II, vol 1, p. 904, Baxter to Benjamin, November 30, 1861.

[16] *Ibid.,* ser. II, vol. I, p. 903. The reference is to the Brownlow letter of November 22.

and he enclosed a copy of Brownlow's November 22 letter.

About December 1, Carroll was superseded at Knoxville by Crittenden, but before leaving he informed his successor of the negotiations with Brownlow. As soon as Crittenden took charge he was besought by one of Brownlow's sons and some friends to let the Parson return to Knoxville. On their guarantee of the Parson's innocence of any crime against the Confederacy and on their agreement that he must submit to civil authorities, preparations were made for the Parson's return. Then on the fourth of December John Baxter who had just returned from Richmond, in company with another of Brownlow's sons, called upon Crittenden and presented to him the letter Benjamin had written him on November 20 concerning letting Brownlow out of the Confederacy. Now for the first time did Crittenden learn that Baxter had been negotiating with Benjamin and had induced him to adopt the attitude assumed in the letter. As further proof of Baxter's influence, he had secured the letter to Crittenden to be delivered in person, or perhaps, not at all, as he might find expedient.[17]

Immediately (December 4) Crittenden directed A. S. Cunningham, his assistant Adjutant-General, to inform Brownlow that if he would call at the army headquarters in Knoxville within twenty-four hours he could get a passport to go into Kentucky.[18] The Parson came in within the specified time and accompanied by Baxter he agreed to Crittenden's stipulations about departing, with the exception of the time. The General wanted him to leave the next day, but the Parson wanted to remain a day, and on that day, December 6, he was arrested by the Confederate marshal on a warrant charging high treason against the Confederacy. Thus had the civil authorities interfered.

J. C. Ramsey, the Confederate States District Attorney, whom Brownlow denominated a "*corrupt scoundrel* and unprincipled knave," had made application for the warrant to Robert B. Reynolds, the Confederate Commissioner, whom

---

[17] *Ibid.*, ser. I, vol. VII, p. 763, Crittenden to Benjamin, December 13, 1861.
[18] *Ibid.*, p. 806.

Brownlow declared to be "a third-rate county-court lawyer, a drunken and corrupt *sot*, who had been kicked out of a grocery a few days before by a mechanic, and who was afterwards taken up from the pavements of the street, in a beastly state of intoxication, by Rebel troops, and lodged in the guard-house!" Commissioner Reynolds issued the warrant which stated in part that Brownlow, a citizen of the Confederate States,

being moved and seduced by the instigation of the devil, and not having the fear of God before his eyes, did wilfully, knowingly, and with malice aforethought, and feloniously, commit the crime of TREASON against the Confederate States, by then and there, within said district and *since the 10th day of June last*, publishing a weekly and tri-weekly paper known as "Brownlow's Knoxville Whig," said paper had a large circulation in said district and also circulated in the United States, and contained, weekly, divers of editorials written by the said Brownlow, which said editorials were treasonable against the Confederate States of America, and did then and there commit treason, and prompt others to commit treason, . . . and did give aid and comfort to the United States, both of said Governments being in a state of war with each other.[19]

This was the answer of many of the Confederates in Knoxville and East Tennessee to the person who had so bitterly denounced them and who had made himself guilty of treason. The Parson had apparently convinced them that he had not been mixed up in the bridge-burning, but he could not erase the editorials in his *Whig*, some of which it was charged constituted treason. The civil authorities had acted quickly in seizing Brownlow and they immediately prepared to defend their actions before Secretary of War Benjamin and President Davis, fearing that they would be ordered to release him. On the day of Brownlow's arrest, Ramsey informed Benjamin of his action and asked the Secretary to postpone his decision until he should receive the facts.[20] The next day, December 7, he wrote Benjamin at length telling of Brownlow's devilment in East Tennessee and expressing the belief that he knew the bridges were

---

[19] *Ibid.*, pp. 806-7; *Parson Brownlow's Book*, pp. 295-96.
[20] *Official Records*, ser. II, vol. I, p. 905.

to be burned. Certainly it would be in the interest of justice for all concerned to hold a trial to find out. "His newspaper," he declared, "has been the greatest cause of rebellion in this section, and most of those who have been arrested have been deluded by his gross distortion of facts and incited to take up arms by his inflammatory appeals to their passions and infamous libels upon the Confederate States." The soldiers guarding the passes into Kentucky were disgusted at the way in which Brownlow was about to be escorted out of the state by a military guard, while his dupes were being arrested and thrown into prison. They felt that it would be a degrading service to escort him to the Kentucky line, where he could stir up more trouble for the Confederacy than Johnson and Maynard combined. Before he slipped out of Knoxville in early November it was reported that he had been "confined at home by a bleeding of the lungs." It should therefore be to his advantage to be sent south to Tuscaloosa where the climate would help his lungs, instead of being allowed to go off into the bleak Northern winters. If he had been anxious to go north, they insisted he could have done so when President Davis issued his proclamation in the early fall calling upon all who were dissatisfied with the Confederacy to leave and they would be unmolested.[21]

Others added their protests against allowing Brownlow to go. W. G. Swan, the recently elected Confederate Congressman from the Second District, wrote President Davis that he was surprised at Benjamin's dealings with Brownlow and that he found "the citizens and soldiers almost unanimously indignant."[22] J. G. M. Ramsey and W. H. Tibbs, the latter the Confederate Congressman from the Third District, signed a joint protest against letting Brownlow go while his deluded followers were being severely dealt with. They were especially surprised that he was to be allowed to go to Kentucky where he could direct the invasion of East Tennessee and cause much other mischief to the Confederacy. They pleaded, "Let the civil or military law take its course against the criminal leader

---

[21] *Ibid.*, ser. I, vol. VII, pp. 744-45.
[22] *Ibid.*, p. 742.

in this atrocious rebellion, as it has already done to his ignorant and deluded followers."[23]

The Knoxville *Register* reiterated these sentiments. Brownlow was the ringleader in the troubles in East Tennessee; he should be imprisoned at Tuscaloosa until the war was over and then sent to "Abe Lincoln and abide with him forever." "East Tennessee," it declared, "has been a heavy expense to the State and to the Confederate Government, in consequence of the teaching and leading of Brownlow and others; and now to let him go in peace seems to be the height of folly or we cannot

This scene represents the Parson entering the Knoxville jail. "I have found many old acquaintances here and long-tried friends; whilst some were glad to see me in no worse condition, and in expectation of hearing the current news of the day, as well as from their families, others shed tears upon taking me by the hand, grasping it in silence." From Brownlow's *Sketches of the Rise, Progress, and Decline of Secession.*

see right. It will cool the ardor of many a soldier and cause the community to lose confidence in the hope that they entertained of the speedy independence of the South."[24]

Brownlow immediately upon his arrest notified General Crit-

[23] *Ibid.*, pp. 743-44.
[24] December 13, 1861. Quoted in *Official Records,* ser. II, vol. I, pp. 924-25.

tenden of his predicament and reminded him that he had come
in at the General's invitation and promise of a passport.[25]
Crittenden answered on the same day, through his Aide-de-
Camp Harry I. Thornton, that "he does not consider that you
are here upon his invitation in such a manner as to claim his
protection from an investigation by the civil authorities of
the charges against you, which he clearly understood from
yourself and your friends you would not seek to avoid."[26]
Brownlow demanded an immediate trial and bail, both of which
were refused, though according to him, "my friends voluntarily offered a bond of ONE HUNDRED THOUSAND
DOLLARS." He had changed his mind since the October day
on which he had written in his "last editorial" that he would
rot in prison before he would accept bail.

In the meantime the Parson was lodged in the Knoxville jail
while the Confederacy tried to solve the knotty problem of
what to do with him. The jail was crowded with about 150
Unionists, many of them well-known to him, and upon his entry
they fell upon him grasping his hand and shedding tears in
silence. He had a speech ready for them, and as soon as the
greetings were over, he cheered them with the prediction that
the Federal Government would "crush out this wicked rebellion
and liberate us, if we are not brutally murdered," and he would
let them know that whatever they might think about their own
predicament "I regard this as the proudest day of my life."[27]
He also on the first day began keeping a diary which he continued to the end.[28]

He found the jail a most unattractive place, so crowded that
some of the prisoners were forced to stand to permit others space
on the floor where they might sleep. The jail was void of all
furniture, not even a chair, unless a "dirty wooden bucket and
a tin cup" could be considered furniture. The Parson claimed
that the Rebel soldiers were accustomed to washing their hands

[25] *Ibid.*, ser. I, vol. VII, p. 807.
[26] *Ibid.*
[27] *Parson Brownlow's Book*, p. 309.
[28] The original diary is now in the possession of the Brownlow family in Knoxville.

and faces in the water supply, and when he complained, one of them replied, "By G—d, sir, we will have you know that where a Jeff Davis man washes his face and hands is good enough for any d—d Lincolnite to drink." The guards, he declared, were a set of drunkards who sang "blackguard songs" for the benefit of the prisoners, and at times these white prisoners were insulted by insolent Negroes whom the Confederates set over them as guards. When complaints were made, the answer came that any sort of treatment was "too good for a set of d—d Union-shriekers and bridge-burners." He found the food very bad, so bad that it was "not fit for a good and trusty dog to devour." It was the Parson's misfortune to discover that the jailer was a person whom he had once published as a forger, and it seemed certain to the Parson's mind that this erstwhile forger would now take his spite out by putting arsenic in his food. Brownlow, therefore, had his meals brought into the jail three times a day, and in sufficient amounts to take care of the wants of two Baptist preachers—to such humility or heroism had the distempers of the times reduced the Parson that he was found providing food for and eating with Baptist preachers!

Each day in the jail there were scenes of terror, heroism, and touching fortitude, as old and young were pushed in or sent out on their way to the prison at Tuscaloosa — or, indeed, dragged before the court-martial to be tried for bridge-burning and if found guilty later to be executed. On one day, in came "a Union man from Campbell county . . . leaving behind six small children, and their mother dead," and his only offence was holding out for the Union; on another, out went fifteen prisoners to Tuscaloosa there "to be treated like dogs." Then, "old man Wamplar," a Dutchman, seventy years of age, was brought in from Greene County, "charged with being an *Andy Johnson man.*" Some were rounded up for praying for the President of the United States, others for cheering the Stars and Stripes.

As nothing appeared too dastardly for the Confederates to do, the Parson began to develop a hallucination that he would be hanged. He determined to meet the occasion like a man, by being ready with a speech which he intended to demand the right

Another of the Parson's "Rebel atrocities." Madison Cate, a captured Union Guard, is being visited by his wife, in the Knoxville jail. The Parson, though appearing in the doorway in this illustration, according to his statement, held the baby during the interview. "I hope I may never look upon such a scene again. Oh, what oppression! And yet this is the *spirit* of Secession." From Brownlow's *Sketches of the Rise, Progress, and Decline of Secession.*

to speak from the gallows. He believed they would have granted his request "from an intense curiosity to hear what I had to say in such a trying moment; and I believe I could have stood forth and said it in the face of ten thousand people." He began composing his speech at intervals, "compelled day by day to contemplate the near prospect of a brutal death upon the gallows." Conscious of the fact that this would be the last chance he would ever have to denounce his enemies, he added a venom even beyond his custom; for, as he later said, "if I have any talent in the world, it is that talent which consists in piling up one epithet upon another."

With his vivid imagination and his inborn prejudices and hatreds, he set his speech to circumstances most derogatory to the Confederacy. He supposed in the beginning that he had been tried and convicted by a court-martial sitting in Knoxville —"I say I *suppose* so, for I have never had any trial, or even a notice of a trial being in progress." Selecting the bridge-burners' court-martial for his withering denunciation, he declared Thomas J. Campbell, the judge-advocate, to be "a perfidious man, as destitute of real honor and purity of purpose as he is of true courage and manly virtue"; from among the remaining members of the court he picked James D. Thomas for this excoriation: "a man who was expelled from the Methodist ministry for whipping his wife and slandering his venerable old father-in-law." Colonel W. B. Wood was an "arch-hypocrite and would-be murderer," William G. McAdoo was guilty of "treachery and insincerity," while Campbell Wallace was the "prince of hypocrites and great embodiment of human deceit." Now the Parson would take a last fling at the traitors high in the Confederate Government. William L. Yancey was "a convicted murderer, who killed his uncle" and was pardoned by the governor of South Carolina; L. T. Wigfall to escape assassination had fled from South Carolina to Texas where he became a swindler and murdered "as many as two men"; John Floyd stole $30,000 from the Washington Monument Fund and filled Southern forts with Federal guns; John Slidell was an "intriguer, who never had an honest emotion of soul in his life";

Judah P. Benjamin "was expelled from a New England college for stealing money and jewelry out of the trunks of his fellow-students"; Jacob Thompson was a thief, who fled from Washington "by night to avoid persecution"; Howell Cobb was a speculator in stocks, "using Government money"; Jefferson Davis "led the way in the work of repudiation and in defrauding Mississippi's honest creditors"; Robert Toombs aided Lawrence M. Keitt and Preston Brooks "in their attempt to assassinate Sumner"; W. G. Swan, a Confederate Congressman, was a forger and a swindler. With such words on his lips did the Parson choose to plunge into eternity, and so heroic did he feel in thus talking before his imaginary ten thousand that he made provision to continue his onset from the grave: He would leave behind some "hostile reminiscences" in documents which he requested his "sons to publish . . . even at the cost of their lives."

"But I must close. Solemn thought! I die, with confidence that the United States Government will crush out this rebellion during the coming spring and summer." He hoped the Union men would take care of his family and teach them that their father died an honorable death. And then the Parson chose his last words: "Let me be shrouded in the sacred folds of the Star-Spangled Banner; and let my children's children know that the last words I uttered on earth were—

> Forever float that standard sheet
>> Where breathes the foe but falls before us,
> With Freedom's soil beneath our feet,
>> And Freedom's banner streaming o'er us !"[29]

The Parson was a great actor; and he knew his East Tennessee audience.

Again was the Parson doomed to disappointment, for the Confederate authorities refused to hang him or even to try him —rather they would keep him in prison. The broadcasting of all of his righteous indignation and the suffering of sweet mar-

---

[29] Most of his prison diary, including his last speech, is published in *Parson Brownlow's Book,* pp. 308-70. For additional information on his prison days, see *Portrait and Biography,* pp. 32-59.

tyrdom were denied him except in his imagination and his diary. Another proof could he thus add to the perversity of the Confederates. But, as he later said under the influence of a patriotic speech, "I told them if they would give me the privilege of making a speech, one hour long, under the gallows, that I might speak to the people and pronounce a eulogy on the Southern Confederacy, that I would be willing to die. And I really think I could have swung in peace."[30]

The Parson had been troubled with a throat and lung affliction before he had slipped out of Knoxville in November; his experiences in the gorges and defiles of the Great Smokies had not increased his strength, and now to be thrown into a crowded jail made too great a hardship to be borne. Soon the *Nashville Patriot* was saying "We learn that W. G. Brownlow, imprisoned at Knoxville, refuses to eat any thing, *desiring to starve himself to death.*"[31] The Parson wrote from the jail a hot denial of this hunger strike, and charged the Confederates with bad faith in keeping him in prison. But he was really ill, and on December 19 the prison doctors offered to remove him to the hospital, but he declined, as he "did not want passports to where I would likely be poisoned in twenty-four hours." Yet he found life almost unendurable in the Knoxville jail. The sentinels were often like howling wolves, "rushing to our windows with the ferocity of the Sepoys of India, and daring prisoners to show their heads—cocking their guns and firing off three of them into the jail, and pretending that it was accidental. Merciful God! how long are we to be treated after this fashion?" On Christmas day the Union women of the community sent him a basket of good things, which he generously divided with the other prisoners. The next day he completely lost his appetite and came to the conclusion that he was getting the fever.[32] Various rumors were flying over the country concerning the Parson. Jere T. Boyle, up in Kentucky, heard at one time that he was on his way northward with 1,500 or 2,500 troops, and at an-

---

[30] *Portrait and Biography,* p. 47.

[31] December 17, 1861, quoted in *Parson Brownlow's Book,* pp. 321-22.

[32] *Parson Brownlow's Book,* pp. 320-26.

other, that he was in the Knoxville jail, certain to be hung.[33]

During these twenty days while the Parson had been in prison, his case was not being neglected by the Confederate Government, nor was he tamely submitting. His imprisonment constituted one of the most disquieting and troublesome problems of the Confederacy, taking up the time of officials and officers from the President in Richmond to the District Attorney in Knoxville. There can be no doubt that Secretary Benjamin and General Crittenden were taken by surprise when civil authorities arrested Brownlow. The confusion between the military and civil authorities was sufficient to give the Parson an excellent opportunity to play up the charge of bad faith on the part of the Confederacy. He made the most of it. In the first place he declared that the warrant was preposterous, for "Every man of legal knowledge will see that the publication of a newspaper, however objectionable its matter may be, does not amount to treason."[34] Then, the Confederacy had grossly tricked him. It had invited him in, under the promise of a safe conduct to the Union lines, and thereupon had arrested him and thrown him into jail without bail. "I am not willing to believe," he declared, "that the representatives of a would-be great Government struggling for its independence, and having in charge the interests of twelve millions of people, intend to act in bad faith to me." On December 16, he wrote Secretary Benjamin reminding him that he had authorized General Crittenden to give him a passport and that the General had invited him in for that purpose; but "a third rate County Court Lawyer, acting as your Confederate Attorney, took me out of his hands and cast me into this prison. I am anxious to learn which is your highest authority, the Secretary of War, a Major General, or a dirty little drunken Attorney such as *J. C. Ramsey* is!" In concluding the Parson said, "You are reported to have said to a gentleman in Richmond, that, I am a bad man, dangerous to the Confederacy, and that you desire me out of it. Just give me my passports, and I will do for your

---

[33] *Official Records,* ser. I, vol. VII, p. 508.
[34] *Parson Brownlow's Book,* p. 303.

Knoxville Jail, Dec. 16. 1861.

Hon J. P. Benjamin:

You authorized Gen. Crittenden to give me passports, and an escort to send me into the old Government, and he invited me here for that purpose. But a third rate County Court Lawyer, acting as your Confederate Attorney, took me out of his hands and cast me into this prison. I am anxious to learn which is your highest authority, the Secretary of War, a Major General, or a dirty little drunken Attorney, such as J. C. Ramsey is!

You are reported to have said to a gentleman in Richmond, that, I am a bad man, dangerous to the Confederacy, and that you desire me out of it. Just give me my passports, and I will do for your Confederacy, more than the Devil has ever done; I will quit the country!

I am, &c,

W. G. Brownlow—

A specimen of the Parson's handwriting and language. Reproduced from a copy of a letter which appeared in his *Sketches of the Rise, Progress, and Decline of Secession.*

Confederacy, more than the Devil has ever done, I will quit the country!"[35]

Securing no results from his onset against the Secretary of War, Brownlow decided to climb a step higher and address his cause to the President of the Confederacy. After reciting voluminously the history of his case, he declared the Confederacy was guilty of "a gross breach of faith."[36]

Not waiting to be pushed into some course by Brownlow, the Confederacy continued its efforts to clear up the Parson's case from the day of his arrest. On December 8, President Davis called General Crittenden to Richmond for a military conference, but it is not too much to infer that Brownlow was discussed.[37] A few days later Secretary Benjamin called upon District Attorney Ramsey for the facts concerning Brownlow's arrest. Ramsey replied that he believed Brownlow had information of the plot to burn the bridges and he knew that the Parson had been the first to suggest the possibility of destroying the bridges. Public sentiment approved the arrest and Ramsey believed Brownlow should be imprisoned in Tuscaloosa but he would "cheerfully dispose of the case according to your own better judgment."[38]

The situation resolved itself into a mild contest between Secretary Benjamin and General Crittenden representing the military power on the one side and District Attorney Ramsey representing the civil authority on the other. Crittenden and Benjamin had been placed in a position sufficiently suggestive of bad faith as to cause both to want to get out of it by ridding the Confederacy of Brownlow. Crittenden wrote Benjamin on December 13 that there was no bad faith on his part, for the understanding was that Brownlow would submit to civil trial, but "if the civil authorities release Mr. Brownlow, I shall proceed at once to give him a passport and send him with an escort beyond our lines."[39]

---

[35] *Official Records*, ser. II, vol. I, p. 910; *Parson Brownlow's Book*, p. 318. See facsimile of this letter on p. 198.

[36] *Official Records*, ser. II, vol. I, p. 919-21. This letter was undated, but it was marked "Received January 2, 1862."

[37] *Ibid.*, ser. I, vol. VII, p. 745.

[38] *Ibid.*, ser. II, vol. I, pp. 908-10, December 10 and 17.   [39] *Ibid.*, pp. 908-9.

Benjamin threshed out the case with Ramsey and came to the conclusion that the Parson ought to be let loose. He admitted that the courts had the right to take the prisoner from the military authorities but the thought never occurred to him that it would be done. But since it had happened, he had only one regret—"that color is given to the suspicion that Brownlow has been entrapped and has given himself up under promise of protection which has not been formally kept." Both Benjamin and Crittenden felt sensitive on the point. "Better that even the most dangerous enemy however criminal should escape than that the honor and good faith of the Government should be impunged or even suspected." Crittenden had promised Brownlow protection against a court-martial; Benjamin had promised a passport. Both had carried out their promises, which in the latter case had not resulted in Brownlow's full expectation, though due to no fault of Benjamin's. The Secretary ended his communication to Ramsey with this rather pointed remark: "Under all the circumstances therefore if Brownlow is exposed to harm from his arrest I shall deem the honor of the Government so far compromised as to consider it my duty to urge on the President a pardon for any offense of which he may be found guilty and I repeat the expression of my regret that he was prosecuted however evident may be his guilt."[40]

The hint was sufficient. On December 27, Ramsey called up Brownlow's case in court, had Benjamin's letter read, and thereupon entered a *nolle prosequi*.[41] Brownlow was now a free man again. He had undoubtedly been indicted by Ramsey on account of the extreme personal enmity between the two, but in carrying out a private grudge Ramsey had given the Confederate Government a great deal of trouble. But even with Brownlow in jail, the Confederacy could not rightly be charged with bad faith. When the promise of a passport for the Parson was being extracted from Benjamin and Crittenden, Brownlow had no desire nor intention of leaving East Tennessee and he had no knowledge that the passport was being requested. His

---

[40] *Ibid.*, pp. 916-17, Benjamin to Ramsey, December 22, 1861.
[41] *Ibid.*, p. 917.

negotiations with General Carroll concerning his return to Knoxville clearly established the understanding equally well with
both, that a civil trial was to be expected, welcomed, and almost
demanded. Then when on December 4 the Parson wrote Carroll refusing to come in, because he felt he would not be given
protection against the *military* authorities, the agreement concerning a *civil* trial was not invalidated. For since this letter
was never delivered, it was doubly well understood that the Parson still expected a civil trial. This understanding was trans-
mitted to Crittenden, who succeeded Carroll; and had the Parson not been suddenly confronted with the possibility of being
escorted out of the Confederacy, he would have come in to stand
a civil trial, and no chance would have been presented to him to
declare the Confederacy guilty of bad faith. It was no part
of the Parson's original plan to leave East Tennessee; the passport was entirely the idea of his friends; and now he used
the mix-up for all it was worth in trying to discredit the Confederacy. In his letter to President Davis in the latter part of
December he said, "Until very recently he had intended to continue a citizen of the Confederate States but the events of the
last three weeks have convinced him that laws can afford no
protection to himself or family."[42]

Unappreciative of Secretary Benjamin's scrupulous regard
for avoiding even the appearance of bad faith, Brownlow, when
he got beyond the power of the Confederacy, stated that he had
been having some dealings with "a little Jew, late of New Orleans" but that he had expected "no more mercy from him than
was shown by his illustrious predecessors toward Jesus Christ."[43]

Although Secretary Benjamin and the War Department
were glad to have the Parson off their hands and conscience,
the local Confederates in East Tennessee still saw Brownlow as
the most dangerous and cunning man with whom they would
be forced to deal. He was a "diplomat of the first water," who
never undertook a task "unless he sees his way entirely through
the millstone." He covered "over his really profound knowledge

---

[42] This letter was written in the third person.
[43] *Portrait and Biography*, pp. 19-21.

of human nature with an appearance of eccentricity and extravagance." The Knoxville *Register* continued its characterization: "Crafty, cunning, generous to his particular friends, benevolent and charitable to their faults, ungrateful and implacable to his enemies—we cannot refrain from saying that he is the best judge of human nature within the bounds of the Southern Confederacy." By "a species of diplomacy and legerdemain" he had convinced Benjamin that he was "quite a harmless individual." In fact he had outwitted the Secretary. The *Register* had not decided whether it should laugh or get mad "with the manner in which Brownlow has wound the Confederate Government around his thumb," but it did not doubt for a moment that he was "laughing like the king's fool in his sleeves." Brownlow should not be underestimated: "In brief Brownlow has preached at every church and schoolhouse and made stump-speeches at every cross-road and knows every man, woman and child and their fathers and grandfathers before them in East Tennessee. As a Methodist circuit-rider, a political stump-speaker, a temperance orator and the editor of a newspaper he has been equally successful in our division of the State." When he should once reach Kentucky, from "among his old partisan and religious sectarian parasites he will find men who will obey him with the fanatical alacrity of those who followed Peter the Hermit in the first crusade."[44]

Brownlow's case had been attracting attention throughout the Confederacy, and there were few people who were willing to treat him as leniently as Benjamin had done. In Columbus, Georgia, the *Times* concluded, "Now, this hoary-headed and persistent traitor is occupying too much of the time and attention of the country. HE DESERVES DEATH, AND WE VOTE TO KILL HIM."[45]

Brownlow was too sick to appear in court when his case was dismissed; and although he was now technically free, the military authorities took charge of him to await the day when he should be properly escorted out of the Confederacy. Soon the

[44] Quoted in *Official Records,* ser. II, vol. I, pp. 925-26.
[45] Quoted in *Parson Brownlow's Book,* pp. 347-48.

Parson had become "*salivated* from an excess of mercury," and
the doctor declared that unless he should be removed from the
jail there would be little hope for his recovery. Thereupon the
Parson was taken to his home where he might have the comforts
of a feather-bed and the attention of his family. Here Captain
G. H. Monsarrat, commander of the post, kept him under strict
surveillance, both in the interest of the Parson's safety and for
safeguarding the public peace.[46]

The Parson was still a white elephant on the hands of the
Confederacy. He was evidently sick, but there was some suspicion as to how sick he was, and there was a wholesome fear
that he might plot with Unionists and might possibly make
his escape. An East Tennesseean begged Benjamin to get rid
of the Parson and his family "and everybody else that desires
to leave," for if this were done "it would be worth 10,000 men
to the Southern cause."[47] During the month of January Brownlow continued very sick, yet Colonel Danville Leadbetter, whom
Brownlow denominated the "prince of villains, tyrants, and
murderers," placed heavy guards over him and denied him
the right to see various callers whom the Colonel doubtless considered potential plotters. As Colonel Leadbetter had neither
love nor respect for the Parson, he got little pleasure out of
guarding him. Near the end of January with an air of impatience he inquired of Brownlow when he would be ready to
leave. The Parson replied that he was as anxious to go as some
people were for him to leave, but that he was still unable to
travel. Fearing that the Parson might be simulating sickness,
Leadbetter ordered his transfer to the hospital where he could
not plot treason with the Union leaders. Brownlow protested
with great vehemence that it was one of "their hellish schemes
to get me out where they could poison me or have me assassinated." Leadbetter let the Parson have his way, but he doubled
the guard and made life uncomfortable for him in many other
ways, with the hope of driving him either to the hospital or outside
of the Confederacy. By the middle of February Brownlow had

[46] *Official Records*, ser. II, vol. I, p. 919; *Parson Brownlow's Book*, pp. 337-38.
[47] *Official Records,* ser. II, vol. I, pp. 923-24, J. J. Craig to Benjamin, January
3, 1862.

had enough; he was now, feeble as he was, ready and anxious to leave the Confederacy or go back to jail—anything to "secure the repose of an afflicted, insulted, and outraged family." As for Leadbetter, when the Federals should capture East Tennessee, the Parson expected to see him hanged if hands could be laid upon him. To Leadbetter's successor, Robert B. Vance, whom the Parson esteemed, he poured out his heart's woe: His guards had turned his office and library into a barracks, where they had broken up his rocking-chairs, ruined his carpet, and damaged his books; they had used up his coal and wood, burned his candles, and consumed three meals a day, which he had set before them; they had introduced mumps and measles into his family with the result that only his wife, his son John, and two Negroes were well; sentinels stood day and night at his windows and doors, and on being changed every two hours they made a great and unnecessary noise. All of these persecutions and abuses the Parson had put up with without complaint, but one night the guard tried to keep the Parson's door open against the protests of his wife, who forcibly closed it and locked it in the face of the guard. Now, this last bit of treatment was too much. He had never appealed to Leadbetter, "for he never had a gentlemanly emotion of soul in his life"; but he would now appeal to Colonel Vance for better protection.[48]

The Parson had no complaints to make under Colonel Vance's régime, and his health seemed to mend so fast that on February 24 he sent for Captain G. H. Monserrat, who had recently succeeded Colonel Vance, to make arrangements for leaving the Confederacy. In early January, A. T. Bledsoe, Chief of the Bureau of War at Richmond, had instructed Monserrat to have Brownlow sent out with a proper escort; now in February the plan was to have Brownlow directed through Richmond. Brownlow fearing trickery charged bad faith again. On the 27th he addressed Secretary Benjamin a note in which he declared that personal safety forbade his going by way of Richmond. He wanted to leave through the Cumberlands or to go to Nashville.[49]

[48] *Ibid.*, pp. 926-28; *Parson Brownlow's Book*, pp. 353-61.
[49] *Official Records*, ser. II, vol. I, pp. 923-28; *Parson Brownlow's Book*, pp. 367-68.

Arrangements were hurriedly made to forward him to the Federal lines. Especial precautions were taken to ensure his safety, for Blanton Duncan, an old acquaintance of the Parson's had emphasized in a letter to Benjamin what he doubtless already knew, that Brownlow was bitterly hated. Duncan said, "He is hated and pursued with a virulence beyond belief, and if proper steps are not taken there is great danger that he will be assassinated during his journey and the Government thereby disgraced. I heard threats against him everywhere on the road."[50] On March 1, Benjamin instructed Monserrat to send Brownlow out by the passes in the Cumberland Mountains or any safe road. The Parson chose to go to Nashville, and his wishes were complied with. The Confederate authorities took the utmost precaution with him; they even permitted him to select the two officers who were to command the squad of ten soldiers who should make up his escort.

Early on the morning of March 3, Brownlow with the two officers left Knoxville for Loudon where the squad of soldiers were to join the party. The captain of the squad cautioned his men to protect the Parson at all hazards, after which they set out for Athens. Here they found it necessary to ward off a rush of soldiers from a troop-train. They spent the night in Bridgeport and reached Wartrace the next day. At this place trouble developed over a flag of truce, and for a time it appeared that the Parson might be returned to East Tennessee or released on the spot. After three days, arrangements were made and the party went on to Shelbyville where for a week they were halted by the refusal of General Hardee to permit the Parson to pass to the Federal lines. While in Shelbyville, the Union element lionized the Parson and one of the ladies sent him a bouquet which he acknowledged with high sentiments for the Union and damnation for the Confederacy. At twelve o'clock noon on March 15, he landed in the Union lines.[51]

A wave of relief might well have swept over the Confederacy as the Parson crossed no-man's land into the Federal army,

---

[50] *Official Records*, ser. I, vol. LII, pt. 2, 254 January 8, 1862.

[51] *Official Records*, ser. I, vol. VII, pp. 913, 917; vol. X, pt. 2, p. 39; ser. II, vol. I, pp. 928-29; *Parson Brownlow's Book*, pp. 369-79.

but the Brownlow problem was not entirely solved until East
Tennessee could be pacified. On January 28, while Brownlow
was still in jail, Secretary Benjamin had ordered the release
of all political prisoners who would take the oath to support
the Confederacy, an invitation to which Brownlow replied, "Before I would take an oath to support such a hell-forsaken institution, I would suffer myself to rot or die of old age"[52] East
Tennessee was far from pacified even with all the offers of forgiveness, for on March 1, in the local elections that were held,
the Union candidates largely prevailed. On April 18, General
E. Kirby Smith, who was now in command in East Tennessee,
offered amnesty and fair treatment to all who would come forward and take the oath to support the Confederacy. About this
time he suspended all draft laws in East Tennessee as an inducement to bring back the refugees in Kentucky. He promised that
they should not be molested if they would return and settle
down on their farms and take care of their families. The destitute families of fugitive Unionists were a great drain on the
resources of the Confederacy. These fugitives had thirty days
in which to return, at the end of which time, if they had not
returned, their wives and children would be sent to them at their
own expense. "The women and children must be taken care of
by husbands and fathers either in East Tennessee or in the
Lincoln Government."[53]

This policy, which was designed to help relieve an economic
situation and to promote Confederate patriotism, would affect
the families not only of the ordinary fugitive but also of the
ringleaders like Brownlow, Johnson, and Maynard. It worked
with particular aptness in connection with the Brownlow family, for the Parson was spreading the report that his family was
being held in East Tennessee as hostages for his own conduct
in the North. A speedy answer was thus made to these un-
founded charges when on April 21 the Confederacy ordered
Mrs. W. G. Brownlow to prepare herself and family to pass
beyond the Confederate lines within thirty-six hours. She ob-

---

[52] *Portrait and Biography,* pp. 19-21; *Official Records,* ser. II, vol. I, p. 879.
[53] *Ibid.,* pp. 882-83, 886; *Parson Brownlow's Book,* p. 369.

jected and a few days of grace were allowed her, but on April 25 she and her family had made ready and on that day they left Knoxville, arriving in Norfolk on their way north, three days later. About the same time the Brownlow family had been ordered to leave, the Johnson, Maynard, and W. B. Carter families were given the customary thirty-six hours to make their preparations for removal, and by the end of the month all had taken their departure for the North.[54]

[54] *Official Records,* ser. II, vol. I, pp. 883-86, 929-31.

CHAPTER X

A TOUR OF THE NORTH[1]

IN TIMES of stress people must have heroes. Robert Anderson, of Fort Sumter fame, became the rallying cry to raise up soldiers for the first battle, but his reputation tarnished as the feeling developed that he had given up the fort too easily. Oliver Ellsworth marched his comical Zouaves up hills and down and made himself known to many people; and then when he took to serious war and sought to cut down the Confederate flag on the Marshall House in Alexandria, Virginia, he was himself shot down by the hotelkeeper and thereby was made for his country into another hero, though a dead one. Charles Wilkes humbled Great Britain when he stopped the *Trent* and took off Mason and Slidell, the Confederate agents, and awoke to find that his name led all the rest in a country that needed another hero and a live one. But soon the people were to see that Wilkes had done nothing more than what the British themselves had been doing for centuries, and there straightway developed a vacancy in heroes.

It was, therefore, an opportune time for Brownlow to make his appearance, and ride upon a reputation made in a fashion quite different from any one so far used. He was, indeed, not entirely unknown in the North, for he had gone to most of the Whig national conventions and he had carried on his memorable slavery debate with Parson Pryne in Philadelphia a few years before. But the North had never known the hero that was now in the making; heretofore, he had been an intense partisan of the Southern people and Southern slavery; now through a miraculous transformation he would devastate those people with as

[1] This chapter was published in substantially its present form in *The East Tennessee Historical Society's Publications,* VII (1935), 3-27. For permission to reprint it here, I wish to thank the Managing Editor of that journal.

terrible destruction as he had formerly dealt out to his worst enemies in the North. He was now to sweep across the Northern sky, and in every lineament and characteristic become familiar throughout the land.

This is what Northerners saw and admired: He was six feet tall, but somewhat short of the 175 pounds which he had at one time weighed; he was almost fifty-seven years old, "and, although rather *hard-favored* than otherwise," he would "pass for a man of forty years." He was high-strung and taut, vibrating with restless energy. Though no orator he spoke in a loud voice, and revelled in making speeches bristling with pointed darts of venom and vituperation. Three years previously he had suffered an attack of bronchitis which had left him for two years unable to speak above a whisper, though he had gone at various times to the best doctors in New York for treatment. Yet he had known the time when he "could be heard by an audience of any size"—when, indeed, he had "been able for four or five dreadful hours on a stretch to speak in the open air." This voice which had seemed to be so stubborn that it could not be coaxed back through temperance talks or even sermons was upon the Parson's new introduction to the North, to the Stars and Stripes, and to freedom, to reappear as he told of his wrongs and as he poured out hot hatred and vengeance upon the South. The farther he penetrated the North and the more terribly he condemned the traitors, the stronger his voice got, until it could be heard again for a half mile. This was the physical Parson.[2]

The mental and moral Parson followed these specifications: He had a pugnacious and decisive nature, which led him to take part in all the religious and political controversies of his time. As he told his awe-stricken readers and listeners, "For the last thirty-five years of my somewhat eventful life I have been accustomed to speak in public upon all the subjects afloat in the land, for I have never been neutral on any subject that ever came up in that time."[3] Though known "throughout the length and breadth of the land as the 'Fighting Parson,' " he maintained

---

[2] Temple, *op. cit.*, pp. 281-84; *Portrait and Biography*, p. 26; *Suffering of Union Men*, p. 9; *Parson Brownlow's Book*, p. 18.

[3] *Ibid.*; *Suffering of Union Men*, p. 8.

14

that there was no one more peaceably inclined toward his neighbors than himself. He further introduced himself as an extraordinary person. He had never been arraigned in his Church for immorality; he never played a card; he was never a profane swearer; he "never drank a dram of liquor, until within a few years,—when it was taken as a medicine"; he never smoked a cigar or chewed a quid of tobacco; he never attended a theatre; he never saw a horse-race except at the fairgrounds of his own county; and he never courted but one woman and her he married.[4]

At twelve o'clock noon, on March 15, 1862, the Parson with a flag of truce up alighted from his buggy in the Union lines, five miles out from Nashville, and once again breathed the pure air of the *United States*. On his trip he had been somewhat wrinkled and drawn in his countenance, but on seeing the Federal lines, he swelled up, his wrinkles disappeared and he shouted out, "Glory to God in the highest, and on earth peace, good will toward all men, except a few hell-born and hell-bound rebels in Knoxville."[5] He announced that he was "Parson Brownlow" and then began shaking the hands of the soldiers who crowded around him. Soon officers made their appearance, and the Parson was conducted to General Buell, who greeted him with great cordiality and sent him to the St. Cloud Hotel. The General did not neglect to find out all the Parson knew about the Confederate armies and fortifications through which he had recently passed. On reaching the hotel the Parson's identity was discovered by a group of soldiers who crowded in upon him to gaze at this fighter from East Tennessee and to listen to the conversation which he had struck up with some acquaintances in the lobby. Horace Maynard, Emerson Etheridge, and other expatriated East Tennesseeans soon learned that the Parson was in town and hurrying to the lobby they enacted amidst gaping straggling soldiers scenes of tears and pathos.

Brownlow was undoubtedly one of the greatest attractions that had come to Nashville since the arrival of the Federal army. And here fate was to play some of its strangest pranks. Andrew

---

[4] *Parson Brownlow's Book*, p. 19.   [5] Temple, *op. cit.*, p. 315.

Johnson and Parson Brownlow may not have travelled a great distance geographically to meet in Nashville but they had travelled an infinite distance mentally. They both arrived about the same time, the one Brigadier-General Andrew Johnson, Military Governor of Tennessee, the other plain William G. Brownlow, the Fighting Parson of the Southern Highlands. It seemed the Parson was about to become a greater attraction than the Governor; the two certainly must meet. Brownlow had fought Johnson "systematically, perseveringly and untiringly, for the last twenty-five years. . . . He has scored me on every stump in the state of Tennessee, and I have paid him back to the best of my ability." And then the two former enemies met, "rushed into each other's arms, and wept like children." They sank the hatchet in a briny effusion and parted fast friends. Though not ecstatic in his praise of the new Governor, Brownlow felt sure that the choice would please Union men generally. It pleased the Parson particularly to know that Johnson felt "all the malice and venom requisite for the times."[6]

Brownlow remained in Nashville a week during which time he continued to be a great attraction. There was much Union speechmaking going on in this center of sullen secessionists. The Parson heard Etheridge speak to 1,200 people for two hours; he would soon hear Maynard speak for two and a half hours; he would certainly make a speech himself, for the crowds around the St. Cloud Hotel would demand it. His time soon came. He spoke out in the biting March wind in front of the hotel, but he had not been away from the "bogus Confederacy" sufficiently long to regain his voice completely. He spoke only a few minutes but he had strength enough to tell the crowd that he had been thrown into jail in Knoxville, that he had served his time, and that on seeing the Federal troops he "felt like a new man." Declaring that the Confederacy was tottering, he ended his speech with the cry, "Grape for the Rebel masses, and hemp for their leaders!" Henry Villard heard him and thought that he "was a very entertaining talker, and spoke more movingly, with

---

[6] *Portrait and Biography*, pp. 28, 55; Temple, *op. cit.*, p. 316; *Independent*, May 22, 1862; *Putnam's Magazine*, III, no. 16 (April, 1869), p. 434.

flashing eyes and pointing finger, of the wrongs to himself and his fellow-Tennesseeans."[7]

The Parson found the ladies in Nashville more rebellious and bitterly unyielding than any other class of citizens, but they were not all so, for a Union lady presented him with a bouquet. There were also other Union ladies in and about Nashville, for he attended a tea given by some of them, and with others he planted himself on Spruce Street to help them wave handkerchiefs as the Union army marched by. And this little patriotic party did not stand unnoticed by the troops. Each regiment halted, played a patriotic air, and cheered for "Parson Brownlow and the ladies."[8]

When Brownlow reached Nashville he could not forget that here had been the capital of Southern Methodism, and that the Baptists had made it one of their strongholds. He could not help but think that the worst class of men in the South were preachers, and as for Summers, McFerrin, and McTyeir he learned that they had fled, leaving their Book Concern vacant. But God be praised for good old Bishop Soule, now eighty years old! A Federal chaplain who had recently visited him at his home near Nashville, had found him reading—the Constitution of the United States. But the "notorious J. R. Graves, the Baptist editor," had fled ingloriously before the oncoming Federal troops.[9]

The Parson had left Knoxville with few if any plans for the future except to speed the day when the Federal troops would rescue his East Tennessee. There quickly passed through the minds of certain people great possibilities. The country was in bad need of a hero who would make Northerners hate their erstwhile Southern brothers so intensely that they would be willing to shoulder arms and slay them if they could. It was soon evident that the Parson had no equal in beating the war tom-toms and firing the minds of the people. This was so both because of the story he had to tell and because of his manner

---

[7] *Memoirs of Henry Villard, Journalist and Financier, 1835-1900*, I, 234; *Portrait and Biography*, pp. 17-18.

[8] *Parson Brownlow's Book*, pp. 384, 390-91.

[9] *Ibid.*, pp. 392-94.

of telling it. Soon, therefore, came in a stream of invitations from Northern cities whose citizens were not sufficiently interested in the war, begging the Parson to come and make a speech. He should be well paid for his trouble. Even Lincoln urged him to visit Washington. Here was the Parson's chance; he would make a triumphal procession through the North, inciting Northerners against Southerners, gratifying his own very natural desire to be lionized for what he had done and suffered in East Tennessee, and at the same time accumulate enough money to make it possible to return home, when it should be rescued, and begin where he had left off with his *Whig* newspaper.

He set out for the North down the Cumberland, on the *Jacob Strader*, "that floating palace," and on March 23 he arrived at Fort Donelson, "where the late terrible battle was fought." He saw arms and legs of dead soldiers, protruding from their shallow graves, and the stench was so offensive that he stayed as far away as possible. The boat hooked up here for the night, but there was no rest for the Parson, for his reputation had already got too far ahead of him. Troops from the Northwest, passing up the river, heard that he was on the boat. They immediately surrounded the craft and insistently demanded a speech. Forced out on deck, he made them a short talk in which he riddled the Confederacy and tried to madden his hearers by declaring that that government was torturing women and children. The Confederates were fleeing southward, and he predicted a great battle would be fought if the Federals could catch up with them.[10]

Resuming his journey down the Cumberland into the Ohio, he continued up this river and arrived in Cincinnati on March 28. He was met at the wharf by representatives of the Gibson House who offered him their hospitalities as long as he should remain in the city. The Union Committee immediately called upon him and escorted him to the Merchants' Exchange where he made a short address before "a vast assemblage of the best men in the Queen City." He was then taken sightseeing to view the wonders of the "most populous city of the West." For the

---

[10] *Ibid.*, pp. 396-99.

next few days the city revolved around the Parson, biding the time when he should deliver his principal address. In the meantime he was making himself handy, praying at a funeral at one time and becoming the center of animated conversation at another.[11]

On April 4, the Parson addressed an immense audience in Pike's Opera House. Every seat was filled and the crowd overflowed into the aisles. According to the *Cincinnati Gazette* the opera house had likely never before accommodated such a large and refined assemblage. The house was decorated with flags. Across the front part of the stage were two tiers of seats for the honorary vice presidents and toward the rear was a raised platform on which were seated 372 school children, who sang a special song of welcome ending with the lines:

> "Thus speaks he, the hero! Then sing with one voice:
> We love and revere him, in his presence rejoice!
> Then hail him again, and forever and aye!
> His country he loves, and for it he would die!"

Thereupon the Parson was introduced as the model patriot whom the historians would pick out from all the other heroes for his matchless courage and patriotism. Then for an hour and twenty minutes Brownlow held up before his audience his ancestry, his politics, both recent and remote, his experiences in East Tennessee, and the heart-rending jail scenes. He did not fail to mention his bronchitis and the fact that his voice was getting stronger the more he denounced the vile heresies of secession. He was a Southerner and his opinions did not change with the section of the country in which he might find himself. He still believed in slavery but he was for the Union first, even "*though every institution in the country perish.*" The South was more to be blamed for the war than was the North. But he would say:

If I had been authorized, some two or three years ago, to select about two or three hundred of your most abominable anti-Slavery

---

[11] *Cincinnati Daily Commercial*, March 29, April 1, 1862; *Parson Brownlow's Book*, pp. 399-400; *Irreligious Character of the Rebellion*, p. 33.

agitators in the North, and an equal number of our God-forsaken and most hell-deserving Disunionists at the South, and had marched them to the District of Columbia, hanged them on a common gallows, dug for them a common grave, and embalmed their bodies with *jimson-weed* and *dog-fennel*, there would have been none of this trouble, nor should I have been here to-night!

He would have the property of all rebels, including their Negroes, confiscated and used to recompense the losses of the Unionists. He declared that the rebellion had pretty well "played out" and predicted that the Federal troops would "wind the thing up this spring and summer." The blockade had already almost starved out the South, and he closed his speech on this key, concluding, "It has been remarked on the streets of Knoxville that no such thing as a fine-toothed comb was to be had, and all the little Secession heads were full of squatter sovereigns hunting for their rights in the territories."[12]

Short addresses were then made by General S. F. Cary, a native Cincinnatian and a widely travelled temperance lecturer, and by John F. Fisk, the President of the Kentucky Senate. Then came a lengthy set of resolutions declaring that the Union must be preserved and maintaining that Brownlow was a true and intrepid patriot. The meeting ended with the song, "Hail Columbia." As the admission fee had been fifty cents, the Parson was doubly grateful for his large crowd, for he was enriched in the amount of $1,125. He gratefully accepted this sum with a reference to the plight in which his wife and children found themselves.[13]

Preachers preyed much on Brownlow's mind. He addressed a meeting of the ministers of Cincinnati and seized the occasion to condemn again the Southern clerics. He declared that "High functionaries in the Episcopal Church are now drinking and swearing." In the South many of the ministers preached on Sunday, "but swear and get drunk during the week." He spoke of a recent meeting in Knoxville where a minister had prayed

---

[12] *Cincinnati Daily Commercial*, April 5, 1862; *Portrait and Biography*, pp. 22-26; *Parson Brownlow's Book*, pp. 401-25.

[13] *Cincinnati Daily Commercial*, April 7, 1862.

that the Lord would sink Burnside's fleet and raise Lincoln's blockade. "And at it they went," continued Brownlow, "composed of many old clerical rips, who besieged a throne of grace, raising their hands heaving and setting like an old Tennessee ram at a gate-post, that God would send lightning and storm and raise the blockade." Instead, the Lord gave Roanoke Island to Burnside. There was just one thing the Parson would put before the Union—the Christian religion.[14]

Brownlow set out northward in tow of General Cary, who received his title through his position in the recruiting service.[15] The General considered the Parson his best means for raising Federal armies. The *modus operandi* consisted of the Parson's set speech, which he had first tried out on Cincinnati, and then while the heat was white the General would strike a blow for the recruiting service. They stopped first at Dayton, where they addressed a large audience, and on April 8 they arrived in Indianapolis. On the trip they had been accompanied by the mayor of Indianapolis and they received "one continued ovation during the journey." On their arrival at the Indiana capital they became the guests of Governor Morton. The Parson spoke in Metropolitan Hall to a crowd equal to any that had ever gathered there. The Governor and Mayor Maxwell and many other eminent people sat upon the stage as the Parson delivered his set speech. When he concluded, "Glory Hallelujah" was sung. Then the Governor announced "a brilliant victory" which the Federal troops had won. This news greatly excited the audience and the "patriotic Parson joined with the assemblage, and waved his handkerchief exultingly."[16] It was the opinion of competent judges that this meeting was "the most intellectual and spirit-stirring entertainment Indianapolis has ever had."[17] Governor Morton knew the Parson well enough to realize how much he would enjoy going out to Camp Morton to see 5,000 Rebel prisoners, some of whom no doubt were the very soldiers

---

[14] *Portrait and Biography*, pp. 30-45.

[15] Cary was later elected to Congress in 1866. Ten years later he was nominated vice president on the Greenback ticket.

[16] *Portrait and Biography*, pp. 49-64.

[17] *Ibid.*, p. 64.

who had pestered him back in Knoxville. He could not resist making them a speech, now that he had them where they could not run away. He spoke to them after a manner which got for him "no very cordial reception." In fact, some of them cried, "Traitor to the South," "Put him out."[18]

The Parson and the General left Indianapolis and passed through a continuous ovation en route to Chicago. They had decided to go because the Chicagoans had adopted such complimentary resolutions that the Parson felt that he could do nothing less than visit them. The Board of Aldermen appointed a committee to which were added representatives from the Commercial Exchange, to go out to welcome him as he neared the metropolis. They awaited him at Michigan City where Federal Judge Drummond honored him with a complimentary speech. The party now passed into Chicago and deposited the Parson on the bountiful hospitality of the Sherman House. As soon as possible after his arrival he went out to Camp Douglas to take a triumphant look at the Rebel prisoners there—again 5,000 of them. He made them a short speech, but he seems to have pursued tactics different from those he employed at Camp Morton, for they made no harsh remarks or menacing motions at him.

He and General Cary made their first formal speeches before the Merchants' Exchange. Mayor Ramsey introduced the Parson to "the immense throng" and a member of the Board of Trade sang his praises, declaring that when the history of the rebellion should be written, "it will be sadly deficient if its pages do not tell, in words that burn, the story of your wrongs, your fortitude, and your unswerving devotion to your country in the hour of her great trial. Our children will need no romance to stir their young hearts; but the truthful picture of your sufferings and heroism will fill the place of high-wrought fiction." No longer, he declared, would it be necessary to turn to the Greeks and Romans for mighty heroes. On the following night Brownlow and Cary made their customary speeches to "an overwhelming audience."[19]

---

[18] *Ibid.*, pp. 48-49; *Parson Brownlow's Book*, p. 426.

[19] *Portrait and Biography*, pp. 65-72; *Parson Brownlow's Book*, p. 429.

The Parson now doubled back on his trail to Cincinnati, passing through Lafayette, Indiana, where he addressed a "large and enthusiastic audience." Ohio at this time had a hero in the person of Clement L. Vallandigham whom the Union element desired strongly to replace. Recruiting had shockingly slowed up under his teachings. A loud cry, therefore, went up for the Parson and the General. The legislature, seconded by both branches of the Columbus City Council, called upon Brownlow to visit the capital city to perform his act. He arrived on April 14, and was met at the station by the 69th Regiment with their brass band. They escorted him to the capitol amidst cheering throngs. The speaking took place in the afternoon in the House Chamber, crowded with Senators, Representatives, and "a great number of ladies." Governor Tod and the Parson, arm-in-arm, marched to the platform where the Governor introduced the Parson to the audience and turned him over to James Monroe, the President of the Senate. President Monroe spoke lengthily on the noble traits the war had brought out in many people, and held up the Parson as one of the best examples. Thereupon Brownlow spoke his piece "which stirs and fascinates by its tones of earnestness." In the evening, introduced by ex-Governor Dennison he spoke for more than an hour. As it was very difficult to make politicians into soldiers, the General waited until the meeting in the theatre to spread his recruiting net. Before leaving for the East, the Parson was entertained by the president of the City Council, at a magnificent banquet attended by many senators and representatives and also by "many handsome ladies."[20]

Brownlow was now about to pass out of a region somewhat disaffected with the war because many people here were of Southern ancestry, because it made little money out of the war, and because it felt the depression and horror of men killing men in wholesale fashion. He no doubt left with the feeling that he had whipped up against the South fury sufficient to drive whole armies into General Cary's recruiting nets. He would soon enter a region which was not sending recruits up fast enough because

---

[20] *Parson Brownlow's Book*, pp. 429-36.

too many of its people were too busy making money out of a
national calamity. They did not think much about the horrors
of war because they had no time left for such diversions amidst
the enjoyment of those things which their newly-got fortunes
would buy for them. Soon the American correspondent of the
London *Times* was sending back dispatches on this order:
"There is something saddening, indeed revolting, in the high
glee, real or affected, with which the people here look upon what
ought to be, at any rate, a grievous national calamity."[21]

On April 17, he reached the forks of the Ohio, where he
was met by the combined governmental forces of Pittsburgh
and Alleghany City. They gave him the keys to both cities and
conducted him to the best hotel, the Monongahela House. In the
evening he spoke for an hour and a half to "a crowded hall," and
left early the next morning for Philadelphia. He was invited to
ride on the locomotive in order that he might while crossing the
mountains better enjoy the beautiful scenery. The romantic
beauty of it all gripped him, suggesting his own Southern Highlands, and thus he expressed his emotions:

> Poets and tourists may sing and write of "a life on the ocean
> wave," or "a home on the rolling deep"; but give me a seat in an
> open locomotive at the head of a long passenger-train, and let me
> cross the Alleghany Mountains from Pittsburg to the new mountain-
> city of Altoona, gazing on the dashing streams on the one hand,
> and the lofty and romantic mountains on the other. The sun was
> high in the hill of heaven, and rolling his chariot through a cloud-
> less sky; all creation was calm, and sleeping on the bosom of serenity,
> until aroused by the heavy tread and clear whistle of the iron horse![22]

At Altoona the Parson was met by a group of outriders from
Philadelphia including, "that prince of clever fellows, George
W. Childs, the extensive and energetic Philadelphia publisher."
After a ride across more mountains they arrived at Harrisburg,
the "ancient capital of the Keystone State." An "immense con-
course" gathered around the train and demanded a speech from

---

[21] Quoted in E. D. Fite, *Social and Industrial Conditions in the North during the Civil War*, p. 259.

[22] *Parson Brownlow's Book*, pp. 436-37.

the Parson. Introduced by Governor Curtin and invigorated by his mountain scenery, he made a fiery pass at the Confederacy. He would not speak of his troubles "in the kingdom of Jeff Davis," but he would say that the Apostle Paul had fought only with the "beast at Ephesus," while he, himself, had "fought the 'devil and Tom Walker,' and the infuriated legions of the so-called Southern Confederacy!" His greatest ambition was to go back to set up his *Knoxville Whig* again. "I want to go back," he declared, "and point out to the triumphant Federal army such men as deserve to hang, and suitable limbs upon which to hang them! Nay, I desire to tie the rope around some of their infernal necks." The rebels had hung, shot, tied to trees, and whipped to death East Tennesseeans, but a change was coming. After speaking a few minutes the Parson excused himself to go into the "Refreshment Saloon" to join in a cup of coffee the Governor, ex-Governor Porter, and other celebrated people.[23]

Then he was off for Philadelphia, "being immensely cheered at every station on the railroad, and loudly called for." Though it was about midnight when he arrived, he was met by an official delegation from the city government and welcomed with a short speech. After making his bow in a few remarks he was driven rapidly to the Continental Hotel—"perhaps the most elegant house in America." After being introduced to a number of people who could not wait until the morning to meet him, he was shown to his rooms, tired though happy. A few years had produced a wonderous change in the Parson's relation to Phila-delphia. The city was now to accord him a reception much dif-ferent from that which had taken place when he was debating Parson Pryne. It was only natural that this patriot of '61 should be early driven to Independence Hall, the cradle of the liberties he had been so valiantly defending, and that when there he should think of Washington, and Franklin, and Robert Morris, and of the signers of the Declaration of Independence. A reception was held in the Hall where he was properly welcomed by the city. At eleven, he appeared on a flag draped stand erected in front of the Hall, where he spoke to an "immense audience." He made

---

[23] *Ibid.*, pp. 437-40.

his set speech with few changes. Varying his "squatter-sover-eign" thrust somewhat, he said, "They were out of soap with which to wash their dirty faces; they were out of every thing, including fine tooth combs, while every little rebel head was full of squatter-sovereigns, looking for 'their rights' among the tangles." Forgetting their dignified Quaker heritage the audience roared with "tremendous applause and laughter." After he had finished, his admirers were given a chance to meet him. So great was the rush that he retired to the interior where groups were admitted and received behind locked-doors. One timorous lady who asked about her son in East Tennessee fainted when the Parson told her that he was a Rebel.[24]

On reaching Philadelphia Brownlow could consider that he had completed one of his major campaigns. But it seemed there could be no rest in the North for a person of his characteristics. He was being called for in every direction. The report was spread that he had been offered $1,000 a night to "go on the lecture platform," but that he had refused because that would give him more money than he needed.[25] It was also reported that Lincoln invited him to come to the White House.[26] Before he had reached Philadelphia, the city of Baltimore invited him to make his speech there.[27] All these offers he refused, for the sound reason that George W. Childs had not gone all the way to Altoona for no good purpose beyond being the first to welcome the Parson to Philadelphia. Being a successful publisher, he naturally knew that Brownlow could write the kind of a book that people would buy. The contract was made and the Parson retired to the little village of Crosswicks, New Jersey, to do the work, and a book resulted whose significance will later appear.

Crosswicks was a quiet sleepy little country village, which until the Parson's arrival had never experienced greater excitement than to have as a neighbor four miles away in Bordentown, first "the celebrated infidel Tom Paine" and later for a quarter

[24] *Daily Evening Bulletin* (Philadelphia), April 18, 1862; *Parson Brownlow's Book,* pp. 440-42.
[25] *Daily Evening Bulletin,* April 18, 1862.
[26] *Ibid.*
[27] *Parson Brownlow's Book,* pp. 442-44.

of a century Joseph Bonaparte, the ex-king of Spain and brother of the great Napoleon. But with the arrival of Brownlow this little Quaker settlement awaked from its long sleep. Three Quakers soon asked him to speak in their meeting house, a favor never before bestowed upon outsiders. He regaled a "crowded house" with an hour and a half of fervent speaking. In fact the Parson was so much himself on this occasion that, on his own admission, he gave the building such a shock as it had never felt since the days of the Revolution when a cannonball had plowed a hole through the north wall.[28]

While Brownlow was busily whipping his book together, his family was making its way out of the Confederacy, under a special escort. As before stated, the policy of the Confederacy in East Tennessee required this expulsion, but the Parson hastened the departure by his unwise and untrue remarks in Cincinnati and elsewhere that his family was being held as hostages for his good conduct. With much effect he informed his Northern audiences that he had told his wife on his departure that she might well prepare to be executed, for he was going to assail terrifically the Confederacy, in the North.[29] He was now in such a heroic mood that it appeared he was willing to sacrifice his wife on the altar of his patriotism.

With his family now safe at Crosswicks, he launched an attack against Colonel W. M. Churchwell, Confederate provost-marshall in East Tennessee, who had ordered the expulsion, declaring that the provost-marshal was taking his spite out on helpless women and children because the Parson had once exposed him in a case of personal dishonesty. And General E. Kirby Smith, for allowing himself to become the tool of Churchwell, was "little," "sordid," "mean," and "contemptible." There was only one person connected with the expulsion who had gentlemanly instincts, Lieutenant Joseph H. Speed of Virginia. The Parson attributed Speed's good manners to his background of Whiggery and Methodism. Brownlow was especially excited by a report published in a Confederate newspaper that his family

---

[28] *Ibid.*, pp. 444-46.
[29] *Cincinnati Daily Commercial*, April 1, 1862.

were good Confederates. With great force he denied the slander, and explained that the "only difference between us is, that I claim to be capable of despising the wicked concern, and all connected with originating it, with more *intense hatred* than they can."[30]

Less than a month after arriving in Philadelphia, Brownlow was ready to resume his campaign. He was being called for in all directions. New York, the largest city in all the land, was anxiously waiting to welcome him; and certainly Washington, the seat of those who held the destiny of the Union in their keeping, had claims upon the Parson which amounted to an obligation on his part to visit that city. But he was as near Washington as he expected to approach, as long as he could well keep away. He was considerably disgusted with Lincoln and the government for their delay in rescuing East Tennessee, and he was not afraid to speak out his sentiments. In early May he exclaimed, "In God's name, I call upon President Lincoln, and upon his Cabinet and army-officers, to say how long they will suffer a loyal people, true to the Union and to the Government of their fathers, to suffer in this way." With growing impatience he declared, "Let the Government, if it have any regard for its obligations, redeem that country at once, and liberate these people, no matter at what cost of blood and treasure. They have suffered these outrages for the last twelve months, and are now desponding,—nay, despairing of any relief."[31] With such thoughts he set out for New York City.

He knew there would be further adulation for him in that direction; there would also be many dollars to be garnered which he would promise to use in restoring his newspaper in Knoxville; and he might build up so much indignation against the Government's neglect of East Tennessee that Lincoln would be forced to the rescue. So he set out for South Amboy, taking with him his heroic daughter, Susan, who was now Mrs. Sawyer. Her exploits in defending the flag in the Parson's yard back in Knoxville, had appealed to the Northern mind and had sug-

---

[30] *Parson Brownlow's Book,* pp. 252-53.

[31] *Ibid.,* pp. 453-54.

gested that the daughter would be almost as great an attraction as the father. The New York newspapers were now proclaiming her as a "chip off the old block." The city had already formed its opinions of the great Southern Unionist—a man original in his way of thinking, eccentric in his manner, invincible in his determination, and never giving up an opinion he thought right; a crusader who had fought with his hands, pen, and tongue—"a name which, though coupled with roughness of exterior, lack of polish and absence of refinement, has not yet been associated with dishonor, or tainted with secession."[32] The editor of the *New York Times* sang forth:

We have learned here to regard him as the true type of what the Southerner ought to be, and of what in tale and tradition he is represented to be. Daring, self-reliant, earnest, truthful, gentle, in the right cause eloquent, and against the wrong unsparing; patient and unconquerable in persecution and adversity; the soul of honor, with the heart of a woman—these are the elements of genuine chivalry, and all these are the possession of Brownlow.[33]

New York City awoke early on the morning of May 13, for the Parson was coming. A reception committee of distinguished citizens boarded the ferry boat at 5:30 for South Amboy to meet the train bringing the Parson and his party. For four hours they waited and listened before the belated train, decked in flags, pulled into the station, and then "Shout after shout went up from the expectant crowd, and various amusing mistakes were made by people who took and mistook everyone but the right person for the Parson." When he stepped down from the train, everyone was disappointed. "They expected to see a rough, hardy, keen-featured man, who might pass for a prize-fighter, a bully or a rowdy; instead of which they saw a man slightly built, with stooping shoulders, a round, bullet head, a quiet, pleasant countenance, and an air somewhat depressed, with a travel-stained, dust-laden *tout ensemble* very unlike the ideal."[34]

---

[32] *New York Times,* May 14, 1862.
[33] *Ibid.*
[34] *Ibid.*

Though disappointed in his appearance, the people were none the less enthusiastic in their welcome. After being ferried across the bay, he landed amidst a throng of people who lined the street and cheered him as he was driven to the Astor House where he was assigned to superb apartments. Masses of people swarmed into the hotel to meet him, but he now felt important enough and sufficiently used-up to deny most of them the privilege. What a difference a war had made in the Parson's standing with old Father Knickerbocker! A few years before, he had visited the city unnoticed, to seek treatment for his bronchitis; now he was peddling patriotism—and the difference was mighty.

He was soon performing in his best fashion. The day after his arrival he gave his stock speech before the Chamber of Commerce after a glowing introduction of fulsome praise. He also spoke at a banquet given by the New England Soldiers' Relief Association. New York was a large city even in the 1860's; the Parson must make many speeches before all who wanted to hear him could be accommodated; and there were various causes to be served. The people must be entertained by an eccentric and unusual performer; the cause of the Union must be served by the Parson whipping up patriotism through singing his hymn of hate; and he must raise enough money to reëstablish himself and his newspaper in East Tennessee, if the tardy Government should ever clear out the Rebels. It was this last purpose that would be served in a speech which it was announced he would deliver in the Academy of Music on the fifteenth. A grand reception was to be held for him, and Governor Morgan was to preside at the speechmaking. The price of admission was to be fifty cents the person, and all the proceeds should go to the reëstablishment of his *Whig*. A vast crowd attended with New York's best in the forefront. Governor Morgan finding it impossible to attend, Hon. William M. Evarts supplied the vacancy and introduced Brownlow. Again did the Parson recount the suffering of the Union men in East Tennessee, and boldly did he tell what he thought should be done. "If nothing else will satisfy the crazy people of the South," he exclaimed, "I believe in exterminating them, and in supplying their places with men who

15

would be of some benefit to the country." The way in which the Government had neglected East Tennessee was a crying shame, and those in charge should be called to account for it. He declared, "I avoided Washington, because I didn't want to see anybody there until justice had been done East Tennessee."[35]

This speech not only enriched his fortune by more than $2,500, but it also enhanced his reputation with additional praise. According to the *New York Times* this speech greatly stimulated the patriotism of his hearers. "He is himself a legion," it said, "and might safely be pitted against the whole Confederacy."[36] Mr. Greeley's *Tribune* sang out:

Seldom has more triumphant welcome been vouchsafed to warrior or statesman than was given last evening by the city *en masse*, or at least as much of it as could be compressed within the walls of the Academy of Music, to the sturdy and much suffering lover of the Union—Parson Brownlow. Long before the hour of commencement the aisles and lobbies were crowded and the stage was covered with leading citizens.[37]

He was loath to leave New York City, for he had developed into a hero of vast proportions, so great that he eclipsed President Lincoln's flickering reputation and could make slighting remarks about him. His plan to reëstablish his newspaper received wide acclaim and support. At this time it became one of the best methods of making a patriotic display to go about getting subscribers for the Parson's new paper; and the task was not difficult among those who had seen and heard the editor. If the paper was to be like the Parson it would be entertaining enough. A dry goods house early reported that it had secured 200 subscribers. Such loyalty to his cause the Parson felt deserved nothing less than a visit from him, so he sought them out and brought the business to a standstill as the people crowded around him. He soon mounted a table and made a "few remarks to the curious hundreds who thronged around and wished to hear him." He told his "squatter sovereign" joke and

[35] *Ibid.*, May 15, 1862.
[36] May 16, 1862; *Boston Evening Transcript*, May 21, 1862.
[37] *New York Daily Tribune*, May 16, 1862.

"brought down the house." Naturally more names went on the subscription list, and the *New York Tribune* hoped "a list a mile long may be obtained to aid him."[38]

Brooklyn was near enough to New York City for its residents to cross East River for one of the Parson's performances, but the city would not be satisfied without a visit from the Parson. On May 17 he spoke before the Brooklyn Mercantile Library Association. An immense audience was present, with Mayor Kalbfleisch presiding. The proceeds, which amounted to $1,200, went to Brownlow's newspaper venture. Naturally the churches would lay claim on some of the Parson's time and strength. He promised to preach at the Hedding Methodist Episcopal Church in New York City. At the appointed time he appeared and announced that he was too weak to preach. Nevertheless, he told much about his hard lot in East Tennessee, metamorphosing an abbreviation of his set patriotic speech into a sermon. General Cary, who had been little in evidence in New York, filled out the time with a speech on temperance.[39]

Before leaving New York City, the Parson made one speech somewhat different in substance though not in performance and effect, from the set speech which he had used so often. On May 19, he spoke before the Young Men's Christian Association at the Cooper Institute. He named his performance the "Irreligious Character of the Rebellion," and in it he reached an intensity in feeling and an extravagance in language which he had heretofore not been able to attain. In unmeasured terms, to his heart's content, he poured out his bitter condemnation of the South and its leaders, lay and religious. No doubt his performance suggested in his mind the prophets of old as they smote mightily for Jehovah. He thundered out, "All the iniquities that ever prevailed anywhere on the face of God's green earth they have in full blossom in every state south of Mason and Dixon's Line." Again were the Southern preachers the beloved object of his attacks. Every preacher in the South supporting the Confederacy was a drunkard—"a more unmiti-

---

[38] May 15, 16, 1862.
[39] *Ibid.*, May 17, 19, 1862.

gated, God-forsaken set of scoundrels do not live than the preachers of the Gospel down South." As an example of a Southern prayer and a recommendation of the proper response, he described an incident which he held had happened in East Tennessee. A Methodist preacher kneeled down and prayed, "O Lord, we thank Thee for having inaugurated this Revolution. . . . Judge Pickens rose up in his seat, and taking his hat, says he, 'God d—m such a prayer to hell!' " The audience greeted this sally with loud laughter.[40] The *New York Times* complimented him in an editorial which it entitled "A Martyr Missionary," and declared that he was "doing good service to the Union cause by his speeches in the Northern States."[41]

To an Englishman in America at this time, the Parson did not appear in such a favorable light. He wondered about the intelligence, culture, and mental balance of a people who could make a hero out of a person like Brownlow. George Augustus Sala introduced this subject in his diary, by writing, "Parson Brownlow you may have already heard of." He then recorded that his "gabble was not only listened to, but loudly cheered by a large and respectable audience in the Empire City of the Republic." He had not been able to determine whether Brownlow was "more bad than mad, or whether his eloquence was inspired by depravity, by delirium tremens, or by the dog days." He then quoted this as a specimen of the Parson's style:

If I had the power, sir, I would arm and uniform in Federal habiliments every wolf, and panther, and tiger, and catamount, and bear, in the mountains of America; every crocodile in the swamps of Florida and South Carolina; every negro in the Southern Confederacy; and every devil in Hell and Pandemonium. . . . This war, I say to you, must be pursued with a *vim* and a vengeance, until the rebellion is put down, if it exterminates from God's green earth every man, woman, and child south of Mason and Dixon's Line. . . . And we will crowd the rebels and crowd and crowd them, till I trust in God we will rush them into the Gulf of Mexico, and drive the entire race, as the devil did the hogs into the Sea of

---

[40] *Irreligious Character of the Rebellion*, pp. 29, 32; *New York Tribune*, May 20, 1862.

[41] May 22, 1862.

Galilee. . . . We can whip the Southern Confederacy; we can take in England and France; and I want to carry it on till we whip out all creation.[42]

The Parson may not have greatly appealed to Englishmen detached from the dementia of a contest of wholesale slaughter, but he was a vast sensation to those Americans who had become so maddened by blood that they were willing to see a civilization fall and life itself disappear from the land rather than give up a political organization. So, loud and persistent calls for the Parson continued to come—from all parts of the Empire State and from New England. There was money in it, and the Parson wanted very badly to reëstablish his *Knoxville Whig*. Before the end of May he had completely capitulated to the New England demands; he set out on a sweeping campaign which carried him into every New England state with the exception of isolated Vermont. The first city he honored with his presence was the foremost city. The people were prepared for his coming by peans of praise sung out for him. The "reputation of the 'Parson' had long preceded him, and there are but few who have not heard of and desired to know him."[43] He had supported the Union "where it costs something to make that profession—costs property, social standing, peace and quiet, reputation, and life itself. Few communities, since the days of the early Christians, have been worse persecuted for principle's sake than have been the Union men of East Tennessee."[44]

On May 22 the Parson arrived in Boston. The reception committee immediately drove him to the Revere House and quartered him in the historic "Daniel Webster Rooms." Governor Andrew and his staff called upon him and escorted him out to Fort Warren, where the Parson had the pleasure of looking over some Rebel prisoners. One of the prisoners caught the ear of the Parson and convinced him that he was an East Tennesseean who had been forced into the Confederate army. Brownlow inter-

[42] George Augustus Sala, *My Diary in America in the Midst of War*, II, 403-4.

[43] *New York Tribune*, May 21, 1862; *Boston Morning Journal*, May 24, 1862.

[44] Editorial in *Boston Morning Journal*, May 23, 1862.

ceded and got his release. He held his first performance on the second day after his arrival, and made his old set speech, at Music Hall, announcing beforehand that the proceeds of the meeting would go to the resurrection of his *Whig*.[45] Boston, being a large city, required more than one speech and more than one day's visit. He was in demand at the churches. At one religious exercise, he "made a short and characteristic exhortation, and offered a pungent prayer," according to a news item.[46] He could not refrain from visiting the business district. The next day he drew the headlines, "Parson Brownlow among the Pearl Street Shoe Dealers," with the news that he had visited a big shoe store where "hundreds of persons rushed in to catch a glimpse of the Doctor." Thereupon he leaped upon the counter and delivered his East Tennessee atrocities speech.[47]

Leaving Boston, his plans carried him down to North Bridgewater, and thence northward to Salem and on to Lowell where he spoke on May 29 and thence to Portland, Maine, the next day.[48] On his return through Dover, New Hampshire, the crowd gathered around his train and demanded a speech. He gave them a synopsis of his main speech, vigorously adding that he was "good for eight more campaigns and three more rebellions."[49] He swept on through Roxbury, Providence, in Rhode Island, over into Connecticut where he spoke at Norwich and then at Hartford. He was highly entertained in Hartford, the ammunition center. Here following his speech the workmen from Colt's factory presented him with a revolver, holsters, and all other needed equipment. In a fiery speech he accepted this armament, and so emboldened did it make him that he threatened to put a bullet through anyone who should dare to insult the flag. He then raised the hue and cry for a manhunt to seek out the Hartford secessionists and ride them out of town on a rail. So effective was this grandiloquent gesture that he scarcely ever forgot to use it in the other towns he visited. It was a happy and be-

[45] *Boston Evening Transcript*, May 24, 1862.
[46] *Ibid.*, May 26, 1862.
[47] *Ibid.*, May 28, 1862.
[48] *Boston Morning Journal*, May 24, 1862.
[49] *Ibid.*, June 2, 1862.

fitting thought that led the workmen to present a revolver also to the daughter who had so boldly defended the flag against ninety Rebels back in Knoxville.[50]

He turned northward from Hartford to the arsenal city of Springfield, Massachusetts, and thence on to Amherst and Worcester. At Worcester he spoke to an immense crowd, and according to the local newspaper "He kicks, smites, chops, butchers, and crushes them, and then delivers them over to be roasted by hell-fire."[51] Truly, as a Bostonian concluded, he was "one of the most remarkable men of the time," a statement that the Englishman would agree to but not with the same meaning.[52]

Philadelphia liked Brownlow, and Brownlow liked Philadelphia. The Parson had scarcely got well started in the New England states before the Quaker City was calling for him again. The war-makers of the City of Brotherly Love wanted him to speak on secession at the Academy of Music. The price of admission would be fifty cents, and the entire proceeds should be "appropriated toward the reëstablishment of the Knoxville *Whig.*"[53] The urgent invitation was broadcast: "Let our citizens turn out by thousands to show the brave preacher how highly they estimate his services."[54] On June 14, he spoke much according to his old custom with the same old story of Southern atrocities. "No larger or more fashionable audience ever assembled in the Academy of Music," according to competent opinion. Brownlow's family was present and occupied a box. His flag-defending daughter Susan was made the center of an interesting ceremony preceding the Parson's speech. Not to be outdone by Hartford, which had presented her with a Colt's revolver, Philadelphia would now present her with a fine silk flag, which she might yet be forced to defend with her Colt's revolver.[55]

[50] *Boston Evening Transcript,* June 9, 1862.
[51] *Worcester Daily Spy,* June 10, 1862.
[52] *Boston Evening Transcript,* May 26, 1862; The Parson's itinerary is given in the *Boston Morning Journal,* May 28, 1862.
[53] Philadelphia *Daily Evening Bulletin,* June 7, 1862.
[54] *Ibid.,* June 11; W. G. Brownlow, *Brownlow, the Patriot and the Martyr showing his Faith and Works, as Reported by Himself,* p. 105.
[55] Philadelphia *Daily Evening Bulletin,* June 14, 20, 1862.

Philadelphia could never tire of hearing about atrocities in East Tennessee. On June 20, the Parson was bracketed with a Mr. Bokum in a great war festival, where the former would speak his accustomed English and the latter would inform those people who understood only German. The sanitary fairs and relief meetings worked the Parson constantly but he helped them much, and the Philadelphians felt duly grateful. The war women who conducted these relief agencies, according to the *Daily Evening Bulletin* "have recently possessed a lion of the first magnitude in the brave Parson Brownlow, who is besieged with invitations every day, and presented with bouquets and huge cakes every evening. The noble Tennesseean generally says a few words in his vigorous style on such occasions, and retires after a process of hand-shaking, which is no mean test of his power of endurance."[56]

Soon the Parson left his beloved Philadelphia, taking his family with him, and settled down in Cincinnati for a time.[57] But before the end of June he was called to Washington as a witness in the impeachment trial of Judge West H. Humphreys, and only such business could induce him to go to the nation's capital, so thoroughly did he disapprove of the Government's neglect of East Tennessee. He had already made up his mind to dislike the pettifogging politicians controlling affairs there, and he was not sure that he would look with much favor on the city itself. A day or two after his arrival he expressed himself as unfavorably impressed by the Government, not only because it did not clear the Rebels out of East Tennessee, but also because it treated them too leniently. There were Rebels even yet in office in Washington. The Government treated the Rebel sick and wounded in its possession with too much care. He would confiscate all their property and besides he would stretch the necks of lots of them. As for the head man, Lincoln, the Parson had never seen him. He had called around at the White House, but the President was "holding a 'council of war,' " and so the Parson was not allowed to see him. Brownlow confessed that this

[56] *Ibid.*, June 21, 1862.
[57] *Cincinnati Daily Commercial*, June 25, 1862.

was "a matter of small moment," and added "The Mountain having gone to Mahomet, Mahomet must come to the Mountain next time."[58] Undoubtedly the Parson felt piqued at the way Lincoln was neglecting him. He had been received with much greater acclaim in the North than Lincoln had ever been accorded—so why should he not have some little pride in the matter.

He did consent to speak his piece on the Rebellion and to tell the Washingtonians a thing or two. On the last day of June he performed in Ford's Atheneum, but little notice was taken of his presence in town.[59]

With an impatient disposition on the conquest of East Tennessee and with a feeling that he was a great man in all the towns and hamlets in the North, manifestly Brownlow would spend as little time as possible in cold and unappreciative Washington. So, during the summer and fall he carried out various speaking trips which took him through Central and Western New York, through Utica and Buffalo, and on into the Middle West again. He wrote his friend and publisher, George W. Childs, a letter from Utica in August, saying that he showed the Rebels "no quarter, and the people shout amen."[60] By October he had carried his campaign into Illinois. David Davis heard him speak at Bloomington and wrote about it as follows: "Have just heard Parson Brownlow's speech. He spoke in East door Court House. Wind was so high that he could not speak longer than an hour and a half. He finishes tonight in the hall and is to be followed by Deacon Bross of the *Tribune*. His speech was the most denunciatory of any I ever heard. His talk is all random shots, no argument at all. Adjectives he used in abundance and the whole vocabulary of expletives he has at command. There was at least 2,000 persons present and went away disappointed that he quit. He tells many anecdotes but never

[58] MS letter to the *New York Weekly,* written in Washington, June 28, 1862. The manuscript is in the Library of Congress.

[59] The only reference to Brownlow made in the *Daily National Intelligencer* was the brief announcement that he would speak, June 30, 1862.

[60] MS letter, Brownlow to Childs, Utica, New York, August 7, 1862, in the Library of Congress.

smiles. His nostrils are like a race horse. His face is iron and you can see by his eye that he does not fear the face of man."[61]

Brownlow had undoubtedly become a radical and he had arrived at that position through his contact with the people of the North and through his inherent disposition to go to extremes. He shot venom and spleen and fire and brimstone at the Southerners, he told how they should be hanged, drawn, and quartered. He was a fighter; he was unusual to look at; his language was decisive, vitriolic, and unpolished; in the excitement of a speech he lost all sense of proportions and largely the limits of good taste. But these things made a good show and afforded rare entertainment for the commonality of the North. The Parson mistook their applause as meaning complete agreement with his policy of extermination for the Southerners. The mass of people are never really blood-thirsty except at a distance or under the influence of mob psychology.

---

[61] MS letter, David Davis to Wm. M. Orme, Bloomington, Ill., October 21, 1862, in Library of the University of Illinois.

CHAPTER XI

BACK IN TENNESSEE

The North made of Parson Brownlow a great generator of war enthusiasm and hysteria. He sang his hymn of hate throughout the country and purveyed shocking accounts of Southern atrocities. In pushing the cause of Northern patriotism he was not unmindful of personal advantages to be reaped and opportunities to be seized. He had left the Confederacy with the stern purpose of coming back as soon as possible to force vengeance upon his enemies. As he could not return until the Federal armies should have driven out the Confederates he never ceased to demand a military strategy which should make its principal object the rescue of East Tennessee; and as he knew the more money he should carry back with him the easier his work would be, he never left his audiences uninformed on his financial needs in restoring his *Knoxville Whig*.

Naturally, then, he readily consented to write for George W. Childs a book which would tell how the South had provoked the war and how it had harried the Union people in East Tennessee. Such a book would make a great deal of money for the Parson, it would enrich Childs, and it would fire up the furnaces of Northern wrath and indignation and set them at the throats of their erstwhile Southern partners in the Union. Being an enterprising publisher, Childs had hastened from Philadelphia to Altoona to meet the Parson on his first trip east and to engage him to write the book. Brownlow accepted $10,000 for the manuscript and immediately set to work preparing it. Thus he busied himself in his Crosswicks, New Jersey, home, and before setting out on his campaign into New York and New England in May, he had finished the book.[1]

---

[1] Temple, *op. cit.*, p. 317.

A work so hastily got together could not have been a model in diction or composition, but the Parson stood out on every page—and the North liked the Parson and his extravagant style. He called his work, consisting of 458 pages, *Sketches of the Rise, Progress, and Decline of Secession; with a Narrative of Personal Adventures Among the Rebels*. Perhaps only a person with the sharp perspicacity of the Parson could have noticed an appreciable *decline* in the rebellion by May of 1862. The bookbinders, finding the Parson's title too long for their skill, reduced it to *Parson Brownlow's Book*, and by this title it became known to hundreds of thousands. In the first part of a long and fulsome flow of language he dedicated the book to all species of people who loved the Union and despised rebellion and especially to his "companions in the Knoxville Jail"; the second part he gave over to himself, who had opposed recklessly that Rebellion; to Washington, who had revered the Constitution; and to Jackson, who had demanded the preservation of the Union. Then followed as the text, a great conglomeration of editorials from his *Knoxville Whig*, written during 1860 and 1861, most of a diary which he had kept in the Knoxville jail, and withering denunciations of the Southerners which expressed his opinions in April and May of 1862 and which acted as beginning, end, and fillings for the gaps between his quoted material. In part of one chapter, he restrained his burning anger long enough to introduce his readers to the climate, soil, topography, and productions of East Tennessee, but he ended it with the cry of "fraud and villainy" against the secessionists and the declaration: "The Union men of the State are now in the majority, and will have the State back or die in the last ditch!"[2]

One of the most interesting contributions the Parson made to his work was, in his capacity as spokesman of the Lord, to report the divine opinion and pleasure concerning the Rebellion Since the remotest ages, warring nations have had their god of battles. The Hebrews wrought mightily under their Jehovah; but when the great nations of the earth became Christian and

[2] P. 223.

when deserting their Christian principles they plunged themselves into savage war, both sides perforce must call upon the
same God for contradictory blessings. Each belligerent, assuming complete justification for his actions, has sought to appropriate for his own exclusive use the God of all. It vexed the
Parson terribly that the wicked Southerners should in "unpar-
donable prayers" assume to call upon the God he was serving.
From the beginning of this Rebellion the Rebels had "arrogantly
claimed that God was on their side," and had promised their
soldiers that if they should fall in battle the cause for which
they fought would constitute "a passport sufficient to introduce
them to all that exceeding weight of joy at God's right hand!"
The Parson would readily admit that the Lord had had something to do with the secession movement but only to the extent
of permitting the devils to enter the chief leaders "just as He
permitted them to enter the herd of swine and precipitate them
into the Sea of Galilee!"[3]

In the opinion of the Parson there was no argument on this
earth more sure and compelling than that by statistics. With
the feeling of divine sanction and finality he proclaimed the
wondrous works of the Lord as culled from the trade reports and
census volumes, and showed how unmistakably they proved that
God was on the side of the North. He exclaimed, "How wonder-
fully has God arranged all the conditions of this great drama,
to favor the Government of the United States and the millions
of loyal citizens adhering thereto!"[4] The proof he found in the
following facts. The South by an immense cotton crop in 1859
richly supplied the wants of Europe and overstocked England.
During the same year and the two years following, the Lord
smiled upon the North and gave to her great grain crops, while
at the same time He was apparently ungenerous to Europe, in
lean crops—but there was a hidden purpose back of it all.
Europe was now forced with the wealth the Lord had allowed
it to accumulate from the evil South to purchase the surplus

---

[3] Pp. 177-79.
[4] P. 182.

grain crop of the North and keep the balance of trade in favor of the Federal Government, even with all the exports of Southern cotton cut off.[5]

If this argument should seem far-fetched to some people, Brownlow had more direct proof that God was a Northerner: "In a review of the battles lost and won in this war, it is plain to be seen which army has the approbation of Providence." Thereupon he called the roll of Union victories and found that there had been seventeen in 1861 and twelve in 1862, up to the early part of May. The Rebels had won in some inexplicable way seven victories during the first year, but had been completely shut out during 1862. But even in a more eloquent fashion had the divine approval been shown in the number of towns which the Federals had taken "with the Lord's *permission*." The Parson counted fifty-six towns and cities and twenty-five forts, all safely in the hands of the United States. He banteringly asked, "Do the clergymen who play at this game of Secession brag call this backing up one's friends?"[6]

Instead of the Lord smiling on the South, the devil had it well under his control. The Parson declared that there was "in the South a mass of corruption that would poison the atmosphere of Paradise, were it to come in contact with it." Profane swearing was almost universal among both officers and privates in the Southern army, and "Drunkenness, swindling, fighting, Sabbath-breaking, and gambling are the order of the day." All of these facts and many others went to show that the Lord was on the side of the Federal Government. As overwhelming and final proof, the Parson cited statistics on the lot that had befallen many Confederate generals. Eight had been killed in battle, one had committed suicide, six had been captured, two had been suspended in disgrace, four had resigned and only one had been allowed to die a natural death.[7]

The Parson was not always perfectly convincing to the skeptical in his charges of Southern outrages and atrocities,

[5] The Parson did not originate this argument, but he eagerly appropriated it from an "able writer . . . in a religious periodical of high standing." Pp. 181-82.
[6] P. 186.
[7] P. 190.

but now and then he cited as additional proof for the doubters the engravings in his book. He offered this species of proof of the atrocity where a Union man was "tied upon a log, his back stripped bare, and cut all to pieces with hickories."[8] He not only wanted to select the limbs from which the sorry carcasses of his enemies should dangle, but he would even destroy some of the states. Of the "Old Dominion" he would make only "a historic cognomen in all time to come." A new rule must arise on her ruins and a new race occupy her soil. "What a fate, and what a retribution!" he exclaimed. He would divide the state among Maryland, Delaware, West Virginia, and East Tennessee.[9]

In the preface to his book the Parson said:

Extreme fastidiousness of taste may, perhaps, shrink with over-sensitiveness from some of the language I have employed. . . . The traitors merited a sword-thrust style, and deserved the strongest epithet I have applied. My persecution by them was such that I had a fair right to handle them roughly: they were not worth any other mode of treatment; and I have written what I have written.

In concluding his four hundred and fifty-eighth page of terrible vituperation and abuse and of exaggeration and pathos, he admitted "I have spoken plainly, vehemently,—perhaps bitterly: I could not do otherwise in so dear a concernment as my country's good."

Brownlow naturally expected everybody in the North to read his book, and he was going to see to it that the Southerners should swallow it. He declared in New York, "They shall see it, read it at home, and tremble in their boots, as I give a fair and honest but scathing version of their villainy and their murderous course and conduct from beginning to end."[10]

The book was published in the summer of 1862 and it was estimated that by September a hundred thousand copies had been sold and it was predicted that a half million would ultimately be marketed. In early July, George W. Childs sent Ben

---

[8] P. 274.
[9] P. 276.
[10] Brownlow, *The Irreligious Character of the Rebellion*, p. 26.

Butler a copy autographed by Brownlow, with the intelligence that the Parson highly approved of Butler both as a man and a soldier. In fact Butler was "just his style," and the Parson would be willing to support him for the presidency of the United States.[11]

The principal Northern magazines reviewed the Parson's literary production, but due to the blunting effect their patriotism had upon their critical judgment, they found the book far better than they could possibly have adjudged it in peace-time, if indeed they had noticed it at all. *Harper's Magazine* considered it a little too severe in its language but felt that the fiery Parson had much provocation.[12] The *North American Review* declared: "The writer commands our high respect as a man of massive, though unpolished intellect, of tenacious integrity of purpose, of no ordinary capacity in political satire, invective, and argument, and of a patriotism impregnable equally to bribes and to threats."[13] *Godey's Lady's Book* spoke more of the deserving Parson than it did of his literary skill. It believed that most people in the North would read the book, and especially would they be glad to do so when they should find out that the Parson got a liberal royalty on every copy sold. It continued, "When we remember the persecutions that Mr. Brownlow underwent, the loss of all his property, the danger to his life, his separation from his wife and children, his long imprisonment, who will not purchase a copy of this book, and help the long persecuted Editor and Parson to get his rights and money enough to purchase the outfit for his printing office."[14]

So great a favorite had the Parson become with the literary élite of the North, that he and his publisher, George W. Childs, decided that for the sake of profits they might reissue another literary product of the Parson's, slightly out of date in the Civil War, but as intemperate and blistering in language as his war

---

[11] *Private and Official Correspondence of Gen. Benjamin F. Butler during the Period of the Civil War,* II, 51.

[12] *Harper's New Monthly Magazine,* July, 1862, pp. 263-64.

[13] October, 1862, p. 568.

[14] September, 1862, p. 301.

book and as much in keeping with the peculiar literary tastes that seemed to prevail at that time. So it happened that *The Great Iron Wheel Examined* which had revolved more than 100,- 000 times during the great religious warfare of the 1850's was now once more set in motion. The only patriotic excuse that could be devised for the reissue would be to help the Parson raise money for his *Whig* and to keep alive the reputation of Parson Graves, who was now, according to Parson Brownlow, a cowardly Rebel.[15]

The Parson in person or the Parson in print was equally attractive to a sufficiently large number of Northerners, because he either entertained them or maddened them, as to make him a financial and patriotic asset in almost any guise. For those who could not afford to buy so stout a work as *Parson Brownlow's Book* there were two other productions which would give them much the same impression of the Parson and of the Rebellion. There was the *Portrait and Biography of Parson Brownlow, the Tennessee Patriot. Together with his Last Editorial in the Knoxville Whig; also, his Recent Speeches, Rehearsing his Experience with Secession, and his Prison Life.* It was published as a pamphlet in Indianapolis in 1862 and was sold for twenty-five cents. It declared that there were no greater exploits in modern times than those of the "patriotic exile, Parson Brownlow, of Tennessee." For those who could spare fifty cents there was published in Philadelphia in July of 1862 another pamphlet entitled *Brownlow, the Patriot and Martyr. Showing his Faith and Works, as Reported by Himself.* To popularize Brownlow's speech in New York City on May 15, 1862, at the Academy of Music, the text was published in a pamphlet, under the title of *Suffering Union Men.* This production contained one of his most delectable Southern atrocities: Rebel soldiers on their return through Knoxville after the Battle of Bull Run proudly held in the windows of their coaches the heads of Union soldiers they had decapitated.[16] His Cooper Institute

---

[15] This re-publication was announced in an advertisement in the rear of *Parson Brownlow's Book.*

[16] P. 17.

16

speech, which he made on May 19, 1862, was published in pamphlet under the title, the *Irreligious Character of the Rebellion.* Even when not in the center of the picture, the Parson was made to do service for patriotism and profit. This method of exploitation was used by resourceful Allen M. Scott, who wrote in 1863 his *Chronicles of the Great Rebellion,* in which using the Biblical style of language, he devoted two chapters to Brownlow.[17]

When it seemed that the Parson had been sufficiently portrayed in book and pamphlet, and his speeches in the North properly circulated, enterprising newspaper editors afforded their readers amusement or made them more patriotic by reproducing some of the literary gems formed and polished by the Parson while he was yet in East Tennessee. Making such industrious use of him, the *Boston Evening Transcript* published his undelivered gallows speech;[18] and the *Boston Morning Journal* reproduced his famous answer to Jordan Clark, informing him when he expected to join the Democratic Party.[19] The exploitation of the Parson was not complete, however, until he should be taken in hand by Erastus Beadle and made the hero in one of his dime novels, which were now beginning to be read so widely by soldiers and civilians alike. And, so, there appeared *Parson Brownlow and the Unionists of East Tennessee,* published in New York, 1862.[20]

The North had shown its high regard for Brownlow in many ways, but it remained for Lee & Walker, 722 Chestnut Street, Philadelphia to set him to music and publish, on January 12, 1863, the "Parson Brownlow Quick Step." No other form of music, of course, could so appropriately express the excitable Parson. His picture adorned the centre of the sheet.[21]

There were many people who were his admirers but who had never had the opportunity to see him or to behold his likeness on

---

[17] Published in Cincinnati, by C. F. Vent & Co.

[18] May 28, 1862. See pp. 192-95.

[19] May 21, 28, 1862. See pp. 127-28.

[20] For the significance of the Beadle dime novels, see A. C. Cole, *The Irrepressible Conflict, 1850-1865,* p. 224.

[21] A copy of this piece of music is in the Library of Congress. During the progress of the Civil War the dedication of music to the principal heroes became a widespread custom.

the "Quick Step." They must be served and at the same time a few honest and patriotic pennies turned by the resourceful photographers, who heralded his approach by advertising fine likenesses of him which they held for sale. The Parson would also make a remarkable addition to the numerous picture albums which patriotic citizens kept and filled with the nation's heroes. His first visit to New York City in May, 1862, led one photographer to announce that "GLORIOUS PARSON BROWNLOW" was for sale and that "Twenty-five cents in stamps will bring the Parson by return mail." Another photographer advertised

"PARSON BROWNLOW
a
CARTE DE VISTE
IN
SIX ATTITUDES
Ready this day."[22]

As he proceeded over the North he set the photographers into a whirl of activity and gave them one of their greatest opportunities to exploit a patriotic figure. Philadelphia offered the Parson on a card for twenty-five cents, and in a steel engraving for only ten cents.[23] The energetic Boston photographers secured a supply of photographs of the Parson and had them on hand before his arrival.[24]

But things were never done quite as well in other parts of the country as in Boston; so, it remained for those artists who captured the Parson after his arrival to offer the best likenesses. This notice was posted, "The very best photograph of this Apostle of Freedom was yesterday taken by Black." It could be had either in wholesale lots or by retail. One, assuming to be an authority on Brownlow's appearance, declared, "There have been many pictures of him made, but none equal to this work of our Boston artist." As Brownlow progressed over the country many other pictures of him were made.[25]

[22] *New York Times,* May 15, 1862.
[23] Philadelphia *Daily Evening Bulletin,* April 18, 1862.
[24] *Boston Evening Transcript,* May 21, 1862.
[25] *Boston Morning Journal,* May 24, 1862.

Among many people in the North the name of Brownlow became as well known and more favorably than that of Lincoln. In the name of patriotism he exploited the North, and the Northern war-makers exploited him equally as much. In addition to these two principals who profited, was a third party as has appeared, made up of those enterprising and resourceful business men who were not so fortunate as to be manufacturers of war materials but who nevertheless produced things which the spirit of war made the people buy. This third class printed books and pamphlets about the Parson, put his likeness upon paper, and set him to music; and after they had fully exploited him they began upon his flag-defending daughter. There came out of Philadelphia a brochure by Major W. D. Reynolds, "late acting adjutant of the Western Army," entitled *Miss Martha Brownlow; or the Heroine of Tennessee. A Truthful and Graphic Account of the Many Perils and Privations endured by Miss Martha Brownlow, the Lovely and Accomplished Daughter of the Celebrated Parson Brownlow, during her Residence with her Father in Knoxville.* It was "beautifully illustrated" with the vigorous heroine on the front cover and at the end of the text. It contained, in addition, two drawings of fights with the Rebels by Union people and a third, whose artist might well have been recently whetting his imagination on Dante's Inferno. He represented a terrible monster with a face half hidden by a cloak thrown around its shoulders, concealing a dagger in the left hand and brandishing a flaming torch in the right, accompanied by a drove of venemous snakes, and trampling upon the Constitution. In the background was a flaming city. The whole was the spirit of the Confederacy. The Parson's daughter defended the flag in Knoxville for a page or two, but soon the story got far beyond. Brownlow came to the front and was jumbled into scenes, bringing in the slaying of Zollicoffer at Mill Springs and the fall of Fort Donelson. He hid out again in the Great Smokies and finally reappeared in Knoxville, with his reunited family. The author freed a few Negro slaves and made of them heroes slightly less in magnitude than the Parson himself. They spoke the purest English on proper occasions, but now and then, the writer, nodding, allowed them to drift into "nigger talk." Though declared to be "truthful," many elements in the account were highly imaginative, and the whole assumed a level of intelligence among Northerners far lower than must have been the fact.

Such books were highly entertaining, but everybody in America could not read English—some people could read only German. They must be told in their own language the exciting experiences of the Parson's daughter. So the enterprising Philadelphia firm of Barclay and Company published in 1863, *Miss Maude Brownlow oder Die Helden von Tennessee*. It mattered not that Reynold's Martha Brownlow now became Maude, for her real name was Susan, and most of her exploits were fictitious.

Before the end of 1862, Brownlow was ready to return to East Tennessee. He had made a triumphal procession through the North, and receiving for many of his lectures an average of $1,000 each, he had accumulated enough money completely to reëstablish in Knoxville himself, his family, and his newspaper. He had also collected enough proverbial rope for hanging all his enemies. Why tarry when the harvest was ripe for its reaper? The answer must be given by the Federal army and the National Government, and Brownlow often impatiently pressed for action. He wanted the army to start immediately; he would accompany it and point out those rebels who should receive attention. "We will shoot them down like dogs," he declared, "and hang them on every limb we come to."[26] He pleaded, "Let an army—'a terrible army, with banners'—go at once into East Tennessee, and back up the loyal citizens, while the latter shoot and hang their persecutors wherever they can find them. I want the army to serve for me as a forerunner,—a sort of John the Baptist in the wilderness,—so that I may go back with a new press, type, and paper, and resurrect my Union journal, and tell one hundred thousand subscribers, weekly, what is going on upon the borders of civilization."[27] The Confederates had

<hr />

[26] *Suffering of Union Men*, p. 19.
[27] *Parson Brownlow's Book*, p. 454. Letter to the *Philadelphia Press*, May 3, 1862.

been doing all the hanging; now he would like to do some.[28] If the Federal Government should never do anything else, "it ought at least, and at any cost of money and blood," to rescue East Tennessee.[29]

While waiting for his country to act, Brownlow had been continuing his speechmaking in the North through 1862, but by the beginning of 1863 he had determined to come closer to the center of operations. Shunning Kentucky on account of her lack of enthusiasm for her armies of occupation, Brownlow left his family north of the Ohio and ventured down into the domains of his former bitter enemy, Governor Andrew Johnson. On February 22 (1863), he spoke to the soldiers, in the capitol at Nashville, on the virtues of George Washington.[30] When jobs with the government were so plentiful, especially for those with the proper influence, it seemed almost preposterous that Brownlow should be left out. Perhaps, he had been too critical of the government to expect to be favored like Andrew Johnson, or perhaps, at this time, he had no great ambition for political or financial preferment. So it came about that he became only a United States Treasury agent with headquarters at Nashville. It was his duty to permit or prohibit the ordinary trading and commercial activities of all classes of people, powerful or insignificant, and especially to keep close watch on all cotton which should come into the possession of the Federal army, to guard it from the cupidity of speculators, whether private or officer or civilian.[31]

As has previously appeared, it was not the fault of Lincoln or of McClellan that the Federal armies had not marched into East Tennessee. The President held this movement as one of the most important that could be made and the occupation of East Tennessee "nearly as important as the capture of Rich-

---

[28] *Portrait and Biography,* p. 47.

[29] *Parson Brownlow's Book,* pp. 216-17.

[30] "Major Connolly's Letters to his Wife, 1862-1865," *Transactions of the Illinois State Historical Society for the Year 1928,* p. 235. During October he had engaged in a speech-making trip through Michigan and had run across the "venerable Gen. Cass." Brownlow's *Knoxville Whig and Rebel Ventilator,* June 1, 1864.

[31] *Official Records,* ser. I, vol. XXIII, pt. 2, p. 524.

mond."[32] When Buell had in the spring of 1862 moved on Nashville instead of Knoxville, Lincoln set about some other scheme for getting what he wanted; but it should have left no hope with intelligent people that there could be success when the marplot John C. Frémont, lately removed from Missouri, was intrusted with the task. Taking command of the "Mountain Department," which extended as far south as Knoxville, Frémont planned to find a path through the Southern Highlands to East Tennessee, but the sudden incursion of Stonewall Jackson into the Shenandoah Valley in May, 1862, so completely disrupted Frémont's plans to take possession of the East Tennessee portion of his Department that he never made the attempt.[33] Brownlow had vivid expectations of accompanying Frémont to Knoxville. He declared to a Chicago audience, "I want a big war-horse and military suite, and the General and myself will ride down among those rebels, and, if you will excuse my apparent egotism, I do believe the scoundrels had rather see the Devil coming after them."[34]

The Parson was doomed to disappointment. He declared that if he were the governor of Tennessee like Andrew Johnson he would resign "on the ground of not being backed up by the government." He was completely out of patience.[35] It seemed preposterous to him that the loyal part of Tennessee should remain in the hands of the Confederates, while only the disloyal part should constitute the Tennessee over which Andrew Johnson should rule. It was pleasant enough to hold under domination the Rebels, but it was entirely distasteful to allow the Rebels to dominate the Unionists.

After the fall of Nashville the armies of Grant and Buell, instead of directing their attention to East Tennessee, marched southward into Mississippi and began preparations for clearing the Mississippi River of every Confederate obstruction. Mem-

---

[32] J. G. Nicolay and John Hay, eds., *Complete Works of Abraham Lincoln*, VII, 247, E. M. Stanton to Halleck, June 30, 1862.

[33] R. U. Johnson and C. C. Buel, eds., *Battles and Leaders of the Civil War*, II, 278.

[34] *Portrait and Biography*, p. 71.

[35] C. R. Hall, *Andrew Johnson, Military Governor of Tennessee*, p. 58.

phis fell in June and West Tennessee was soon overrun. Then the Confederates made a great rebound northward into Kentucky, which might have carried them far had a wiser commander than Braxton Bragg been the leader. In October (1862) they retreated back into Tennessee after the battle of Perryville, and now at last Lincoln felt sure Buell would pursue Bragg and go to the rescue of East Tennessee. Instead, Buell went back to Nashville, seemingly his first love; and so after having begged Buell for two years to seize East Tennessee, Lincoln now removed him from command and put Rosecrans in his place, with the order to seize and hold East Tennessee. Union generals seemed to shun East Tennessee as they would a plague—Rosecrans stayed in Nashville for weeks before marching eastward to Murfreesboro there to fight at Stone's River a battle during the last days of 1862 and the first two of 1863. Now the capture of Vicksburg became the chief concern in the West for the first part of 1863, and not until after its fall in early July, was East Tennessee made a major objective.

In the summer, plans were put into play for the final conquest of this long-sought region. Rosecrans was ordered to march southeastward to drive Bragg out of Chattanooga, while Burnside was to lead an army from Lexington, Kentucky, across the Cumberland Mountains to Knoxville. Rosecrans flanked Bragg out of Chattanooga, and in the last days of August Burnside's entry into East Tennessee led Simon B. Buckner to evacuate Knoxville. During the first days of September the Federals marched in, more than two years after Brownlow, Johnson, and the other East Tennessee Unionists had begun their frantic calls for help. Now that this region was in the hands of the Federals, Lincoln determined that they must hold it, for if they did, the "rebellion must dwindle and die."[36]

The importance of East Tennessee was vividly brought home to the Confederates when after Lee's retreat into Virginia, following the battle of Gettysburg, he ordered Longstreet with about 11,000 men to go to the support of Bragg. With Knoxville now in the hands of the Federals, the direct railway connections were

---

[36] Nicolay and Hay, *op. cit.*, IX, 129, 154.

broken; as a result, Longstreet entrained his troops by way of Petersburg, Wilmington, Augusta, Atlanta, and northward to Ringgold, Georgia, requiring ten days to make the trip. In the meantime the hard-fought battle of Chickamauga had taken place, and the Federals were now bottled up in Chattanooga. Arriving on September 25, Longstreet marched northeastward through East Tennessee and laid siege to Knoxville. After delaying an attack that might have succeeded, he remained around the city until December 3 when he retreated northeastward to the region between Russellville and Greeneville, there to spend the winter. He lived off a country already famished. His foraging parties were often attacked by the bushwhacking Unionists, who developed the habit of taking no prisoners, so bitter had they become in their privations.[37] In the spring he rejoined Lee in Virginia and East Tennessee was freed from any further major molestations by the Confederates.

After Longstreet's retreat from Knoxville in December, Lincoln on the 7th issued a proclamation of thanksgiving for the deliverance, and called upon all loyal people everywhere to assemble in their churches and thank God "for this great advancement of the national cause."[38] East Tennessee had rested heavily on Lincoln's heart, and it was with genuine joy that he saw it back in the hands of the Federals. Since the beginning of the war its recovery had been a question of sentiment, politics, and military strategy inextricably bound up.

Brownlow was vastly pleased with the recovery of his old home. He had been much in evidence in the preparations by Burnside for the march and in supporting it later with fresh reënforcements. While Knoxville was under siege by Longstreet, Brownlow declared, whether Burnside should hold the city or not he was "a glorious moral and military hero, and deserves everlasting honors."[39] He had done more than any other Union general could be induced to attempt. The old idea of the military railroad from Lexington to Knoxville arose again, and

---

[37] Johnson and Buel, *op. cit.*, III, 745-51.

[38] Nicolay and Hay, *op. cit.*, IX, 217-18; A. B. Lapsley, ed., *Writings of Abraham Lincoln*, VII, 27.

[39] *Official Records,* ser. I. vol. XXX, pt. 4, p. 25; vol. XXXI, pt. 3, p. 277.

Burnside made preparations to construct it. Brownlow informed Lincoln that "all men of sense" agreed to the wisdom of such an undertaking, and asked the President to press it on Congress in his next annual message.[40]

The Parson returned to Knoxville on the heels of Burnside's army and before the end of September he had secured an order from Secretary of War Stanton for enough ambulances for Burnside's army to transport his wife and children and those of Horace Maynard from Cincinnati to Knoxville.[41] He immediately made preparations to set up his newspaper, and carry out the promise he had been making all over the North. He had held up to his prospective subscribers a paper which would take a hand in all the controversies of the day, which would be independent in everything and neutral in nothing. It would be an

unconditional Union Journal, holding up all participants in the *late* Rebellion—now almost played out—as a choice collection of men for a Rogues' Gallery! At the same time, it will make war upon all the gamblers, the thieves, North and South,—those whose trade it is to rob the public, as well as private pilferers, the whiskey-bloats, the bullies in elections, oppressors who grind the face of the poor, extortioners in trade, who swindle by wholesale and retail, and all foul-mouthed Secession sympathizers and other disturbers of the peace in the various sink-holes of society![42]

To help carry out such a laudable undertaking for the promotion of Unionism, the United States Government and the Federal armies lent their aid. A Federal brigadier ran upon "a new printing-press, type, and some ink" in the little town of Alexandria in Middle Tennessee, and immediately informed General Rosecrans that he would turn them over to Brownlow, unless he were otherwise instructed.[43] The Government gave him $1,500 to aid his paper, together with the use of five army wagons to bring paper and other material from Cincinnati.[44]

---

[40] *Ibid.*, p. 278.   [41] *Ibid.*, vol. XXX, pt. 3, p. 745, September 19.
[42] Prospectus in *Parson Brownlow's Book.*
[43] *Official Records*, ser. I, vol. XXX, pt. 3, p. 26, August 31, 1863.
[44] *Knoxville Whig*, April 14, 1869.

At last there would be a rallying point for Unionism south of the Ohio and the Potomac, and the truth would once more be spread out over the land.

On November 11, 1863, the first issue of the revived *Whig*, phoenix-like, made its appearance from the ashes of its former existence, after a silence of more than two years. It came out under a more extended title, speaking defiance in the addition. It was now Brownlow's *Knoxville Whig and Rebel Ventilator*. The pent-up anger, indignation, and vengeance of two years' standing were now to find their old-time channel of expression. The first issue contained his old valedictory and a new salute to the faithful. The halter awaited the intelligent and crafty leaders and forgiveness, the deluded masses—"With high regards for our friends, a decent respect for honorable enemies, and the lowest contempt for the leaders in the Rebellion, this Journal, with whatever of talents its editor can muster, launches upon the troubled sea of life!" On each page appeared a waving United States flag surmounting a selected stanza of poetry.

The Parson was taut and ready for the fray. Lincoln had been too lenient, he would likely make a soft peace. "The *mediation* we shall advocate, is that of the *cannon* and the *sword;* and our motto is—no armistice on land or sea, until *all* ALL the rebels, both front and rear, in arms, and in ambush are subjugated or exterminated! And then we are for visiting condign punishment upon the leaders in the rebellion, who may survive the struggle, in the unholy crusade against civilization."[45] He was soon digging into the happenings of 1861 to draw out terrible indictments of his dearest enemies. He burdened his paper with scathing attacks against them and with the threat of terrible vengeance that should go out against them. Those aristocrats who had lorded it over East Tennessee for the past forty years should now be driven out. They were a class of people "whose consciousness of superiority has been sticking out, whenever a family has owned from three to ten kinky-headed Negroes. This was an aristocracy founded alone upon the nigger, and so far

---

[45] *Knoxville Whig and Rebel Ventilator,* November 11, 1863.

has it carried its insolence for years" that its members spoke to mechanics only with an air of great condescension.[46]

Brownlow saw many things to dislike and conditions to reform. Though gallant among the Northern ladies, he thoroughly detested the "female rebels," and frequently cried out against them. As time went on they seemed to become more incorrigible. "Female rebels," he declared, "old and young, married or single, widows or orphans, ought to be required to behave themselves, and failing to do so, they ought to be sent beyond our lines where their disloyalty and bad behavior will be appreciated. And those who complain of their bad treatment in sending them out, ought to be sent after them."[47] "Ill-bred soldiers and insolent negroes" riding up and down the sidewalks of Knoxville should desist. He wondered whether such maneuvers were born of military strategy or necessity.[48] Knoxville had suffered much in its manners under Confederate control.

Brownlow had seen much violence, personal and national, and it seemed to have unbalanced his better judgment. He not only used violent language but he counselled personal and private violence on the part of the people in preserving their rights and punishing their enemies. Perhaps he did not see that there was a difference between violence organized and stamped with the governmental approval and violence unorganized and willed by individuals. East Tennessee, though held in its principal strongholds by the Federal troops, was in the country districts subjected to the raiding parties of both armies, and the boundary lines between organized troops and guerillas were not always clearly drawn. In a conflict with a group of seventeen men, whom the Parson denominated guerillas, a Union man had been killed. This deed aroused in him a burning vengeance on the seventeen. He published in his paper the names of all he could discover, to serve as their decree of banishment or death: "We tell the world that such men can't live in East Tennessee. They *must* die if they ever return to this country. Let Union men kill them like dogs if they ever meet with them. We have procured all

---

[46] *Ibid.,* February 20, 1864.
[47] *Ibid.,* November 2.   [48] *Ibid.,* January 30.

the names but four, and record them that Union men and soldiers may shoot them down wherever they find them."[49]

It pleased Brownlow much when he learned that General A. C.
Gillem in a somewhat questionable manner had seen to it that
John Morgan had not been taken prisoner in the fatal brush
at Greeneville, Tennessee. He praised Gillem "for the timely and
religious act for terminating the life, robberies and wholesale
thefts of *John H. Morgan,* the most renowned land pirate of the
nineteenth century."[50]

The disorganizing effects of warfare in East Tennessee were
keenly felt in the realm of private property. Each government
in the day of its power had seized the property of its enemies,
but with the passing of time the process of restoration entered
the slowly emerging courts. Brownlow favored a hard and even
course against the Rebels here. He believed that the Federal
court at Knoxville was entirely too light in its dealings with the
Rebels, in both property and personal rights. He called it "a
complete farce."[51] The magical and powerful title of "A Union
man" the Parson would not lightly bestow on former Rebels, unrepentant and unashamed. "A Union man" was fine metal that
had passed through the fiery furnace. He warned Governor
Johnson against making it possible for so-called Union men to
establish claims for damages done by marching armies or over-
zealous patriots.[52] He also believed that the slaveholding Unionists should not receive pay nor expect it for any of their slaves
which the government found it necessary to use. Other Unionists had suffered losses; let the slaveholders do likewise.[53]

It was an outrage that Rebels should be suing Union men to
recover their property. The courts might aid the Rebels and
restore it, but the Union man still had one last resort. He might
slay the Rebel as a discharged soldier had recently done, and
the Parson would applaud. The courts might do whatever they
pleased, "but injured, insulted and oppressed Union men will

---

[49] *Ibid.,* April 30, 1864.
[50] *Ibid.,* September 21.
[51] Hall, *op. cit.,* p. 135.
[52] Andrew Johnson Papers, Brownlow to Johnson, January 28, 1865.
[53] *Knoxville Whig and Rebel Ventilator,* April 16, 1864.

redress their own wrongs—and, for the life of us, we are not able to see that they are in error."[54] The Parson was giving dangerous counsel for the peace and repose of East Tennessee.

But all courts were not bad; their wickedness depended on the character of the decisions they handed down. Brownlow, himself, resorted to the courts to settle certain matters which he had not been able to dispose of in his *Knoxville Whig and Rebel Ventilator*. He had roasted over the brimstone pits of hell Sneed, Crozier, and Reynolds, whom he charged with causing his arrest, imprisonment, and banishment; but newspaper abuse was of no monetary value. Therefore, he would sue them for damages, in the courts. In the circuit court for Knox County he brought suit against the demon trio, and within five minutes after the case had gone to the jury, a verdict for $25,000 damages came out. Had he asked for double the amount, he might have got it just as easily, he boasted. Another Unionist who had been outraged to the extent of $25,000 was likewise pacified. In such matters, this was the Parson's article of faith: "Impoverish the villains—take all they have—give their effects to the Union men they have crippled and imprisoned—and let them have their 'Southern Rights.' "[55]

There was one governmental authority in East Tennessee that could not be imposed upon or terrified; Parson Brownlow was still a United States Treasury agent, and until a great amount of red tape should be pulled and time consumed he was judge, jury, and executioner for matters that came within his province in East Tennessee. He was East Tennessee's dictator in its commercial affairs. No one might sell goods, buy goods, or import goods without his consent. This power he exercised through his right to determine who were Union men, and he let it be known that he could easily detect impostors. No Rebel should be allowed to engage in any sort of commercial activities, and taking a prescribed oath did not make a Rebel into a Union man, the Parson held. "They may take all the oaths prescribed by the President, by Congress, by the military, and by Gov. Johnson,"

---

[54] *Ibid.*, February 22, 1865.
[55] *Ibid.*, March 1.

but they would still remain Rebels to the Parson. Besides being the arbiter of trade relations, Brownlow was also the custodian of much Rebel property such as abandoned farms and plantations. These lands he offered to rent out to persons properly qualified.[56]

Brownlow was not only the dictator of the economic welfare of East Tennessee; he was also its journalistic lord. Between these two absorbing duties and his proclivity to be interested in everything that engaged people's attention, he found the days were likely to be made up of insufficient hours. He gave notice of the division of his time: He allotted his mornings before ten o'clock to his newspaper; the rest of the day he devoted to his Treasury duties. He warned the public to respect those hours: "We don't want to be stopped and bored on the streets, and in the mud, on our way to and from our meals, and don't intend to be in the future."[57]

Instead of having her trade and economic recovery stifled by nice considerations of personal hatreds and political proscriptions East Tennessee should have been treated to a broad program of humanitarianism. This region suffered fearfully from both armies. Its horses and mules had been driven off, its cattle and swine slaughtered, its granaries emptied, its crops devastated, and its fences burned. The Federal armies marched into a destitute region, only to use up what substance there was left. This situation was soon on the road to developing into a major disaster. Outside aid must come or starvation would actually begin its ghastly work. In order to call the attention of the country to the dire needs, there was formed the East Tennessee Relief Association, made up of the Unionists of the region. On February 9, 1864, they sent an appeal to Lincoln, which the President on April 28 submitted to Congress. The appeal recounted the destitution that prevailed and suggested again the great desirability of building the railroad from Lexington to Knoxville. In sending the document on to Congress Lincoln expressed his deep commiseration for "these most loyal and

---

[56] *Ibid.,* February 20, 27, April 23, 1864.
[57] *Ibid.,* April 23.

suffering people," and recommended again to Congress the construction of the railroad.[58]

Brownlow was a member of the Relief Association and one of the signers of the appeal to the President. His sympathy for the starving was excelled only by his bitterness against the Rebels, for according to his reasoning they were responsible for the situation. He declared that only the Union destitute should be fed "and none others"—and he would say so "unhesitatingly." He termed as "barbaric" the plan advocated by some of the military experts to evacuate the civilian population. He declared that the East Tennessee Unionists "understood the government of their choice was sending an army here to *protect* them, and not to *banish* them cruelly from the land of their nativity, and the graves of their relatives. We will fight this unjust, cruel and inhuman order to the last, no matter by whom made or defended."[59]

The call went out to the North for aid, but wiser heads than the Parson saw to it that humanitarian considerations were somewhat broadened. No Rebels of fighting age should be fed with the proceeds, but if anything should be left after the Union element had been taken care of, the old men and women and the young children of Rebel taint should share it.[60] The generosity of the North for the destitute quickly expressed itself. Cities such as Philadelphia, New York, and Buffalo raised over $100,000, and widespread contributions throughout the North brought to East Tennessee sufferers more than $252,000. Northern relief organizations made appropriations from their funds or set about raising a specific East Tennessee donation. The Sanitary Commission gave many articles of comfort, the Pennsylvania Relief Society busied itself, and Edward Everett aided the cause with his oratory.[61]

East Tennessee was made to assume the position in national

[58] *Report to the Contributors to the Pennsylvania Relief Association for East Tennessee*, pp. 29-38; Nicolay and Hay, *op. cit.*, X, 86, 87; Richardson, *op. cit.*, VI, 204.

[59] *Knoxville Whig and Rebel Ventilator*, April 16, 1864.

[60] *Report to the Contributors to the Pennsylvania Relief Association for East Tennessee*, pp. 11-12.

[61] *Ibid.*, p. 25; Humes, *op. cit.*, pp. 316-33.

sentiment which Belgium was later to occupy in the Great World War. It had its atrocities to be believed and its destitute to be fed, and it became the subject as well as object of much promotion writing. J. R. Gilmore, assuming the name of Edmund Kirke, wrote his *Down in Tennessee and Back by Way of Richmond*, and had it published in 1864. He described the pathetic plight of a suffering people against whose sorrows the government had closed its eyes and ears, and predicted that this story would "be read of and wondered at, when this generation has passed away."[62] In 1863, J. T. Trowbridge wrote his *Cudjo's Cave* to direct the attention of the country to the sufferings of the East Tennesseeans. This book sold in immense numbers, touching the hearts of the North for Southern Unionists in much the same way that Harriet Beecher Stowe's *Uncle Tom's Cabin* had appealed to them concerning the slaves. In the estimation of a poet too modest to sign his name, East Tennessee was worthy of an epic poem if not two, so he wrote *Secession or Prose in Rhyme and East Tennessee A Poem by an East Tennesseean*. In these two poems he told of the crimes of the barbarous Rebels and the coming of the rescuers. This book was published in 1864.

As tenacious a form of Unionism as existed in the whole country was to be found in East Tennessee; yet this region was not an equal partner in the object of its devotion. It was neither a state nor part of a functioning state—fully neither in the Confederacy nor in the United States. On the attack of Fort Donelson on February 15, 1862, the Tennessee Government fled to Memphis where the legislature convened on the 20th. Exactly a month later it adjourned *sine die*, and never again did a Confederate legislature meet in the state. With the overrunning of middle and western Tennessee, civil government went out of existence and Governor Harris joined the Confederate army. On February 22, Grant had declared civil government suspended and martial law in effect. On March 3, Lincoln appointed Andrew Johnson military governor of Tennessee, and on March 12 he assumed his duties in Nashville.

---

[62] P. 105.

It was no easy task to distill out of the alarms of war a civil government, yet during 1862 Johnson busied himself with trying to set up civil rule in local affairs. The spectacular raids of Nathan Bedford Forrest and John Morgan and the great sweep of Bragg's army made Governor Johnson's efforts futile. But the Governor was not alone in his attempt to restore civil government; the Confederates had not yet abandoned the state. In June, 1863, they held a convention at Winchester, near the Alabama border, and nominated a governor and candidates for the Confederate Congress. The elections were held in the following August, and a governor, Robert L. Caruthers, and congressmen were chosen. The congressmen took their seats in Richmond, but Caruthers was never inaugurated.

On the first day of July (1863) the Unionists held a convention for the purpose of deciding on what step to take next. East Tennessee was still under Confederate control and Brownlow was still an exile, but he and other East Tennesseeans attended. Brownlow was made a member of the important committee on Federal Relations. It was distinctly to the advantage of the East Tennesseeans to delay all important steps until their section were freed from the Confederates, otherwise they would play little part in a government which they considered to be peculiarly their own. Furthermore, they had in the person of Governor Johnson the chief position as long as the military régime prevailed. But Lincoln would hurry the process and make Tennessee function again as a state as soon as possible. In September, after the fall of Knoxville and Chattanooga, he instructed Johnson to prepare the state for civil government, and on December 8 he issued his first amnesty proclamation and plan for reconstruction.

Tennessee now had the plan; the President had laid down the conditions the National Government would require. The next month Governor Johnson ordered local elections for March in those regions under Federal control, and established qualifications for voting more stringent than those Lincoln had required. The attempt ended in failure, since too many people either refused to vote or found themselves unable. East Tennesseeans, who considered themselves the only unterrified and uncorrupted part of the state and the only "truly loyal," now decided to succeed to their heritage. They recalled the old Greeneville Convention, which had adjourned in 1861 with the right to reassemble, to consider the situation. It met in Knoxville on April 12, 1864, and was soon torn with dissensions as to whether it would seek to secure civil control of all Tennessee or confine itself to demanding statehood for East Tennessee. After four days of confusion it adjourned to ward off a worse fate. It recommended Lincoln for president and came out for its own Andrew Johnson for vice president, and placed East Tennessee in an advantageous position for any eventuality in civil developments by appointing a state central committee.

East Tennessee's past devotion to the Union would be a sacrifice almost worthwhile if it could now seat its favorite son in the vice presidency.The National Union (Republican) Convention was held in Baltimore in June, and among the delegates present was the inevitable Parson Brownlow. The perplexing question of the admission of delegates from Tennessee immediately arose, for the status of Tennessee as partner in the Union was an issue with which legal minds had been tussling considerably. Was Tennessee a state? If not, what was it? While the question was uppermost, Brownlow was spied in the Convention. A clamor went up for a speech, a voice which he always heeded. As he made his way to the platform "he was greeted with deafening applause. The Convention and audience rose to their feet, and amid the waving of hats and handkerchiefs, the gallant old loyalist of East Tennessee" mounted the rostrum. He declared that he was sick, very sick, and could not make a speech. Yet he would say that the Tennessee delegation must be seated. Down in Tennessee the people did not recognize secession; this Convention must not. He remarked that Tennessee might have a candidate to propose for the vice presidency. The delegates were seated with full rights; Andrew Johnson was nominated for Lincoln's running mate; and Tennessee was thereby through inference recognized as a state, for vice presidents must be residents of states.[63]

If Tennessee was a state it should vote in the coming presidential election. This duty emphasized the fact that all Tennesseeans competent to take part in elections did not agree on political matters. Many people in middle and western Tennessee who had either been amnestied or had never departed from the faith, were not anxious to come under the domination of the radical East Tennesseeans. They were conservatively constructed and were inclined to think that there were other men who would make a better president than Lincoln had been or gave promise of being. The trouble broke out in a convention called by the East Tennessee Central Committee to meet in Nashville on September 5. The East Tennesseeans and their radical allies seized control of the convention and named Lincoln and Johnson men for the electors. The Conservatives later put out a McClellan and Pendleton ticket, representing the Democratic Party, but so restricting and stringent were the voting qualifications made by Johnson that the McClellan ticket withdrew. The Lincoln and Johnson electors received a straggling vote. Congress refused to count the Tennessee returns, presumably because the group did not want to consider Tennessee a state, and yet she nevertheless elected a candidate from Tennessee. If Tennessee was not a state then Andrew Johnson was not vice president.

Now that Johnson would be inaugurated on the following March 4, East Tennessee must be prepared to maintain her dominant position in Tennessee. The East Tennessee Central Committee, therefore, called a convention to meet in Nashville in December, but General Hood's operations prevented its assembling until January 9, 1865. Its control by the East Tennesseeans was cleverly provided for by allowing every county one vote and one additional vote for every 150 Union votes cast in the secession election of June, 1861. Thus East Tennessee Unionism was finally rewarded and its adherents placed in a position of dominance. This convention became the all-powerful

[63] *New York Times,* June 8, 9, 1864; Milton, *op. cit.,* pp. 52-53, 122.

dictator of Tennessee's civil restoration, as far as state power could be exerted. It provided for amending the constitution in various particulars, including freeing the slaves; it repealed the secession ordinance, dissolved the military league with the Confederacy, repudiated the Confederate debts, and declared all acts of the secession government null and void.

Before adjourning it provided for two elections, one to be held on Washington's birthday for the purpose of ratifying the constitutional amendments, the other to be held on the Lincoln and Johnson inauguration day for the election of a governor and legislature. This body not only acted as constitutional convention and legislature, it also served as a political convention—it nominated Parson Brownlow for governor, and selected the legislative ticket. The Parson was the logical choice for the convention to make, for he had been in the midst of the East Tennessee leadership which had now got control of the whole state. He had served continuously on the Central Committee which had brought about East Tennessee's present good fortune. He was the most prominent East Tennesseean outside the vice presidency—Johnson had received his reward, Brownlow must have his.

In the February 22 election the constitutional amendments were adopted by a vote of 26,865 to 67, and on March 4 Brownlow was elected by a vote of 23,352 to 35. According to Lincoln's plan, if the number of voters in the election for restoration should be as large as one-tenth of the votes cast in the presidential election of 1860, the state should be considered validly in the Union again. In each election Tennessee had met the test.[64]

---

[64] For the main facts concerning Tennessee's political history during the Civil War, see J. W. Patton, *Unionism and Reconstruction in Tennessee, 1860-1869*, pp. 26-50; Fertig, *op cit.*, pp. 34-60; Temple, *op. cit., passim; The South in the Building of the Nation*, II, 517-22.

CHAPTER XII

A NEW GOVERNOR SEEKS VENGEANCE

To THE TITLES "Parson" and "Editor," Brownlow now added "Governor," but whether he was preaching, writing, or ruling he was still the Parson. His election was, of course, a grim wartime act, secured in the same manner as battles are won. In time of war the laws are silent, a comment as true in Tennessee as in ancient Rome. The thirty-seven who voted against him were either jolly humorists or the forlorn but unterrified rear guard of the routed Rebels. Now as later the right to vote was based upon support of Brownlow. Abraham Lincoln, Andrew Johnson, and the East Tennessee Unionists wanted Brownlow; that was enough.[1]

It was a strange and dangerous act to set a person of Brownlow's record to rule over a million people. In peaceful times it would have been perilous; in the confusion incident to the closing of a civil war, it might well seem preposterous. Unless the wild threats of his terrible vengeance upon the majority of his fellow-citizens, made constantly for the previous five years, were merely deep acting upon a broad stage, Tennessee might look forward to conditions worse than war. For the promoting of the orderly progress of peace, it would have been impossible to make a worse choice; for carrying out a war of vengeance of a minority against a majority, Brownlow was incomparably the best selection that could have been made throughout the land. As a master in whipping up hate and revenge, he had no peer.

It therefore became Brownlow's program from the beginning to use his power as dictator of Tennessee to punish those against

---

[1] Moore, *op. cit.,* I, 526; Edward McPherson, *The Political History of the United States of America during the Period of Reconstruction* (Referred to hereafter as *History of Reconstruction*), p. 27.

whom he had a grudge, public or private, and to introduce to Tennessee that new variety of democracy which made it possible for a small minority to dominate completely the civil and political existence of the vast majority. His program was broadly political, and he succeeded in carrying it out. In politics he had grown strong and efficient; in the other and more important fields of human development he had little vision and no ability. He found Tennessee financially bankrupt and he proceeded to whip her down into far deeper distress; he found her an economic desolation and he left her as he had found her; he found social chaos among Unionists and Rebels and he added to the turmoil by setting the Negro upon the back of his former master; in the church organizations he found Christ left out and he locked the door against His return. The Parson had throughout his past life promised such a program; no one should have been surprised. He was chosen for a purpose; he efficiently carried it out; by this standard he was a success.

Brownlow was elected governor on March 4; on the same day Andrew Johnson ceased to be military governor of Tennessee and became vice president of the United States. A month later the Parson was inaugurated. During the interregnum the governor-elect was in theory the military governor also, but as there were no duties that engaged his time, he set about divesting himself of obligations which he could not well perform while governor. He resigned his Treasury agency in favor of his son John B. Brownlow, who continued it until the end of the year, when it went out of existence—the office having handled from start to finish over $100,000 of business.[2] He also gave over the active management of his old friend the *Knoxville Whig and Rebel Ventilator* to his son, John, with the announcement that the latter would likely make "rather a sophomoric display" of himself, but he hoped that the public would bear with the new editor for he would learn fast. The son disappointed no one, for he so completely adopted the style of the father and carried on the campaign against the enemy so successfully that it was regarded safe to remove on February 21,

---

[2] *Knoxville Whig and Rebel Ventilator*, January 10, 1866.

1866 the *Rebel Ventilator* from the title of the *Whig*. But there was still much work to be done, and vigilance was ever the watchword, for there were about forty newspapers in the state at this time and only seven were counted unconditionally loyal. The Parson did not completely give up writing for the *Whig*, and many things the son wrote were as much the father's as if he had written them.[3]

Now that Brownlow was to become governor there were some so hopeful as to believe that the leopard could change his spots or the Ethiopian his color. The *New York Times*, more dubious than hopeful, advised him to "make some attempt to infuse a little moderation into his language and demeanor," to smother his feelings of revenge, and to try to forget his war memories.[4]

Early in April the Parson left the invigorating and patriotic atmosphere of East Tennessee and journeyed to Nashville to be inaugurated governor of all Tennesseans in theory, but of the East Tennessee Unionists in fact. In preparing for his coming, the capitol was given a scrubbing and the American flag was draped about everything which would support one. The day broke in rare splendor upon an immense crowd either in Nashville or on its way thither. Soon cannon were booming forth and bands of music were blaring out. The Parson had come to take charge of the government; let the people rejoice! Amongst a great war display and amidst three major-generals and five brigadier-generals with their staffs in full uniform, the new governor was invested with power.[5]

On the sixth he delivered his message to the legislature, a requirement of the governor which the Parson as time went on made more and more into a strange mixture of a sermon, a political harangue, and a *Whig* editorial. He was weighed down by no sense of traditional dignity in such documents. He immediately launched an attack against the evils and evil-doers of the

---

[3] *Ibid.*, March 29, 1865, April 4, September 26, 1866. A partnership was soon formed among the Parson, his son John, and T. Haws, which lasted until February 5, 1867, when John withdrew, but continued to act as editor. *Ibid.*, February 20, 1867.

[4] March 22, 1865.

[5] *Knoxville Whig and Rebel Ventilator*, April 12, 1865.

times. He declared that secession was "an abomination that I cannot too strongly condemn, and one that you cannot legislate against with too much severity." The Rebels were terrible monsters and their robberies and disorders were upsetting the state. He submitted the Thirteenth Amendment for ratification, though he still disliked Negroes, free or in bondage. He hoped none would come to Tennessee and those already there could be colonized. In order to add the earmarks of a message to his talk he discussed finances, the penitentiary, the insane asylum, and the railroads. An important financial move he recommended was an increase in the salaries of the state officials.[6]

He not only prepared his regular message for the beginning of each session of the legislature, but he also wrote many special messages as each session wore on. In addition he issued proclamations in great abundance, for in that manner could the governor speak to the people, argue with them, browbeat them, do all the talking and have the last word. On account of this proclivity he won the nickname of "Old Proc," and his enemies declared that he issued many proclamations for no other reason than to impress upon the people the fact that he was governor. With no desire to violate the law, but because there was none other like him, Brownlow now and then, and especially after he fell out with his secretary of state, would issue proclamations by merely inserting them in the *Whig*, without the signature or seal of the secretary. This certifier of the authenticity of state documents would on occasion see in the *Whig* a proclamation for the first time.[7]

Brownlow found no governor's mansion to receive him when he arrived in Nashville, a deficiency which he hoped to remedy later when in a message to the legislature he recommended the construction of such a building. Throughout his tenure of office

---

[6] For the text of the message, see *Senate Journal of the First Session of the General Assembly of the State of Tennessee, 1865* and *Acts of the State of Tennessee Passed at the Second Session of the Thirty-fourth General Assembly for the Year, 1865-66.*

[7] *Knoxville Whig,* October 30, 1867; "Digest of Election Cases. Cases of Contested Election in the House of Representatives from 1865 to 1871," *House Misc. Docs.,* no. 152, 41st Cong., 2nd sess., p. 908.

he was forced to live in a room fixed up in the state capitol or in some boarding house out in the city. Depending most of the time on the boarding house, he would drive with a friend to the capitol every morning with horse and buggy and arrive strictly by nine o'clock. Being conscientious as to the time requirements of the office, he remained at the capitol during the day and left not before five o'clock in the afternoon.[8]

The Confederate evacuation of Nashville early in the war and the occupation of the capitol by Federal soldiers and generals had not left the archives of the state in perfect order or completeness. Those carried away by the Confederate government were captured at the end of the war near Augusta, Georgia, "three miles from Buzzard Roost station, near Gum Swamp." The state records were packed into 41 boxes and the state's money, made up to a great extent of Mexican gold, was heaped into 56 boxes and two casks. These spoils were returned to Nashville soon after Brownlow's government had been set up. To do honor to the occasion the Parson and his secretary of state, A. J. Fletcher, went to the railway station, and loaded this precious cargo upon six army transport wagons. The Parson mounted the foremost wagon in the caravan, and seating himself on a box of archives with a gold-headed walking cane in his hand and his feet resting upon a box of treasure, he drove through the streets of Nashville amidst the cheering throngs of people up the high hill to the capitol. It was freely predicted that Tennessee would soon go on a gold basis and beat all the other states and even the nation in this respect.[9]

Acting upon an obscure and ambiguous amendment made to the constitution by the convention in January, 1865, Brownlow proceeded to appoint a great many people to office, for the state was being remade *de novo* now, as only the governor and legislature had been elected in March. It was of vast importance to him and his party that the various judges be sympathetic; he secured that sympathy by appointing only those who had it.

---

[8] *Knoxville Whig,* February 20, October 9, 1867. Message to Legislature, October 7, 1867.

[9] *Knoxville Whig and Rebel Ventilator,* June 7, 1865.

Though elections were permitted occasionally, still by the end of 1867 the vast majority of state judges from the highest to the lowest were Brownlow's appointees.[10] He acted upon two restrictive principles in making his appointments: He would honor the too common practice of nepotism, and he would see that East Tennessee should rule supreme. He appointed his son James P. Brownlow, and later his nephew, Sam Hunt, adjutant-general and made liberal provision for many others of his kin-folk, who were not tainted with rebelism. As one of his sons-in-law had been a Confederate captain and a brother-in-law had cast his lot with the Confederacy, he found opportunity to apply this latter principle.[11] Aided by a legislature dominated by East Tennessee, Brownlow either appointed or secured through legislative action the appointment of a great many East Tennesseeans to the various offices. So generous were the legislators that the governor declared, "They literally gave East Tennessee all the offices; and one good-natured fellow said to me that he believed they would give us both Senators if we claimed them."[12]

But Brownlow was not all of the government, though he was the chief power. The legislature had a separate existence, and occasionally some of its members had a separate mind. It had met on April 2, a week before Lee's surrender. It had been nominated by a Brownlow-East Tennessee convention, and elected on a general ticket bearing Brownlow's name for governor, by a species of restrictions which placed most of the voters in East Tennessee. Many of the legislators were inexperienced men who had risen to the top when the depths had been stirred, and it was charged that a large sprinkling of them were "mere birds of passage, camp-followers, and hangers-on of the Federal army." Brownlow objected to this characterization, but the best

---

[10] *Knoxville Whig*, October 9, 1867. For the amendments to the constitution see, F. N. Thorpe, ed., *The Federal and State Constitutions, Colonial Charters, and Other Organic Laws of the States, Territories, and Colonies, now or heretofore forming the United States of America*, VI, 3445-48.

[11] Price, *op. cit.*, III, 359-62; *Knoxville Whig and Rebel Ventilator*, November 29, 1865, October 2, 1867, February 3, 1869 (note by John B. Brownlow on margin of office file).

[12] *Knoxville Whig and Rebel Ventilator*, April 12, 1865.

defense he could make was to say that most of them were natives of Tennessee and of the surrounding states and to promise to investigate their former careers and publish the results. He did so and made out for them even a better record than he had anticipated.[13]

The impressions of one of the imported statesmen, J. J. Noah, "atty Gen. of the 11th judicial District," appear in this letter he wrote to Thaddeus Stevens: "We have a fine working majority in the Legislature and we are busily engaged in making more stringent our laws against traitors. We are endeavoring to hold the state in our power and expect our friends in Congress will do all they can for us. We have a respectable number of Northern men, ex-officers of the army (like myself) who have settled in Tennessee who intend to incorporate as much of Yankee enterprise and loyalty to our Government as we can. The mass of the people do not meet us hospitably or kindly but we intend to stay with them and not be driven out."[14]

The chief concern of this legislature was to entrench in authority a small unterrified and aggrieved minority of Tennesseans and to give them whatever advantage could be had through the government. Therefore, the work of this legislature was largely political; whatever social or economic legislation there was came as an incident to the minority's enjoyment of what the state had to offer. In this program they expected completely to recommend themselves to the national government. They quickly ratified the Thirteenth Amendment, finishing the process by April 7. To guarantee to themselves the government in all future elections they passed a law which disfranchised all Tennesseans who had not been "publicly known to have entertained unconditional Union sentiments from the out-

---

[13] Fertig, *op. cit.*, pp. 62-63; *Knoxville Whig and Rebel Ventilator*, March 29, 1865; *Testimony Taken by the Joint Select Committee to Inquire into the Condition of Affairs in the Late Insurrectionary States*, I (Report of Committee, referred to hereafter by the binder's title, *Ku Klux Conspiracy*), p. 420; *Why the Solid South? or, Reconstruction and its Results* (referred to hereafter by the binder's title, *Noted Men of the Solid South*), p. 178.

[14] Stevens MSS, No. 53337, November 27, 1865. In Harvard University Library.

break of the rebellion until the present time." These were divided into two classes according to the heinousness of the crime they had committed. Those who had been intelligent or cunning enough to secure the position of leadership either in civil or military affairs, measured by the various standards set up by Lincoln, Ben Wade, Henry Winter Davis, and Andrew Johnson, were to be denied the right to vote for a period of fifteen years. Measuring the seriousness of their crime by the intelligence of the criminals, the law placed the remainder of the Confederates in another class and disfranchised them for five years.[15] Brownlow, in pushing this law through, had gone far beyond Johnson's program as outlined in his Amnesty Proclamation, of May 29, 1865. The Governor, in reconstructing his own Tennessee disfranchised all the Confederates, high and low; Johnson in reconstructing the part of the South that fell to him, permitted all Confederates to vote except the small class of leaders.

Tennessee, led by Brownlow, not only disfranchised the overwhelming majority of its citizens, but pursued them with much other hostile legislation. The avenging leaders in their zeal sometimes passed even beyond the bounds that a heresy-hunting legislature had fixed. The house passed a bill which would have forced many Confederates into nakedness, by fining from five to fifty dollars anyone caught wearing the Confederate uniform. The senate headed off this bill, but its record in other respects left it little advantage in liberality over the house. It passed a bill, which vastly pleased Brownlow, depriving ministers who had sympathized with the Confederates, of the right to perform the marriage ceremony and requiring them to work on the roads, pay a poll tax, and serve in the militia. This bill failed in the house. The senate entertained a bill for a time which would have required women to swear allegiance to the United States before they could be married. Brownlow, with his well-known contempt for Rebel women, was unable to convince the senate that this bill should pass. But this body failed by only

---

[15] McPherson, *History of Reconstruction*, p. 27. The law was passed June 5.

one vote to strike a most serious blow to the civil rights of Confederates by requiring the plaintiff in all suits to take a test oath, which very few could do.[16]

The Tennessee majority was now in subjection to the minority and to keep them from resisting, legislation was passed to tie their hands and close their mouths. They were disarmed by a law which permitted only returned Federal soldiers and "all citizens who have always been loyal" to carry "any and all necessary side arms." If anyone should utter "seditious words or speeches, spreading abroad false news," or utter false libels against the state or the United States, or incite riots, rebellions or "any manner of unlawful feud or differences," such person should suffer fine and imprisonment, and be deprived of that privilege which was dearest to the minority's heart—he should be prohibited from holding office for three years.[17]

Authority and responsibility had not the slightest sobering effect upon Brownlow. He was no less wild and extravagant in his speech as governor than he was as parson. He made himself feared as an unrestrained despot rather than revered as a protector against violence. The masses looked upon him as a usurper who had seized the government for diabolical ends. The Confederates might and many of them did applaud when he said of the assassination of Lincoln that it was "the most villainous affair that ever blackened the records of Crime";[18] but when he spread the report that Jefferson Davis had been captured in his wife's clothing and predicted the former Confederate president's speedy entrance into Hell through the hangman's noose, there was less accord. It gave Brownlow much pleasure to be able to say, "Fallen preachers, pray for the Confederacy! Hell opens wide to receive the hypocrites as they come from the gibbets of the felon. Truly the mighty have fallen! May they fall still lower down!"[19]

Brownlow bitterly resented the return of the Confederate

---

[16] Fertig, *op. cit.*, p. 67; *Noted Men of the Solid South*, 180.

[17] Fertig, *op. cit.*, p. 66; *Ku Klux Conspiracy*, I, 421, 454, 455; *Knoxville Whig and Rebel Ventilator*, July 5, 1865.

[18] *Knoxville Whig and Rebel Ventilator*, April 26, 1865.

[19] *Ibid.*, July 19.

soldiers to Tennessee, and especially to East Tennessee, where the Unionists were still receiving some aid from the East Tennessee Relief Association. He considered this portion of the state to be the special abode of Unionists, and if he could help it he would not have the Rebels eating from the fat of the land or out of the larder of the relief association. He was sure that the Rebels would give trouble, so he decided to whip up such a fury against them that they would be forced to flee the country. He failed to realize what Grant, and Sherman, and many others had sensed, that the returning Confederate soldier would be the most law-abiding citizen in the Union if it were permitted to him.

In his campaign to rouse up hate against the returning Rebels he began early to publish in his *Whig* long accounts of Confederate "atrocities" which had taken place in East Tennessee during the early part of the war. The scenes in the Knoxville jail were reënacted with great vividness, and the heroic bridge-burners were rehanged in all the realism that the imagination of an expert at invective could produce. *Parson Brownlow's Book* was advertised regularly at $1.50 per copy, the reading of which would make any person of undiluted Unionism set out on a man-hunt for the returning Rebels. Firearms and daggers, which only the unconditional Unionists might legally carry, were displayed in a menacing and alluring fashion in *Whig* advertisements.

There were some Unionists in East Tennessee, however, who were less fearful of the Rebels and more generous toward them; and these people attempted to convert the Parson. One of them signing himself "Rednaxela," which was "Alexander" reversed, wrote the *Whig* and counselled conciliation. He declared that he was a Unionist and he had suffered as much as anyone in East Tennessee; but, "Let passion and mad impulse no longer rule the hour. Let us, by conciliation and kindness, win back to a reverence of the old flag the thousands of our unfortunate countrymen, so lately estrayed, who are now wishing to acknowledge its supremacy. To seek revenge may be human, but it is God-like to forgive."[20]

---

[20] *Ibid.*, June 7, 1865.

Brownlow's whole past life was eloquent proof that he was incapable of forgiveness to his enemies. He issued on May 30 a proclamation taking note of the difficulties that had sprung up between Unionist and Rebel. He called upon the Unionists to be lenient and to take their troubles to the courts, but the mollifying effect of this part of his proclamation was then smothered out by the recounting of the terrible crimes that Unionists had suffered at the hands of Rebels. Although the Parson had appointed the judges, he suggested in his proclamation that if the courts did not do justice, then no power on earth could prevent the individual from taking his case in his own hands. Those who were guilty of having aided the rebellion had "forfeited all rights to citizenship, and to life itself. Every field of carnage, every rebel prison, every Union man's grave unite with a violated law and demand the penalty, and if the courts do not administer it, an outraged people will. I call upon all Rebel robbers, bushwhackers and guerillas to cease their wicked ways and betake themselves to honest toil." And as governor he warned the chief Rebel sinners "to quickly and forever withdraw from the country." Here was the spectacle of a governor attempting to banish an important element from his state.[21]

Brownlow speaking unofficially could scarcely have been more violent. To the Parson it was a patriotic duty for the Unionists to maintain control in Tennessee, and he could see no difference between doing so through violence and through franchise laws. He asked whether any man "in his sober senses" supposed that the Rebels could "escape killing or such a beating as will disable them for life?" "If they are acting under this delusion," he continued, "their erroneous notions will be corrected by the development of time."[22] He was not for pacification; he would not compromise with evil. Under his teachings his Unionist neighbors held a meeting in Knoxville and resolved that if any Union men were assassinated "we pledge our lives and sacred honor that ten Rebels shall forfeit their lives for every Union man assassinated."[23] When the Confederates cried out against this proscription and violence, the *Whig* quickly retaliated by repub-

---

[21] *Ibid.*, June 7, 1865.   [22] *Ibid.*, August 30.   [23] *Ibid.*, September 6.

lishing a chapter of "Rebel atrocities" which had been heaped upon Unionists from 1861 to 1863.[24] Brownlow was in truth fulfilling all the promises of vengeance he had made after his expulsion from the Confederacy in 1862.

Under such discouragement, law and order almost ceased to exist in East Tennessee. So near extinction did orderly existence approach that Brownlow felt it necessary to announce: "The Executive will distinguish between who are resenting injuries done to them and their families, and bands of robbers who seek to live without work."[25] So near engulfed with whippings, robbings, and murderings was Washington County that a meeting of the better citizens was held at Jonesboro to try to re-institute the forms of government whose destruction the policies of Brownlow had brought about. It recommended that each civil district hold a meeting and appoint six honorable men "to hunt down and bring to justice such violators of the law as ought to be punished."[26]

Brownlow never gave up the idea that banishment of the Rebels would be the best solution for the troubles in East Tennessee. He repeated, "My most religious advice to those active leading Rebels and bad men, throughout the length and breadth of East Tennessee, is to sell out and go to a new country, take a new start in life, and cease to boast of the part they took in the rebellion."[27] Many East Tennesseeans accepted Brownlow's advice and left. Considerable numbers settled in Georgia, especially in Atlanta. Others drifted into the smaller towns and almost remade them.[28] General Nathan Bedford Forrest testified in 1871 that a great many people "had to fly the country in East Tennessee" and that many men "who had been in the Southern army were killed, when they returned home, by Union men." He declared that there was more bitterness in East Tennessee "than in any other part of the country."[29]

---

[24] For example, *ibid.*, September 13, 1865.
[25] *Ibid.*, September 6.   [26] *Knoxville Whig*, June 13, 1866.
[27] *Knoxville Whig and Rebel Ventilator*, August 30, 1865.
[28] As an example, many of the East Tennesseeans came to the little town of Crawford, Georgia. Athens, Georgia, *Banner Herald*, February 1, 1926.
[29] *Ku Klux Conspiracy*, XIII (Florida and Misc.), 15.

The Brownlow disorders in East Tennessee did not escape the notice and condemnation of people north and south. The Parson gave his answer in a letter to the *Cincinnati Gazette* in which he declared that there was much more violence in Middle Tennessee than in East Tennessee, that the former region "abounds in thieves and robbers, any of whom would murder a man for his watch or for a $5 bill." In fact the whole South was full of disorders and he would tell the American people why: "I am one of those at the South who believe this war has closed out two years too soon! The rebels have been whipped, but not whipped enough. For saying these things I expect to be abused by all rebel papers South, and by all traitorous sheets North. Let them say out; I am able to stand their abuse. I am for the American Union, regardless of the hate of sections, the war of parties, or the malice of individuals."[30]

It might appear that a more orderly way by which to drive the Rebels out of Tennessee would have been through court actions. Brownlow had early thought of this method, and by September, 1865, he had all the state courts functioning.[31] There was also the Federal district court, but he distrusted and hated the judge, Trigg, because he had criticized the governor's disregard for law and order. Trigg also had permitted certain lawyers to practice in his court whom Brownlow claimed were disbarred by the oath required. The Parson ended up his argument by referring to Trigg's court as a "one-horse concern," and the judge retaliated by taking his legal advertising away from the *Whig*.[32] Yet attempts were made to use the court against the Rebels. J. A. Sperry, a former editor of the Knoxville *Register*, was tried for saying mean things about the Unionists during the war. His acquittal was recorded in the *Whig* as a burning outrage. John E. Gamble, of Blount County, was tried for treason, in that he had been a Confederate enrolling officer, but he also was acquitted.[33] But there was another Federal tribunal which Brownlow expected to deal out justice in a

---

[30] Quoted in *New York Times*, November 18, 1865.

[31] *Knoxville Whig and Rebel Ventilator*, September 20, 1865.

[32] *Ibid.*, June 21, September 6.   [33] *Ibid.*, December 20.

sufficiency. He had been preparing the way by reminding the readers of the *Whig* of the horrors which Union soldiers had suffered at the Andersonville Prison.[34] In due time Henry Wirz fell a victim to post-war hysteria and a military commission, and the *Whig* exclaimed, "A more righteous execution has not taken place since the hanging of Hayman [*sic*]."[35]

The Federal court in Tennessee was dismissed as devoid of patriotism, but the Parson had faith in the state courts because he had made them and he led other bitter Unionists into a like attitude. By the fall of 1865 the *Whig* was teeming with many advertisements from the county courts of East Tennessee of attachments, sheriff's sales, and other such acts. The Rebels were being made to pay with their property. Old Parson W. T. Dowell, who had shared the hardships with Brownlow in his flight from Knoxville in 1861 and who later left Tennessee, now decided that the quickest way to get rich would be to return and sue the Rebels for damages.[36] Parson Brownlow soon found it necessary to resort to the courts again. In his suit against Crozier, Reynolds and Sneed the previous year, he had got a judgment of $25,000 damages against them and he executed it by selling them out of their property in Knoxville. But when the war ended, the defendants reopened the case and succeeded in having the original judgment annulled. Brownlow now declared he would institute a new action and sue for $40,000 damages.[37]

The Rebel leaders should also be sued in criminal actions. Brownlow attempted to establish the doctrine that all Rebels were criminals, because in engaging in war they had made themselves guilty of treason. The fact that they were obeying the orders of the Confederacy, a *de facto* government, did not make a difference in his opinion. True enough the Federal courts were admitting this interpretation, and General Grant had fully agreed with it, but Brownlow would not be turned aside. Three

---

[34] For example, *ibid.,* November 15, 1865.

[35] *Ibid.,* November 29.

[36] *Ibid.,* December 20.

[37] *Knoxville Whig,* December 25, 1867. Of course Brownlow was never able to enrich himself to the extent of $40,000 in such an easy manner.

Confederates who had been concerned with the execution of the decree of the Confederate court martial which had condemned to death the bridge-burner, C. A. Haun, were tried in the circuit court for Knox County, and acquitted. They were then tried for hanging the two Harmons and again acquitted. Before the end of the trial President Johnson had suggested through Secretary Stanton that Governor Brownlow pardon them. Brownlow resented this interference, replying that he had no power to issue a pardon at that time.[38] The circuit court for Jefferson County was more patriotic in Brownlow's opinion, for it had tried and sentenced to 14 years in the penitentiary, DeWitt C. Williams for "Treason against the State of Tennessee in aiding and abetting the late rebellion."[39] Williams appealed to the state supreme court and got a *nolle prosequi* on the ground that the treason was against the United States and not against Tennessee.[40]

Brownlow considered that eternal vigilance was the price of minority supremacy in Tennessee. He was somewhat perturbed by the uncertainty as to whether he was the governor of a state in the Union or of an unclassified political division. In early January, several months before he had become governor, he was clamoring for the admission of Tennessee but for the exclusion of the rest of the Confederacy.[41] Soon after the legislature met in April it elected David T. Patterson, Johnson's son-in-law, and Joseph S. Fowler to be the state's two senators in Washington and on April 21 it passed a resolution requesting the president to proclaim Tennessee no longer in a state of insurrection.[42] When on May 29 President Johnson began appointing his provisional governors for the various Southern States preparatory to their admission into the Union again, he naturally took no notice of Tennessee; but on June 13 he proclaimed Tennessee in a state of peace again and thereby assumed that it was a state in the Union.[43]

---

[38] *Ibid.*, June 27, 1866.   [39] *Ibid.*, April 25.   [40] *Ibid.*, September 26.

[41] *Knoxville Whig and Rebel Ventilator,* January 3, 1865.

[42] *Noted Men of the Solid South,* pp. 179-80; *American Annual Cyclopaedia,* 1865, p. 778.

[43] McPherson, *History of Reconstruction,* pp. 13-14.

It would now be necessary for Tennessee to take one more step before she would be ready to participate fully in the Federal government; she must elect her representatives in the lower house of Congress. As the state's regular election would be in August, it was determined that representatives should be elected at that time and a few legislative vacancies filled. Brownlow and his minority party looked forward to this occasion with some apprehensions. In fact from the very beginning of his régime, he felt that an army would be one of the most welcome safeguards his government could have. In his message to the legislature in April, he asked that a military force be put at his disposal; the lawmakers responded by passing a law authorizing the sheriff in each county to raise a squad of twenty-five men as a patrol to enforce order (and without mentioning it, to harass returning Rebels). To put down riots and major disturbances the sheriff might raise as large a force as he deemed necessary.[44] So small was the Brownlow minority party that it felt there was still danger. The legislature, therefore, on May 9, called for Federal troops in addition to those who had remained in the state after the war, to guarantee a republican form of government to Tennessee.[45]

As the Brownlow government had not yet established its legitimacy with a great majority of the Tennessee people, it seemed that the August election might well be made an auspicious occasion on which to turn it out. It was argued that the famous convention of January, 1865, had resulted from the self-appointment of a microscopically small minority which had presumed to direct the amendment of the constitution and then had nominated largely its own members to the legislature. Some said that it had not been based on more than one-seventh of the people; others maintained not more than one-twentieth. Since the election in August, 1865, would be the regular time for the selection of all state officers according to the old constitution, a clamor sprang up, aided by many conservative Union men, that this procedure be followed.[46]

---

[44] Fertig, *op. cit.*, pp. 65-66.   [45] *Noted Men of the Solid South*, p. 180.
[46] *Ibid.*, pp. 178-79, 184; *The South in the Building of the Nation*, II, 525-26.

Emerson Etheridge, a Tennessee Unionist leader in 1861, now led the opposition against the Brownlow minority government. Toward the last of June, anticipating the Fourth of July celebration, he wrote that until law and order returned there could never be an old-fashioned Fourth. At that time the people would be much happier than now, "with no law but force, and no semblance of civil government, State or Federal, but usurpation enforced by the bayonets of negroes."[47] He took part in a meeting at Dresden, which resolved that a "few desperate political and pecuniary adventurers, assembled mainly from the military camps in and out of the State of Tennessee" had met in Nashville inside the fortifications, had fraudulently and without the knowledge or consent of nineteen-twentieths of the people set up a government, that Brownlow had usurped the office of governor, and their nominees, that of the legislature. They were all "scarcely less treasonable, revolutionary and lawless than were the original authors and instigators of the rebellion." For such direct language Etheridge was later tried in his absence, at Columbus, Kentucky, by a military commission.[48]

If the Tennesseeans expected to get rid of Brownlow, they must either resort to violence or overturn the franchise law. As they had no intention of trying the former method, a few attempted the latter. They endeavored to weaken the law's effect by applying for registration, but the rule was strictly adhered to that the voter must have been *publicly* known to be a Unionist from the beginning of the war. The Brownlow courts ruled strictly on all points, including the Conservatives' contention that the law did not refer to municipal elections.[49]

Unquestionably the majority of Tennesseeans had no visions of success or had no intentions of trying to vote—they were resigned to their fate for the time being; but they bitterly condemned Brownlow's government and aroused in the Governor words of burning denunciation and threats of his vengeance. In answer to the contention that a complete state government

[47] *Ku Klux Conspiracy,* I, 456.   [48] *Ibid.,* p. 455.

[49] *American Annual Cyclopaedia,* 1865, p. 779; *Knoxville Whig and Rebel Ventilator,* July 12, 1865.

should be elected in August, he said, "To call for an election of Governor and members of the Legislature next August, is an open declaration of war, and if persisted in, will be treated as *rebellion*."[50] He flooded the state with his proclamations and addresses during July, and in these he explained who could vote and what would happen to those disfranchised if they attempted to cast ballots. On July 10, he called for the arrest of all pretended candidates "travelling over the state denouncing and nullifying the constitution and laws of the land, and spreading sedition and a spirit of rebellion." He also warned the county clerks that he would hold them accountable for their faithful carrying out of the law. In an address a few days later he defended the basis on which his government rested, declaring that it was the President's plan, and that the number of people on which it was based was immaterial. He announced that he would unseat by military force anyone illegally elected. The Rebels should not with bloody hands deposit their ballots and attempt to seize by numbers the government they had sought to destroy. A word to the wise was sufficient: "The civil and military authorities understand each other, and will act in harmony."[51]

At this time the Governor and the President were enjoying friendly relations, and Johnson had twice telegraphed Brownlow to carry out the law, praising him for his vigor, and promising him all the Federal troops necessary. Brownlow with two armies back of his government might well feel that he could disregard the will of Tennessee. Though martial law had not been formally declared, the *Whig* rightfully admitted what was the fact, that Tennessee was under martial law and would remain so until the Rebels should learn how to behave themselves.[52]

On August 3, the election took place and was unaccompanied

---

[50] *Ibid.*, June 28, 1865.

[51] *New York Times*, July 15, 1865; Fertig, *op. cit.*, pp. 67, 68; *American Annual Cyclopaedia*, 1865, p. 779; *Ku Klux Conspiracy*, I, 456-57; *Noted Men of the Solid South*, 181-82.

[52] *American Annual Cyclopaedia*, 1865, p. 779; McPherson, *History of Reconstruction*, pp. 27, 199; *Official Records*, ser. I, vol. XLIX, pt. 2, p. 1083; *Knoxville Whig and Rebel Ventilator*, July 19, 1865.

by violence—eloquent proof of the remarkable forbearance of a people trained to respect the forms of law. A total of 61,783 Tennesseeans went to the polls and elected eight Congressmen. Two features of the election Brownlow disliked. Half of the Congressmen were conservative Unionists, who were opposed to the Brownlow régime; and 61,783 voters seemed to be too many unless they should vote the Brownlow ticket—only 23,352 had voted directly for Brownlow in March. He immediately called upon the county clerks and sheriffs for a report, and after studying their methods of registering the voters, declared that they had permitted 22,274 disfranchised Tennesseeans to register and vote. He proceeded to throw out these votes but the evidence was so overwhelming that the Conservatives had been properly elected that he was unable to dispose of but one of them. As Dorsey B. Thomas had defeated the Parson's good friend Samuel M. Arnell, he was selected for the slaughter. Brownlow refused to bare the complete evidence on which he acted, but he saved his friend. Thomas later contested the election before Congress, but this body saved itself from making a decision on the merits of the contest by contending that Thomas had not instituted proceedings soon enough. The August election had been fought out entirely among the Unionists—no Confederates voted. The rift had come between the Conservatives who opposed disfranchisements and test oaths, and the Radicals, who were willing to follow Brownlow to any limits.[53]

The Brownlow government, assisted by the United States army and the sheriffs' posses of twenty-five each, had successfully leaped the first hurdle. His old legislature met in its second session on October 2 and strung out its life in uproarious debate, in inaction, or in suspended animation for the next 239 days. The Parson found so much to be thankful for that his message to the legislators took on much of the nature of a sermon. "I cannot, therefore," he declared, "neglect to call upon you, again and again, to bow your heads in adoring thankfulness before 'Him who rides upon the storm and calms the roaring seas,' that

---

[53] Fertig, *op. cit.*, p. 69; *Noted Men of the Solid South*, pp. 182-83; "Digest of Election Cases," pp. 162-63.

he still rules the armies of earth and heaven, and that the American people are still the people of His special care." It might
almost be inferred that he was also thankful that there were still
the Rebels whom he might belabor to his fullest pleasure. He
recalled the parable of the Prodigal Son, but showed in many
words that the forgiveness implied there was not intended for
the Rebels. The Prodigal Son had never been guilty of seceding
from the Union and becoming a traitor; and in that circum-
stance the Parson found a mighty difference. The mass of the
Rebels should still be kept from voting from five to ten years
longer "so as to give them time to wash the blood of loyal men
from their hands." As for the ring-leaders, who had pressed
forward in rebellion "with all the malignity of fiends and the
cruelty of savages; . . . who, through rapine, arson, perjury
and butchery, have filled the land with mourning; they are
entitled to neither mercy nor forbearance."[54]

Despite the splendid victory Brownlow's party had won in
the August election, there were disturbing elements in the situation, and these could have no more certain effect than to make
the future uncertain. There could be no doubt that in throwing
out the 22,274 votes he had exercised a right that could be based
on no other ground than might. He never wove fine-spun theories
out of the principles of a democracy which held that the majority
had the right to rule. He knew his party was in a minority and he
was disturbed over the fact that it was a hopelessly small one;
he was also wise enough to know that it could never become
larger, except through artifice. His only hope was through the
continued disfranchisement of the majority and the enforcement
of this course by the use of troops. But he never doubted the
justice in the situation. Because the majority had tried to
destroy the Union, he let his spirit of vengeance blind him to
the fact that that act did not disqualify the mass of Tennesseeans from continuing to participate in the government of the
state. Brownlow failed to see that secession was not a movement

---

[54] *Senate Journal of the Adjourned Session of the General Assembly of the
State of Tennessee, 1865-66,* pp. 6-8; Fertig, *op. cit.,* p. 72; *Noted Men of the
Solid South,* pp. 184, 189.

against the institution of government, which in itself would brand its participants as enemies of organized society. Rather, he acted on the theory that those who favored secession favored anarchy. As for securing the results of the war, it did not fall within the province of the state to assume this duty. It was the peculiar duty of the Federal Government to guard what had been won; secession was not a movement against Tennessee but against the United States. But human nature favored the position Brownlow had taken, and as he had a bountiful supply of this he pushed his use of it in Tennessee to an extreme.

It was, therefore, entirely logical for the Parson to defend the rule of the minority; but the construction of his mind did not lead him to delve into the intricacies of political science and political theories like a John C. Calhoun might have done. Being a parson and a Methodist, he resorted to the Bible and to his religion. He recalled that Noah had been in a minority in the flood, that Lot had been among the few to escape the flames of Sodom, and that Jesus Christ on the cross was in a minority. According to the *Whig* "He reflects that, at this time, *minorities* are occupying the palaces in and bivouacking on the plains of glory, while *majorities* are crowding the deep caverns and pitching their tents on the hill tops of hell."[55] He also remembered the old Methodist hymn, which ran:

> "Broad is the road which leadeth to *death*,
> And thousands walk together there;
> But *wisdom* shows a narrow path,
> With only here and there a traveller!"[56]

The majority might at times with great wisdom submit to the rule of the minority, if the minority were wise and just; but the disfranchised Tennesseans reflected ruefully on the fact that in their predicament the wise were being ruled by the unwise. The power, wealth, culture, and natural leadership of Tennessee were being forced to submit to a minority which had

---

[55] *Knoxville Whig*, March 21, 1866.
[56] *Ibid.*, March 7.

gained its position through accident. The *Nashville Banner* pointedly reflected, "But in honest truth the great majority of the so-called Union or Loyal men of the South were the merest trash that could be collected in a civilized community, of no personal credit or social respectability."[57]

Nothing could be gained through arguments; Brownlow would act. In January, 1866, the *Whig* openly admitted that as there were twice as many Rebels as there were Unionists, if the latter expected to maintain themselves in the next general state elections (August, 1867), the franchise law would need to be strengthened. There was something radically wrong with a law that gave the vote to 22,274 Tennesseans, who should have been kept away from the ballot box.[58] The Governor should not be forced to use up his time preserving the purity of elections by throwing out fraudulent votes. So a new stringent law was introduced in the legislature, making registration more difficult and giving Brownlow unusual powers. Acrimonious discussion immediately began and continued until the legislature developed into a brawling mob which finally broke up in confusion and bedlam. The Parson had become too radical to hold together a legislature of Union men elected under a severely restricted ballot in the midst of war. James Mullins, white-haired and sixty-five, led the Brownlow forces. To many it appeared that the law was being forced through by a determined and insane majority without proper discussion. On February 13, for the purpose of destroying a quorum a sufficient number of members withdrew from the house. Mullins declared that this procedure was the result of a prearranged program. Speaker Heiskell asked if he was being accused, whereupon Mullins said he would suspect the speaker as soon as anyone else. In a rage Heiskell sprang from his chair, called Mullins "A G—d d—d old liar and a d—d thief," and threw his gavel at him, barely missing another member. Mullins then exclaimed, "You are a G—d d—d liar, a d—d old scoundrel, a partial presiding offi-

[57] Quoted in *Knoxville Whig,* March 21, 1866.
[58] *Knoxville Whig and Rebel Ventilator,* January 31, 1866.

cer, and one of the conspirators," and with his hand in his pocket moved toward the speaker. The house broke up in an uproar.[59]

The legislature adjourned from day to day until the 19th when Heiskell decided to issue warrants for the doorkeeper to arrest and bring back eleven members. Two days later a resolution was introduced to expel four members for "seditions and revolutionary" conduct. To head this off, mutineers, twenty-one in number, left the house. Heiskell refused to entertain a motion to have warrants issued for their arrest and return, on the ground that a member had the right to decide whether he would vote or not. To make the situation more difficult some of the members then resigned.[60]

The Parson now stepped into the breach and declared that the seceders were bent on paralyzing the state government and destroying its influence with the national leaders. He furthermore charged them with attempting to destroy the state's credit, to prevent the passage of appropriation bills, to abandon the lunatic asylum and the penitentiary, to keep Northern immigrants out of the state and "prepare the way for a second rebellion."[61] On March 3, he issued a proclamation declaring the seceders' seats vacant and calling for a special election on the last day of the month, for new members. In his proclamation he declared that they "by factions and revolutionary proceedings, have succeeded in breaking up the Legislature, and paralyzing the State Government." They had "arrested the machinery of State Government as effectually as if the same had been done by force of arms."[62]

Not only had the Parson by his extremism outraged the great majority of Tennesseeans, but thus had he also disrupted his Union following and stripped his government of almost every vestige of dignity and decorum, and made of it a grim brawl. Even some of his East Tennesseeans were among the seceders.[63]

---

[59] *Knoxville Whig*, February 28, March 7, 1866.
[60] *Ibid.*, February 28.
[61] *Ibid.*, April 4.
[62] *Ibid.*, March 14.
[63] *Ibid.*, March 21.

All told there were twenty-four seats in the house to be filled and two in the senate. All the bolters ran for reëlection and with five exceptions were returned by big majorities; but the legislature refused to readmit twenty-one of them.

The Parson had been defeated in his strategy, but this very defeat convinced him still more that the franchise law needed remaking, for otherwise members supporting his program would have been returned. The legislature now came to life again, and on April 18, Brownlow sent in a message urging them to hurry the passage of the franchise law.[64] But the members were in no better humor on their return. Soon the member of the house from Carter County, in the midst of East Tennessee, fell to savagely attacking Brownlow. He declared that the Governor who had run away to a place of safety during the war, now presumed to teach patriotism to those who had remained in Tennessee. "While the people of the North were throwing *gold* at Gov. Brownlow, the rebels were throwing lead at me," he shouted. At this moment James P. Brownlow, the adjutant-general and the son of the Governor, walked up to the member from Carter, thrust his hat into his face, and called him "a d—d Liar and Coward."[65] The Governor undoubtedly had developed the chief branch of his government into the greatest brawling mob in America. Henry Watterson, not yet become the famous Marse Henry but now only an inconspicuous newspaper helper in Nashville, declared the majority of the legislature were "LIARS and SCOUNDRELS, who ought to be in hell or the penitentiary. . . ." The *Whig* dismissed him as "Little *henry watterson,* of the *Nashville Banner.*"[66]

Although Brownlow extremism had been rejected in the special election by the return of the seceding members, the Governor was doubly determined to push the new franchise bill through. The Conservatives seeing the futility of further physical obstructions hit upon the strategy of universal suffrage and universal amnesty. According to their plan all Negroes should

---

[64] "Special Message of Gov. William G. Brownlow to the General Assembly of Tennessee, April 18, 1866," *Appendix Senate Journal.*
[65] *Knoxville Whig,* April 25, 1866.   [66] *Ibid.*

be given the ballot but at the same time all Rebels also should be allowed to vote. This was a clever move for it would put into operation a part of the Congressional radical program which was so extreme that the Thaddeus Stevens oligarchy had not yet applied it anywhere. Negro suffrage ought, therefore, to endear and recommend Tennessee, not yet admitted into the Union, to the Radicals in Washington. But to Brownlow, Negro suffrage was only a little less outrageous than Rebel suffrage. The Parson was wise enough also to see that if the Conservatives gave the Negro the suffrage they might induce many Negroes to vote their ticket out of gratitude. But the Conservatives knew that the Rebel vote would greatly outweigh the Negro vote, so in either case they would be the winners. Risking the displeasure of their Radical allies in Washington, the Brownlow party followed their antipathy to Negroes, and rejected the Conservative scheme.[67]

The Brownlow party now pushed through their franchise bill, which became a law in May. It was the old law reënacted with important changes. Under the old law the county clerks had registered the voters and in Brownlow's opinion they had been too lax in their work. As they had been elected locally, some of them were conservatively inclined and had allowed men to register whose Unionism was subject to suspicion. By the new law "commissioners of registration" were to register the voters, and Brownlow was given the power to appoint these commissioners. These appointees of Brownlow were to guard with extreme care the sacred suffrage jewel, and before anyone might wear it he must successfully pass through a definite procedure and be awarded a certificate. He must produce two witnesses who could vote, to swear that he was not disqualified by any of the provisions of the law, and then he must swear an extensive oath in which he should recount what he had done, what he had not done, and certify to the pleasure he had experienced at the news of Union victories and Confederate de-

[67] McPherson, *History of Reconstruction*, p. 28; *American Annual Cyclopaedia*, 1866, p. 728.

feats. The oath also included other emotions and psychological reactions he must have had. The old registration lists were annulled.[68]

Brownlow was greatly pleased. Only in Tennessee, throughout all the former Confederacy, did he see Union men in control and Rebels disfranchised. President Johnson had been careless in his reconstruction rules and had allowed Rebels to vote; Brownlow had done differently.

The Brownlow minority had riveted the yoke on the necks of the Confederates in Tennessee, but there were others against whom it felt equally as bitter. On them its laws could have no effect, but it would not forego passing joint resolutions against them. A few days after dealing with its own Rebels it called for the death penalty to be assessed against Jefferson Davis, James M. Mason, R. M. T. Hunter, Robert Toombs, Howell Cobb, Judah P. Benjamin, John Slidell, Robert E. Lee, and John C. Breckinridge, and recommended that they should be "held as infamous forever."[69]

Disfranchising the Rebels did not completely solve the difficulties in the position of the Brownlow minority. A year of Brownlow had sadly defaced the solid front of the Union party and there had already begun to crumble away a respectable number of Conservatives. In casting about for accretions, the immigrants, Northern and foreign, readily suggested themselves. Brownlow believed that Northerners would naturally sympathize with his party and that foreigners could be made quickly to learn who their friends were. A considerable number of Federal soldiers had remained in Tennessee after the war and others freshly mustered out of the army were looking for a place in which to begin life. Brownlow spread the news throughout the North that East Tennessee was "the Eldorado of the late revolted South," and soon he was getting so many inquiries that he printed in reply a form letter, in which he described the

---

[68] *Ibid.;* Fertig, *op cit.,* p. 73; *Ku Klux Conspiracy,* I, 421; McPherson, *History of Reconstruction,* pp. 27-28; *Noted Men of the Solid South,* pp. 185-86. This law was tested in the State Supreme Court, and held constitutional.

[69] *Acts of Tennessee, 1865-66,* pp. 450-51.

pleasures and profits that came to those wise enough and fortunate enough to live in East Tennessee.[70]

In keeping with the movement common throughout the South
to secure foreign immigrants, he set up an immigration bureau
in his government and put at the head Hermann Bokum, a German. The Parson was partial to the Germans and the Swiss
and made a special drive for them. In the Civil War he had
come in contact with the Germans and had found them almost
uniformly on the Union side. A few were already in Tennessee,
and these he courted with a special fervor. In Knoxville he spoke
to the Germans for an hour and a half and praised them for
their fine qualities and patriotism. He made it a practice to
have his message to the legislature reprinted in German and
widely distributed. Of his message in October, 1865, 6,000
copies were printed in German and 15,000 in English, but of a
later message, 1,000 copies were set in English and 2,000 in
German—a fact which led the *Messenger of Peace* to make the
pointed inquiry: "Are Americans in a minority in Tennessee?"[71]

Tennessee never acquired a very large number of foreigners,
though she gave them the right to vote before they should become
citizens. Brownlow had greater success in inducing Northern
immigrants, though he was much disappointed in some of them
after they arrived. Many of them in failing to follow his leadership in politics won from him harsh words. The *Whig* declared,
"For those *Northern sneaks* who turn *Southern men* after fighting three or four years on the Federal side, no party ought
for a moment to entertain a particle of respect."[72] Brownlow
said he would welcome to Tennessee all Northern men who
favored the Federal government, but "if there be one class of
men in Tennessee today, meaner than another, it is that class
of Northern rebels, copperheads and adventurers from the

[70] *Knoxville Whig and Rebel Ventilator,* January 3, November 15, 1865, June
6, 1866.

[71] *Knoxville Whig and Rebel Ventilator,* October 11, November 1, 15, 1865;
Knoxville Whig, April 4, August 1, 1866.

[72] *Knoxville Whig,* August 8, 1866. Brownlow attributed the failure of foreign immigrants to come to Tennessee to "the intolerant and proscriptive spirit
of a large faction of those lately in rebellion." *Ibid.,* November 7, 1866.

North, who are in sympathy with the Rebels of the South. May God in his mercy put it into the heads of such *cattle* to stay away from Tennessee, and especially from East Tennessee."[73]

In the opinion of some of the Conservatives, Brownlow in his attempt to win over the Northerners, had filled the offices with them to the exclusion of many capable Tennesseeans. Among the foremost was his private secretary, H. H. Thomas, who during many days while Brownlow was sick, acted in almost the full capacity of governor. A. J. Fletcher, the secretary of state, publicly condemned Brownlow for his outrageous court- ing of Northerners by putting them into office. He declared, "We have put them on the bench and made them Attorneys General. Some of them are very shrewd in the pursuit of office." To one of them Brownlow had given a commission for an office not yet vacant "long before he was eligible, and a life time before he had any fitness for the office."[74]

There was another element in the population of Tennessee which gave Brownlow concern—slaves in the ante-bellum days, now the freedmen. He had had an inherent antipathy toward Negroes in any other position in life than slavery. Toward them now as freedmen he found it difficult to change his old attitude. Largely out of respect for him and Andrew Johnson, Lincoln had not included Tennessee in his Emancipation Procla- mation, though this state by every test should have naturally come within its effect. Out of the burning fire of Unionism and from a sense of expediency, Brownlow had favored the aboli- tion of slavery in the convention of January, 1865. Likewise he was impelled to advise his first legislature to ratify the Thir- teenth Amendment. But he had much the same attitude toward the freedmen that Lincoln had; they should be got out of the way. Brownlow would have them colonized in some Southern clime where they might do their own governing. As a just pun- ishment to the Rebels, he would not object to having one of the former Confederate states confiscated and turned over to the Negroes—a movement which at the moment was being started

---

[73] *Knoxville Whig and Rebel Ventilator,* September 13, 1865.
[74] *Knoxville Whig,* October 2, 1867.

19

by Dominican carpetbaggers for Louisiana.[75] Brownlow was certain no more should be allowed to come into Tennessee.

When the Negroes got their freedom they flocked to the cities where they became a menace to peace and property. Brownlow observed them in Knoxville and was readily confirmed in his low opinion of the Negro race. The Freedmen's Bureau soon came along to protect the Negroes and to plague the whites. Brownlow declared that they refused to work since they believed that the United States owed them a living and that they should be furnished houses even if the white people should be turned out. "They fiddle and dance at night," he observed in disgust, "and lie around the stores and street corners in the daytime."[76] And in Negro soldiers, some of whom were stationed in East Tennessee, he found a more serious disgust. They used their guns too freely and assumed a general attitude toward the whites which Brownlow could not endure. He declared that none was needed in East Tennessee and that the whites "don't propose to be shot down like dogs by men of any color, or to be run through with the bayonets at every corner of the street."[77] Believing that the Rebels of Middle and West Tennessee had the same antipathy to them that he had, he wanted Negro troops stationed in these regions to bedevil and madden the people there.[78] In early 1866, a Negro soldier shot and killed Lieutenant-Colonel Dyer on the streets of Knoxville and the East Tennesseeans immediately lynched him in front of army headquarters. With evident approval the *Whig* recounted how he had been "discovered, dragged out by the infuriated populace, shot and hanged by the neck, in front of headquarters until he was dead."[79] Soon thereafter all Federal troops were removed from East Tennessee, and this region was now free from Federal

[75] See H. C. Warmoth, *War, Politics and Reconstruction, Stormy Days in Louisiana.* Hinton Rowan Helper, who had stirred up a tempest in ante-bellum days in his *Impending Crisis,* was now advocating the banishment of the Negroes or their destruction in some other fashion. See his book *Nojoque.* See also *Knoxville Whig and Rebel Ventilator,* August 23, 1865; *Acts of Tennessee, 1865,* p. 5.
[76] *American Annual Cyclopaedia,* 1865, p. 781.
[77] *Knoxville Whig and Rebel Ventilator,* August 30, 1865.
[78] *Ibid.,* September 27, 1865.
[79] *Ibid.,* February 14, 21, 1866.

soldiers for the first time since Burnside had captured Knoxville.[80]

From the first days of their freedom the Negroes began to develop ambitions for a participation in the government. They made a friendly gesture toward Brownlow on the eve of his departure for Nashville to assume the governorship. Through Horace Maynard they presented him with a gold watch.[81] Soon thereafter the Tennessee Negroes petitioned the legislature for the right to vote. The most that body would do was to print 500 copies of the petition.[82] As gifts and petitions seemed to have no effect, the Negroes next held a convention in Nashville on August 7 and 8 to awe the lawmakers and to stir up public sentiment for Negro suffrage. They resolved that they were opposed to the admission of the Tennessee Congressmen at Washington until the legislature acted on their petition.[83]

The thoughts of Negro suffrage did violence to Brownlow's whole past. He hated to think on the subject. If the country was not ridded of them by colonization, he believed most of them would soon die out. In June, 1865, it was his belief that "Idleness, starvation, and disease, will remove a majority of the Negroes in this generation." The better class he thought would go to work, and, perhaps, they might be allowed to vote "on the ground that a *loyal Negro* is more worthy than *a disloyal white man.*"[84] During the summer and fall Thaddeus Stevens, Salmon P. Chase, and other Northerners whom Brownlow thought he could not afford to displease began advocating Negro suffrage. Sumner informed President Johnson that he was disappointed in Brownlow's attitude and believed that the President ought to interfere.[85] So it happened that in his message to the legislature in October, 1865, Brownlow took a somewhat more liberal attitude toward the Negro, but nevertheless a belabored, grudging one. He pleaded again a natural prejudice

---

[80] *Ibid.*, March 7, 1866.
[81] *Ibid.*, March 29, 1865.
[82] *American Annual Cyclopaedia*, 1865, pp. 778-79.
[83] *Ibid.*, 780-81; *Knoxville Whig and Rebel Ventilator*, August 23, 1865.
[84] *Ibid.*, June 28, 1865.
[85] Milton, *op. cit.*, p. 178.

against Negroes, but thought eventually the most intelligent might be allowed to vote; but the ballot box should not be opened to "the uninformed and exceedingly stupid slaves of the Southern cotton, rice and sugar fields." He feared they would be controlled by their former masters for years to come. With an air of impatience he met outside suggestions: When the loyal people of Tennessee thought the Negroes should have the suffrage, they would get it "and not before." And when the time came, it would be the state and not the national government that should give it to them. He was, however, willing that the Negroes should be given certain civil rights immediately—a promise of the very same development which was taking place in some of the Johnson reconstructed states in their Black Codes.[86]

On January 25, 1866, long after both South Carolina and Mississippi had conferred certain civil rights on their Negroes, Tennessee made the Negro a competent witness in the state courts to the same extent that Congress allowed him to testify in the Federal courts; and not until May 26, 1866, was he given full civil rights, except that he might not serve on juries or attend the same schools as the whites. As soon as this action was taken the Freedmen's Bureau abolished its troublesome courts in the state.[87]

Brownlow had no enthusiasm for this legislation but he felt that it was necessary to relieve the outside pressure. East Tennesseans, generally, felt no responsibility toward the outside; for a hundred years they had looked upon the Negro with contempt as belonging to a lower order of life; it was now too late for them to change their views. The Negro testimony law had been pushed through, because the legislature felt that only by so doing could they get the Freedmen's Bureau out of the state. But most of the East Tennessee members were uncompromising to the last; only eight of them voted for the law.[88]

---

[86] *Senate Journal of Tennessee, 1865-66,* pp. 11-13; *American Annual Cyclopaedia,* 1865, p. 781; *Noted Men of the Solid South,* pp. 184, 189.

[87] *Noted Men of the Solid South,* p. 185.

[88] *Knoxville Whig and Rebel Ventilator,* December 27, 1865, January 31, 1866.

The Negroes believed Brownlow was their friend, and the Governor did not object. February 22, 1866, several thousand of them gathered in front of his lodging house in Nashville to greet him. Pleading that he was too sick to make them a speech, he told them that they had "a right to form processions, to march to the music of LIBERTY, to throw the star spangled banner to the breeze, to wear your emblems and badges, and wear them proudly."[89]

The situation held forth possibilities. Perhaps sometime Brownlow would find it necessary to call in the Negroes as allies to be added to the immigrants in ruling Tennessee and holding in subjection a chafing set of Rebels becoming more dangerous the longer they reflected on their degradation.

---

[89] *Knoxville Whig*, March 7, 1866.

CHAPTER XIII

THE MINORITY ESTABLISHES ITSELF

THE BITTEREST HATRED Brownlow was able to distill he had flung out against the religious leaders of the Confederacy. He made the Methodist preachers the particular object of his attacks. Since they were of his own Church he knew them best, and they appeared to him to be the most hardened sinners. He might have been able to forgive them individually of their treason, but when he saw them stampeding the Church organization into the Rebellion, he feared they were bent on disrupting religion. By 1862 he had declared that it would "take years of fasting and prayer to heal the divisions."[1]

Under the direction of Bishop Early, the aristocratic brother of the General, the Holston Conference did what religious organizations have always found it expedient and wise to do; it acknowledged the supremacy of the government under which it lived, and loyally supported it. At its conference in 1861, at Greeneville, the home of Andrew Johnson, it inserted in its exercises prayers for the Confederacy, and did not stultify itself by including the United States, the public enemy. The next year it met at Athens, Tennessee, where it logically expelled nine Union preachers and naïvely elected to life membership in the "Parent Missionary Society," President Davis, and Generals Sterling Price, John Morgan, Simon B. Buckner, Robert E. Lee and Stonewall Jackson. The next year (1863) it met at Wytheville, Virginia, and standing true to its policy, expelled more Union preachers.[2] In 1864, Bishop Early held the conference in Bristol. It scanned its membership and found addi-

---

[1] *Parson Brownlow's Book,* p. 190.
[2] Price, *op. cit.,* IV, 266, 299, 341; W. B. Hesseltine, "Methodism and Reconstruction in East Tennessee," *East Tennessee Historical Society Publications,* III (January, 1931), 7.

tional traitors to the Confederacy and promptly expelled them. It also forbade anyone taking the oath to support the public enemy, which was trying to conquer the country. The Confederate Government aided the Holston Conference by arresting and imprisoning those ministers who were too outspoken in their love for the United States.[3]

When the Confederacy lost the war, the Holston Conference bowed to the inevitable. At its meeting in Marion, Virginia, in September, 1865, with the same Bishop Early presiding, it passed a series of resolutions of loyalty to the United States, and as consistent as ever, declared that it was obeying the Scriptures which taught loyalty to the supreme civil authority. It showed contrition by admitting that it had been hasty in expelling some of its members during the war.[4]

The course of the Methodist Church in East Tennessee during the war, had been an outrage in the eyes of the Parson. In the first number of his resurrected *Whig*, issued on his return from the North in 1863, he began a fierce denunciation of the "revered traitors." He charged:

They have aided in the work of devastating the country; they have contributed to fill the land with mourning; they have caused tears of tens of thousands of widows to flow, they have done their full part, in handing to posterity an army of orphan children; they have aided materially in filling thousands of graves with the best citizens of the country, North and South; and fearful to relate, they have mainly contributed to send thousands to hell, who might have been redeemed by the blood of Christ, but for this war! We can never hear one of these base hypocrites preach, if we can get beyond the sound of his hateful voice.[5]

The Parson declared that the Confederate Methodists were a depraved set of people, and were wicked beyond compare. They had recently held a religious picnic and they had amused themselves mostly by fiddling and dancing.[6] Throughout the remainder of its existence Brownlow's *Knoxville Whig and Rebel*

---

[3] Price, *op. cit.*, III, 358-59, and IV, 352, 361.
[4] *Ibid.*, pp. 400-8; *Knoxville Whig and Rebel Ventilator*, October 4, 1865.
[5] *Ibid.*, November 11, 1863.   [6] *Ibid.*

Ventilator held the Confederate Methodists to be the worst element in all rebeldom, and pursued them relentlessly.

The situation demanded something more than condemnation. Brownlow was still a Methodist and he would remain so, but he would not fraternize or commune with the Rebel Methodists. The remedy was simple. The Southern Methodist Church, which had by agreement in 1844 been given the South as its vineyard, should now be dispossessed by the Northern branch of the Church. The violation of an agreement did not seem to matter with the Parson; it was sufficient that the Southern Methodists had been guilty of treason. He now, seconded by the Federal army chaplains, began a correspondence with the Northern organization for the purpose of inducing it to take over the Church in Tennessee.

With the coming of the Federal armies into East Tennessee, many of the churches had been left without pastors and some without congregations. This property Brownlow felt should be seized, and the process was soon started. Bishop Matthew Simpson, who may have believed in the separation of church and state but who certainly believed that the Northern Methodists should join the Republican Party, became interested in extending his Church southward. Such a program would increase the power of his Church and at the same time punish and dispossess the Rebels. He appeared in Tennessee in January, 1864, and organized a few congregations in Nashville before visiting East Tennessee. The Parson invited him to Knoxville, but the Bishop was unable to reach the citadel of Brownlowism on account of high water on the Tennessee.[7]

The General Conference of the Methodist Church in Philadelphia in 1864 had sanctioned the religious invasion of the South. After attending to some political matters at the Republican National Convention at Baltimore in June (1864) Brownlow had continued his journey to Philadelphia where he consulted with Bishop Simpson. He returned by way of Cincinnati in order to confer with Bishop Kingsley under whose watch-care the South had been placed. Brownlow urged the organization

---

[7] *Ibid.*, February 23, 1864; Hesseltine, *op. cit.*, pp. 10-12.

of the Holston Conference as a part of the Northern Branch of the Church.[8] In more immediate and direct pursuance of this scheme, the Parson and a few other Methodists in May, 1864, issued a call for a convention to meet in Knoxville the following July. In the meeting that took place "fire and brimstone" resolutions were hurled at the Southern Methodists and a committee was appointed to decide on the next step. The decision was quickly made to secede from the old Holston Conference, seize the property and join the Northern branch. The report was adopted unanimously. There were 55 delegates present, 27 being preachers. Brownlow was in chief command.[9]

Thus far had the religious revolution progressed when Brownlow became the civil head of Tennessee. According to the new governor, Tennesseeans had committed more grievous sins religiously than politically, if such were possible. Therefore the Rebel Methodists should expect religious reconstruction no less surely than political reconstruction. The Parson in time past had often accused the Democrats of wanting to unite church and state, but as governor he would not refrain from using the increased power of his position in dealing with the Methodists. In August, 1865, he promised to let them meet and take up their Church affairs if they properly demeaned themselves—otherwise he would arrest them. As for Bishop Early, he should not play bishop within the Parson's dominions.[10]

Just as the Governor began the process of rescuing the state from the Rebels with the meeting of his legislature in April (1865), the Parson began the first important work of rescuing the Church in the following June. Bishop Clark was directly in charge of the new Holston Conference, which was called together in Athens, and organized as part of the Northern Methodists. With joy the assembled preachers of religion and patriotism

---

[8] Strictly speaking the terms applied to the two branches of the Methodist Church were Methodist Episcopal Church South, and simply Methodist Episcopal Church. The terms *Northern* and *Southern* are used for clearness and to emphasize the contrast.

[9] *Knoxville Whig and Rebel Ventilator*, July 23, 1864; *Southern Watchman*. August 2, 1865; Price, *op. cit.*, IV, 353-57.

[10] *Knoxville Whig and Rebel Ventilator*, August 16, 1865.

recorded the success of Federal arms over "a gigantic, unprovoked and wicked rebellion" and announced the dispersal of the Rebels "who crimsoned the land with the blood of our sons and brethren, swept our homes with desolation, and filled our hearts with anguish." They resolved such traitors out of all possibilities of entering Heaven and consigned them to the nether world. Those ministers who entered the rebellion "and imbibed the spirit thereof, are guilty of a crime which is sufficient to exclude them from the Kingdom of Grace and Glory" and they should not be admitted into the Conference until "full confession and thorough repentance." This new Holston Conference of the Northern wing started out with more than a half-hundred preachers, more than 6,000 members, and 51 Sunday schools.[11]

Violence both in language and in act for the next half dozen years characterized the Brownlow church régime in its relations with the Southern Methodists. They were plainly informed that the Federal soldiers would soon be returning home, with both the mind and the means for tolerating little from Rebel Methodists.[12] One soldier regulator declared, "We Federal soldiers regard horse thieves and the Southern Methodist Church as the only two rebel organizations but what surrendered with Lee's army."[13] Brownlow characterized the Southern Holston Conference at Marion, Virginia, in September, 1865, as nothing better than a "Rebel Court Martial," and the *Whig* advised the Northern Methodists to "show no quarters to traitors and treason." The Southern Methodists were a "politican rebel organization."[14]

Brownlow attempted to stampede all East Tennesseans of Union proclivities into his Northern Methodist organization, fearing that the Rebels might predominate in Church as they undoubtedly did in state. This new organization should be designed also to capture the Negroes and immigrants. As an effort to capitalize on former Union patriotism, the Northern Method-

[11] *Southern Watchman*, August 2, 1865; Price, *op. cit.*, IV, 393-94.
[12] *Knoxville Whig and Rebel Ventilator*, September 20, 1865.
[13] Price, *op. cit.*, IV, 457.   [14] *Knoxville Whig*, May 30, December 19, 1866.

ists in some places labelled themselves the "United States Church."[15] So utterly worthless and depraved were the Southern Methodist preachers that Brownlow was not sure they should be allowed to assume the various stations they were attempting to fill. Of them he said, "With souls panting, no doubt, for spiritual comfort and refreshment, these lovers of *Southern* religion will groan around the altars of these pious divines!"[16]

The onset against the Southern Methodists became one of the chief activities of the Northern Methodists of East Tennessee. J. L. Mann, pastor of the Greeneville church, gave fourteen extensive reasons why he "would not fellowship" with the Southern Methodists, ending up with the charge that they were striving "by all means, both fair and foul, and especially by the latter, to build up and perpetuate one of the most *intensely treasonable* organizations now out of perdition."[17] Apart from Brownlow, whose time was somewhat divided on account of his gubernatorial duties, the greatest clerical gladiator in East Tennessee was Rev. T. H. Pearne, the presiding elder of Brownlow's Knoxville district. He kept up a continual agitation against the Southern Methodists and sought to exterminate them with harsh words. After accusing them of all the crimes in the Decalogue, he asked when did they "put away and renounce their treason-abetting and rebellion-promoting political meddling?"[18] He declared, "I have no terms to express the supreme contempt and utter loathing which they deserve." Though accusing Southern Methodist pastors of having engaged in politics, he saw no inconsistency in plunging headlong into the game himself. In 1868, he attended the Republican Convention in Nashville and offered a resolution of praise for Brownlow.[19] He wrote many attacks in the *Whig* against the Southern Methodists and became so proficient in the Brownlow style of journalism that he later took over the paper and became the sole editor.

Under the tutelage of Brownlow, Pearne, and others, the

---

[15] Price, *op. cit.*, IV, 476.
[16] *Knoxville Whig and Rebel Ventilator*, October 4, 1865.
[17] *Ibid.*, November 14, 1866.
[18] *Ibid.*, December 19.
[19] *Ibid.*, February 28, 1868.

Northern Methodists of East Tennessee grew strong in numbers and vindictive in spirit. Brownlow attended a conference
in Greeneville in the summer of 1866 and declared that he had
never heard better preaching than there. He reported that the
Holston Conference contained 6 presiding elder districts, 60
stations and circuits, 200 preachers, and 18,300 members.[20]
The pestilential condition of the times, aided by the leadership
of the Northern Methodists in East Tennessee, led to a veritable
reign of terror in certain parts of the Holston Conference. The
Northern Methodist transformed himself into a modern crusader
who looked upon every Southern Methodist minister as an unspeakable Turk to be assaulted and his house of worship as a
new Jerusalem to be stormed. The Southern preachers were
locked out, barred out, and thrown out of their pulpits and if
they showed a disposition to dispute or remain on the church
grounds they were cowhided or ridden away on rails. So zealous
were these crusaders that even Elder Pearne sought to call them
off their warfare of violence.[21]

The particular occasion for most of the trouble with the
Southern Methodists developed out of the seizure of their church
property. The Northern Methodists seized about a hundred
churches in East Tennessee and drove their Southern brethren
to resort to "public halls, courthouses, private dwellings, and
groves."[22] In a land where the Southern Methodists were disfranchised and deprived of valuable civil rights, their only
recourse left was to plead the injustice of the seizures and beg
for their property to be returned. In 1867, the Southern Holston Conference appointed a committee to memorialize the general conference of the Northern Methodists, meeting at Chicago,
to restore their property, and resolving at the same time not
to shake the hand of ministers of the Northern Holston Conference until it released from its grasp "all the property of ours
which it now holds."[23] Receiving no satisfaction, the Southern

---

[20] *Knoxville Whig,* May 30, 1866.
[21] *Knoxville Whig and Rebel Ventilator,* December 20, 1865; Price, *op. cit.,* IV,
460-77, 492-508.
[22] *Ibid.,* V, 11.
[23] *Ibid.,* IV, 444-45.

Methodists petitioned the general conference again the next year, but Bishop Simpson being too busily engaged in directing the prayers and resolutions of the conference toward the removal of Andrew Johnson from the presidency, had the memorial referred back to the Northern Holston Conference.[24] The struggle to regain their property was long drawn out, but they gradually made headway. By 1873 the Northern Methodists still held eighteen churches and one parsonage. The controversy was finally settled by the so-called Cape May agreement a few years later.[25]

The Northern Holston Conference, backed by the government of Tennessee and the Northern Methodist Church, forged ahead of the Southern Holston Conference in membership. Their numbers were increased also by the flocking in of the Negroes. But in this situation there was great need for the most astute diplomacy.[26] East Tennesseeans had such a strong antipathy for Negroes that even their extreme Unionism could not efface it. When the Negroes obtained political equality in Tennessee, they believed that religious equality was included. Following out this idea three colored preachers, uninvited, partook of the communion with whites in the Knoxville congregation. Much explanation was necessary to keep the Southern Methodists from gaining a major victory here, as they spread the news of what had happened.[27] In the name of patriotism the Parson and his religious lieutenants had succeeded in setting East Tennessee as far back religiously as politically.

Brownlow's religious program was not his only excursion into the field of organized morality. Temperance had long interested him, and now that he was governor, he would strike a blow in its behalf. In his various messages to the legislature he dealt with the subject, and though he used some vehemence in arguing for it, he was never able to translate it into legislation. He advocated a tax on whiskey so high that no one could afford to pay it, and if he could not win support for this plan, he pro-

---

[24] *Ibid.*, pp. 455-58.
[25] *Ibid.*, V, 5-31, 89.
[26] *Ibid.*, IV, 411, 433, 446.   [27] *Knoxville Whig*, November 6, 1867.

posed to give the counties the right to abolish completely the manufacture and sale of whiskey within their borders. As he looked around over the state he saw "Intemperance . . . blowing up steamboats, upsetting stage-coaches, and through the carelessness of drunken engineers or switch-tenders, . . . bringing trains in collision or running them off the track."[28]

Having the Tennessee government securely in their hands, the Unionists decided they would make it serve their purposes, whatever they might be. They early hit upon the plan of extracting from the treasury, pensions for those East Tennesseeans who had borne the brunt of Confederate tyranny. A bounty of $100 each to every widow and orphan of an East Tennessee Unionist was much advocated during the fall of 1865, and the *Whig* was insistent in its support of the plan, berating all who opposed it.[29] The bill was finally defeated, but in his messages to the legislature on April 13 and 18, 1866, Brownlow changed the scheme somewhat by broadening it and demanding that the state pay all loyal Tennesseeans who had suffered losses in the war. He counted on the United States ultimately reimbursing Tennessee. He was already mildly disgusted with the Federal Government for being so slow in doing this elementary justice to Tennessee, especially since it had already paid for damages suffered by Indiana, Pennsylvania, and other Northern states. To raise this money, awaiting the time when the United States would act, he advocated the state issuing small bonds in the denominations of $50 and $100. He was confident the Federal Government would reimburse Tennessee before the bonds should fall due, and so the state would be put to no expense. This became a Radical scheme of first importance after the passage of the franchise act, but it never became a law. Perhaps too many people would share its benefits; the few were the ones who were

---

[28] *Senate Journal of Tennessee,* 1865-1866, pp. 23-24; *Knoxville Whig,* October 9, 1867.
[29] *Knoxville Whig and Rebel Ventilator,* November 22, 1865; *New York Times,* November 10, 1865.

successfully to plunder this state, as was true in most of the other Southern states.[30]

There were, indeed, benefits to be had by the East Tennessee Unionists in their control of the government, but there were also hazards. In the spring of 1866, when the "little rebellion" had broken out in the legislature over the attempt to force through the franchise law, the hazards began to loom up as too certain. At this time a large mass meeting was held in Knoxville for the purpose of determining what should be the wisest course for the Unionists to follow. The old idea of a state of East Tennessee was immediately brought out and refurbished again. They declared that if the franchise law did not pass they would immediately demand a new state to escape the tyranny of the Rebels who largely predominated in Middle and West Tennessee. They had fears of the wrath of those whom they had degraded. Brownlow's *Whig* seized the new state plan and pushed it with vigor. In March, 1866, it reported that the new state enthusiasm was "increasing very rapidly," that the course of feeling and events in Middle and West Tennessee was "increasing the desire to be separated from them, and to have a loyal State organized here." Middle and West Tennessee had plunged the state into secession and had brought down upon East Tennessee all her woes. She could, therefore, never live in peace and friendship with those parts of the state.[31]

Beside the feeling of certain retribution ultimately for what they had made the rest of the state suffer, the East Tennesseeans had additional reasons for a new state. East Tennessee had always differed from the middle and western portions of the state in politics and in economic developments and ambitions. East Tennessee might well become a great mining and manufacturing state. It would not be too small; it would, in fact, be eleven

---

[30] *Senate Journal of Tennessee*, 1865-1866, p. 425; *Knoxville Whig*, April 25, May 2, 1866.

[31] *Knoxville Whig*, March 14, April 4, 11, 1866; *American Annual Cyclopaedia*, 1866, p. 732.

times as large as Rhode Island; it would include 31 counties.[32]
A more important immediate reason would be the certain admission into the Union of the new state of East Tennessee. The
Whig declared Congress would admit it at once, as it would be
"greatly superior to West Virginia."[33] The Congressional Radicals were the friends of industrialism in the North, so they would
not be frightened by the appearance of hostile agriculturalist
Congressmen as they held Southerners generally to be, for East
Tennessee had already embraced the industrial program.[34]

A propaganda campaign was started to popularize the new
state idea and to arouse the people into a demand for it. A convention was called to meet in Knoxville in May, 1866, and various
meetings were held to arouse interest and to elect delegates.[35]
To the objection raised that if East Tennessee were set up as
a state, it would lose the beautiful capitol building in Nashville,
a new-state enthusiast replied, "We had rather be governed
by good laws made in a hog pen, than rebel laws made in the
grand Capitol at Nashville."[36] The meeting took place on May
3 and 4 in the courthouse, with 22 counties represented.
Oliver P. Temple set forth in a long report the reasons why East
Tennessee should become a new state, emphasizing the possibility of the state passing into Rebel hands at the next election
and leaving to the imagination what would happen to East
Tennesseeans in that event. The convention resolved to issue an
address to the people and to immediately petition the legislature
for permission to divide the state. On May 16 a new-state
memorial was presented to the legislature. It was referred to a
committee which reported it back favorably. But by this time
the franchise law had passed and the keenest edge of the movement was dulled.[37] Brownlow declared that the East Tennesseeans favored a new state "and if the measure were left to the
people at the ballot-box, they would carry it by as great a
majority as they voted down secession in 1861."[38]

---

[32] *Knoxville Whig*, April 4, 1866.
[33] *Ibid.*, April 11.
[34] *Ibid.*, April 25.   [35] *Ibid.*   [36] *Ibid.*, May 9.
[37] *Ibid.; American Annual Cyclopaedia*, 1866, p. 732; Fertig, *op. cit.*, p. 76.
[38] *Knoxville Whig*, May 30, 1866.

In fact the East Tennessee politicians were opposed to dividing the state as long as there was any possibility of their ruling the whole, since it would have reduced their power and spoils; and the masses of people in East Tennessee could never be made to see the wisdom of legislating themselves into poverty by the erection of a new state with all the expense of setting up a new government. Proof that East Tennesseans did not want a new state is to be seen in the fact that they had control of every branch of the government when the movement was at its greatest strength, and if they had wanted the new state or had been convinced that the people wanted it, they had it within their power to cut off East Tennessee and apply to Congress for admission. But statehood agitation was destined never to die. In the early part of 1869, when the Radical Tennesseeans saw definitely the end of their road, they introduced again the statehood resolution in the legislature, but now they had waited too long. The Morristown *Gazette* sized up the situation thus, "That party sees that power is certain to slip from their grasp if the State continues as it is, and hence they want East Tennessee, which is so intensely Radical, cut loose from the other portion, so they will have something to fall back upon."[39]

The whole Brownlow régime, political, constitutional, and religious, was watched throughout the United States with feelings as diverse as the watchers. Some comments were far from friendly, and if Brownlow considered his critics worthy of his wrath, he replied with double the venom they used. The quarrel most bitter and spectacular in the language used grew up with George D. Prentice, the brilliant editor of the *Louisville Journal*. It had its innocent and obscure origin back in 1864 when Prentice, who had come to distrust Lincoln and had been bold enough to publicly say so, accused Brownlow of suddenly departing from his coolness toward the President and entering into a full support of him because of a Federal job that had been bestowed upon the Parson. This accusation led to a mild passage of arms between the two, but the full fury of the fight did not develop until 1866 when Prentice began to find fault with Brownlow's management

[39] Quoted in *Knoxville Whig*, February 17, 1869.

of Tennessee. The Parson had early in the quarrel struck back with the charge that Prentice had swindled the United States Government in connection with army contracts during the war.[40] He then, as was his custom, drifted into personal and private abuse. He declared that Prentice was no longer a person of influence, that "For more than a year he has been in a state of beastly intoxication."[41]

Prentice now began a denunciation of Brownlow which, perhaps, equalled in its severity anything the Parson had ever been able to produce—a denunciation so extreme and devoid of good taste as to suggest the disintegrating effects of old age. He became brutally personal. The Parson's face looks "like that of a dead man, who mistaking a boy's tooting horn for Gabriel's trumpet has got up for judgment before his time." He professed to guide people to "heaven and curses them to hell." "He lies with his pen, lies with his tongue, lies with his gestures, lies through every pore of his shrivelled hide." He was as extreme as "the lowest and worst radical in the nation. He would gladly bathe his hands and feet and wash his face in the blood of every man who is not a radical." No state had ever been disgraced by such a governor as Brownlow. "He is a parody, a caricature, a broad burlesque on all possible Governors. He is a monstrosity. He is a thing as much out of nature as Barnum's wooly horse, or his giants and dwarfs, or his calf with two heads and eight legs—four of the legs pointing toward the zenith. His blood is hell broth, which Satan will one day sup with a long spoon." Prentice declared, "He never argued a question in his life, approaching no subject but with fierce, bitter, coarse, low and vulgar objurgations." He called himself a clergyman.

He preaches, prays and exhorts, draws down his face, drops the corners of his mouth, and undertakes to look sanctimonious. . . . He can't offer up a prayer in the House of God without telling the Lord what an infernal scoundrel, that or the other neighbor is. From his youth up to his old age, he has had no personal contro-

[40] *Knoxville Whig and Rebel Ventilator*, November 9, 1864, May 9, 16, 1866; Temple, *op. cit.*, p. 289.
[41] *Knoxville Whig*, April 4, 1866.

versies without attacking the wives, fathers, mothers, grandfathers, grandmothers, brothers, sisters, children, uncles, aunts, and nephews of his opponents. He has sought to strew his whole path of life with the dark wrecks of wantonly ruined reputations. He has never had an hour's happiness except in the unhappiness of others. He never had a friend on earth outside of his own family.

He was destined to go down in disgrace a prey to his own conscience.[42] He was in fact a wild animal and Tennessee ought to catch him "with a lasso and cage him."[43]

The Parson having met in Prentice his match in the art of vituperation, and having many less skillful enemies to fight soon began to devote his attention to the latter. Among these he found John Baxter, an East Tennessee Unionist who nevertheless had had sufficient standing with the Confederacy in 1861 to secure the promise of a passport for the Parson when he was hiding out in the Great Smokies. Baxter aroused the anger of the Parson by refusing to support his régime as governor. Brownlow now devoted many columns of his *Whig* to low abuse of Baxter, taking up his career from 1861 on down. In 1867, when the fight was at its height, he denounced Baxter through three columns of the *Whig*, and then declared "As a LIAR you are at the head of the list, and if a Liars' Fair were to be held in Tennessee, you would take all the premuims."[44] He also fell to fighting W. B. Carter whom he charged with stealing and embezzling.[45] Editor Fleming, who ran the Conservative newspaper in Knoxville, the Parson notified should have his attention as soon as he had finished with writing his message to the legislature. The Parson disliked Fleming because of uncomplimentary remarks the latter had made about him in his paper. He also found it easy to castigate terribly Frederick S. Heiskell.[46]

John B. Brownlow, who edited the *Whig*, either inherited or

---

[42] Quoted from the *Louisville Journal* by the *Southern Watchman,* May 2, 30, 1866.

[43] *Knoxville Whig,* May 16. 1866.

[44] *Ibid.;* March 7, 1866, May 15, 22, June 5, 1867.

[45] *Ibid.,* October 31, 1866.

[46] *Ibid.,* May 2, 1866, September 4, 1867.

developed the propensities of his father for combats both mental and physical. He naturally disliked J. W. Patterson, the editor of the Knoxville *Commercial* in 1866, and to show his contempt for him, he informed the readers of the *Whig* how he had accosted Patterson on the streets of Knoxville and would have caned him properly had a gentleman not interfered. He added a generous amount of cowardice to the other characteristics he gave the editor of the *Commercial*.[47]

The longest and most constant fight the Parson ever engaged in began early in his long life and with few interruptions lasted until the candle was finally snuffed out. This was his feud with Andrew Johnson. Their ante-bellum differences had been buried in the common cause they made for the Union from 1861 to 1865, and with the coming of peace goodwill continued to prevail. Governor Brownlow became the President's chief adviser concerning the granting of pardons to Tennesseeans and during the early part of Johnson's term all pardons went through Brownlow's hands. As has appeared the Governor and the President worked together in the early development of the Brownlow régime to the extent of the President's promise of the United States army if it should be needed. In November, 1865, the Parson's son, John, visited Washington and was so cordially received by the President that he returned to Tennessee a Johnson enthusiast. The Tennessee Unionists were equally pleased with the President and as proof, the legislature in October, 1865, passed resolutions of endorsement, though they carefully specified why they liked him—they liked "especially his declaration that 'Intelligent treason must be made odious, and traitors punished.' "[48] Their faith in him continued on into January, 1866, when they passed another resolution of support.[49]

The situation was not, however, without its dangers to the continuance of the *entente cordial*. Thaddeus Stevens had early laid plans to control the presidential policy concerning the

---

[47] *Ibid.*, May 2, 1866.
[48] *Knoxville Whig and Rebel Ventilator*, July 19, August 16, November 29, 1865; *Acts of Tennessee*, 1865-1866, p. 413.
[49] *American Annual Cyclopaedia*, 1866, pp. 727-28.

South even if it were necessary to break the President. When Congress met in December, 1865, there were signs of discord, and in less than three months there was open and bitter warfare between Johnson and the slowly forming Congressional oligarchy, led by Stevens. The break came on the Freedmen's Bureau bill, which Johnson successfully vetoed in February, 1866. East Tennesseans, who had always disliked Negroes, were much pleased with the veto and redoubled their support of the President, though they were somewhat upset by Johnson's pardon of too many Rebels too soon. They hoped he would not forget his dictum about treason being made odious.[50]

Brownlow was not entirely pleased with the President's course. He was soon saying that the Freedmen's Bureau veto was the greatest victory for the Rebels since the battle of Bull Run, and he became especially suspicious of Johnson when he noticed who in Tennessee were loudest in his support.[51] As has appeared the Parson had been having some trouble among his own Unionists. In the session of his legislature, in November, 1865, there had been rumblings of discontent when a member wanted Brownlow impeached for his extravagances and violation of law, and again when a resolution was introduced to require Brownlow to tell why he threw out so many votes in the August, 1865, election.[52] Undoubtedly there was developing an anti-Brownlow party among the Unionists, and William Heiskell, speaker of the house, was gradually becoming their leader. This group held a Union State Convention in Nashville on February 22 to endorse Johnson's stand on the Freedmen's Bureau measure and to stand behind him in his Reconstruction policy.[53] So it happened that the Parson, if he had had no other reasons for breaking again with Johnson, would have been forced into conflict by his enemies in Tennessee embracing the President.

It would be a grave matter to desert the President, for East Tennessee was no less the home of Johnson than of Brownlow,

---

[50] *Knoxville Whig,* March 28, 1866.

[51] *Ibid.,* April 4, 1866.

[52] *Knoxville Whig and Rebel Ventilator,* November 15, 29, 1865.

[53] *Ibid.,* February 28, 1866; *Ku Klux Conspiracy,* I, 461-62; *American Annual Cyclopaedia,* 1866, p. 731.

and the Parson could not be sure how this region would react. He knew that East Tennesseeans liked Johnson's Negro policy. For a month or two the *Whig* ceased to praise Johnson, yet it feared to blame him. Within a month the period of groping gradually disappeared and the Parson began to assume a critical attitude.[54] On March 24, in a speech in Knoxville before the Germans, he declared he had not yet been able to determine clearly what the President had in mind, but if it was to resurrect the Democratic Party, then he would part company with Johnson. His suspicions had already been aroused by the President's leniency toward Rebels. After all it was becoming more evident every day that the Congressional party were the true patriots, and the Parson declared, "I hold that a more talented, and patriotic body of men never occupied the Halls of Congress since the foundation of the Government."[55] On April 2, he spoke in Knoxville for an hour, and pulled farther away from the President. For a month or two the Parson and his *Whig* were able to keep their quarrel from developing into the stage of personal abuse, by centering their attacks largely against the Tennessee supporters of the President. The Johnson Conservatives were "secessionists whitewashed"—"They are the Southern Democratic party resurrected."[56] In June, 1866, the *Whig* declared, "If such a pack of men were to join in our praise, we should doubt our own integrity, and therefore it is that we will not fall into the support of any man they favor."[57]

Soon the floodgates of wrath were opened and the fight with Johnson began to resume its ante-bellum severity.[58] In a letter to Salmon P. Chase, the politically ambitious Chief Justice of the United States Supreme Court, Brownlow confided that he had once thought the President would remain true but he had "long since given him up." He declared that East Tennessee was full of Johnson emissaries, forming clubs and drumming up support. Out of nine newspapers in that region seven were for

[54] *Knoxville Whig*, February 21, April 4, 1866.
[55] *Ibid.*
[56] *Ibid.*, March 14, April 4, 25.
[57] *Ibid.*, June 13.
[58] *Ibid.*, June 20.

Johnson. If the Rebels should get control of Tennessee, "we Union men will have to leave the State."[59] Brownlow believed Johnson had helped to promote the "little rebellion" against the passage of the franchise act, for he charged him with appointing six of the bolters to Federal jobs.[60] Brownlow was soon announcing that back in 1862 when he and Johnson met in Nashville and were reconciled, he had forgiven Johnson with mental reservations and that all the praise he had given him since that time was to be taken as merely a comparison of what he would have thought of Johnson if he had become a Rebel.[61] Brownlow now discovered that Johnson had opposed his nomination for governor in 1865, because he wanted to be both vice president of the United States and military governor of Tennessee at the same time.[62] Now did Brownlow bitterly repent of his support of Johnson for the vice presidential nomination in 1864. He would admit that "it was the worst act of his protracted and somewhat eventful life."[63]

The national issue on which Brownlow completely broke with Johnson and joined the Congressional Radical party was the Fourteenth Amendment. After the veto of the Freedmen's Bureau bill, warfare between the President and Congress developed fast. Stevens, Sumner, and their lieutenants malignantly abused the President and cast out his Reconstruction program and by June, 1866, they developed the Fourteenth Amendment as a part of their Southern scheme. At first Brownlow had not felt that Tennessee was being given proper consideration, for when Congress met in December, 1865, the Tennessee Congressmen were not admitted. In fact Stevens had seen to it that not even their names should be called in the organization of the

---

[59] "Diary and Correspondence of Salmon P. Chase," *Annual Report of the American Historical Association,* 1902, II, 515-16.

[60] *Knoxville Whig,* June 27, 1866.

[61] *Putnam's Magazine,* vol. III, no. 16 (April, 1869) p. 434. An examination of thirty volumes of the Johnson Papers in the Library of Congress, shows that little correspondence passed between Johnson and Brownlow during the period of their truce (1862-1866). Brownlow's communications were generally short telegrams.

[62] Temple, *op. cit.,* p. 344.

[63] *Knoxville Whig,* August 22, 1866.

House—even the staunch old Unionist Horace Maynard was unacceptable, though he was allowed the courtesy of the floor. But Brownlow had kept in touch with Johnson and, therefore, knew how bad he was; there was no course left but to join the Congressional Radicals, even if he had not been otherwise willing. He wanted Congressional recognition of Tennessee by her admission into the national legislature, and he also wanted pay for the damages suffered by the Tennessee Unionists. If Tennessee's course so far had not been radical enough to please Stevens and Sumner, Brownlow would oblige them by doing whatever else they might require. So when the Fourteenth Amendment was submitted to the states he made immediate preparations to ratify it. He called a special session of the legislature to meet on July 4 (1866), for what could be more patriotic than to prepare for ratification on the "Glorious Fourth"![64] The Tennessee Radicals also made merry in their celebrations over the state, both for the Fourteenth Amendment and for the Fourth of July. To honor Brownlow and the legislature, the symbols of patriotism in Tennessee, the merry radicals at Loudon boomed forth their cannon ten times.[65]

On the meeting of the legislature Brownlow submitted the amendment with his reasons. He was undoubtedly somewhat perturbed over the possibilities of difficulties in persuading the legislators to ratify, for a storm of opposition had been raised throughout the South on this stern measure of the Congressional Radicals. There were already mutterings that the South would never be a party to its own dishonor, and in this determination the President seemed to agree, for he had let it be known that he was opposed to its ratification. In his message Brownlow put great stress on the necessity of ratifying the amendment for the purpose of getting Tennessee into the Union again—he had the most complete assurance that if Tennessee ratified she would be immediately admitted. And after all, the amendment was a most gracious act of Congress. It exhibited "a magnanimity on the

---

[64] *Noted Men of the Solid South*, p. 186; Fertig, *op. cit.*, p. 62; *The South in the Building of the Nation*, II, 528-29; *Knoxville Whig*, June 27, 1866.

[65] *Ibid.*, July 11, 1866.

part of the American people ... which challenges our admiration. .... Viewed as terms of final adjustment between the conqueror and conquered, their mildness and freedom from all penalties is without a parallel in the history of nations."[66]

The senate ratified the amendment without a struggle, but there were an unterrified few in the house who had agreed with the rest of the South that the amendment would cause a revolution in the old form of the national government and would bring degradation and vengeance upon the South. They acted immediately. Some who were in Nashville refused to attend the session and others appeared only to resign. M. E. W. Dunnaway resigned his seat the day following the first meeting. Brownlow replied, "As it is evidently the design of your resignation to reduce the House below a quorum, and to break up the Legislature, the same is not accepted."[67] It seemed that there was in the making a second "little rebellion" and that the disorders attending the passage of the franchise bill were to be reënacted. Eight bolted in the house, and either fled to their homes or took to hiding in Nashville. They succeeded in preventing a quorum. Brownlow was so determined to have the amendment ratified that he now called upon the United States army to aid. General Thomas, to whom he applied for troops, was instructed by the President through Secretary Stanton, to take no part in the political turmoil. The Federal army had not yet been given the additional duty of ratifying Federal amendments. The house instructed Speaker Heiskell to issue warrants for the arrest of the absent members, and Captain Heydt, the superintendent of the capitol and the sergeant-at-arms, set out to serve them. Pleasant Williams, of Carter County, who had taken part in the first "little rebellion," and was now a leader in the second one, fled to his home in the mountains of East Tennessee, only to be followed by Captain Heydt, who arrested him and returned him to Nashville. Another member defied the Captain and was defended against arrest by a group of his friends who had armed

---

[66] *House Journal of the Called Session of the General Assembly of the State of Tennessee, July 4, 1866*, p. 27; *Knoxville Whig*, July 11, 1866.
[67] *Ibid.*

themselves. By July 19 the house had been able to round up enough members to make a quorum provided two in the custody of the Captain were brought to the floor. To prevent their escape they were held in a committee room in the capitol. Speaker Heiskell ruled that there was not a quorum present, but the house overrode his decision, voted the two prisoners in the committee room present, and ratified the Fourteenth Amendment. Heiskell then refused to sign the resolution, and thereupon abdicated the chair. John Norman, the speaker *pro tem* then signed it. In the meantime Williams and A. J. Martin, the two legislator-prisoners, sued out a writ of *habeas corpus* before Thomas N. Frazier, judge of the Criminal Court for Davidson County, who ordered the prisoners to be released. The house disregarded the decision of the judge and held them. Heydt, for his zeal in arresting and detaining citizens of Tennessee against the orders of a judge, was himself arrested in his quarters in the capitol building early one morning by the sheriff of Davidson County with twenty-five assistants. He was brought before Judge Frazier and fined ten dollars. Williams also brought suit for damages against each member of the legislature who had aided in his arrest, but when the sheriff attempted to serve the warrants he was ordered from the house.[68]

The boldness of Judge Frazier amazed the Radical legislators. He was declared a Rebel, though he was one of the East Tennessee Unionists who had fled to Nashville during the war and who had been appointed to his judgeship by Military Governor Andrew Johnson. The *Whig* declared that rather than see traitors trample upon the law, "we would see our beautiful State converted into a vast battle-field."[69] At its next session, in May, 1867, the house brought impeachment proceedings against Frazier, and the next month the senate convicted him, removed him from office, and declared him henceforth ineligible for a public trust in Tennessee. The constitutional convention in 1870 restored his rights to him and him to his old judgeship.[70]

---

[68] For the ratification of the Fourteenth Amendment by Tennessee see, *Knoxville Whig*, July 18, August 1, 1866; Fertig, *op. cit.*, pp. 77-78; *American Annual Cyclopaedia, 1866*, p. 729; *Noted Men of the Solid South*, pp. 186-88, 191.

[69] *Knoxville Whig*, July 25, 1866.   [70] Fertig, *op. cit.*, pp. 77-78.

The senate having ratified the amendment on the eleventh, the action of the house on the nineteenth completed the process, and on the same day Brownlow telegraphed the clerk of the Senate, John W. Forney: "A battle fought and won. We have carried the constitutional amendment in the House. Vote—43 to 11, two of A. Johnson's tools refusing to vote. My compliments to the 'dead dog' in the White House."[71] A few days later Forney replied: "All honor to the fire-tried Unionists of Tennessee. The loyal millions are everywhere celebrating your fortitude and courage, and praising Congress for preparing to admit you into the National Council."[72]

Brownlow's violent course in forcing the Fourteenth Amendment through his legislature led many people throughout the country to wonder what he would next do in the name of law and patriotism. Gideon Welles, the Secretary of the Navy, recorded in his diary that news had arrived from "the coarse, vulgar creature who is Governor of Tennessee" that the amendment had been ratified by a legislature chosen "under circumstances and animosities which would not be justified or excusable in peace." The method he used to secure ratification was "an exhibition of Radical regard for honest principle, for popular opinion, and for changes in the organic law."[73] The *Richmond Examiner*, wearied and disgusted, said, "If there is any law, written or unwritten, which can reach this old scoundrel Brownlow, it should be appealed to at once. Patience has ceased to be a virtue."[74]

Congress immediately passed a joint resolution admitting the Tennessee delegation, after reciting that Tennessee had passed the Thirteenth and Fourteenth amendments, had repudiated the Confederate debt, had organized a state government, and had "done other acts proclaiming and denoting loyalty." They had now admitted Johnson's home state into Congress but under conditions that were galling to him. With evident joy they now placed the President in the dilemma of indirectly approving the

[71] *Knoxville Whig*, July 25, 1866.
[72] *Ibid.*, August 1.
[73] *Diary of Gideon Welles*, II, 557, July 19, 1866.
[74] Quoted in *Knoxville Whig*, August 8, 1866.

Fourteenth Amendment or making himself the instrument for the attempted continued exclusion of his own state. Johnson immediately signed the resolution stating that it was merely the expression of an opinion and an unnecessary act, as Congress was the sole judge of the qualifications of its own membership. He had serious doubts that Tennessee had constitutionally ratified the amendment, and furthermore, no notice had been sent to the President or to the Department of State.[75] Brownlow had with evident contempt for the President ignored the regular form of notification. On July 24, the day the statement was written, it was read in the house with sarcasm and laughter, and on the same day Horace Maynard and two of his associates were sworn in. The next day Senator Fowler was seated in the upper chamber, but Senator Patterson, the President's son-in-law, was insulted and kept waiting three days while a committee investigated his war record, and he was seated only a few hours before final adjournment.[76] The Tennessee legislature thanked Congress and adjourned to the strains of "Hail Columbia, the Star Spangled Banner and Yankee Doodle . . . played in the Halls of the Capitol on a full band."[77]

Tennessee was, thus, the first Confederate state to be readmitted, having been the last to secede. She escaped the heavy hand of Congress later exhibited in the military reconstruction of the rest of the Confederacy, but her deliverance was at the hands of her own Radicals, who in their extremism antedated and even surpassed the Congressional Radicals. Tennessee, thus, became the first Radical stronghold in the South, who proudly pointed to her record of accomplishments in bold contrast to the Rebel-ridden state of Kentucky to the northward.[78]

Brownlow's haste and extreme methods employed in forcing

---

[75] McPherson, *History of Reconstruction*, pp. 105, 151-53.

[76] E. P. Oberholtzer, *A History of the United States Since the Civil War*, I, 187-88; *Noted Men of the Solid South*, p. 183.

[77] *Acts and Resolutions of the State of Tennessee passed at the Extra Session of the Thirty-fourth General Assembly, July, 1866*, pp. 29-30, 34. The music was provided for by a senate resolution.

[78] See Brownlow's message to the legislature, November 6, 1866, in *Senate Journal of the Second Adjourned Session of the General Assembly of the State of Tennessee*, 1866-1867, pp. 10-22.

ratification through the legislature were due, first to his rekindled and burning hatred of Andrew Johnson and to his knowledge that the President was opposed to the amendment; and secondly, to the professed fear that Johnson was planning to destroy the state government and supplant Brownlow with a military governor. The state having been saved by Congress should now be placed under the watch-care of that body. The Parson declared that the amendment had been ratified "in the face of the direct opposition of the Federal administration, and in defiance of its power and patronage." He directly charged Johnson with encouraging the bolters, and otherwise attempting to defeat ratification by letter-writing and bribery. Some people had criticized the Governor for his reference to Johnson as "the 'dead dog' in the White House"; in answer Brownlow wrote three columns for the *Whig* in which he defended his "dead dog" expression, heaped further abuse upon the President, and recalled for those who might have forgotten, the drunken exhibition Johnson had made of himself when he was inaugurated vice president.[79]

The Parson now considered it his patriotic duty to attack the President at every possible opportunity, for a new rebellion was in the making and Johnson would be its head. On August 9, he wrote, "We are to have another war. Johnson has gone over to the rebels, and in the next rebellion, will take the place of *Jeff Davis*. . . . We want another war to put down the rebellion." Then there would be an opportunity to do "a large amount of hanging."[80] The *Whig* said, "That we are to have another conflict of arms we have no sort of doubt. . . ."[81] When it should break out, a million loyal men would surround the Capitol and White House and soon be *"disposing of the heads of leading traitors* after the most approved style of the age, in which the King of England lost his head."[82] Then, the Parson declared,

---

[79] *Senate Journal of Tennessee,* 1866-1867, pp. 10-22; *Knoxville Whig,* July 25, August 8, 22, November 7, 1866.

[80] MS letter in the Library of Congress, to "My dear Sir," written at Knoxville, August 9, 1866.

[81] *Knoxville Whig,* August 29, 1866.

[82] *Ibid.,* August 1.

the loyal masses will "make the entire Southern Confederacy as God found the earth when he commenced the work of creation, 'without form and void.' They will not, and ought not leave a rebel fence-rail, out-house, or dwelling in the eleven seceded States." Taking a hint from some of Thaddeus Stevens' speeches, he would exterminate the Rebel population and confiscate and sell their land to pay the expenses of the war.[83]

Johnson's course had lost him many friends throughout the country, but there were still many left, and they would show their faith in his plan of reconstruction by holding a convention in Philadelphia in August, 1866, to be followed in September by a soldiers' and sailors' convention in Cleveland. These meetings would be valuable for developing sentiment favorable to Johnson in the Congressional elections in the fall. The Radicals, not to be outdone, prepared to hold similar conventions. Their first convention met in Philadelphia and their soldiers and sailors convention came together in Pittsburgh, both in September.

As the main purpose of the Philadelphia convention was to prove to the country that the South favored the Congressional leadership, a great effort was made to produce as many Southern delegates as possible. It met in two divisions, a Southern and a Northern. The latter division was made up of the "honorary delegates," consisting of such well-wishers as Anna Dickinson and Frederick Douglass, and was presided over by Governor Curtin of Pennsylvania. Brownlow appeared with a group of Tennessee Radicals and immediately became the greatest attraction in Philadelphia, where he was well-known on account of his various visits for conventions and speechmakings. He headed all processions and sat in the front row on the rostra. A grand parade of delegates, who according to the *New York World* were "self-appointed, representing nobody but themselves," accompanied by fire-wagons, and various other vehicles decorated with flowers and flags, made its appearance on the streets. Brownlow and other important Radical leaders in a carriage, headed the procession, followed by the seventy-five members of the Tennessee delegation. In another display of strength on the

[83] *Ibid.*, August 22, 1866.

streets, Brownlow and Andrew Jackson Hamilton, the late provisional governor of Texas, headed the march in an open ba-
rouche. In the assembly halls Brownlow was equally prominent.
At one of the meetings he was introduced by Judge W. D.
Kelley, and for five minutes the applause swept the hall. The
Parson was obsessed with the idea that another war was imi-
nent, and on almost every occasion he spoke of it. He had already
decided that this war would be fought in three divisions, and he
wanted "a finger in that pie." The first division should be armed
with rifles and artillery "to do the killing"; the second should
"be armed with pine torches and spirits of turpentine, and let
them do the burning"; and the third should be equipped with
compasses and chains "to survey the land into small parcels and
give it to those who are loyal in the North." "Great applause"
followed this short speech—short because the Parson was very
sick with the palsy. At another time he informed the convention
that if Johnson should win in the approaching election the
Union men would be forced to flee from the South, but as for
himself, when he hid out in the Great Smokies in 1861 he had
decided that that would be his last time to flee from the Rebels.
"I will sooner expire on a lamp-post under the shadow of the
Capitol of Tennessee!" he exclaimed. At the mention of Andrew
Johnson, three groans "for the dead dog in the White House"
were given and three cheers for Brownlow.

Brownlow was in demand at all times of the day and night.
The Liberty Cornet Band serenaded him at the home where he
was staying. To show his appreciation the Parson came out and
delivered from the steps "a short and telling address." On the
Sunday preceding the meeting of the convention "The Nitro-
Glycerinical Parson," as he was called by a friendly reporter,
had promised to preach in the Methodist Church, but when the
time came he found himself not well enough, but not to disappoint the congregation he "gave the audience a little hell-fire,
by way of a closing exhortation before pronouncing the
benediction."

Before the two conventions went home they held a joint
meeting in front of the Union League House. The Parson in

order to see the crowd to better advantage, Zacchaeus-like, climbed up and secured a perch on top of the building and soon found himself in the company of Chief Justice Chase and General Cameron, who had developed similar strategical plans for viewing the multitude. Brownlow declared that he looked down upon 100,000 people—some appraisers said more. The Johnson "Bread and Butter Convention," he declared, in comparison looked like a common town meeting. In the confusion the League House caught fire, but Brownlow declared that the "Copper-Johnson incendiaries" had set fire to it and had damaged it to the extent of $40,000.

These Southern Radicals did much parading and engaged in much loud noise-making, but when it came to resolving their articles of faith, they broke up in confusion. The Rebel states representatives, in order to secure and maintain control back home, seized upon Negro suffrage as the remedy. The convention refused to follow. As for the Parson, he favored it. He would rather be elected by loyal Negroes than disloyal whites; he would rather be buried in a Negro graveyard than in a Rebel one; and when he should go either to hell or heaven, he would rather go with Negroes than with white Rebels. The convention agreed on its hatred of the President, and according to the Parson the document issued was "the most powerful bill of indictment ever presented to the world against any offender." Inside Independence Hall or in its shadow, the main activities of this convention had taken place—according to the *Whig* the "grandest Convention which ever assembled on this continent (save that of 1776 when independence was proclaimed.)"[84]

Thus had the influence of the President's "Bread and Butter Convention" been snuffed out by the Southern Radicals, aided by the "honorary delegates" from the North. At the very time they were carrying out this task, Andrew Johnson accompanied

---

[84] For the main facts concerning these conventions see, *Knoxville Whig*, September 12, 19, October 24, 1866; *Cincinnati Daily Commercial*, September 3, 4, 7; Oberholtzer, *op. cit.*, I, 391-95; H. K. Beale, *The Critical Year. A Study of Andrew Johnson and Reconstruction*, p. 331. The Parson was much pleased with A. J. Hamilton, and especially glad to know that his father had been born in Knox County, Tennessee.

by William H. Seward, Ulysses S. Grant, Admiral David G. Farragut and other notable people, was making his "moccasin tracks" in his "Swing around the Circle" to attend the ceremonies in Chicago incident to the laying of the cornerstone of the Douglas monument. These "tracks" must be "wiped out," and no person would be better able to do so than the Parson with a flying squad he would organize. The conspiracy of newspaper reporters, mayors, and governors to misquote and insult the President of the United States might have seemed sufficient to discredit Johnson before the country, but Brownlow was sure there was a type of work to be done which only he and his helpers could do. The Parson selected twenty-seven Southern Radicals from the Philadelphia collection and set out across New Jersey for New York and the New England States. They would properly expose Johnson's "bush-whacking pilgrimage" and answer well his "abusive speeches, made for the most part under the influence of liquor."[85] Though Brownlow's body was filled with pain and shaken with the palsy, he felt he had a patriotic duty to perform. He generally spoke from fifteen to twenty-five minutes, and gave his plan for the conquest of the South in the next war, which he had exposed at Philadelphia. For this sentiment and because he was the inimitable Parson, he received louder and longer applause than any other member of his party. This small army operated somewhat after the fashion of cavalry raiders. They deployed and broke up their group into as many as seven divisions in some regions, rejoining one another preparatory to a new invasion. The Parson carried the warfare as far into New England as Rutland, Vermont, and then headed his forces westward through Albany and central New York. Never since the days of "Tippecanoe and Tyler Too" had the Parson seen such enthusiasm as greeted the raiders. They made an excursion to Auburn, New York, the home of Seward, to disperse his forces in that region. They successfully carried that stronghold amid a rousing reception, with bells ringing, cannon roaring, and beautiful ladies waving handkerchiefs, and tossing bouquets. They reached Buffalo on Sep-

[85] *Knoxville Whig*, October 3, 1866.

tember 19, having during the past two days held twenty-two mass meetings.

They now set out for the Middle West, passing through Erie and Cleveland and on to Cincinnati, holding thirty mass meetings on the way. The reception they received in the "Queen City of the West" was "grand beyond conception, and excelled anything that has come off in Cincinnati for years." Here the next war was made to assume the character of a recruiting campaign. One placard prominently displayed in the demonstration bore the inscription: "250,000 OHIO MUSKETS FOR THE SECOND REBELLION." Brownlow declared that Johnson was already making preparations for evacuating Tennessee and leaving it to the Rebels, by his recent removal of General Thomas' headquarters from Nashville to Louisville.

Leaving Cincinnati, the party now reduced in number to twenty, set out for Indianapolis with the intention of holding from thirty to forty mass meetings on the way. Much weakened by his strenuous campaigning, the Parson now deserted the main party, and boarding a sleeping car, set out for Chicago. Here he was entertained by Lieutenant Governor Bross in his mansion on Michigan Avenue, in full view of Lake Michigan. Though now primarily taking the rest cure, Brownlow could not refrain from engaging in the excitement when the army arrived and began operations in five divisions. Chicago was soon ablaze with processions of marching pedestrians, rumbling carriages, blaring bands of music, waving flags, and "shouts that rent the air, with torch lights that illuminated the Heavens, and every other conceivable display, and the story is not half told." William B. Stokes introduced Brownlow, who made a short speech; he was too sick to speak long. He informed the crowd that the Radicals would carry Illinois by a vast majority, as indeed they would carry all other parts of the country.[86]

Governor Brownlow returned to Tennessee in triumph. Recommendations began to be made that he run for the vice presidential nomination, and there were even suggestions that he

[86] *Ibid.*, September 19, October 3, 10, 24, 1866; *Daily New Era*, October 12, 1866.

would make a good president. Not all Tennesseeans, however, agreed with his campaign of vilification of the President; they felt that it was not the Governor's business to be touring the country in a seven ring circus. In answer the Parson declared that he had at least not run up liquor bills of $400 each in the various towns he had visited and then absconded without paying them.[87]

With Brownlow in such complete control of Tennessee it seemed needless for him to give much attention to the campaign there. Yet the fight was exhilarating and he would not rest. He published again his classic answer to Jordan Clark in 1860, informing the expectant Arkansan when he would join the Democratic Party; he also ran every week at the head of the editorial page of the *Whig*, a radical speech Johnson had made in September, 1864, to draw the contrast with his present position. He also formed the determination that the Johnson party in Tennessee should not interrupt the unanimity of feeling in the state for the Radicals. A Johnson ratification meeting had been announced for Knoxville to be held on September 19. The *Whig* declared that such a convention would be treasonable and revolutionary and that it must not be held; "LET THEM CALL IT IF THEY DARE.—Whenever they do so it shall be dispersed at the point of the bayonet, or the loyal militia in the State will perish in the attempt."[88] The Parson declared that this corrupt party had been "sired by a Massachusetts traitor and born of a South Carolina harlot. Baptized in a wigwam at Philadelphia, in the august presence of a vast army of government dependents, political turncoats and apostate Republicans, Rebel Congressmen and Rebel Generals, the ceremonies were gone through with by an association of old clerical hacks, who had lied and drank themselves out of countenance during the rebellion."[89]

In the Congressional elections the Radicals gained a two-thirds majority in Congress and made a clean sweep of the

[87] *Knoxville Whig,* October 24, 1866.
[88] *Ibid.,* September 19. See also *ibid.,* October 3, November 7.
[89] *Daily New Era,* October 12, 1866. This was part of a speech the Parson delivered in Chicago.

Tennessee delegation. The President had been terribly worsted in the nation, and Brownlow had annihilated him in Tennessee. The Parson's war talk and the general campaign of the Radicals to assassinate the character of Johnson had stampeded the people to support the policy of extremism. Brownlow had been a good general and strategist. He had chosen the winning side and had placed Tennessee in a strong position with the rulers of the nation. Now he need not fear anything that Johnson could do. He hated the President so profoundly that he was unable to recognize in him a friendly act. Soon after the election the President promoted in the Federal army, James P. Brownlow, the Parson's son, who had been the adjutant general of Tennessee, and detailed him to San Francisco. Instead of regarding this as a favor to his son, the Parson declared that Johnson had sent him to the wild West to fight the savage Indians and doubtless be scalped by them—and this after all James had done in taking care of the President's drunken son during Civil War days![90]

There was one person, however, whom Tennessee delighted to honor, the commander of the Federal troops in the state, whose headquarters the President had transferred from Nashville to Louisville. The legislature made preparations to celebrate the battle of Nashville, on December 15 (1866), and invited General Thomas, the hero of that conflict, to be present as the chief guest of honor, and to receive a gold medal which it had voted him. A downpour of rain forced the ceremonies into the capitol, where Brownlow made the presentation speech. During the ceremonies Captain Heydt presented to General Thomas, Governor Brownlow, and Speaker Frierson of the senate, large bouquets of flowers.[91] It was felt that General Thomas would have been much more liberal in his use of the troops in aiding Brownlow to secure the ratification of the Fourteenth Amendment if the President had permitted.

Brownlow had succeeded in intrenching himself and the Radicals in Tennessee and in tying the state to the Radical juggernaut of the nation. His position was strong, but there were yet forces which must be reckoned with.

---

[90] *Knoxville Whig*, December 5, 1866.   [91] *Ibid.*, December 19.

CHAPTER XIV

THE REIGN OF THE TENNESSEE RADICALS

HAVING DEFEATED his old enemy, Andrew Johnson, Brownlow came out of the struggle elated and satisfied. But success is sometimes more difficult to endure than defeat, for it leads on to ambitions which must also be satisfied. The great stir the Parson had made in the world up to this time had been incited more through fear and vengeance than ambition. Now, the pleasure that comes from being an important man began to work its insidious influence, and Brownlow took on a new characteristic in Tennessee politics.

The regular election for all state officials and a new legislature was due in August, 1867. Having tasted of power Brownlow discovered that he liked it. Being governor for only two years seemed too short; though physically worn out, his mind was still strong and his hatreds were as keen as ever; he would accept two more years. Being a skillful politician, he outwardly assumed the attitude of a Caesar rejecting a crown. But there were many Radicals in Tennessee who knew that they would rise or fall with the Parson; they would be bolder than Anthony, they would force the crown upon the brow of the Parson. Preparing for the Radical convention which would meet on February 22 and nominate a governor, they began in January to promote a great number of county meetings throughout East Tennessee which called loudly for Brownlow. Their resolutions, being much alike in their wording, bespoke a central direction. The Radicals of Bledsoe County declared that whereas it had pleased God "to give us a Governor in the almost miraculously preserved person of William G. Brownlow, whom we have tried and found to be *not* wanting," they were determined to work for his renomination.[1]

---

[1] *Knoxville Whig,* January 23, 1867. For other county meetings, see *ibid.,* January 16, February 13.

The feeling was soon expressed and spread that only the Parson could properly punish the Rebels and save East Tennessee from the vengeance they would wreak if they should secure power.[2] The *Whig* quoted with approval the discovery which the *Press and Times,* the chief Radical newspaper in Nashville, had made, that the clamor for Brownlow "grows more and more manifest" and that he "can stay at home and outrun any other nominee of the Republican party who can be put on the track."[3] Under the circumstances no Radical was so bold or ambitious as to oppose the Parson.

The convention met in Nashville on Washington's Birthday eager to deify the Parson and damn the President. On the walls of the house of representatives chamber, where the delegates gathered, there were hanging in the gallery of notables the pictures of Lincoln and Johnson. The martyred President was decorated with flags, the living President was left bare. The contrast was soon noted, whereupon a delegate moved that thirty-six men be appointed to hold the United States flag in front of it "to keep his Accidency quiet during the session of the convention." Another member moved that the President should be stood upon his head. Before the convention had scarcely come to order a letter from Brownlow was read in which he protested that he was not seeking the nomination, but he quickly added, "Even in my feeble state of health, if I were nominated by your Convention, I would not feel at liberty to decline the nomination." He followed this hint with a characteristic abuse of Johnson.[4]

The Convention immediately nominated the Parson unanimously and loudly called for him. Being near-by he quickly entered the hall, amidst a roar of applause, the waving of handkerchiefs, and the tossing of hats high in the air. Brownlow accepted the nomination with alacrity and predicted that he would be charged with "dictation, usurpation, a violation of the Constitution—with lying, perjury, stealing, forgery and counterfeiting!" He would be held to be the friend of the Negro, but

---

[2] *Ibid.,* February 13, 1867.
[3] *Ibid.,* January 16.   [4] *Ibid.,* February 27.

he would "sooner be elected by dark skinned loyalists, than to be elected by the votes of fair-skin traitors." Though it would be more than two years before a new president of the United States would take his seat, the convention declared that General Thomas was its choice—"the man who never made a mistake and never lost a battle."[5]

Before adjourning, the Radicals thanked God for saving from traitors "the best government ever known to man" and for proving the "heretofore doubtful problem that man is capable of self-government." It held as self-evident truths that those who saved the state and nation should govern them, that those who sought to destroy them should repent of their sins, that rebellion was a "treasonable expatriation," that law should be made a "terror to evil-doers," that the Constitution of the United States and the Declaration of Independence should be "*living truths* and *practical maxims* in Tennessee," that the Radicals in Congress had the sole right "to restore, preserve, and govern the country," that "we honor the firmness, courage, and wisdom which have characterized the administration of our Chief Magistrate, the Hon. Wm. G. Brownlow, and while we sympathize with him in his bodily suffering, we admire the healthy mind, conscious to itself of rectitude, which bears with like equanimity the throes of pain and the perilous cares of State; and that we declare him the unanimous choice of the loyal people of Tennessee for our next Governor." But as for Andrew Johnson, "we cover our faces with shame when we contemplate the disgrace brought upon our beloved State by the defection and degeneracy of her unprincipled adopted son, who by the bullet of an assassin has ascended to the Chief Magistracy of the nation; and we shall cordially endorse any action of Congress which shall legitimately deprive him of continued power to disturb the peace of the country."[6]

Brownlow received the congratulations of his fellow Radical, Salmon P. Chase, the Chief Justice of the nation.[7]

[5] *Ibid.*, March 6, 1867.
[6] McPherson, *History of Reconstruction*, pp. 248-49.
[7] R. B. Worden, *An Account of the Private Life and Public Service of Salmon Portland Chase*, pp. 657-58.

The Conservatives met in April and nominated for the governorship Brownlow's bitter critic, Emerson Etheridge. They favored peace, order, and obedience to the laws, opposed the military domination of the state, and expressed their support of Andrew Johnson.[8]

Brownlow had for the past few months been moving rapidly toward Negro suffrage, not because he had lost any of "those prejudices of caste, resulting from education and life-long habits," but because he saw he would need the Negro votes to maintain himself in power. Under the contagion of the Northern atmosphere at the Philadelphia Convention in September, 1866, he had shouted for Negro suffrage, and had declared that he "would sooner go to a Negro heaven than a white Rebel's Hell."[9] As has previously appeared, the Radicals in Tennessee had already given the Negro full civil rights, except to sit on juries. When the legislature had met in November, 1866, he had uncorked "his bottled thunder" and had delivered his message made up of a "mass of political crudities, unstatesmanlike dogmas and revolutionary doctrines, more radical and startling than have ever been propounded by any similar functionary in the Republic."[10] Remembering how strong was the race feeling among his East Tennessee supporters, he approached the subject of Negro suffrage cautiously. He had found that the Negroes had "shown greater aptitude for learning and intelligence than was expected" and the Rebels had, under Johnson's leadership, got worse. Despite the most strenuous suffrage laws, traitors in large numbers had been voting in Tennessee. Should the Negroes, then, not vote? Even Andrew Johnson had advocated since his accession to the presidency a scheme for Negro voting. But the Parson's most compelling argument was that it would keep the state out of the hands of the Rebels and greatly please the Radicals in Washington, who were undoubtedly moving toward Negro suffrage for the rest of the South.[11] Tennessee

---

[8] *American Annual Cyclopaedia*, 1867, p. 706. [9] Warmoth, *op. cit.*, p. 50.

[10] Nashville *Union and American*, quoted in *Daily New Era*, November 10, 1866.

[11] *Senate Journal of Tennessee*, 1866, p. 12; *American Annual Cyclopaedia*, 1867, p. 729.

was the only Radical state in the South; it should not disappoint Congress.

The Conservatives in the legislature, who had long favored the removal of the disabilities against the Confederates, immediately seized upon the Parson's recommendation and cleverly changing it, introduced a bill for universal suffrage and universal amnesty. This trick which they had tried once before, failed again. The Parson was now more than ever determined that the Negroes should have the vote and he believed that it would be calamitous if the Radicals should not be responsible for giving it to them. So on the day before Christmas, as if he were giving a Yuletide present to the Negroes, he sent a special message to the legislature in which he boldly came out for complete and immediate suffrage for the Negroes. "Onward is the watchword which shields and inspires two continents!" declared the Governor. "Now is the time for Tennessee to show to the world that she belongs to the advanced guard on the great question of equal suffrage! With the loyal men of the State allowed to vote, the Government thereof will remain in loyal hands. Without their votes, the state will pass into disloyal hands, and a reign of terror not so easily described as realized will result."[12] The Parson was determined that the Conservatives should not have the credit of giving the Negro the vote, through their scheme of connecting Rebel voting with it.

During January and February (1867) Negro meetings, properly directed, began to spring up in various parts of the state, calling for the right to vote and for Brownlow's renomination for the governorship. In Knoxville they met and noisily cheered Brownlow's name every time it was mentioned.[13] Negroes in Blount County met at Maryville and resolved for Brownlow and Negro suffrage. They had afforded soldiers who had "fought and vanquished on the battlefield the bloody minions of a slaveholders rebellion, and who are ready and willing to mete out justice to traitors at the ballot box."[14] Such resolutions showed

[12] Ibid., 1866, p. 730.
[13] Knoxville Whig, February 20, 1867.
[14] Ibid., February 6.

that the Negroes knew how to vote. The McMinn County Negroes met at Athens, resolved for the ballot, and thanked for their present blessings Almighty God, the Radical Congress, and Brownlow.[15]

Now that the Parson had set his heart on Negro suffrage, with the majority he could command in the legislature it was inevitable. Sensing that they were about to secure their "Place in the Sun" the Negroes filled the gallery of the house to look and applaud. The *Whig* reported in early February, "The gathering clouds of dusky humanity which settled down in the galleries of the House early in the day, plainly portending a storm —some wordy encounter in which Sambo could not be otherwise than an interested spectator."[16]

On the 20th the Negro suffrage law was passed, and the Parson thereby gave to Tennessee the distinction of being the only state in the South to permit the Negro to vote—an even greater accomplishment when it was remembered that the Congressional Radicals had not yet forced it upon their military districts now about to be set up in the former Confederacy. Thus were the Tennessee Conservatives forcefully reminded that the rule of their own native Radicals was more extreme than that of the Northern Radicals.[17]

Brownlow occupied a proud pinnacle in the Southern States. Only Tennessee was a state in the eyes of the Congressional Radicals; the other divisions which Johnson had called states were dragging out through the sufferance of Congress a weak existence, which was soon to be terminated when they should lose their names, become military districts, and receive numbers. Naturally Brownlow looked upon these Johnson states with contempt. When Virginia, North Carolina, and Georgia, at various times, had made requisitions upon him for the return of escaped criminals, he vigorously refused their requests. To the governor of Virginia he made "such an answer that no further correspondence took place between us on the subject."

---

[15] *Ibid.*, February 27, 1867.   [16] *Ibid.*, February 6.
[17] *American Annual Cyclopaedia*, 1867, p. 706; *Noted Men of the Solid South*, p. 193.

Brownlow declared he would "not surrender Union officers and soldiers to the horse-thieves and bush-whackers of the rebel states to be imprisoned and hung because of their Union sentiments."[18]

The objective toward which all eyes in Tennessee were now turned was the August election. The movement for Negro suffrage had been developed largely with this point in view, and now that the Negro would vote in the next election both parties sought his support. Naturally the Radicals had captured the colored man's affections, but the Conservatives did, none the less, attempt to garner what dusky votes they could. In their April convention they had agreed to full political and civil rights for Negroes. Each party was able to organize supporting Negro conventions.

But even with the Negroes voting, Brownlow was somewhat fearful of the outcome of the election, for the Conservatives were organizing with a determination to capture the state. It was therefore necessary for the franchise laws to be further dealt with, and on February 25 (1867), the old law of May 3, 1866, was amended and reënacted. The chief purpose of the new law was to place the machinery of elections more completely in Brownlow's hands. By giving him authority to set aside registrations in any county, it made him supreme dictator, and really made elections an unnecessary farce.[19]

Since Brownlow's government was based on force and fear, it was highly important that these elements be not allowed to deteriorate. The sheriffs' "County Guards" which had been provided for in 1865 had never worked effectively, and Brownlow had been forced to depend much on the Federal troops. But as Johnson was president and still had some authority left in dealing with the army, he made no greater use of the troops in aiding Brownlow than the national exigencies demanded. Fully sensing this situation, Brownlow had gone out among the governors of the Northern States and had got the promise of all necessary arms and ammunition. A trained and enthusiastic

---

[18] *Knoxville Whig,* January 23, 1867.
[19] *Noted Men of the Solid South,* pp. 190-91.

army always at his command Brownlow felt he must have. So on February 20, 1867, Tennessee passed a new army law providing for the raising of a force to be called the Tennessee State Guard, and to be composed of one or more regiments from each Congressional district. Brownlow was their commander-in-chief and in order to make of them modern "Ironsides," no person might enlist who could not pass a test on loyalty, which included taking the franchise oath.[20] Now that Tennessee was about to have an army of her own, she called upon the United States for arms and the gift of a fort or two in the vicinity of Nashville where the equipment could be kept when not in use.[21] To translate his army from paper to living flesh and blood required effort and expense which the Governor and Commander-in-Chief would not undergo immediately, if he could use the threat of it as a club to brandish over the heads of Tennesseeans. So, a few days after the law had been passed, he issued on February 25, a rousing proclamation, reciting the terrible crimes that were taking place in the state, quoting the law which would make possible his army, and threatening proper punishment if the people did not become law-abiding immediately. "Atrocious murders and numerous outrages" had been committed by "violent and disloyal men," and since "these bad men are banding themselves together" he proclaimed that he intended "to put a stop to all such outrages." He had "no concessions to make to traitors; no compromises to offer assassins and robbers; and if, in the sweep of coming events, retributive justice shall overtake the lawless and violent, their own temerity will have called it forth." The Brownlow Government would be sustained "despite all the efforts of disappointed traitors and disloyal newspapers." The Rebels were "giving forth their vile utterances in railway cars, in public hotels, on the streets, and through the newspapers" and were doing great damage to the good name of the state. He closed with the threat, "I mean what I say."[22] This proclamation actually called out no troops, for his army was

---

[20] *Ibid.*, p. 192.
[21] *Ibid.*
[22] McPherson, *History of Reconstruction*, p. 208.

yet unorganized. The Parson hoped to subdue the people with fear.

Still his Tennesseeans did not subside in their restlessness and in their preparations for the coming election; so, on March 1, the legislature requested the United States Government through General Thomas to afford Tennessee, Federal troops sufficient to preserve order. The General replied that as the rebellion had been declared at an end in Tennessee, the Federal army had no right to assume one of the principal duties of the civil government. Federal troops could be sent only in answer to a specific request of the governor reciting the nature of the disorder and the authorities to whom the troops should report.[23] Finding that he could not secure the United States army to aid him in governing the state, Brownlow set about organizing his own army.

He issued Order Number 1 on March 6, calling for volunteers for three years unless sooner discharged. Captains whom he had commissioned were to raise companies of 100 men, 25 of whom should be mounted to act as scouts. To restrain the vengeance of his picked "Ironsides," he warned them against trespassing and pillaging. General Joseph A. Cooper was placed in direct command.[24] Negroes, now being able to take the franchise oath, could be enlisted especially for Middle and West Tennessee, and to facilitate their volunteering, it was reported that at least one Negro captain was among those commissioned.[25] The first company was organized in Jonesboro in the early part of May, where they received their guns and paraded through the streets.[26]

With the Negroes voting and his army organized Brownlow was now ready for the campaign and election. Henry Ward Beecher, who had in the beginning supported Johnson but who was now the religious overlord of the Radicals, had been looking on Brownlow's work and had pronounced it good. He

---

[23] *American Annual Cyclopaedia,* 1867, p. 705; *Nated Men of the Solid South* p. 192.

[24] *Ibid.,* pp. 195-96; *American Annual Cyclopaedia,* 1867, p. 706.

[25] *Daily New Era,* March 27, 1867.

[26] *Knoxville Whig,* May 8, 1867.

extended his blessings and wished him godspeed. In January he had written him, "I hope God will be gracious to you and invigorate your frame. He has made your life precious to those who wish well to the country. Into the struggle of the next campaign you will carry not only the fate of Tennessee, but of the whole South, and so of the nation. May God go with you and bless you and bring you victorious; then if you wish to depart we will rejoice with you in the inheritance of that rest, which remaineth for the people of God."[27]

Now, for the first time in American history, the Negroes would play a major part in an election. It was a solemn experiment in government to turn over voluntarily the power of a state heretofore exercised by a people with a background of a thousand years of political training, to a mass of ignorant people a year or two removed from a line of bondage and servility reaching back to the beginning of written records. Even the most extreme Radicals saw the possibility of criminal disaster that might follow, if the Negroes were not properly directed in their political activities. To avert this calamity and to make secure their own control of the offices, they organized the black voters into Union Leagues. Northern and Southern Radicals directed their activities. By using a ritual consisting of robes, sashes, pass words, secrecy, and a few military maneuvers they found the easiest road to the Negroes' heart and affections. Lodge meetings sprang up all over the state, and these drew the Negroes into the Union League as irresistibly as the candle attracts the candle fly. According to General Forrest, who was himself disfranchised but whose former slaves could vote, "The Negroes were holding night meetings; were going about; were becoming very insolent; and the Southern people all over the State were very much alarmed."[28] Through the Union Leagues the Negroes received their registration and their ballots; and those who did not join found the greatest difficulty in voting.

These newly-enfranchised people were greatly aroused; they

---

[27] *Ibid.*, January 16, 1867.

[28] *Ku Klux Conspiracy*, XIII, 7. See also *Knoxville Whig*, August 14, 1867; *Noted Men of the Solid South*, p. 191.

believed that the Millenium was near at hand. They held their meetings all over the state and were addressed by both white and black speakers. Brownlow's *Whig* published the peregrinations of one black orator, "a gentleman of talent," who announced his coming for 26 places.[29] At Murfreesboro 1,500 of these groping children of Radicalism held a political picnic to cheer the name of Brownlow. In fact, the Parson became so great a hero in the minds of these simple people that they visualized him as a Black Napoleon. At Gallatin, a Negro preacher declared that Brownlow was "a colored man, and he meant to go for him, and wanted every colored man to do the same, at which the crowd cheered heartily."[30]

It was maddening for the Rebels to see their former slaves marching and meeting, excited by their right to vote, while they, themselves, were disfranchised. Unable to restrain themselves, they attempted to break up Negro gatherings and thereby precipitated bloody collisions. In July, a marching column of Union Leaguers in Franklin led to a riot in which one person was killed and 40 wounded.[31] At Brownsville a Radical meeting swayed by two Negro orators resulted in a collision in which 100 shots were fired.[32]

The Conservatives were too intelligent to expect many Negro votes. Even if a Negro should want to vote their ticket, he would find it virtually impossible, as the road to the ballot box led through the Union League, which was under the complete control of the Radicals. Nevertheless, the Conservatives hoped to scare away from the Radical ticket many native white Unionists, by raising the race question and arousing their feeling against Negroes. With gleeful malice they dug up the Parson's ante-bellum debate with Pryne and exposed some of his degrading remarks applied to the Negroes. Brownlow, twisting the facts a bit, answered by declaring that Pryne had challenged him to defend the South, "and I done so, with an ability credit-

[29] *Knoxville Whig*, May 29, 1867.
[30] *Ibid.*, April 17, 1867.
[31] *American Annual Cyclopaedia*, 1867, p. 708.
[32] *Knoxville Whig*, May 22, 1867.

able to me, although I was on the *wrong side of the subject!*"[33]
In preparing for a great Fourth of July celebration and political meeting to be held in Knoxville, three Negroes had been
placed upon the committee of arrangements to hold their race
true. In publishing the names of the committee the *Whig* omit-
ted the Negroes. The Conservatives immediately very trouble-
somely inquired why they had been slighted by the omission.
The Parson declared the names had been left off without his
knowledge, and angered by Conservative deviltry, he threw off
his racial hesitancy and boldly stated that "if week-kneed Union
men and time-serving partizans can't stand this, let them stay
at home on the 4th of July."[34]

The old custom in Tennessee required a joint campaign, in
which the opponents would abuse each other and delight their
partisans. As Brownlow's health did not make it possible for
him to take to the hustings, he contented himself by campaigning up and down the columns of the *Whig*, while Etheridge
travelled around over the state. He called Etheridge a "vulgar
blackguard, a professional gambler and political seditionist"
and charged that he had received his nomination by "a treasonable conclave at Nashville."[35] As Tennessee revolved around
the Parson, he became the object of bitter attacks and the subject of poetry and praise. A Radical poet wrote his "Brownlow
and Tennessee," in which this stanza appeared:

> When midnight shrouds the sacred spot
> Where traitors 'gainst their country plot,
>   What man is damned the first and most,
>   Damned while they tremble lest his ghost
> Should haunt them with a hangman's knot,
> And visions grim of gallows-post?
>   Brownlow.[36]

The Conservatives turned to burning condemnation of the
Radicals. The *Bolivar Bulletin* said:

---

[33] *Ibid.*, May 8, 1867.
[34] *Ibid.*, June 5.
[35] *Ibid.*, May 8, June 5.
[36] *Ibid.*, February 13.

The foul-mouth Radicals of this woe-befallen State are going to have a "powerful time" this coming summer. In order to win advocates to their lawless clan, they are going to import a dozen or more of the spoon-lifting, eel-skinning fraternity of the North, and have them stump every county in the State. Among them will be Fred. Douglass, the negro orator (?). Nigger Douglas and Beast Butler to stump Tennessee! Good Lord, deliver us.[37]

Etheridge characterized the Tennessee Radicals as "the party paying no taxes, riding poor horses, wearing dirty shirts, and having no use for soap."[38]

The Conservatives early realized that they were fighting a lost battle; yet they continued to grasp at every straw of hope and prod the Radicals wherever possible. In May, in answer to a question from a Conservative as to whether his party would be permitted to make a canvass, Brownlow stated that there would be no interference with them unless they delivered "incendiary speeches" and advised "the overthrow of the State government by mob violence." They tested the franchise law in the courts, only to be told that it was constitutional.[39] The state supreme court heading them off from having the whole law declared void, they next planned to take advantage of a weakness in the law, which threw the Parson into a panic. The tenth section being badly worded seemed by an honest and logical construction to indicate that the county courts might appoint the election judges, and that only if they should not act, the Brownlow commissioners of registration should appoint them. If this interpretation had stood, it would have taken the control of the local election machinery out of the hands of Brownlow, and in many cases would have made it possible for the Conservatives to register. The State Central Committee of the Conservatives sent out a notice for the county courts to immediately appoint the judges. Brownlow quickly, on July 1, issued a remarkable proclamation in which he declared that the law

---

[37] Quoted *ibid.*, February 20, 1867.

[38] *Ibid.*, August 7.

[39] McPherson, *History of Reconstruction*, p. 257. The court later changed its mind and declared the law unconstitutional.

22

gave to the commissioners of registration the right to appoint the election judges, and that if any court attempted to exercise the right or any judge so appointed attempted to serve, collision with the state government would result. He announced that General Cooper would disperse his troops over the state to enforce the law despite the threats of seditionists, and if necessary Brownlow would call out all the troops at his command. Overpowered by the threat of soldiers the Conservatives gave up what they believed to be a legal right, and gradually lost interest in the campaign. Some of their candidates resigned their nominations and returned home.[40]

The Radicals, however, did not lessen their guards or remove their sentries from the watch-towers. In the early part of the year, in addition to giving the Negro the vote, they granted the franchise to all foreigners who had been in the United States one year and in Tennessee six months, and who had not participated in the rebellion.[41] The poll books were the sacred registers of the loyal, and by properly guarding and purging them the election could be won before the voting was done. According to the law those who had voted in the elections of February and March of 1865 could automatically be registered; but in order to prevent the Conservatives from being able to offer proof of this qualification, the old poll books were in some places stolen or destroyed. One Union man who had been a captain in the United States army but who had become a Conservative was by Brownlow's direct orders prevented from registering, because he had married into an influential Rebel family.[42] The registrations in some of the counties, made by the Governor's own appointees, he set aside.[43] As the day of the election approached Brownlow's army was scattered widely over the state, the Negro companies being concentrated in Middle and West Tennessee. Their presence in some places provoked trouble which resulted

---

[40] *Knoxville Whig*, July 24, 1867; *American Annual Cyclopaedia*, 1867, pp. 707-9.

[41] McPherson, *History of Reconstruction*, p. 257.

[42] *Ku Klux Conspiracy*, I, 462-63.

[43] *American Annual Cyclopaedia*, 1867, p. 708.

in bloodshed.[44] In Franklin County they dragged a man from
his home and shot him.[45] There was also a comical side to their
activities, as the infantry rode around on the trains making
a show of their strength and the horsemen parading through
the country districts. In one of their engagements they rode a
man out of town on a rail, in another they settled a family
quarrel, it was said, by ordering a divorce.[46] In all there were 19
companies distributed over the state, consisting of 1,500 men.
The people of Tennessee were indebted to these troops to the
extent of $93,822.36, for their efforts in seeing that Brownlow's
party should win the election.[47]

There were a few Federal troops stationed in Tennessee but
they operated under strict orders from General Thomas' headquarters, which orders forbade them to engage in any activities which could be construed into managing elections. They
should interfere only to prevent riots and bloodshed.[48]

In the election Brownlow's forces made an almost complete
sweep of the state. The Parson beat Etheridge by a vote of
74,848 to 22,548. All of the Congressmen were Radicals. The
only successes the Conservatives secured were four members of
the lower house of the legislature.[49]

The experiment of Negro suffrage had been tried and it was a
success for the Radicals, though it left in all others a feeling
of melancholy and an anxiety for the future of a state at the
mercy of such ignorance, some of it innocent and some vicious.
A. A. Steele, a Union man who had been a member of Brownlow's first legislature, declared the Negroes as they voted reminded him "of a drove of sheep huddled to be driven into an
inclosure, or a flock of partridges into a net." Few could read
their ballots, which had been given them by their white man-
agers. "The election," he said, "was not what I would consider

---

[44] *Ku Klux Conspiracy,* I, 421, 463.
[45] *American Annual Cyclopaedia,* 1867, p. 708.
[46] *Noted Men of the Solid South,* pp. 196-97.
[47] *Knoxville Whig,* August 7, October 9, 1867.
[48] *American Annual Cyclopaedia,* 1867, p. 708.
[49] *Ibid.,* p. 709; *Noted Men of the Solid South,* p. 198.

a free one; it was a burlesque on republican government, and conducted entirely in the interest of the dominant faction and its candidates."[50]

Raphael Semmes, the former Confederate raider, whom the Parson called "Pirate Semmes," now editor of the *Memphis Bulletin*, wrote down his reflections on the melancholy sight: "To our eyes, the long procession of dusky figures, making their way slowly to the judge's stand, bore the semblance of a funeral procession. Liberty was dead, we thought, and those were her pall-bearers. The white people, those unfortunate individuals who had been tabooed on account of their color, were looking on from a distance, pretty much as they would look upon the realization of some Eastern tale in the 'Arabian Knights.' We scanned the countenance of the dusky voters. Childish curiosity and simplicity, stolid indifference, blank ignorance, wretchedness and crime were the main characteristics.

"And these were the voters of America, the men who are to be the future guardians of the constitutional liberties of the States, the law-givers and judges of a land of white men. We turned away sick at heart." Semmes explained that he had been denied the right to vote on account of a "supposed defect in patriotism."[51]

Tennesseeans had now the prospect of two more years of the Brownlow régime, some congratulating themselves on their good fortune, others consoling themselves as best they could. All the country was watching Tennessee, for she was a unique experiment in the art and science of government. The Philadelphia *Press* admitted that Brownlow was rough and violent, but just the sort of man Tennessee needed to bring her out "from the fiery furnace of slavery and vested wrong. . . . We would not willingly see him Governor of Pennsylvania, but we do want him for, and rejoice in seeing him Governor of Tennessee."[52] As a scourge for Tennesseeans the Philadelphians had high praise for the Parson.

---

[50] *Ku Klux Conspiracy*, I, 461.
[51] Quoted in *Knoxville Whig*, August 7, 1867.
[52] Quoted *ibid.*, August 14, 1867.

On October 10, Brownlow was inaugurated governor for a second time. The ceremonies took place in the hall of the house of representatives, where members of the house and of the senate were assembled. At the door his coming was announced, and immediately he entered the hall assisted by a senator and a representative. "He looked emaciated, pale and feeble, and moved slowly down the aisle," the members rising as he was assisted to the rostrum. Being too feeble and hoarse to deliver his inaugural address, he was given permission to have his secretary, H. H. Thomas, read it. It was short and fierce. He boasted of being elected by the biggest majority in the history of the state, and he ridiculed and condemned the Conservative party, whose record was so bad that "it only remains for it to advocate Poligamy, in order to have sounded every known depth of political infamy!"[53]

Brownlow had scarcely got himself elected to office a second time before he was confronted with a complicated election situation in Nashville. As his régime rested mostly on the less intelligent people in the rural districts and small settlements, the larger cities appeared to him as danger spots to be feared unless he could curb their power. In May, 1866, Memphis had disgraced his state by rioting against the Negroes; Chattanooga had never been friendly; and Nashville had been sternly hostile. Only in Knoxville, of the larger cities, was he a hero.[54] Soon metropolitan laws were passed for the special benefit of Memphis and of Chattanooga.[55] Nashville had escaped, perhaps because it was the capital city, where the Governor would naturally be able to keep a close watch.

Brownlow had an inherent prejudice against Nashville, because it was not in his beloved East Tennessee. It was in a region infested with Rebels, who had precipitated the state into rebellion. He stayed there only when it was absolutely necessary; most of the time when the legislature was not in session he lived

---

[53] *Ibid.*, October 16, 1867.

[54] For an account of the Memphis riot see *American Annual Cyclopaedia*, 1866, pp. 730-31.

[55] There was great excitement in Memphis; the *Avalanche* defied Brownlow. *Daily New Era*, March 8, 1867.

in Knoxville. In the latter place he always felt much better, for East Tennessee was "redolent with patriotism, refined as the finest gold. That of Nashville a deadly, treasonable exhalation."[56] And, furthermore, the Nashville people consistently insulted Brownlow and his legislature. In the old days the Nashville papers and people would "flatter and praise and toast and feast the members with oyster and wine suppers," but now they blackguarded them without ceasing.[57]

Therefore when Nashville prepared to hold its municipal elections in September, 1867, Brownlow determined that the city should be made to realize that it was in the state of Tennessee. The trouble arose when Mayor W. Matt Brown held that the franchise law did not apply to municipal elections, and hence the Board of Aldermen should appoint the election judges. Brownlow ruled otherwise and ordered General Cooper to occupy Nashville with his army and prevent the city authorities from holding the election. Cooper appeared with the troops at his command; and the city proceeded to recruit extra policemen. Civil war seemed certain. The city appealed to the President for protection against its Governor, and Grant wired General Thomas at Louisville to hurry to Nashville to confer with Brownlow and the city authorities. Thomas appeared but found the Governor conveniently absent in Knoxville. Thomas now had great difficulty in extracting from Grant the exact duties and powers he should assume. Grant informed Thomas that his troops should not interfere between the two sets of election officials but should "confine their actions to putting down hostile mobs." He should prevent a conflict. As the election machinery was in the hands of the city, this order seemed to indicate that Thomas should prevent Brownlow officials from interfering, for only in that manner could a conflict arise. Grant befuddled Thomas more in attempting to clear up the cloud by telegraphing another enigma: "Nothing is clearer than that the military cannot be made use of to defeat the Executive of a State in enforcing the laws of a State. You are not to prevent the legal

---

[56] *Knoxville Whig*, April 11, 1866.
[57] *Ibid.*, April 22, 1868.

State force from the execution of its orders." But Thomas
wanted to know whether he should aid in executing them. Thomas finally sensed that he should support Brownlow if he called
for aid. On September 27, the Governor proclaimed Nashville
in a state of insurrection and called upon the United States
Army to put it down. Mayor Brown, now seeing that it would
be foolish to expect his policemen to defend the city against
Brownlow's army reënforced by United States troops, withdrew
from the contest, protesting "against this most unjust, illegal,
and high-handed course."[58]

The Radicals now carried the city of Nashville by the same
means they had used in securing the state. They elected mayor
a disreputable stranger by the name of A. E. Alden, whom
Brownlow had appointed commissioner of registration, and
thereby they handed the city over to a "band of freebooters,"
who set up the "Alden Ring," which within less than two years
stole $700,000 from the city. Brown determined to remain in
possession of the office and thereby force the courts to pass upon
the legality of the election. But Brownlow would not be so easily
defeated. He ordered General Cooper to march his army against
the Mayor and dispossess him. Seeing the inevitable, Brown
departed.[59]

Browlnow did not use all his waking moments bedeviling the
cities and people of Tennessee. Soon after the Nashville troubles
he exhibited a side of his nature not generally evident in his
public dealings with his Tennesseean enemies; he made it easy
for Isham G. Harris, the governor who had led Tennessee into
the rebellion, to return. His motives were mixed in this show of
forgiveness to a former antagonist. The fact that Andrew
Johnson was a bitter enemy of Harris' may have caused the
Parson to relent; certainly since Johnson had assumed a soft
attitude toward Jefferson Davis and the other traitors, "and

---

[58] *American Annual Cyclopaedia*, 1867, pp. 709-10; *Knoxville Whig*, September
18, October 2, 1867. The text of Brownlow's proclamation of September 27
is in the Brownlow MSS, in the Division of Library and Archives in the Capitol
at Nashville.

[59] *American Annual Cyclopaedia*, 1867, p. 710; *Noted Men of the Solid South*,
pp. 198-200.

the pro-rebel policy of the President warrants the conclusion that none will be punished," the Parson saw no reason why he should continue the pursuit of Harris; there had been worse traitors on the stump in the recent Tennessee election than he; also the ex-Governor's family needed him; and the economy of Tennessee was involved. The last element that entered into the Parson's mixed motives concerned a reward of $5,000 which the legislature on May 1, 1865, had offered for Harris. In his proclamation offering this reward, the Parson proceeded as if Harris had been a low criminal unknown to the people of Tennessee and never seen by them. After giving the weight, age, and complexion of Harris, he further described him by saying, "The study of mischief and the practice of crime, have brought upon him premature baldness and a gray beard. . . . He chews tobacco rapidly and is inordinately fond of liquors."[60]

At the end of the war Harris with other prominent Confederates had gone to Mexico there to develop under Maximilian a New South. On the fall of the Mexican Emperor, Harris had gone to England, but by 1867 he was tired of foreign lands and longed to return to Tennessee. Knowing how bitterly Brownlow hated him, he dared not put himself in the Parson's hands. But the Tennessee governor had now relented, and in his message to the legislature in October, 1867, he had requested the legislature to repeal the reward as the state might be called upon any day to pay it, "and in return, she would have nothing to show for the outlay." The Parson could be as belittling in his message as in his proclamation. The legislature repealed the reward on November 11, and soon thereafter Harris came to Nashville and called on Brownlow, who was said to have exclaimed as he greeted him, "While the lamp holds out to burn, the vilest sinner may return." The Governor and the ex-Governor then for a few minutes held pleasant converse, after which the

[60] *Acts of Tennessee*, 1865, p. 147; "A Proclamation by William G. Brownlow, Governor of Tennessee," *American Historical Magazine*, III (April, 1898), 151-54.

Parson paroled him to appear before the Federal Court the next spring.[61]

About this time Brownlow's health became a subject of wide interest and of particular concern to certain Tennesseeans. His health had been a favorite topic for discussion both by himself and by the public since he had lost his voice on the eve of his debate with Pryne in Philadelphia and especially since he had lain out in the Great Smokies to escape the Confederates. When he became governor in 1865 he was very weak and to facilitate his correspondence he had printed on his official stationery the explanation: "As I shall gradually recover from my nervous prostration, I hope to be able to write better and more at length." But he did not seem to improve, and as a result his secretary, H. H. Thomas, assumed many of the duties of the governorship, including the signing of Brownlow's name. In answer to the charges made now and then that he was too sick to exercise his duties as governor and that he was controlled by others, he declared that he did his own ruling, for had not the "whole Confederacy failed to regulate me five years ago!"[62] For the first year of his term, he scarcely ever made a speech without referring to the poor state of his health as a reason for not speaking at greater length. He seemed at all times to be so feeble both by admission and by appearance that rumors more than once were spread that he had died. A great sensation was created in Knoxville in early October, 1866, when it was reported that the Parson had passed away. There were sighs of relief as the rumor reached the passengers on the trains passing through, and according to the *Whig*, "The large number of traitors from Georgia and other rebel States gave manifestations of great joy." But the *Whig* knew who had spread the report and why—"to witness an exhibition of joy by malignant traitors."[63]

---

[61] *Senate Journal of the Thirty-Fifth General Assembly of the State of Tennessee for the Years 1867-68*, p. 36; *Knoxville Whig*, November 27, 1867; Temple, *op cit.*, pp. 337-38.

[62] *Knoxville Whig*, April 4, 1866.   [63] *Ibid.*, October 10.

Nothing better illustrated the hatred of the Parson throughout the South than the eager expectancy with which they awaited the announcement of his death. According to the Nashville *Press and Times*, "They wish him dead. He never ventures on a railroad train but they hope for a disaster that may bring him to an untimely end. They rejoiced when they heard he had died of cholera in Cincinnati, and sorrowed when they heard that he was alive."[64] People even attempted to give him loathsome diseases—at least, he supposed it to be so. In the latter part of 1866, he received from Adairsville, Georgia, by express with fifty cents charges, a package containing material which he believed to be innoculated with disease germs.[65]

But the ill-health which the Parson had been considering an asset in his political aspirations, was soon to develop into a liability; and now instead of telling how sick he was, he almost invariably declared that he was in as good or better health than he had been for the past twelve months. The first signs of a change came when the clever campaign was started for his renomination to the governorship. Not even the most extreme Radicals would want to renominate him if he were on the point of death, so to head off the reports that he was too sick to be considered for a second term, he declared that the "vindictive rebels and their apostate Union co-workers, are advertising from one end of the State to the other than I *am dying* or *will die*." He affirmed that he had never felt better during the past twelve months.[66]

The Radicals accepted the Parson's word; they renominated and reëlected him, as has appeared. Now that he was to be governor for two more years, some of the other aspiring Radical leaders began to develop logical ambitions for the senatorship which would be vacated by Patterson, the President's son-in-law, on March 4, 1869. Soon Horace Maynard, Andrew J. Fletcher, General Joseph Cooper, and William B. Stokes entered the race for this attractive honor. No one had thought

---

[64] Quoted *ibid.*, November 21, 1866.
[65] *Ibid.*
[66] *Ibid.*, July 10, 1867; *Daily New Era*, October 12, 1866.

of Brownlow, who had just been reëlected to a second term as governor, for those who had watched the feeble old man as he had been helped into the hall to be inaugurated, could not help feeling that he would soon "transfer his citizenship to heaven." In fact, it was reported that he could not live longer than six more weeks.[67] But the Parson startled the Radicals and the whole state by announcing on October 15 his desire to be elected to the Senate. He was quick to say that he was stronger than he had been for a whole year, and unable to conceal the growing ambition that had seized him, he plainly stated that he wanted to be the United States Senator because it was the "highest honor which the State can confer upon a citizen." He also felt that he might be useful in securing for Tennessee that justice, in the form of the payment of Civil War claims, which the United States was "so tardy in bestowing."[68]

Brownlow seemed to have hypnotic powers in addition to his ability as a clever politician. The mere fact that he wanted something was reason enough for most of his fellow-Radicals. Immediately all of those Radicals who had had visions of living in Washington for six years in the capacity of a Tennessee senator, effaced themselves and sorrowfully buried their ambitions —all except Stokes. *General* Stokes, for he had been a soldier in the Civil War, was a man of courage and tenacity, and besides he was ambitious. He believed Brownlow was too feeble to be of any value to Tennessee in the Senate; and therefore, it would be doing the state a patriotic service to oppose him. He fought it out with the Parson in the election, which was held on October 22, but lost by a vote of 39 to 63. Brownlow's hold on the Radicals was thus proved invincible. Stokes sulked secretly and never forgot the "dog-in-the-manger" characteristic which the Parson had so forcefully exhibited. The Radicals generally were jubilant, almost as much for the effect they supposed it would have on Johnson as for the joy it would give the Parson. The Nashville *Press and Times* imagined that when Johnson heard of the election "Doubtless the air around him was filled

---

[67] *Knoxville Whig,* October 30, 1867.

[68] *Ibid.,* October 23.

with curses as thick as a cloud of Nashville mosquitoes and the visits to the consoling demijohn were frequent and long."[69] Possibly the Parson's ambition for the place was whetted when he remembered that he would be discomfiting the President again, by succeeding his son-in-law.

The Tennessee Conservatives reflected that "Old Man Terrible" had now secured for himself six more years of office holding, and that likely he fearing that the days of the Radicals in Tennessee were numbered, had sought a place beyond the reach of his enemies. The *Nashville Banner* took his election philosophically: "He is the Radical King Bee, and we prefer him to any of the gallinippers and horseflies that buzzed after senatorial honors. We will keep him in the Senate as a model of Radicalism and a warning voice! As we had to have a Radical, we preferred him." It hoped that this good fortune might "have a soothing effect, may make him, in fact, as amiable and kindly disposed in his public dealings as he is in his private disposition and personal conduct."[70]

To maintain himself in the supreme leadership of a group of Radicals, able and ambitious, and to secure every honor his fancy should dictate and the people could bestow, marked the Parson as an unusual man. On his return to his home in Knoxville, he was given an enthusiastic reception enlivened by speechmaking, ringing bells, and brass bands.[71]

He was now about to draw up a new lease on life. He would live and grow strong in spite of all his enemies and rivals, and he would prove it to them by going on a deer hunt in the rough Chilhowee Mountains in Blount County among the Great Smokies, which he knew so well from Confederate days.[72] He also would improve his physical frame by resting occasionally at the fashionable Montvale Springs.[73] Was there a new Parson in the making?

---

[69] Quoted *ibid.*, October 30, 1867.
[70] Quoted *ibid.*
[71] *Ibid.*, December 4, 1867.
[72] *Ibid.*, July 1, 1868.
[73] *Ibid.*, July 14, 1869.

CHAPTER XV

THE STORM BEFORE THE CALM

THE TENNESSEE Radicals, led by Brownlow, had beat down all opposition and had gained complete supremacy; the national Radicals under the leadership of Thaddeus Stevens and Charles Sumner, had seized control of the nation, but they were annoyed with having Andrew Johnson around as President. As early as January, 1867, they had decided to get rid of him if possible, by impeachment. Their first efforts to start proceedings against him failed for lack of probable evidence, but after a year of scrutiny during which Johnson committed more crimes in his dismissal of Stanton, his Secretary of War, the House voted impeachment on February 24, 1868, and made preparations to try the case before the Senate.

Brownlow and the Tennessee Radicals were jubilant. They had been as anxious to dispose of their adopted son as had the Congressional oligarchy. On February 7, 1867, the Tennessee senate had called on the President's son-in-law, Senator Patterson, to resign, as he had deserted the party that had elected him, and a few weeks later the Radical convention in Nashville had struck at the President himself, by endorsing "any action of Congress that will legitimately deprive him of continued power." Brownlow had long known that Johnson had committed all the high crimes and misdemeanors required for the impeachment and removal of the President, and that added to a long list of others, he had scared away immigrants from Tennessee. In addition the Parson attributed "the violence of these pestilential disloyalists to the insane policy of the President...."[1]

Brownlow and his Radicals watched closely events in Washington and when Stanton reinstated himself in the President's

---

[1] *Senate Journal of Tennessee*, 1867-1868, p. 31; *Noted Men of the Solid South*, p. 193; *Acts of the State of Tennessee Passed at the Second Adjourned Session of the Thirty-Fourth General Assembly, for the Year 1866-67*, pp. 294-95.

cabinet after Grant had supinely withdrawn, the Tennessee legislature on January 29, 1868, resolved that it had heard "with feelings of mingled pleasure and delight" of Stanton's return to the cabinet.[2] Brownlow, in Tennessee, prayed for Johnson's removal; Stevens, in Washington, worked for it. They were much alike in opinions, ability to hate, and in health. To a mutual friend returning to Tennessee, Stevens said, "Give the Governor my respects; tell him I hope he will be restored to health and live a long time, and that I say *when he dies to die Hurrahing.*"[3] The legislature had instructed the Tennessee Congressmen in the House to vote for the impeachment and now they expected their Senators to vote removal.

There was no doubt in Brownlow's mind that Johnson would be hurled out of office. "The award is light compared with the magnitude and character of his offences," the Parson declared.[4] Brownlow shared Ben Wade's joy at the prospect of becoming President. "Wade" said the Parson, "will be President *ad interim*, whilst JOHNSON will be President *ad outerim*. . . . And the swarm of rebel office-holders under him will roost lower down than they have been doing!"[5] But if by any possible chance, Johnson should not be removed, Brownlow declared the Tennessee Rebels would start another rebellion, seize the state, and reënslave the Negroes.[6]

When the terrible news reached Tennessee that the President had been acquitted, and only by one vote, the Parson took what hope he could from the fact that the Senate would soon ballot again on other counts; but when Johnson was again saved by one vote, Brownlow was enormously disappointed and chagrined, for both Tennessee Senators had voted to acquit Johnson, when if either one had held true the President would have been ousted.[7] Brownlow felt the acquittal of Johnson as keenly

---

[2] *Acts of Tennessee*, 1867-1868, p. 351.

[3] *Knoxville Whig*, February 19, 1868.

[4] *Ibid.*, March 18.   [5] *Ibid.*, May 13.   [6] *Ibid.*, April 22.

[7] Brownlow did not know that other Senators stood ready to sacrifice themselves to national vengeance by voting to acquit Johnson, if their votes should have been necessary.

as if it had been a personal defeat; he as well as all Tennessee was now disgraced in the eyes of the country. He wrote in June, "Tennessee, including Johnson, Patterson & Fowler, have acted so treacherously that I am ashamed to ask the loyal North any longer to confide in any of us."[8] To add further to his woes, Thaddeus Stevens soon died. The legislature resolved on August 14 that it heard with profound sorrow the news of his death, and that out of the respect it held for the memory of the great Radical leader it ordered its members to wear on their left arm mourning signs for thirty days.[9] As the following Thanksgiving Day approached and Johnson issued his Thanksgiving Proclamation, the Parson decided that Tennessee could not be thankful for those things that pleased the President, so he published his own proclamation.[10]

The disfranchised Tennesseeans had long been unable to see much for which they should be thankful. To be deprived of the right to vote was degrading enough, but to see their former slaves placed in a position of power to rule over them seemed unbelievable. The Negroes, true enough, were under the control of the Radical minority, but if this control should weaken, Tennessee might be converted into another Haiti. Not only were a majority of Tennesseeans denied the right to vote, they were also deprived of the elementary civil right of serving on juries. Brownlow had secured the passage of this law to protect Union men and Negroes from the vengeance of Rebel juries. In 1866, he had declared that he believed a fourth of the people in the penitentiary had been put there unjustly, because of their color or antecedents. Hence he had been pardoning them, but he should prefer making pardoning unnecessary by keeping Rebels off juries. Answering the bitterness produced by this act, the *Whig* said, "Over the passage of this law the uncircumcised rebels of this State howl like so many prairie wolves, and yet

---

[8] Letter to F. J. Deer, June 22, 1868, in the Brownlow MSS in the Library of Congress.

[9] *Acts and Resolutions of the State of Tennessee Passed at the Extra Session of the Thirty-Fifth General Assembly Convened at Nashville, July 27, 1868*, p. 45.

[10] *Knoxville Whig*, October 28, 1868.

it is one of the best laws enacted by this General Assembly."[11]

Though the Parson no longer could plead that he was staying the vengeance of Rebel juries, he continued to pardon criminals in increasing numbers—a practice generally regarded as one of the first unmistakable signs of disintegration in the integrity of chief executives. Brownlow was charged with pardoning Radicals as fast as they were convicted, regardless of the crime.[12] During the early months of 1868, he pardoned about 250 criminals. Such an outcry resulted that he offered as an explanation and defense the recommendation of the legislature that more pardons be granted. He admitted the possibility of a few mistakes, but for the most part he had pardoned those people convicted of petty offenses or because they were Radicals.[13] But there were many Tennesseeans who felt that the crimes had been enormous and that life would be made doubly insecure if the pardoning business were unchecked. General Forrest testified before a Congressional committee, on the dangerous situation that had arisen out of pardoning Negroes: "Ladies were ravished by some of these negroes, who were tried and put in the penitentiary, but were turned out in a few days afterwards."[14]

The Black Peril was increasing as the days went by. Emboldened by the prospect of pardons the Negroes were letting their animal natures go unrestrained. In politics they were becoming increasingly bold. In the latter part of January, 1868, the Negroes were given the right to hold office and to sit on juries, and in the following March common carriers were forbidden to make the distinction of color in the services they rendered. The U L A, which was the short designation for the Union League of America and which would rhyme with K K K, was more deeply and widely entrenching itself throughout the state; and under the patronage of Brownlow it was waxing

[11] *Ibid.*, November 7, December 5, 1866; *Noted Men of the Solid South*, pp. 189-90.

[12] *Ku Klux Conspiracy*, I, 421.

[13] *Knoxville Whig*, April 22, 1868.

[14] *Ku Klux Conspiracy*, XIII, 7.

strong and menacing. The state organization was subdivided into councils, and to do honor to the Parson, the unit at Knoxville was called the Brownlow council. The Parson was proud of this organization; occasionally he made trips through the outlying districts to visit the various councils and to instruct them in their politics and other duties. It was forcibly impressed upon the Negroes that if they expected to engage in political activities they must join the League. These leaguers, with guns in their possession, now and then became more than a political menace; they became regulators, and as such they burned barns and mistreated the white population.[15]

The situation in Tennessee was intolerable for most of the people; the times were out of joint; the cup of woe had been drained. "This State continued through the year [1868] to be the most discordant one in the Union," said a contemporary and competent observer.[16] This was a year of storm and stress, the result of a two years accumulation of abuses, debasements, and insults. There was an end to forbearance even in the face of armies; the spontaneous risings of the people throughout the South in secret organizations, generally referred to as the Ku Klux Movement, was the proof. These organizations were variously known as the Ku Klux Klan, the White Camelia, the Pale Faces, the White Brotherhood, the Constitutional Union Guards, the Council of Safety, the '76 Association, the Sons of '76, the Order of the White Rose, and the White Boys.

The name best known and promiscuously applied to all was the Ku Klux Klan, which originated in Pulaski, Tennessee, in the fall of 1865. It was organized for no serious purpose; had there been an Elks club in town the Ku Klux Klan would never have started in Pulaski. It continued for a year or more for fun-making and prank-playing, during which time its value

[15] *Knoxville Whig,* January 29, July 15, 1868; *Noted Men of the Solid South,* pp. 200-201. The Union Leagues when they were first organized in the South had a white membership, but as they were turned into a means for controlling the Negroes in politics, the whites either got out or organized separate councils. For an excellent discussion of the Union League of America, see W. L. Fleming, *The Sequel of Appomattox,* pp. 174-95.

[16] *American Annual Cyclopaedia,* 1868, p. 721.
23

in frightening Negroes was becoming evident, as it paraded around in its white garbs. According to one account:

While the procession was passing a corner on which a negro was standing, a tall horseman in hideous garb turned aside from the line, dismounted and stretched out his bridle rein toward the negro, as if he desired him to hold his horse. Not daring to refuse, the frightened African extended his hand to grasp the rein. As he did so, the Ku Klux took his own head from his shoulders and offered to place that also in the outstretched hand. The negro stood not upon the order of his going, but departed with a yell of terror. To this day he will tell you: "He done it, suah, boss. I seed him do it."[17]

As the Negro became more dangerous in his Union League, the idea of the Klan spread, and a serious purpose was adopted. It would be the secret means of maintaining white civilization. A general organization for the whole South was secretly built up in a meeting in Nashville, in May, 1867, and a constitution or prescript, embracing lofty purposes and sentiments was adopted. And here General Forrest became the Grand Wizard of the Invisible Empire, in theory ruling over Realms, Dominions, Provinces, and Dens, inhabited by Genii, Dragons, Hydras, Grand Titans, Furies, Grand Giants, Goblins, Grand Cyclops, Nighthawks, and Ghouls.

The menace against Southern civilization must now be crushed, even if it were necessary to drive out or hang the dangerous Negroes and carpetbaggers. Organized almost under the very eyes of Brownlow, the Klan could be considered as a personal answer to him and his régime. It quickly spread over the state and by the beginning of 1868 was bobbing up in the very citadel of Brownlowism, in Knoxville. The *Press and Herald*, the Conservative paper in Knoxville, announced that it would seem that the Knights of the Ku Klux Klan "had indeed burst the cerements of the grave and were now wandering through this soil consecrated by the sacred tread of our great apostle of loyalty, the sainted Brownlow."[18] The Parson immediately

---

[17] Quoted in Fleming, *op. cit.*, p. 255.
[18] Quoted in *Daily New Era*, March 17, 1868.

guessed that the Klan was a political organization bent on the overthrow of his government, for he constantly attributed to all who opposed him revolutionary intentions. He had often been enraged by his enemies applying the term "bogus" to his government, and he was now sure that a *coup d'etat* was in the making. He knew the membership was made up of "ex-rebel soldiers, and those in sympathy with them," for they almost invariably rode good horses and drilled and went "through the evolutions of the Confederate cavalry," showing at all times perfect familiarity with Rebel tactics.[19]

He fell upon them with fury, in the *Whig*: "Our counsel once for all is, that whenever those vile miscreants make their appearance among us, mounted, booted and spurred, and however disguised, let the white and colored Radicals meet them promptly, and in the spirit of their own lawless mission, disperse them, and if need require this in dispersing them, exterminate them."[20] The Klan sent the Parson numerous threatening notes, "being accompanied with pictures of coffins, daggers, pistols, and the gallows."[21] Their hatred of Brownlow extended far beyond the limits of Tennessee. A group of Knights in the far South told a Negro that they were Confederate spirits on their way to Tennessee "to evaporate old Brownlow. They would have done it before, but the Devil was not prepared to receive the Governor of Tennessee and Thad Stevens, so they had to wait."[22]

As the Negroes became bolder and wiser through their Union League, they became less easily frightened by the mysterious and supernatural performances of the Knights. They began to fire into processions of Klansmen and succeeded in killing some of them. In an affray with the Knights, a Negro succeeded in capturing a coat, which Brownlow immediately concluded had once been worn by a slaveholding planter. It was a "long-waisted, swallow-tailed one, with flat tin buttons nearly as large as tea-saucers."[23] But the Klansmen were determined and in-

---

[19] *Knoxville Whig,* August 19, 1868; *Senate Journal of Tennessee,* 1867-1868, pp. 22-24; *American Annual Cyclopaedia,* 1868, p. 721.

[20] *Knoxville Whig,* March 25, 1868.

[21] *Ibid.,* April 15.

[22] Warmoth, *op. cit.,* p. 73.   [23] *Knoxville Whig,* August 26, 1868.

exorable in their purpose to allay the Black Peril; they spread terror among the Negroes in certain parts of the state, and according to Brownlow, drove 300 of them to seek safety in Nashville, where they were lodged in refugee camps.[24]

But, perhaps, in Brownlow's home town there was as much violence as in any part of the state. John B. Brownlow, the *Whig* editor, naturally disliking T. B. Kirby, the editor of the *Press and Herald*, met him on the streets of Knoxville, one day in June (1868), and said to him, "Kirby, you are a d—d scoundrel." Thereupon each slapped the other's face, and Brownlow drew a cocked pistol, but before further execution could be carried out, bystanders interfered.[25] About this time a Radical politician slew Henry M. Ashley, in Knoxville, and the *Whig* in recounting the murder, said he had been "righteously slain." When Ashley's friends threatened revenge, Governor Brownlow, in a statement most remarkable to come from the head of an organized government, called upon the Radicals to come to the support of Ashley's slayer, "and if he shall fall let the loyal men of the town and country fall with him. Let every loyal man in the town, white and colored, arm himself for the conflict."[26]

The height of impertinence seemed to have been reached by the Ku Klux Klan, when on June 13, according to Samuel M. Arnell, a Radical Congressman and a fast friend of Brownlow's, some of the Knights boarded the train near Columbia with "pistols and rope in hand" and searched for him. Arnell immediately telegraphed Brownlow for permission to call upon the military, if necessary, "to suppress all armed and masked parties in this vicinity."[27] Brownlow's army, organized for the election of the preceding year, had now melted away, and the only Tennessee troops that he could now command were the guards that the

---

[24] *Ibid.*, August 19, 1868.

[25] *Ibid.*, July 1, 1868. The editor recounts in the *Whig* with much bravado the details of the encounter.

[26] *Ibid.*, July 22.

[27] *American Annual Cyclopaedia*, 1868, p. 721; *Noted Men of the Solid South*, pp. 203-4. The Conservatives maintained that the Ku Klux Klan had never sought Arnell; it was merely an attempt on his part to get the United States army sent to Tennessee. *Nashville Banner*, quoted by *Knoxville Whig*, August 12, 1868.

sheriffs were allowed by a law of February 1, 1868, to raise at large over the state. As there were few if any of these militiamen in existence, Brownlow found himself a commander-in-chief without an army to command.

The Parson now fell back upon General Thomas, the infallible soldier according to the Tennessee legislature, and on June 15, called upon him for five companies of troops to take charge of Lincoln, Marshall, Obion, Dyer, Gibson, and Fayette counties. Without these forces the Governor declared, "the civil laws cannot be enforced, nor loyal men allowed to exercise their rights and liberties." The General had been appealed to so much by Brownlow to maintain his rule in Tennessee, that he was coming to be wearied. He answered that as Tennessee "was in the full exercise of all the civil functions of a State, the military authorities of the United States cannot legally interfere, except in aid and support of the civil authority." Believing that Brownlow wanted the troops for other purposes, he declined, especially as he had no troops to spare.[28] The General was opposed to making out of his army a police force for Brownlow. Thomas a few days later informed Brownlow that the state laws allowing sheriffs to raise forces seemed to afford a remedy sufficient to take care of the present emergency. Brownlow was forced to admit in his reply that his sheriffs would not act—likely they were themselves members of the Klan.[29]

Denied the aid of Federal troops, Brownlow was forced to depend on his legislature. Many Radicals began bombarding him with requests to call it together in extraordinary session. On July 1, the *Whig* intimated that the Governor would likely issue the call soon, and continuing, said, "The Governor is daily in receipt of letters showing a horrible condition of affairs in about six or eight counties of the State. Every night armed bands of assassins and thieves, calling themselves, 'Klansmen of the Kuklux,' are murdering loyal men, white and colored, and applying the torch to their dwellings." On July 6, he

---

[28] *American Annual Cyclopaedia,* 1868, pp. 721, 722; *Noted Men of the Solid South,* pp. 201-2.

[29] *Knoxville Whig,* July 29, 1868.

issued a proclamation calling the legislature to meet on the 27th for both the political and financial defense of the state. The proclamation was brought out in a highly irregular fashion; Brownlow issued it over his name without the signature or seal of the secretary of state and first made it public in the columns of the *Whig*, with the request that all newspapers which had been designated for carrying legal advertising, copy it three times. Perhaps, the Governor was intending a slight for the secretary of state, Fletcher, whom he did not like.[30]

The Tennessee Conservatives, whether members of the Ku Klux Klan or not, looked upon the situation as rapidly becoming desperate. If the legislature should meet and organize and turn loose upon the state another army of avengers, civil war would certainly result. In a final effort to come to an understanding with Brownlow, a group of former Confederate officers—B. F. Cheatham, John C. Brown, W. C. Whitthorne, A. M. Looney, E. S. Cheatham and others—who were undoubtedly either members of the Klan or who were able to control it, held a conference with the Parson in Knoxville immediately before the assembling of the legislature.[31] They promised that the Klan should desist from further activities if the Parson would guarantee protection to the people.[32]

Brownlow had set out and he was not to be turned back. He would not compromise with Rebels and traitors on any grounds. In his message to this Ku Klux session of the legislature, he recited the record of terrorism that the Klansmen had made for themselves, and how they had taken advantage of his generosity in demobilizing his former army by organizing themselves into this violent secret society. He had asked for Federal troops and had been refused; and now that he had called the legislature in answer to many requests, he hoped the members would not hesitate to be as stern in their legislation as the situation demanded and the pleadings of outraged Radicals suggested. If they thought the Governor too violent and if they did not act

---

[30] *Ibid.*, July 8, 1868.　　　[31] *Ibid.*, July 29.

[32] This information appears in a note written with pencil by John B. Brownlow on the margin of the office copy of the *Whig* for July 29.

vigorously, he intimated that he might resign and not be responsible for what should follow.[33]

A vigorous and widespread effort was now being made to settle the impending troubles and finally compose the Tennessee people by removing all disabilities. Attempts were made to excite Brownlow's pride and generosity by inducing him to adopt such a program and crown his term of office with the complete reconstruction of the state. Brownlow was too fearful of the vengeance he himself had been taking to make such an agreement. In the early part of the year he had sent a letter to the Radical convention in Nashville, warning it against adopting universal suffrage since such a step would result in turning the state over to the Rebels.[34] Now in his message he referred to the appeals that had been made to him by prominent men of both parties to enfranchise the Rebels. He declared that their conduct was such that he could not consent. "They have a military organization in this State," he said,

whose avowed object is to trample the laws under foot and force the party in power to enfranchise themselves and their sympathizers. I cannot stultify myself by yielding to this request, accompanied by threats of violence. If members of the General Assembly are alarmed for their personal safety, and feel disposed to sue for peace upon the terms proposed by an armed mob, they will, of course, take a different view of the subject.

Furthermore, it was not proper for an extra session to take up such matters as the suffrage. It would be better to wait until the next regular session and in the meantime strictly observe "the conduct of those unreconstructed Ku-klux Rebels and their sympathizing supporters."[35]

Despite the Parson's sharp words in his message, a large number of petitions were presented to the legislature praying for an "equal participation by all in the future prosperity and onward march of our noble state." A petition containing nearly 4,000

---

[33] *Senate Journal of the Extra Session of the Thirty-Fifth General Assembly of the State of Tennessee*, pp. 6-8; *Knoxville Whig*, July 29, 1868.
[34] *Ibid.*, January 29, 1868.
[35] *Ibid.*, July 29.

names was presented by Judge Shackleford, who begged the legislators to forget the past and look toward the future development of the state. Henry S. Foote, a former governor of Mississippi, was present and added his plea for the petition. While the legislature was considering these petitions Brownlow submitted another plea or plan from John M. Lea, not because he agreed with it but out of his high regard for the patriotism and integrity of the author. The plan was a clever method of giving the voters the chance to insert universal manhood suffrage into the constitution by commissioning the present legislature, in the next election, to act as a constitutional convention.

On August 1, a conference of prominent former Confederate officers, consisting of Nathan Bedford Forrest, Gideon J. Pillow, and eleven others was held and a petition submitted to the legislature. It was a straightforward and high-toned bid for peace—an effort to "avert the precipitation of the crisis which is acknowledged to be imminent." Admitting by implication that they were members of the Klan, they declared that the Governor wholly misunderstood their purpose. They were not seeking to overthrow the state government nor "to do any other act by revolutionary or lawless means. Neither we nor those with whom in our past days we have been associated contemplate any such rashness and folly, nor do we believe there is in Tennessee any organization, either public or secret, which has such a purpose. And if there be, we have neither sympathy nor affiliation therewith." They believed it unwise for the legislature to organize a military force. "And, inasmuch as the supposed danger to the peace of the State is apprehended from that class of the community with which we are considered identified, as inducement and reason to your honorable body not to organize such military force, we pledge ourselves to maintain the order and peace of the State with whatever of influence we possess" and to support and help execute the laws. "For when it is remembered that the large mass of white men in Tennessee are denied the right to vote or hold office, it is not wonderful or unnatural there should exist more or less dissatisfaction among them." Removing these disabilities "would heal all the wounds of our State, and make us once more a prosperous, contented, and united people."[36]

This onset for moderation was met by a convention of Radicals who resolved that the same program of vengeance which they had been enjoying for the past three years should be continued. They sustained and honored Governor Brownlow, "the gallant, fearless, and incorruptible hero" and they commended him for calling the legislature together to protect loyal people "from the wanton violence of Ku-klux banditti and others, aided and encouraged by wealthy and influential rebels." As for removing Rebel disabilities, they held "That so long as loyalty is a virtue, and treason a crime, unrepentant rebels should occupy back seats." And when the militia should be called out to prevent violence, the county in which the violence took place should be made to pay the cost of its suppression.[37]

Disregarding all overtures for peace and friendship, the Parson and his Radical supporters forced through the legislature a bill for organizing the Tennessee State Guards to be composed of loyal men. It should be the duty of the Governor to send troops to any part of the state if "ten or more known unconditional Union men of good moral character, or three justices of the peace" should swear that the laws could not be enforced without them. If the judge and attorney-general of any circuit, the representative and the senator of a county in the circuit, "and ten Union men of good moral character" in the county should swear that the laws could not be enforced without troops, then the Governor was empowered to declare martial law for the region affected, quarter troops there, and assess the costs upon the taxpayers.[38]

To further stamp out the Ku Klux Klan the legislature enacted laws to punish with a fine of not less than $500 and imprisonment for not less than five years any person who should

---

[36] *American Annual Cyclopaedia*, 1868, pp. 723-24; *Knoxville Whig,* August 12, 1868.

[37] *American Annual Cyclopaedia*, 1868, pp. 722-23; *Noted Men of the Solid South,* p. 208.

[38] *Noted Men of the Solid South*, p. 207; *American Annual Cyclopaedia*, 1868, p. 724.

"prowl through the country or towns of this State, by day or by night, disguised or otherwise, for the purpose of disturbing the peace, or alarming the peaceable citizens of any portion of this State." They should, furthermore, be "rendered infamous." Any one who should feed, lodge, entertain, or conceal a member of the Ku Klux Klan should be punished likewise. Every public officer should be forced to swear that he had never been a member of the Klan and that he had never sympathized with it.[39]

As a further precaution the legislature sent a joint committee to Washington to make a report on conditions in Tennessee and to ask the President for troops. They were cordially received by Johnson and J. M. Schofield, the Secretary of War. They informed the President that the outlook was dark in Tennessee, for the state was at that moment in the mysterious grip of 40,000 Ku Klux Klansmen. Schofield promised that the United States would uphold the civil government of the state and protect its law-abiding citizens. The committee returned and made its report on September 16.[40]

Without waiting for the outcome of the mission to Washington, Brownlow proceeded to compose a proclamation calling for the organization of his new army. He was in the midst of this document when he received news that the United States would give Tennessee whatever help she needed; but he would not now be deterred, he had been commander-in-chief without an army long enough. The proclamation was issued on September 16 —it was a remarkable document both in its content and in the method of its issuance. Across the proclamation book in the Executive Office, the secretary of state, Andrew J. Fletcher, wrote that since the proclamation had never been sent to his office and had never been impressed with the seal of the state or countersigned by him, it could not be certified as authentic. There was no original of it in his office; he had first seen the text in the *Whig*. He added, "No mere newspaper proclamation will be received in this office."

---

[39] *Ibid.; Noted Men of the Solid South*, pp. 208-9.

[40] *Knoxville Whig*, September 23, 1868; *American Annual Cyclopaedia*, 1868, p. 724; *Noted Men of the Solid South*, pp. 207-8.

By its direct wording, the Parson called upon every "good" person, "white or colored, of every county in the state, to proceed without delay to raise companies of loyal and ablebodied men" and bring them to Nashville. If all loyal people in the state should choose to raise companies, then the Parson would have an army composed only of officers. Whether he should call this army into active service would depend entirely on the conduct of the people. He hoped it would not be necessary, but he was determined to put down "armed marauders by force," and he would meet them "with such numbers and in such a manner as the exigency may demand, and whatever may be the consequences I will not be deterred from the discharge of my duties herein by threats of violence from rebel speakers or rebel newspapers, nor by any other means of intimidation." Knowing that the Rebels who were "bitterly hostile to the elevation of the colored man" would attempt "to precipitate a war of races," he would not call out the Negro troopers unless he found the white troops were unable to hold the Rebels in check. If with both whites and blacks he could not put down the Rebels, then he would call on the United States Government to assist him. Having special confidence in the East Tennessee troops and hoping to secure as many of them as possible, he would not put a limit on the number that might come from any one county.[41]

This proclamation struck as much fear when it was issued as it produces wonderment today. It seemed to many Tennesseeans to be a vindictive answer of an irresponsible ruler to their overtures for peace. General Forrest had the impression and stated that it was widespread over the state that an army was to be raised which should be allowed to proceed unrestrained against former Confederates. He declared that it was the general belief that if a Brownlow soldier should kill "a man who had been in the southern army, there would be nothing done with him."[42]

It was an example of remarkable self-restraint on the part of Brownlow in promising to delay the calling out of his army, for in November, elections would be held in the state, and armies

[41] *Ku Klux Conspiracy*, I, 458-59.
[42] *Ibid.*, XIII, 6, 14; *Noted Men of the Solid South*, pp. 209-10.

had heretofore been found valuable in connection with such activities. This apparent negligence may be explained on the grounds, first, that the state government was not before the people for election, secondly, that there would be some difficulty in raising and organizing the army, and thirdly, that the threat of it even on paper would be of some value. And it must also be remembered that Tennesseeans had such a horror of another Brownlow army, black and white, that they had made the Parson abject promises to stay it. If they must have an army they would much rather have the Federal troops. Since Brownlow believed that troops were as necessary for elections as were ballots and ballot-boxes, he compromised by calling on General Thomas for troops. In early October he designated twenty-one counties which should be occupied by Federal garrisons, and Thomas complied.[43]

The Radicals held their convention early in the year (January 22) to choose delegates to the national convention which should meet in Chicago in May. Now that the Negroes were an important element in the state electorate and should be held as Radical allies, a representative of their race from each Congressional district was put upon the state executive committee. As Brownlow held one office and had already been elected to another, the convention contented itself with thanking him for his "eminent service rendered to the cause of loyalty, liberty and progress." The Conservatives came together the following month to name delegates to the Democratic Convention to meet later in New York City, and endorsed Andrew Johnson for the presidency. In June they met again and condemned the destructive program of the Radicals in reconstructing the Southern States, and subsequently issued an address in which they vehemently attacked Brownlow for depriving the state of a republican form of government. They also solemnly condemned the attempt to bring about the supremacy of the African race and other "oppressions, usurpations, and miseries to which this state has been

---

[43] *Noted Men of the Solid South*, pp. 210-11; *Knoxville Whig*, October 7, 1868.

subjected by the minions and agents of the party now in possession of the Government of the United States."[44]

With Brownlow's program of military intimidation in full operation, the Conservatives for a time in the autumn considered withdrawing entirely from the campaign, but after consulting "with many able and discreet persons," they decided to push a vigorous campaign for Horatio Seymour and F. P. Blair, the Democratic candidates for president and vice president. Brownlow turned all the forces at his command in the state to the support of General Grant and Schuyler Colfax, the Republican candidates. To the suggestion of an admirer made before the nominations had been voted, that Brownlow run for the vice presidency, the Parson replied that he would rather have six years in the Senate than four years in the vice presidency; and after the nominations had been made and the campaign was on, he reminded his Tennessee radicals to work hard for Grant and Colfax, for in the Senate he would have many choice jobs to bestow on the faithful if the Republicans were successful. He added that the number of offices had been doubled since the war.[45]

The Union League was now in a thriving condition and working efficiently for the Republican candidates. In May twenty-two councils from eight Tennessee counties met in Knoxville to prepare for the coming conflict, and to resolve their anger against the Republicans who had recently brought about the acquittal of Johnson in the impeachment trial. They condemned Senator Fowler and deprecated "the perfidy of those seven recreants who have so greatly disappointed the just hopes of the loyal people." The Parson made a pilgrimage among many of the councils in July and found them flourishing and faithfully supporting Grant and Colfax.[46]

With the United States army scattered over the state, with the Negroes loyally functioning in the Union League, with the

[44] *American Annual Cyclopaedia*, 1868, p. 721.

[45] *Knoxville Whig*, April 8, 15, 1868; *American Annual Cyclopaedia*, 1868, p. 725.

[46] *Knoxville Whig*, May 27, July 15, 1868.

Rebels still disfranchised, and with the constant threat of turning his own army loose upon the state, still Brownlow had some feeling of doubt as to the outcome of the election. The Ku Klux Klansmen were a mysterious lot of human beings. But he had yet another weapon; on October 19, he proceeded to throw out the whole registration of Lincoln county, and thereby thought he had ridded the state of the votes of one of the troublesome Middle Tennessee counties.[47]

In the election Grant and Colfax, of course, were successful. Grant received 56,757 votes to Seymour's 26,311. In the voting for Congressmen the situation was complicated. With all the precautions the Radicals had taken, C. A. Sheafe, the Conservative candidate in the fourth district, had succeeded in defeating Lewis Tillman, the Radical, by a vote of 4,591 to 3,855. Such returns immediately suggested to the Parson that there had been some illegal voting going on, for who would vote for a Conservative but a Rebel? Since he did not want to admit that his policies had divided his former Union supporters and had led many of them to vote against him and his candidates, the Parson concluded that the Rebels had slipped in and voted the Radical down—and they had done so through the violent methods of the Ku Klux Klan. He saw with surprise 559 votes recorded from Lincoln County. Had he not already deprived that county of its suffrage? Since 554 of them had been cast for Sheafe, he did not hesitate to throw out the whole vote of this county. But this action alone would not overcome the Conservative's majority, so he threw out almost 700 votes from Marshall and Coffee counties, and succeeded in electing Tillman, by a majority of 432. Thus, did he again demonstrate his skill as a mathematician and as a magician, too, by transforming a Conservative majority of 736 into a Radical majority of 432. In a three-cornered contest in the eighth district, Brownlow brought about the election of W. J. Smith, the second

---

[47] *Ku Klux Conspiracy*, I, 456, 460. The governor had been given this power in a law passed February 26, 1868. It not only gave the governor this power for the future, but legalized similar acts of Brownlow in the past, whether the laws at the time "justified the governor in his action or not." For the text see "Digest of Election Cases," p. 910.

highest man, by "utterly repudiating" the vote of Tipton County "as the most stupendous fraud perpetrated in the State during the late election" and casting out the vote of Fayette County "as held in open violation of the franchise law." He based his authority for these actions on the ground that the franchise law was supposed to produce a great change—"I may say revolution—in our elective system. It announces that a large portion of our people have made war upon the Government, and are unsafe depositaries of the elective franchise." He knew that the Ku Klux Klan used violence and intimidation to prevent Radicals from voting. His authority for revising the election returns was, therefore, clear. The Parson admitted that his decision was not conclusive as Congress had the last word—a fact Tennessee well remembered from her experience in 1865-1866.[48]

Tennesseeans were undoubtedly much upset in this election, but there seems to have been little or no violence. Although he had the right by the act of February 26, 1868, to dismiss his commissioners of registration and annul their registration, there was grave doubt whether he had the right to prevent the election being held by the coroner. As for the intimidation and violence charged against the Ku Klux Klan or any other group, the captain of the Federal troops stationed in Marshall County, where Governor Brownlow had thrown out 518 votes, declared that the "election was very quiet; every one voted his sentiments, without disturbance or threats; both white and colored; and no one in the county, as far as we are advised and believe, voted except those who had certificates to vote under the franchise law of Tennessee. The citizens of the county are quiet and law-abiding, and treated my command with kindness and due respect."[49]

As the Parson guessed, Congress finally settled the matter; and again as the Parson well knew, a Radical Congress would find a way equally as easily as he had in seating Radical contestants. When Sheafe's case came before Congress, it was referred to the committee on elections, which group admitted

[48] *Ibid.*, pp. 907-9, 916.
[49] *Ibid.*, p. 918.

that Brownlow had no right to throw out votes—an act quite
apart from the right to throw out registrations before elections
were held—but knowing that it could examine the ballot boxes,
it took the Parson's word for the Ku Klux violence and proceeded to throw out the identical votes the Parson had selected.
Hence, Tillman was seated. The minority of the committee opposed this decision and declared that Brownlow's refusal to
award Sheafe the certificate of election "was an act of usurpation committed, and a wrong done to the prejudice of that gentleman, without a shadow of authority by the laws of either the
State of Tennessee or of the United States." It was only through
the management of elections by highly partial laws that most of
the Congressmen during the Reconstruction period were elected.
Tillman in his defense declared that if these laws were unconstitutional, then not only was he not entitled to his seat "but perhaps only a few of the sitting members from Tennessee of the
present or any preceding Congress since the rebellion are or
were entitled to seats." The Tennessee courts later declared
these very laws unconstitutional![50]

The most confusing complication brought forth by the Tennessee Congressional election of 1868 was the matter of seating
two additional Congressmen which Tennessee had taken it upon
herself to elect. Though both were elected in November, 1868,
the state claimed only one additional Congressman, for one of
them had been elected to serve out the remaining part of the
Fortieth Congress and the other expected the full term of the
Forty-first. Tennessee based her claim to this extra Congressman on the ground that the Negro voters which she had enfranchised should now be counted fully in the enumeration of
population for the purpose of apportioning representation, instead of only the three-fifths value allowed when they were slaves.
Having, according to the census in 1860, 275,000 slaves, she
estimated that the two-fifths additional strength that they acquired when they became free would entitle the state to an
additional Congressman and too anxious to await a new ap-
portionment by Congress, the legislature on March 12, 1868,

[50] Ibid., pp. 910, 915, 917, 921.

passed a law calling for the electing of an additional Congressman. The Radicals believed that since Tennessee under their
guidance and without compulsion from the outside had freed
her slaves and had enfranchised them, being the first of the
former Confederate States to do the latter, she should be given
consideration for this great show of Radical patriotism. And,
furthermore, the Fourteenth Amendment implied this additional
representation. The Radicals argued that Tennessee had 40,000
male Negroes 21 years old or more and that none was disfranchised.

Since Tennessee was the first state to attempt to capitalize
her free Negroes in this respect, she felt that an exception
should be made in her case and that her additional Congressmen
should be admitted. Thomas A. Hamilton, who had been elected
from the state-at-large, for the remainder of the Fortieth Congress appeared first. His case, it was thought, would be especially compelling, for he posed as a special delegate from the recently enfranchised Negroes, and if he should be refused "it
would dishearten the freedmen of Tennessee, who are alleged
to regard the claimant as especially their representative, and
would be disastrous to their interests as a race, now in special
need of the recognition and protection of their government."
The committee to whom his case was referred was much impressed
with Tennessee's record and with her Congressman-at-large, but
they were unable to see how a law of Tennessee could give her an
extra Congressman, when Congress itself had always done the
apportioning. And, besides, it would not be fair to the other
states in the South to allow Tennessee an additional representative when some of them, undoubtedly entitled to more than one,
would receive none at all. The minority of the committee was so
impressed with the justice of Tennessee's case that they recommended that Congress pass a special act allowing Tennessee the
extra Congressman. The House failed to act, and Tennessee was
denied her additional representation.[51]

The case of John B. Rodgers was identical with that of Hamilton, except that Rodgers did not argue the point of being the

---

[51] *Ibid.*, pp. 499-516.

24

special representative of the Negroes, and that he was elected for the Forty-first Congress. His case led to the same conclusion which grew out of the previous one. The same special act favoring Tennessee with an additional Congressman was offered, but it was never reached by Congress.[52] It did not entirely please Brownlow that Tennessee had not been better appreciated and given more power in the national legislature.

Brownlow was determined to be unrelenting toward the Rebels to the last day of his power in Tennessee. They should not vote and if it appeared in any election that by trickery they had voted and won office he would revise the returns to replace them with Radicals. In bantering the Rebel aristocracy on their sad lot, he queried whether rebellion had not "left you high and dry upon the old Constitutional hill, to gaze with astonishment upon the fertile valley of *Progress* below, inhabited by native Radicals and 'imported carpet-baggers'?"[53] His last regular message as governor (November, 1868) developed largely into a political harangue, berating his political opponents. He failed to see or recognize a great undercurrent of opinion widespread over the state, among former Union men no less than former Confederates, that revenge had held sway in Tennessee long enough, that Tennessee had been whipped and lashed into a condition which was becoming utterly intolerable, that even Brownlow's own party of incorruptibles was on the verge of bursting into pieces. A faint ray of conciliation broke in upon his message when he stated that the franchise might be extended to the involuntary Rebels, but never to the unrepentant Rebels who had fought to the last—never should the vote be restored to them until the national debt should have been repaid, and they had done the impossible; until they had "restored to the ballot box the half million loyal voters who now sleep in premature graves."[54]

He thought well of the carpetbaggers, and he had a special

---

[52] *Ibid.*, pp. 941-50.
[53] *Knoxville Whig*, October 14, 1868.
[54] *Ibid.*, November 18.

fury against the Ku Klux Klan for attempting to drive them out, and for discouraging more from coming. He was pained to see Union men in Tennessee objecting to these valuable citizens. What if they did fill some of the offices? "What sort of tenure upon any of the offices of the State would any loyal native have had if the carpet-baggers had not come and squelched out rebellion and planted the banner of the government amidst the reeking ruins of war?"[55] One of his own official household, his own secretary of state, whom he had often snubbed by issuing proclamations without his seal and signature, Andrew Jackson Fletcher, assumed a bold outspoken attitude on the subject of carpetbaggers as well as disfranchisement. He has been given the credit of first suggesting the carpetbag title that ever afterwards adhered to the Northern adventurers who fed upon the Southern carcass during Reconstruction days. He said, "No one more gladly welcomes the Northern man who comes in all sincerity to make a home here, and to become one of our people, than I, but for the adventurer and office-seeker who comes among us with one dirty shirt and a pair of dirty socks, in an old rusty carpetbag, and before his washing is done becomes a candidate for office, I have no welcome."[56]

In the early part of 1869, Fletcher openly broke with the Parson on the point of forgiving the Rebels. The secretary of state was beginning to see that the program of revenge had done a vast injustice to the great majority of Tennesseeans and also to realize that it had done great damage to the progress and development of the state. "The man who is disfranchised in a republic," he said,

is not apt to feel that it is his government, or take any pride or interest in it, nor apt to make a useful or even law-abiding citizen of it.

These people are greatly impoverished by the war. They suffered defeat, wounds and captivity. We have emancipated their slaves; we have disfranchised the master, and disabled him from holding

---

[55] *Ibid.*, April 15, December 2, 1868.
[56] Temple, *op. cit.*, p. 126.

office or sitting on juries; we have enfranchised the slave, and given him the right to hold office and sit upon juries, and thus in many localities reversing the relation of master and slave.[57]

Brownlow would soon be leaving Tennessee for the United States Senate. Instead of making a parting gesture of friendship to all Tennesseans, he would do a more characteristic thing; he would spread terror in his wake as he departed. On January 20, 1869, he issued a proclamation setting forth that a reign of terror had broken out in Middle and West Tennessee in which roving bands of Ku Klux were setting civil law at defiance, taking prisoners from jail and hanging them, taking passengers from railway trains, and driving conductors of Northern birth out of the state. These Ku Klux bands were being incited by ambitious people making incendiary speeches advising the overthrow of the state government, and by Rebel newspapers ridiculing the deeds of the night-riders and denying that there was a Ku Klux Klan. He called upon every "good and loyal citizen" in the state to join the army of rectification. He would soon declare martial law in various counties "and turn over offenders to the military to be tried and punished summarily." These outrages had "been long borne, but the Executive is not to be cajoled or trifled with." He soon expected to have Middle and West Tennessee "as orderly and quiet as East Tennessee is today."[58]

By the end of a month he had gathered together at Nashville 1,600 State Guards, armed and equipped, under the command of General Joseph Cooper. On February 20, he issued another proclamation placing under martial law nine counties scattered over Middle and West Tennessee and ordering troops to occupy them and to stay there "until we have unmistakable evidence of the purpose of all parties to keep the peace." He enjoined the "most rigid discipline among the troops," and directed that no quarter be shown "to either officers or privates who shall be found guilty of habitual drunkenness." General Cooper gave special attention to the cradle of the Ku Klux Klan by ordering

---

[57] *Knoxville Whig,* January 20, 1869.
[58] *Ibid.,* January 20, 1869; *American Annual Cyclopaedia,* 1868, p. 725.

five companies to occupy the town of Pulaski and make it their headquarters.[59]

This Second Brownlow War gradually dissipated itself and became of no consequence in the life of Tennessee or of the Parson, for Governor and Commander-in-Chief Brownlow was soon to transfer his activities to a broader stage and become Senator Brownlow.

[59] *Ku Klux Conspiracy*, I, 460.

CHAPTER XVI

THE LIKE SHALL NOT BE SEEN AGAIN

PARSON BROWNLOW was a political governor. He took no greater interest in the economic and social development of the state than was incidental to his political control, unless, indeed, the wasteful expenditures of state funds, and the exploitation of the Negroes and railroads may be considered more than incidental. But to say so is not to deny that toward the end of his governorship he announced a broad program for the state, which, if he had successfully carried it out, would have marked him as much more than a political governor. He talked much against sectional proscriptions which he felt would scare away Northern capital; as has appeared, he strongly favored the encouragement of immigration to the state, which in his mind would serve fully as much for political purposes as economic; he promoted a free school system by word rather than by act; he favored internal improvements through lending the aid of the state to the railroads; he would develop a middle class of small landholders and further punish the wealthy Rebels by breaking up large plantations; and he would encourage mining and manufacturing, especially in East Tennessee, where it seemed to him such activities could best thrive.[1] He also believed that East Tennessee could be made into a great summer resort.

But the economic aspects of the Brownlow régime must be judged by its accomplishments rather than by any announced desires. Activities began first with the state's money and its borrowing power, and a record of extravagance and corruption was made which placed the state in a position rivaling the similar attainments of the most disreputable carpetbaggers and Negroes in the states farther south. It was not so much a reflec-

---

[1] For example see *Knoxville Whig*, December 23, 1868.

tion on the Parson's honesty as on his financial ability and experience and his inability to see guile in a Radical, however disreputable he might be. A man who in private life had never possessed much wealth, and who largely through the kindness of his heart had lost most of the little he had had, would not likely show financial ability in dealing with the monies a state either had or could borrow in the pestilential times of Reconstruction —a period when it became the custom among the high and the low to plunder the public treasury. And to make worse the Parson's chances for an honest administration of the state's finances, he was aided by a legislature of inexperienced men, who for the most part had not the record of private honesty which had characterized his life.

As one of the inevitable results of the loss of the war by the Confederacy, Tennessee was relieved of her Confederate debt; so Brownlow succeeded only to the ante-bellum obligations of the state. Though the land had just passed through four years of the devastations of warfare and its ability to produce revenue had all but disappeared, the Parson proceeded as if he had an inexhaustible treasury. Salaries were increased and extravagant expenditures carried out which cost the state in money raised and used up $9,293,349.99, including a deficit of $269,166.29. The actual running expenses of the two Brownlow legislatures were more than $760,000. In addition, there was left a bonded indebtedness of $16,565,046.60[2] According to a committee which investigated the Brownlow régime shortly after it had passed on, the debt was increased in 1866 "unjustly and illegally" by $4,941,000, and in 1867 nearly $5,000,000 more "was corruptly and unjustly added." As was characteristic of the Reconstruction era, these bonds were sold for any price a speculator would pay, and quite often he bought them from 17 cents to 40 cents on the dollar.[3]

---

[2] Temple, op cit., pp. 319-21; American Annual Cyclopaedia, 1865, p. 780; ibid., 1868, p. 724; Ku Klux Conspiracy, I, 436; Noted Men of the Solid South, pp. 212-13. These figures take no note of the ante-bellum Tennessee debt, which Brownlow inherited.

[3] "The State Debt. Report of the Committee Appointed to Investigate It," Appendix to Senate Journal of the Forty-first General Assembly of the State of Tennessee, pp. 15 ff.

Naturally these bonds began to depreciate on the market, and when they sold as high as 75, Brownlow considered it was time to rejoice at the sound financial condition of the state. And even when the state defaulted the interest, he took comfort in the gloomy observation that Tennessee occupied "a far more desirable condition than any of the states recently in rebellion." But his political enemies rejoiced at the financial discomfiture of the state as they saw him drag it down further and further, for they believed that sometime even the most fanatical Radical would see that a change in the government would be desirable. By the summer of 1868, the bonds depreciated so low that there were rumors abroad of repudiation. To bolster up the waning credit of the state, a "Financial Board" of five men had recently been appointed, but it had broken up in confusion, and had left the state at a lower ebb than ever before. Believing that a Radical could do no wrong, the Parson blamed the state's low financial standing on a conspiracy hatched by the Conservatives and in his message of July 27, 1868, he called upon the legislature to investigate them and "proceed to sue them for damages in the name of the State." About this time he seemed to have lost faith in the honesty of his legislators or in their forbearance to keep their hands out of the public treasury, for he recommended an amendment to the constitution forbidding an increase of the state debt.[4]

The financial irregularities which beset Tennessee were aided by the Governor's physical condition. He was so afflicted with the palsy that he was unable to comply with the law which required him to place his signature upon each bond issued. He, therefore, commissioned his secretary, H. H. Thomas, to sign the required signature, and thereby, he greatly increased the chance of issuing fraudulent bonds; for when once the right to affix his signature passed beyond his own hand, there could be no certain limits to its extent. In 1866, he had been able to sign 200 bonds before he fell exhausted, whereupon he brought in his secretary of state as well as his private secretary to continue the process. In publicly reassuring bondholders that if his signa-

---

[4] *Knoxville Whig,* June 3, July 8, 29, November 18, 1868.

ture did not appear to be genuine it was due to the lack of imitative skill in his secretaries, he invited political manipulators and counterfeiters to begin their work and destroy whatever financial standing the state had left. Soon the rumors were out that the Parson had millions of bonds stacked up in his office which might be signed by anyone who cared to enrich himself, and that such confusion already reigned as to make it impossible to determine how many bonds had actually been issued. It was directly charged that many of the bonds had been signed in New York City where they had been printed, and had never come into the possession of the state at all. Brownlow admitted that some of the bonds had been signed in New York, and that Thomas had done it, going there to begin the work early in order to save time.[5]

Tennessee in the hands of her native Unionists fared financially about as ill as did the other Southern States which were at the mercy of their Negroes and carpetbaggers. It seemed that Radical rule was as pestilential whether it be native or imported. And in either case the most gigantic thefts were being carried out through the manipulation of the railroads. The captains of troops, when peace came, would transfer their organizing ability to industrial pursuits, and the railroads offered easy entrance. But all railroad developments of this period were not actuated by the desire for plunder. There was an urgent need for rehabilitating the roads and constructing new ones, for upon the transportation establishment other economic developments largely rested. The former commanders of armies and the industrially inclined leaders entered upon the business, for the most part, with honest intentions; the native politicians and the carpetbaggers were the ones to play havoc with the state's credit and good name.

Governor Brownlow believed he could well serve his state in giving some attention to the railroads, and especially did he believe that East Tennessee should now receive the aid denied it when Middle and West Tennessee controlled the state. He had much to say on the subject in his official capacity and he

---

[5] "The State Debt," p. 134; *Knoxville Whig,* May 23, 1866, August 19, 1868.

spread additional observations over the pages of his *Whig.*[6] East Tennessee had long felt the disadvantage of her isolation; ante-bellum railroad conventions had always been welcomed in Knoxville; and now the northern link of the long projected Charleston and Cincinnati Railroad, under the name of the Knoxville and Kentucky Railroad, engaged much of his enthusiasm.

Not restricting himself, however, to East Tennessee, Brownlow immediately upon becoming governor took up the question of the railroads, now being turned back to their owners by the Federal Government, so far as Nathan Bedford Forrest, John Morgan, and other raiders had left anything to be restored. As the state itself through its ante-bellum aid had important interests in the roads, there was additional reason for the state to take some action to safeguard its investments. The state now came to the rescue through a method which was logical and wise enough, had the men in charge honestly carried it out. Bonds were issued for the purpose of rehabilitating the war-worn roads and for meeting the interest requirements. Thus would the state be relieved of the necessity of attempting to secure funds through the doubtful expediency of taxation. Bonds were issued at various times and in such a haphazard fashion, as has already appeared, that the exact amount involved has never been definitely agreed upon; but there can be no doubt that it aggregated $16,000,000. To aid East Tennessee, about $5,000,000 was issued which produced in actual money about $350,000, so poor was the credit of the state and so dishonest were those in charge. For the rest of the state the record was little better. Carpetbaggers with a Union record came in and with it blinded Brownlow to their utter dishonesty and disrepute, and when they had seized all the spoils which they thought could be had, they withdrew from the scene. After the Brownlow pestilence had spent itself, a legislative committee which had been appointed to view the ruin, declared that for the immense debt saddled upon the state the people had to show only the Hermitage and the capitol. Any other values received had disappeared,

---

[6] April 4, 1866, November 18, 1868 may be noted as examples.

while the state had nothing but the debt and the obloquy resulting from her inability to pay it.[7]

By 1867, some of the railroads were defaulting in the interest due on their bonds, and certainly no one who knew the condition of the roads and their finances should have been surprised. Brownlow threatened the roads with seizure by the state if they did not pay their debts, and before the end of the year various roads were taken over. But the attempt of the state to run the roads was a great burden on the weak treasury, and before the end of 1868 Brownlow declared that he would recommend the sale of all roads which did not meet their interest promptly.[8]

The story of the methods used by the dishonest railroad plunderers in promoting bond issues in the legislature is an amazing one. Bribery was, of course, common, but the shapes it took and the atmosphere under which it throve were most outlandishly uncommon. The old methods of wine and women were freely used, and so was money, but a somewhat new departure was taken when new suits of clothes were dangled before the eyes of the hesitant legislator. General J. A. Mabry, the president of the Knoxville and Kentucky Railroad, admitted that he had spent from $2,000 to $5,000 in clothing the Tennessee legislature and that he had an agreement with a Nashville clothier to furnish the goods. The legislators for sale, who found themselves well provided with clothes, could generally be satisfied with $500 apiece. It undoubtedly remained for the Tennessee conspirators to discover the use that could be made of ministers of the church in promoting fraudulent legislation. Knowing the high position that religion and its ministers held in Tennessee politics, and realizing how amenable politicians were to such influences, these conspirators hired preachers to pray bills through the legislature.[9]

But the most amazing method of control, which was, however,

---

[7] "The State Debt," p. 16; "Message of Gov. Albert S. Marks, to the Forty-first General Assembly of Tennessee, delivered January 17, 1879," *Appendix to Senate Journal of the Forty-first General Assembly of the State of Tennessee,* pp. 10, 14.

[8] *Knoxville Whig,* February 27, September 4, 1867, June 3, November 18, 1868.

[9] "The State Debt," pp. 30, 55-58, 67, 68, 85; "Message of Gov. Marks," p. 9.

not peculiar to Tennessee at this time, was the use made of mesmerism and spiritualism. These highly scientific, if not occult, schemes were reserved for controlling Governor Brownlow and other important men. In the summer of 1868, the Parson became involved in a transaction which in connection with any other person would take on the ugly aspects unmistakable of a bribe, and which in the case of the Parson can be charitably explained only on the grounds that he was as usual, ill and did not know what had really happened. General Mabry together with C. M. McGhee, John R. Branner, and Thomas Calloway came into the Parson's presence bringing with them five $1,000 bills, most of which amount they had won speculating on Wall Street. According to the evidence sifted out by the investigating committee a few years later, Brownlow, who was lying on a couch ordered the Greeks bearing gifts to give the money to his wife, who accepted it. Gentle Mrs. Brownlow undoubtedly had no knowledge of the meaning of the money and therefore no sense of guilt, and likely the Parson considered it nothing more than a financial act of friendship on the part of a well-wisher who was more blessed with worldly goods than was Brownlow. But not so innocent were the intentions of the bribers, for they had been consulting the spiritualist Madame Mansfield on the easiest approach to the capture of the Parson, and she had informed the General that the best method for controlling the "old scratch" would be through the use of money. And as for the easiest way to obtain it, she advised them to speculate on Wall Street on Brownlow's account, but without his knowledge. Since the spiritualist's advice in speculating for the money had been so successful, the General and his conspirators believed that the gift would miraculously bring the Parson under their hypnotic influence.[10]

The same sort of corruption that crept into the handling of the railroads also destroyed any fair prospects of a free school

---

[10] "The State Debt," pp. 31, 176-78. The Brownlow régime was investigated twice, once in 1869-1870 when a report was issued in about a thousand pages and published as an appendix to the senate journal of 1871-1872, and secondly, in 1879. I have depended for the most part on the findings of the last investigation.

system for the state. Brownlow remembering that a little learning instead of being a dangerous thing had been of vast importance in his making, in the first year of his rule called upon the state "to keep faith with the destitute and long-neglected school children." The Federal armies had destroyed the Tennessee School for the Blind, near Nashville, and the Library of the East Tennessee University, in Knoxville, had also fallen before their onset. The ravages of war against education should now be repaired, for a good school system would have additional value in directing new immigrants to the state. The legislature seemed to have been too busy issuing railroad bonds and following the Parson's advice on how best to harry the Rebels to pay much attention to his recommendations on education. In a message to the legislature in January, 1867, he referred to that body's refusal to pass important school legislation as deeply to be regretted.[11]

Toward the latter part of his gubernatorial career, the Parson saw some school bills pass his legislature, but by this time, corruption and stupidity had largely dissipated the school fund, so that now laws without money could little aid the school children. The state treasurer, R. L. Stanford, of East Tennessee, was prevailed upon to deposit the school fund, which was in the form of Federal bonds, in a Memphis bank and to receive it later in greenbacks. This action marked him as either stupid or corrupt, and the disaster that must inevitably hang over such a transaction soon came tumbling down upon it. He was not forced to await the repayment of money worth one hundred cents on the dollar, in greenbacks worth much less—the bank hastened the disaster by becoming insolvent and dissipating most of the school fund. Treasurer Stanford resigned, and Brownlow accepted his resignation, expressing much indignation that a public servant should be so faithless. Poor Stanford, who must have been more stupid than venal, and who had a keener conscience than many other men of his day, had the courage and politeness to do what the corrupt carpetbaggers

---

[11] *American Annual Cyclopaedia*, 1865, p. 780; *Knoxville Whig*, January 30, 1867.

would never do—he got himself out of the way by drinking laudanum.[12]

Brownlow was only indirectly responsible for the sorry plight of the schools, but it was part of the régime which he headed. Other institutions in the state were in an equally low state. In looking into the State Hospital for the Insane, he found the relatives of many people from other Southern States, sent to Tennessee to be relieved of having them close at hand. The relatives at large were as crazy as the inmates, Brownlow thought, if they expected Tennessee to give this service free. He sent warning that if the bills were not soon paid, Tennessee would quarter these foreign inmates on their relatives back home.

Just as the state hospital was in need of money, so was the penitentiary. This institution was so terribly crowded that he suggested that a branch be built in East Tennessee. His opponents objected that this was merely an attempt to make it possible to mismanage two institutions instead of one. The state hospital and the penitentiary, the Parson knew, were necessary, but there was one institution which he believed to be a silly luxury. This was the Hermitage. Why should the state, of which he was the governor, keep up this expensive monument to his old imperious enemy, Andrew Jackson, especially since it had never been paid for. He advocated its sale in order to help satisfy the debt.[13]

Brownlow had neither a philosophy nor a program on financial and economic questions. Yet he had his likes and dislikes along these lines, whether he clearly saw why or not. He did not wait to be instructed by the national leaders of the Republican Party as to what he should think about the greenbacks. He knew that he liked the idea of such money, for it helped the debtors, and he believed that the bonds of the nation should be paid in greenbacks unless they specifically stated otherwise. This position he took in a letter to the Tennessee Radical convention in January, 1868. But when "Gentleman" George Pendleton of Ohio, led his Democrats into such doctrines in the presidential

[12] Ibid., December 19, 1866, January 30, 1867, August 29, 1868.
[13] Ibid., November 7, 1866, July 29, 1868.

campaign of 1868, the Parson kept his own counsel on the subject.[14]

Though Brownlow did not live in an industrial state he was beset with a railroad strike in 1868, on the Nashville and North-western Railroad. The strikers appointed a committee to explain their grievances to the Governor, but he was so sure that he already knew their purposes, that in answer to their request for a conference, he declared that they were "a mob to stop the trains and destroy the business of the roads" and he flatly charged them with being part of the Rebel warfare against his administration.[15]

As a governor, Brownlow was neither constructive nor recon-structive; he was distinctly destructive. For four years he had threatened revenge upon a people who, he declared, had injured him and the Unionists; and when he became governor, he brow-beat and intimidated a people who should have been helped back to a position in the state commensurate with their importance. He disfranchised most of the intelligent people and made voters out of 40,000 former slaves, and so exacting was he of Unionists that according to a Congressional committee "Everybody was loyal who voted for and maintained Brownlow and his friends, and everyone was disloyal who dared to oppose them."[16] As a result, his own party broke under his burden, and made it possi-ble for his opponents to gain control of the state and forever abolish his control. The same Congressional committee declared that "No State was ever reduced to such humiliation and degra-dation as that unhappy commonwealth during the years Brown-low ruled over her."[17] A Tennesseean forty years afterwards reflected that Brownlow's régime was "four years of misrule more trying upon the brave men and women of Tennessee than the four years of terrible war."[18] General Forrest, who was, him-self, brave enough to stand his ground even against the Fighting

---

[14] *Ibid.,* January 29, 1868.   [15] *Ibid.,* June 24.
[16] *Ku Klux Conspiracy,* I, 454. Minority Report.
[17] *Ibid.*
[18] *The South in the Building of the Nation,* II, 526 (Carey A. Folk, "Tennessee Since the War, 1865-1909").

Parson, testified that the name of Brownlow became a terror to the people generally. "They were very much frightened," he declared.[19] A Tar Heel, up the French Broad, in Asheville, on the passing of the Parson out of the state to the Senate, expressed more eloquently the feelings many had toward him:

> Innocent children will shrink from his polluting touch, and lonely women will shun him as they would a rattle snake. . . . His name will go down to posterity surrounded with a lurid halo of infamy, and will be spoken only in a whisper, on long winter nights, to send a thrill of terror to the hearts of timid listeners.[20]

The feeling of relief that accompanied his departure was mixed with a sense of bitter outrage, mental if not material, suffered at his hands, which was long in dying down. A full-length portrait of the Parson, painted by Dury, to hang in the state capitol, today bears grimly devastating streaks from the waist down, made either according to tradition by the labial effusions of tobacco-chewing legislators, avenging the wrongs of their people, or according to a more charitable explanation, by the gentle drippings from heaven as they poured through an unfortunate leak in the capitol roof.[21]

If Brownlow suffered a regret at transferring himself to the Senate it undoubtedly came out of the necessity of deserting his *Whig*, which had accompanied him for thirty years, from Elizabethton to Knoxville, and which had helped to make his career. During the past few years his quivering frame had not permitted his hand to write, yet he appeared on the editorial page frequently, signing himself "Senior Editor." In explaining to his readers, whether they be doubting or congratulating him, how he managed to write his editorials, he said that he had a little office in his back yard and while he reclined there he kept handily a table with pen, ink, and paper, and when his friends came in he set them to work. He added that while he was "unable

---

[19] *Ku Klux Conspircay*, XIII, 15.

[20] *Asheville News*, quoted by *Knoxville Whig*, March 31, 1869.

[21] *Knoxville Whig*, August 15, 1866. A letter to the author from Mrs. John Trotwood Moore, April 13, 1931, suggested the latter explanation.

A portrait of Governor William G. Brownlow, bought by the state in 1866 for $1,000. It now hangs in the Tennessee State Library, in the Capitol, at Nashville. Reproduced by permission of Mrs. John Trotwood Moore, Librarian and Archivist.

Knoxville as it appeared to the artist about 1875. The Holston River is shown in the foreground. From Edward King's *The Southern States of North America.*

to *write*" he was "able to *think* upon a large scale."[22] On January 6, 1869, he announced that T. Haws & Company were the sole owners and editors of the newspaper. The only souvenirs which he retained were the building in which the paper was printed, and the back files. Thomas H. Pearne, the elder of the Northern Methodists, who had so terribly beset the Southern Methodists for mixing politics with their religion, now became the "political, religious and general editor" of the *Whig*. In relinquishing his long control, Brownlow looked back upon his thirty years of journalism and declared it satisfactory in his eyes—"had I my life to live over, I would pursue the same course I have pursued, ONLY MORE SO."[23] As "Brownlow" was lowered from the masthead, perhaps he and many of his readers felt that a solemn ceremony should have accompanied the act. On January 27, 1869, the last *Brownlow's Knoxville Whig* fell from the press; on February 3 it was the *Weekly Knoxville Whig*. Feeling that this new title did not say exactly what they had intended, the new editors on the tenth, rescrambled the words into the *Knoxville Weekly Whig*, which may have made their predicament even worse.

On March 3, 1869, Senator Patterson would leave his seat in the Senate for Brownlow to occupy. On the next day a new president of the United States would be inaugurated. The Parson, therefore, began in February to make preparations to resign his governorship of Tennessee and to take up his new duties as Senator. On the 10th he issued his farewell address to the legislature in which he announced that he would cease to be governor on the 25th. He was not as fiery as might have been expected. Without admitting failure, he declared that he had sought to build up Tennessee and would have done better had the Rebels let him. If it might appear that he was too weak to make speeches in the Senate, he would never allow his record to be open to the charge that he had not voted in the right way.[24] As this legislature, too, was soon to pass into history, on the 27th,

[22] *Knoxville Whig*, September 16, 1868.
[23] *Ibid.*, January 6, 1869.
[24] *Knoxville Weekly Whig*, February 17, 1869.

25

it resolved that the members part in peace "and that the Great Eternal may bless us for all our good votes"; it hoped that their bad ones might lead to no harm; and to conclude, they resolved "That we will endorse the words of our great General, 'Let us have peace.' "[25] But, of course, as long as the majority of Tennesseeans were disfranchised, spurned, and ruled over by the Radical minority there could be no peace. With the departure of the Parson, the governorship would devolve on D. W. C. Senter, the speaker of the senate and a Tennesseean with much less vindictiveness than permeated Brownlow.

The fates had been kind to the new Senator. He was displacing a son-in-law of Andrew Johnson in the Senate, and General Grant was relegating Andrew Johnson, himself, back to private life. The Parson would set out early for Washington in order to participate in the glories that would surround the inauguration of a president to be controlled by the Radicals. And all of the glory would not be reflected by the new president; Brownlow was a man with a reputation about as widespread as Grant's. Various Washington ward leaders had made preparations to welcome him no less than the General.[26]

Gathering together a group of his friends he boarded a special car on the Virginia and East Tennessee Railroad. He was personally and keenly hated by more people along the way than, perhaps, any other person who ever made the trip to Washington. He was peered and peeped at by people at the railway stations as if he had been a wild animal in a cage. At Bristol, small boys clamored around his car to catch a glimpse of him, and a grown-up who got a better view declared that he looked "like a d—d old turkey buzzard." The *Lynchburg News* carefully noted and published the fact that the car in which the Parson rode was number 9, and recommended that thereafter every person should "avoid it as he would a leper."[27] When the

---

[25] *Acts of the State of Tennessee passed at the Second Session of the Thirty-fifth General Assembly for the Year 1868-69*, p. 417.

[26] *Knoxville Weekly Whig*, February 17, 1869; *Noted Men of the Solid South*, pp. 211-12.

[27] *Knoxville Weekly Whig*, March 10, 1869.

train stopped in Charlottesville, the seat of the University of Virginia, ten or fifteen young fellows, who were thought to be students of the University, invaded his car. One of them whipped out a pistol and pointed it at the Parson, who was asleep, with the remark that he "would rather shoot the d—d old skunk than to eat." The weapon was snatched from his hand. Those who best knew student ways believed that it was intended merely as a student prank; but the *Knoxville Weekly Whig* declared that it was an attempt to assassinate the Parson and that it was proof enough that "Virginia needs further reconstruction."[28]

Brownlow in the Senate became as great an object of interest and curiosity as he had been while making his trip to Washington. Almost everyone who came to the capitol wanted to see him; the Washington *Chronicle* observed that he was "an object of great interest during this session of Congress."[29] He might well have been also an object of pity, for his frame quivered like a shaking aspen as he sat in his seat. He took the oath of office on March 5, sitting down, and so feeble was he that he not only could not stand up, but his "arm had to be supported while being sworn in." It seemed, indeed, that the Tennessee Radicals had sent him to the Senate for no other purpose than to compliment him. He took up living quarters about a hundred yards from the Senate chamber, so that an easier task might be imposed upon those who carried him back and forth. As his voice was also gone, his speeches were read by the clerk. On being asked whether he did not regret his inability to speak, he replied that it was likely best for himself and for the Senate for otherwise he "Would always be in a row."[30]

Though physically more dead than alive, mentally he seemed as vigorous as ever. He took his duties seriously, arriving early each day and remaining late. He continued, miraculously, to exist throughout his six-year term and attended with great

---

[28] *Ibid.*, March 3, 10, 1869.

[29] Quoted *ibid.*, March 24, 1869.

[30] *Congressional Globe*, 41st Cong., 1st sess., p. 8; *Knoxville Weekly Whig*, March 10, April 7, 14, 1869; *Daily American*, May 1, 1877; Temple, *op. cit.*, p. 341; *Knoxville Daily Chronicle*, May 11, 1871.

regularity, though he missed on account of his illness the whole of the second session of the Forty-Third Congress, lasting from December 7, 1874, to March 3, 1875.[31]

Though he took his position with becoming seriousness, he never became the mighty man of valor in the Senate which he had been back in Tennessee. The Radical Senators lionized him in the beginning, but they never went further, beyond doing him the doubtful honor of making him the chairman of the Committee on Revolutionary Claims. Not being a great man even among the species of giants who occupied the Senate in the Reconstruction days, he spent most of his time with what were considered small affairs, but which he considered important enough. He became a sort of claims agent for all the Unionists of Tennessee who felt that the United States owed them for their patriotic losses; and somewhat to his disgust at times, he was besieged by office-seekers. Though specializing on the Tennessee Unionists, he did not turn a deaf ear to all others who were in trouble or distress on matters of pensions and claims. His activities began with the Revolutionary War, which got him his chairmanship, and came on down through the French Spoliations prior to 1801, through the War of 1812, and on into his specialty, the Civil War. The widows did not fail to receive his attention, as was well shown in his successful efforts to secure an indemnity for Malinda Harmon, the widow of Jacob, who had been hanged by the Confederates in the early part of the war for his activities in bridge-burning.[32]

The Parson wrote few speeches on the general policies up for discussion before the Senate. His first speech was on the question of the repeal of the Tenure of Office Act. Remembering how valuable it had been in getting Johnson into trouble, perhaps temporarily forgetful of who was president or perhaps thinking that it might be useful even against Grant, he opposed

---

[31] *Congressional Globe,* 42nd Cong., 2nd sess., p. 1; *Congressional Record,* 43rd Cong., 2nd sess., p. xvi.

[32] *Congressional Globe,* 41st Cong., 1st sess., pp. 231, 262; 2nd sess., I, 298, 377, 772, 805, 2976, 4286; 3rd sess., I, 1, 598; 42nd Cong., 1st sess., pp. 1, 231; 3rd sess., p. 1; *Congressional Record,* 43rd Cong., special session, I, 3; 1st sess., II, 1; *Knoxville Weekly Whig,* April 7, 1869.

its repeal. In this speech he gave the Senators a slight taste of his style of oratory, when in referring to certain ante-bellum conditions he said, "Amid the baying of the hounds that fed upon the flesh-pots of Egypt, the wisdom of Webster and the Genius of Clay went unheeded." All eyes had been glancing toward the Parson as this speech was read, and at its conclusion Carl Schurz, George F. Edmunds, Jacob M. Howard and other Senators went to his seat to congratulate him.[33] Not being very close either in geography or in sentiment to the money interests of the East, in 1874 he opposed the resumption of specie payment as it appeared to him to be a measure directed toward the contraction of the currency, and he opposed the Civil Rights Bill as it seemed to him to make for the "co-education of the races." By this time he had somewhat reverted to his ante-bellum attitude toward the Negroes, especially as the Negroes in a convention in Nashville had recently denounced him for deserting them.[34]

In whatever manner his attitude toward the Negroes might fluctuate, he never lost his complete detestation of the Rebel leaders. Early in his administration Grant had appointed to the surveyorship of customs in New Orleans, General James Longstreet, who had so lightly entrenched himself against the storm of Republican Reconstruction in the South that he soon capitulated and became a part of it. Grant might have forgotten what a terrible Rebel Longstreet had been, but the Parson did not have so short a memory. Especially did he remember that Longstreet had besieged Knoxville in the fall of 1863 and had forced the Parson and his family to subsist on half-rations, and that after abandoning the siege he had for the rest of the winter ravaged East Tennessee of what little food it had.[35] In the mind of the Parson, one of the first qualifications for office was an unimpeachable Union record during the war.[36]

---

[33] *Knoxville Weekly Whig,* March 31, 1869. Yet Brownlow voted for the modification, which the Senate passed.

[34] *Congressional Record,* 43rd Cong., 1st sess., II, 776-77; Claude G. Bowers, *The Tragic Era,* p. 420.

[35] *Knoxville Weekly Whig,* April 21, 1869.

[36] For instance see telegram to Jas. S. Stewart, January 27, 1869. In Charles Sumner MSS, in Harvard University Library.

Just as a Rebel could do no right, a Federal could do no wrong, and if anyone should attempt to do a wrong to a Federal no one was quicker in coming to his defense than was the Parson. In the course of a debate in 1869 Senator William Sprague, of Rhode Island, attacked General Burnside, who having been more successful in politics after the war than during it, had got himself elected governor of Rhode Island in 1866. Brownlow, figuratively speaking, was immediately upon the floor, to defend the soldier who had at last come to the rescue of Knoxville in 1863. But first, as had got to be a custom with him, he introduced his listeners to East Tennessee, one of the richest and most delightful regions on earth, and so large that it embraced thirty-one counties. Then he made the announcement that former Union men might sit in the United States Senate and listen to attacks on men like Burnside, but no one could make such attacks on him in Knoxville and escape bodily injury. "Indeed," he declared, "there are patriotic women enough there who have named their children for Burnside to whale twenty such orators out of the State with broomsticks." Laughter swept the Senate floor and the galleries at the sally of the women with their broomsticks, and the General whom they were defending said he enjoyed Brownlow's speech more than any other one made.[37]

The East Tennessee hills had so stunted Brownlow's sense of propriety that it never fully developed, even in the United States Senate, yet his record for petulance was not much worse than that of some Senators whose health was far better than his. He seemed never to be able to learn that the Senators might not be as much interested in his personal and political antagonisms as he was. In the latter part of 1869 he was having some internal dissensions in his Republican Party in Tennessee, and to him the floor of the Senate was as proper an arena in which to carry on the fight as was Tennessee. He began an attack upon

---

[37] *Knoxville Weekly Whig,* April 28, 1869. The statement concerning Burnside's comment was written by John B. Brownlow on the margin of the office files, for this date.

some of the Tennessee Representatives in the other end of the capitol and was fast approaching the full vigor of East Tennessee tactics when the vice president halted the reading of his speech with the statement that it was unparliamentary for a Senator to attack a Representative. John Sherman, who perhaps, more for the reason of seeing how far the Parson would go than for any other, insisted that the Parson be allowed to continue—and so the storm swept on and spent its force.[38]

At another time Brownlow came forth to defend himself against an "unwarranted insult and attack" made by James M. Beck, a Representative from Kentucky. Beck in painting the villianies and corruptions of Reconstruction, by way of completeness referred to "Brownlow, while in Tennessee, making a pandemonium of that State." This speech enraged the Parson uncommonly; he immediately wrote out his reply and asked permission under the rule of personal privilege to have it read. The vice president objected that the rules of the Senate did not permit one of its members to attack a member of the other House, but as no Senator objected, the clerk was allowed to proceed with Brownlow's speech. When the hour arrived for a new order of business the vice president halted the reading, but such an unusual treat was it that the Senators decided to hear it all. The Parson began by calling Beck a slave-driver and a coward. If the Parson were not so old and decrepit, he declared he would snatch the Kentuckian's slave-whip and cowhide him with it. Brownlow now became personal unto himself and explained that the Rebels had made the physical wreck out of him that he was. They had driven him into the Great Smokies, had put him into jail, and had tried to poison him. Then they banished him from his beloved East Tennessee. Near the end of the war he had come back, become governor of the state, and because he had given the Rebels justice, he was now attacked. After the speech had been read, Brownlow felt that even more might have been said. He, therefore, had the speech reprinted from the *Congres-*

---

[38] *Congressional Globe,* 41st Cong., 2nd sess., I, 137-40.

sional Globe, and included further comments on the Kentuck-ian.[39]

As a Senator, Brownlow did not attract much attention be-yond his idiosyncrasies and picturesque and violent language. Therefore, with his departure from Tennessee for the Senate there was a gradual subsidence of him as a force to be reckoned with in the world. When he left, he decided that he had nursed the Republican Party in Tennessee into strength sufficient to take care of itself; he would, therefore, not take an active part in its affairs. But before the end of the year, he found himself mixed up in a political contest which was destined to demolish the party on which he had spent so many efforts. D. W. C. Senter, who had succeeded to the governorship on Brownlow's depar-ture, decided that he would enter the gubernatorial election which was to be held in the fall. William B. Stokes, who had been cheated out of the senatorship by Brownlow in 1867, decided that now his turn for the governorship had come. Both Senter and Stokes now sought the blessing of the Parson, and instead of playing a neutral, which was, of course, foreign to his nature, he did the apparently enigmatical and unexpected thing of supporting Senter. His espousal of Senter seemed strange, for Stokes was running on the extreme Radical doctrines which Brownlow had long advocated, while Senter had made an agree-ment with the Conservatives, who were really Democrats or Dem-ocrats in the making, that if they would support him, he would advocate the removal of the disabilities of the former Confed-erates.

His party now split wide open with the two parts savagely fighting each other. Brownlow was soon charged with having joined the Rebels and deserted the Negroes. Protesting that each charge was untrue, he sought to mollify the angry Negroes by recalling how much he had done for them, and to satisfy the extreme Radicals by declaring that he favored removing the

---

[39] *Ibid.,* 42nd Cong., 2nd sess., II, 1036-40; *Personal Explanation. Speech of Hon. William G. Brownlow of Tennessee in the Senate of the United States, February 15, 1872.*

disabilities only of the Rebel masses; he would disfranchise for life, if he could, the Rebel leaders. A complete break with Stokes resulted, who bitterly assailed the Parson on every stump. Undoubtedly a certain change had come over Brownlow, temporarily at least, and Stokes was among the first to sense it. The Parson's style of language was greatly toned down, so much so that Stokes declared that Brownlow no longer wrote his letters and speeches, and that when they were read to him he was too deaf to hear them. Stokes was badly beaten in the election, which took place in August.[40]

Perhaps the Parson was temporarily tired of fighting; he would rest a bit. But it was indeed a remarkable lapse on his part when he should find himself on the same side of any question with Andrew Johnson. But such was the case, for the ex-President was supporting Senter, too. Johnson had returned to Tennessee after completing his term as President, with the distinct feeling that he was not a defeated statesman, certainly not in Tennessee. He would return to the Senate to vindicate himself before the very body which had lacked only one vote of removing him from the presidency. He would seek the vacancy which would soon come and which would be filled in the fall, and it was rumored that he had bargained with Etheridge for his support with the understanding that Etheridge should then have the vacancy which Brownlow would soon make by dying. But Brownlow was to live, to continue to harry Andrew Johnson if for no other reason. Soon these two Kilkenny cats were at it again with all their old-time savagery. Brownlow played his part in the defeat of Johnson, and refused to accept any olive branches that the latter might attempt to hand him. In his desire to placate the Parson and his followers he had been spreading the news of the gift he had made the Parson in 1863 for the purpose of aiding in the establishment of the *Whig*. It was the handsome sum of $1,500. Brownlow quickly denied that it had been Johnson's gift; it had merely passed through his hands from the

[40] *Knoxville Weekly Whig,* July 21, September 1, 1869; *Noted Men of the Solid South,* pp. 214-15.

Federal Government. There could be no implications of ingratitude to Andrew Johnson in the whole affair.[41]

Senter's legislature was soon running away with him. It began to demolish all of the Brownlow structure that it dared; and by removing the disabilities against the former Confederates paved the way for the Democrats to seize the state soon thereafter. A constitutional convention met in 1870, cut loose from Brownlowism, and tied the state back to its old moorings as far as new conditions made it possible. The supreme court, composed of Brownlow's appointees, carried away more Brownlow rubbish.[42]

The Parson might well have recalled how wise old Aesop was when he recounted the fable of the farmer and the vipers. The Rebels had now done what he always knew they would do if they got the chance; they had seized the state. Men whom he had warmed into political life had stuck their fangs into his party. He declared that "so many in Tennessee who were at one time the most outspoken Union men, have proved untrue and have turned back to the 'flesh pots of Egypt,' betraying the too generous friends who had warmed them into life, that I can only ask that the Republicans of the nation will trust Tennessee politicians as far as they prove themselves trustworthy and no further."[43] There was left only one chance of restoring the state to the old order; it should be thrown into reconstruction and thereby have its existence as a state terminated. A movement was started which the Parson was not alone in promoting. Radicals in Tennessee joined with the national Radicals and set out upon a hunt for evidence to be used in demolishing the state. Benjamin F. Butler, always ready for any stratagem or spoil, became the chairman of a Congressional committee of investigation. Only by the quick work of conservative elements everywhere was the disaster averted.[44]

[41] *Daily New Era*, April 16, October 15, 1869; *Knoxville Weekly Whig*, April 14, 1869; Milton, *op. cit.*, p. 657; Winston, *op. cit.*, p. 496.

[42] "Digest of Election Cases," p. 921; *The South in the Building of the Nation*, II, 539-41.

[43] *Knoxville Weekly Whig*, September 15, 1869.

[44] "The State Debt," pp. 18, 96; *The South in the Building of the Nation*, II, 537-38.

It was a marvel how Brownlow continued to exist; perhaps, Death was only mocking him by letting him live to see his handiwork crumble. The Ku Klux Klan, it seemed, continued to thrive in the land of its birth, long after Grand Wizard Forrest had officially declared it dead. In 1871, Brownlow was longing for a chance to vote in the Senate to put the state under the Federal army.[45] If he had had a lapse when he supported Senter, he was soon to grow strong in the old faith again. He had no sympathy for the Liberal Republicans in 1872; and in 1876 he called upon the country to support Rutherford B. Hayes. If Hayes were not elected, all that had been accomplished since the war would be lost. The Rebels were "deaf to the lessons of the terrible past"; they were "determined to carry out their purposes, and render their past treason respectable."[46]

On March 3, 1875, he ended his full term as Senator, and such a clown was Fate that it decreed that Andrew Johnson should succeed him.

He returned to Knoxville, not to muse over the scenes of his former battles but to follow the advice of his late friend Thaddeus Stevens—to "die hurrahing." The two objects he loved most in this world were his wife and his *Whig*. His wife he fortunately still had, but his *Whig* he had cruelly sold into bondage. He soon formed a partnership with William Rule and secured a half interest in a newspaper which must have *Whig* in its title, however much out of date the term might be. So, it was the *Weekly Whig and Chronicle*, with a daily edition known as the *Knoxville Daily Chronicle*. Unable to write, he could still think vigorously and he enjoyed as much as ever the aroma of printers' ink.[47]

As the Parson had been ready for Death for a half century, had confidently expected it on many occasions, and had miraculously escaped it on many more, he made no preparations for it in Knoxville, feeling likely that he should live as long

---

[45] *Knoxville Daily Chronicle*, October 20, 1871.
[46] *Republican Banner*, April 23, 1872; *New York Daily Tribune*, November 2, 1876.
[47] *Atlanta Constitution*, May 1, 1877; Heiskell, *op. cit.*, III, 204-5; Price, *op. cit.*, III, 333.

as Methuselah. Yet every day that he continued to live appeared
a marvel, for he had for the past ten years been a helpless paralytic, who could not speak above a whisper—a physical wreck.
On April 28, 1877, he was as active about his home as a person
in his condition could be. With no thought of ever dying he
had workmen patching up his porches and fixing his fences.
That night he was suddenly stricken down—the last tense cord
that held him to this world snapped. He sank rapidly and on
Sunday, the 29th, surrounded by his family, at 2:05 o'clock
in the afternoon he died of "paralysis of the bowels."[48] So long
had his countrymen been expecting his death, that when it came
they were shocked. As a Georgia editor said, "The expected
event of years has been unexpectedly announced. . . ."[49] His
health vied with his political record in attracting the comments
incident to his departure. A Memphis newspaper said, "For
several years past he has not been able to speak above a whisper,
and he has been physically little more than a dead man. His
candle burned down through the very socket."[50] His high-strung
nature which had led to his vociferous use of himself for half
a century, had made of him a living miracle. Few people ever
got more out of their physical frame.

In Brownlow the elements were mixed. He combined oppo-
sites so successfully that he made himself a monster to many
of his contemporaries, and an enigma for future generations.
Without knowing how it could be, his intimates knew that he
was a Dr. Jekyl and a Mr. Hyde. Publicly he could be a raging,
irresponsible terrorist; privately he could be as gentle as the
Good Samaritan. The Memphis *Public Ledger* said, "His private
life was an utter contradiction of the nature he exhibited in
public. Socially he was genial and sympathetic, in his family
almost idealized, and among his immediate neighbors, especially
the poor, he was held in the highest esteem." Privately, he was
kind and charitable; he loaned money and never pressed for
its return, and he went on many surety bonds and lost; he was

---

[48] *New York Daily Tribune,* April 30, 1877; *Daily American,* May 1, 1877;
Public Ledger, May 1, 1877.
[49] *Atlanta Constitution,* May 1, 1877.   [50] *Public Ledger,* May 1, 1877.

easy to approach, the most humble man or woman might get
an audience with him at any time; he was jovial and smooth talking, and he made friends easily. He was accused of many crimes,
but never of personal dishonesty, drunkenness, or licentious-
ness. He never tasted liquor, never used tobacco, never saw a
play at a theatre, never dealt a pack of cards, and never courted
but one woman—and married her.[51] Such was the Parson privately; publicly he was another man.

One of his contemporaries declared:

> He could express more vituperation and scorching hate than
> any half a dozen men that ever appeared in American politics. . . .
> The man was a strange compound, and there are no more like him.
> The style of journalism by which he brought himself into notice
> and became so terrible to his enemies happily passed away before
> its author and is no longer tolerated by an intelligent public.[52]

Borne on by the heat of battle, he forewent no trick of language or procedure, however low and unfair, to beat down his
enemy. Nothing that his enemy possessed or was related to could
be sacred to him; it made little difference whether he attacked
his enemies or their wives and children, and whether the slanders
which he discovered or invented had any relation to the discussion. An annalist, observing without malice, said, "He has
wronged many individuals, he has dropped the bitterness of
gall into many a cup of happiness, he has caused many a wreck
of hopes and ambitions, and has counted many a mile-stone of
hate and contumely upon his downward journey to the Dark
Valley."[53] He had high moral and intellectual qualities, but he
had no sense of taste or fitness. His language could be inde-
scribably coarse both in direct expression and in insinuations,
but on account of his rare ability at picturesqueness, extravagance, and uncommon similes he could succeed in smothering
with laughter the blushes surging upwards. Theodore Tilton,

[51] For comments on his character see Price, *op. cit.*, III, 351, 352; *Public
Ledger*, May 1, 1877; *Knoxville Whig*, November 6, 1867; Temple, *op. cit.*, pp.
274–86.
[52] Price, *op. cit.*, III, 353.
[53] *Atlanta Constitution*, May 1, 1877.

who made much of the Parson, had to admit that he had "an almost unaccountable deficiency of that sense of fitness of things which we call good-taste."[54] In him the coarseness and roughness of the frontier was never polished by his contacts with more polite conditions, as was true in the cases of Abraham Lincoln, Davy Crockett, and Sam Houston. Perhaps the Parson instinctively thought it would be hypocrisy to change; he would be himself. In introducing one of his compositions he said, "Extreme fastidiousness of taste may, perhaps, shrink with oversensitiveness from some of the language I have employed."[55]

Brownlow was utterly fearless; he was reckless. The miracle of how he could continue to survive his ill health was no greater than of his escapes a thousand times from assassination by his outraged enemies. He declared that he feared nothing but the reproaches of his own conscience; and he was blessed with a conscience not celebrated for vigilance.

He had neither the well-rounded sentences of an orator, nor the voice of one. Rather, he depended on the uncommon use of language to draw and hold the attention of his listeners.

As a statesman he had little to recommend him. He had neither the training nor the temperament that should characterize such a leader. As a politician, he was eminently successful. He had a perfect comprehension of the methods of manufacturing and controlling the feelings and passions of the people on whom he depended for his support. It was undoubtedly true that one should lay "his bitterness and vituperation to a diseased style rather than to a real wickedness and unmanly malice."[56] And it is equally true that he developed this style as one of his most effective weapons in securing attention and a following and in holding them. He would never have harried the South, as he so often threatened, if he had ever found it within his power to do so. In Tennessee where he was in complete control, he threatened a reign of terror and worse, but he was never guilty of actual barbarities. He always hoped to kill the soul of his

---

[54] Theodore Tilton, "Sketch of Parson Brownlow," *Independent*, May 22, 1862.
[55] *Parson Brownlow's Book*, p. 8.
[56] Editorial in *Atlanta Constitution*, May 1, 1877.

THE LIKE SHALL NOT BE SEEN AGAIN 399

enemies with fear, rather than kill people physically. He whipped the Tennesseeans with terrorism for four years and almost made of them a nervous wreck, but he was a bad judge of human nature in thinking that he could permanently subdue people by such methods. After his departure for the Senate, the state in an incredibly short time regained its shattered soul and demolished his handiwork.

The people on whom the Parson could practice his peculiar methods of control were the lower classes, intermixed with the more intelligent citizens brought in by their background, their ambitions for promotion, and their prejudices, social, religious, and political. Ignorance and prejudice played a big part in making a hero out of Brownlow and in keeping him in power. But Tennessee was no more beset with these curses than other states of the times, which fared much better. There were other causes, therefore, which operated and by them was the complete but temporary success of the Parson guaranteed. He was temperamentally fitted and wise enough to embrace Radical Reconstruction and secure the backing of the Congressional oligarchy in maintaining his régime in Tennessee. Without the power of outside authority he could never have existed.

Not having the instincts of a statesman he built his structure on the sand instead of on the proverbial rock. Instead of treating the state to orderly development he fed it upon a program of vengeance. In carrying it out he was guilty of excesses unequalled in some instances by the imported carpetbaggers who beset some of the other Southern States. Also, in thinking that he could build up a permanent party on a small ignorant minority, he was again unwise and a poor judge. Therefore, his work was temporary and so was his fame. When he departed this life, his name went with him except as it should be recalled by those whom he had injured and terrorized, to be damned and cursed. Not only in statecraft did he leave nothing permanent, but also in religion and journalism it was likewise true. Yet at one time he was as well known in politics as his contemporary Abraham Lincoln, in journalism as his rival George D. Prentice, and in religion as Bishop Asbury. But as a figure in the development of a peculiar side of America he was unique and important, and to forget him would be to neglect an amazing side of the national portrait, distorted and disagreeable, yet entrancing and true. He was a product of his times, but his times produced none other like him.

BIBLIOGRAPHY

1. MANUSCRIPTS

Archives of Tennessee, in Nashville. There is little material of importance here relating to Brownlow, except his proclamations, which are available elsewhere in printed form.

John Bell MSS. In Library of Congress. There are a few scattered letters relating to Brownlow.

Brownlow MSS. In Library of Congress. Although there is no special Brownlow collection, a few letters are listed in the Manuscript Division.

Andrew Johnson Papers. In Library of Congress. During the period when Johnson and Brownlow were friendly a few short letters and telegrams passed between them.

Manuscript Archives of Macon County, Franklin, North Carolina.

Thaddeus Stevens MSS. In Harvard University Library. Less than a half dozen letters in this collection relate to Brownlow.

2. GOVERNMENT PUBLICATIONS

Acts, Tennessee General Assembly, 1865-1869.

Congressional Globe, 41st Congress, 1st, 2nd, and 3rd sessions; 42nd Congress, 1st, 2nd, and 3rd sessions.

Congressional Record, 43rd Congress, 1st, 2nd, and special sessions.

"Digest of Election Cases. Cases of Contested Elections in the House of Representatives from 1865 to 1871 inclusive," *House Miscellaneous Documents,* no. 152, 41st Congress, 2nd session (serial number 1434).

Eighth Census of the United States (1860). *Mortality and Miscellaneous Statistics.* Washington: Government Printing office, 1866.

House Journal, Tennessee General Assembly, 1865-1869.

Ku Klux Conspiracy. See *Report of the Joint Select Committee.*

Merriam, L. S., *Higher Education in Tennessee* (Bureau of Education, bulletin no. 16). Washington: Government Printing Office, 1893.

"Message of Gov. Albert S. Marks, to the Forty-first General Assembly of Tennessee, delivered January 17, 1879," *Appendix to Senate Journal* of the Forty-first General Assembly of the State of Tennessee, Nashville, 1879.

"Report of Governor Wm. G. Brownlow, to the General Assembly of Tennessee in Answer to a Joint Resolution calling for Information in Relation to the Late State Elections, at the Regular Session [November, 1865]," *Appendix, Senate Journal* of the General Assembly of the State of Tennessee, Nashville, 1865.

Report of [and *Testimony taken by*] *the Joint Select Committee to Inquire into the Condition of Affairs in the Late Insurrectionary States (Senate Report*, no. 41, pt. 1, 42nd Congress, 2nd session). Binder's title, *Ku Klux Conspiracy.*

Richardson, J. D., ed., *A Compilation of the Messages and Papers of the Presidents*, 10 vols. Washington: Government Printing Office, 1896-1899.

Senate Journal, Tennessee General Assembly, 1865-1869.

"The State Debt. Report of the Committee Appointed to Investigate It," *Appendix to Senate Journal* of the Forty-first General Assembly of the State of Tennessee, Nashville, 1879.

Thorpe, F. N., ed., *The Federal and State Constitutions, Colonial Charters, and Other Organic Laws of the States, Territories, and Colonies now or heretofore Forming the United States of America*, 7 vols. Washington: Government Printing Office, 1909.

War of the Rebellion, The: A Compilation of the Official Records of the Union and Confederate Armies, 130 vols. Washington: Government Printing Office, 1880-1901.

3. NEWSPAPERS

Brownlow's *Whig*, 1839-1869. Published under various titles, at several places, with changing editorship. Established in Elizabethton, under the title of *Tennessee Whig*, in 1839; moved to Jonesboro in 1840 and published under the title of *Jonesboro Whig and Independent Journal* (commonly referred to under the title, *Jonesboro Whig*) until 1849; at the latter date moved to Knoxville and appeared as the *Knoxville Whig and Independent Journal* until October 24, 1861, when it was suppressed by the Confederate authorities; reëstablished in October, 1863, under the title of *Knoxville Whig and Rebel Ventilator*. Upon the inauguration of Brownlow as governor in April, 1865, the editorship passed to his son, John Bell Brownlow. February 21, 1866, the title was shortened to *Knoxville Whig*. In February, 1869, the paper was sold, Thomas H. Pearne became editor and it became known as the *Knoxville Weekly Whig*. The many references to the *Whig* throughout this study as the source for remarks uncomplimentary to Brownlow, is not surprising. While he was editor, he was always ready to publish attacks against himself, usually for purposes of refutation.

Banner-Herald (Athens, Georgia), 1926.
Banner of Peace (Nashville, Tennessee), 1860-1862.
Boston Evening Transcript, 1862.
Boston Morning Journal, 1862.
Chicago Tribune, 1895.
Cincinnati Daily Commercial, 1862-1866.
The Daily American (Nashville, Tennessee), 1877.
The Daily Constitution (Atlanta, Georgia), 1877.
The Daily Evening Bulletin (Philadelphia), 1862.
The Daily National Intelligencer (Washington), 1862.
The Daily New Era (Atlanta, Georgia), 1866-1869.
Knoxville Daily Chronicle, 1871.
New York Times, 1862-1865.
New York Daily Tribune, 1862, 1876, 1877.
Pennsylvanian (Philadelphia), 1858.
Public Ledger (Memphis, Tennessee), 1877.
Republican Banner (Nashville, Tennessee), 1872.
The Southern Banner (Athens, Georgia), 1854.
The Southern Watchman (Athens, Georgia), 1865, 1866.
Worcester (Massachusetts) *Daily Spy*, 1862.

4. PAMPHLETS

Brownlow, W. G., *Brownlow, the Patriot and Martyr, showing his Faith and Works, As Reported by Himself*. Philadelphia: R. Weir, 1862.
———, *A Sermon on Slavery: A Vindication of the Methodist*

Church South: Her Position Stated. Knoxville: Kinsloe & Rice, 1857.

Irreligious Character of the Rebellion. An Address by Parson Brownlow, delivered before the Young Men's Christian Association, at the Cooper Institute, May 19, 1862.

Personal Explanation. Speech of Hon. William G. Brownlow of Tennessee in the Senate of the United States, February 15, 1872.

Portrait and Biography of Parson Brownlow, the Tennessee Patriot, Together with his Last Editorial in the Knoxville Whig; also, his recent Speeches, Rehearsing his Experience with Secession, and his Prison Life. Indianapolis: Asher & Co., 1862.

Reconstruction—Tennessee. Memorial of Citizens of Tennessee. February 13, 1866.

Relief for East Tennessee. Address of Hon. N. G. Taylor. New York: Wm. C. Bryant & Co., 1864. Delivered at Cooper Institute, March 10, 1864.

Report to the Contributors to the Pennsylvania Relief Association for East Tennessee. Philadelphia, 1864.

Reynolds, Major W. D., *Miss Martha Brownlow; or the Heroine of Tennessee. A Truthful and Graphic Account of the many Perils and Privations endured by Miss Martha Brownlow, the Lovely and Accomplished Daughter of the Celebrated Parson Brownlow, during her Residence with her Father in Knoxville.* Philadelphia: Barclay & Co., n. d.

Suffering of Union Men. An Address by Parson Brownlow (Rev. W. G. Brownlow, D.D.) delivered before the Citizens of New York, at the Academy of Music, May 15, 1862.

5. PERIODICALS

American Baptist Register for 1852. Philadelphia: American Baptist Publishing Society, 1853.

Armenian Magazine, 1848, 1849. Edited by Russell Reneau at Rome, Georgia.

Calvinistic Magazine, The, 1827—. Edited by James Gallaher, Frederick A. Ross, and David Nelson at Rogersville, Tennessee. It was revived in January, 1846, under the same name and was edited by Isaac Anderson, Frederick A. Ross, James

King, and James McChain and published at Abingdon, Virginia.

Christian Repository, The. A Religious and Literary Monthly, 1852. Edited by John L. Waller and Charles D. Kirk at Louisville, Kentucky.

Cooper, W. R., "Parson Brownlow. A Study of Reconstruction in Tennessee," *Southwestern Bulletin,* new series, vol. XIX, no. 1 (December, 1931).

De Bow's Review, XXIII. Edited by J. D. B. De Bow at New Orleans.

"Diary and Correspondence of Salmon P. Chase," *Annual Report of the American Historical Association,* 1902, vol. II.

Godey's Lady's Book and Magazine, 1862. Published at Philadelphia.

Harper's New Monthly Magazine, 1862.

Harper's Weekly. A Journal of Civilization, 1862.

Hesseltine, W. B., "Methodism and Reconstruction in East Tennessee," *East Tennessee Historical Society Publications,* III (January, 1931), 42-61.

Jonesboro Monthly Review, The, 1847, 1848. Edited by Parson Brownlow at Jonesboro, Tennessee.

Jonesboro Quarterly Review, The, 1847. Edited by Parson Brownlow at Jonesboro, Tennessee.

McDonnald, R. L., "The Reconstruction Period in Tennessee," *American Historical Magazine,* I (October, 1896), 307-328.

"Major Connolly's Letters to his Wife, 1862-1865," *Transactions of the Illinois State Historical Society for the Year 1928,* pp. 217-383. (Publication no. 35 of the Illinois State Historical Library.)

Millennial Harbinger, The, 1830-1854. Edited by Alexander Campbell at Bethany, Virginia.

Niles' Weekly Register. Published by Hezekiah Niles at Baltimore.

North American Review, 1862.

Patton, J. W., "The Senatorial Career of William G. Brownlow," *Tennessee Historical Magazine,* series II, vol. I (1931), pp. 153-64.

Pedobaptist, The, 1829. A Presbyterian monthly published at Danville, Kentucky.

Phillips, U. B., "The Central Theme of Southern History," *American Historical Review,* XXXIV (October, 1928), 30-43.

Presbyterial Critic, The, 1855, 1856. Edited by Stuart Robinson and Thomas E. Peck at Baltimore.

Presbyterian Advocate, The, 1830. Published monthly at Lexington, Kentucky.

"A Proclamation by William G. Brownlow, Governor of Tennessee," *American Historical Magazine,* III (April, 1898), 151-54.

Putnam's Magazine, vol. III, no. 16 (April, 1869).

Quarterly Review, 1847-1854. Edited by H. B. Bascom at Louisville, Kentucky as a Methodist publication. In 1851 the editorship passed to D. S. Doggett at Richmond, Virginia.

Queener, V. M., "William G. Brownlow as an Editor," *East Tennessee Historical Society Publications,* IV (January, 1932), 67-82.

Shanks, W. F. G., "A Political Romance," *Putnam's Magazine,* vol. III, no. 16 (1869).

Southern Baptist Review and Electic, 1855-1860. Edited by J. R. Graves and J. M. Pendleton at Nashville, successively as a monthly, bi-monthly and a quarterly.

Southern Presbyterian Review, The, 1847-1851. Published quarterly at Columbia, S. C.

Tilton, Theodore, "Sketch of Parson Brownlow," *Independent,* May 22, 1862.

Wilson, J. M., *The Presbyterian Historical Almanac and Annual Remembrancer of the Church for 1858-1859.* Philadelphia: Joseph M. Wilson, 1859.

6. Books and Collected Works

Alexander, J. E., *A Brief History of the Synod of Tennessee from 1817 to 1887.* Philadelphia: MacCalla & Co., 1890.

American Annual Cyclopaedia, 1864-1877. New York: D. Appleton & Co., 1869-1884. In 1877, this title was changed to *Appleton's Annual Cyclopaedia.*

Arthur, J. P., *Western North Carolina. A History.* Raleigh: Edwards & Broughton Co., 1914.

Autobiography of a Pioneer: or, the Nativity, Experience, Travels, and Ministerial Labors of Rev. Jacob Young with Inci-

dents, Observations, and Reflections. Cincinnati: Poe and Hitchcock, 1860.

Bangs, Nathan, *A History of the Methodist Episcopal Church,* 4 vols. New York: T. Mason and G. Lane, 1839-1842.

Beale, Howard K., *The Critical Year. A Study of Andrew Johnson and Reconstruction.* New York: Harcourt, Brace and Co., 1930.

Benedict, David, *A General History of the Baptist Denomination in America and Other Parts of the World.* New York: Lewis Colly & Co., 1848.

Birney, William, *James G. Birney and his Times.* New York: D. Appleton & Co., 1890.

Borum, J. H., *Biographical Sketches of Tennessee Baptist Ministers.* Memphis: Rogers & Co., 1880.

Bowers, Claude G., *The Tragic Era; The Revolution after Lincoln.* Boston: Houghton Mifflin Co., 1929.

Brewer, D. J., ed., *The World's Best Orations,* 10 vols. Chicago: Ferd. P. Kaiser Publishing Co., 1923.

Brownlow, W. G., *Americanism Contrasted with Foreignism, Romanism, and Bogus Democracy, in the Light of Reason, History, and Scripture; in which Certain Demagogues in Tennessee, and elsewhere, are Shown up in their true Colors.* Nashville: Published for the author, 1856.

———, *The Great Iron Wheel Examined; or, its False Spokes Extracted, and an Exhibition of Elder Graves, its Builder. In a Series of Chapters.* Nashville: Published for the author, 1856.

———, *Helps to the Study of Presbyterianism or, an Unsophisticated Exposition of Calvinism, with Hopkinsian Modifications and Policy, with a View to a more easy Interpretation of the Same. To Which is Added a Brief Account of the Life and Travels of the Author, Interspersed with Anecdotes.* Knoxville: F. S. Heiskell Co., 1834.

———, *The "Little Iron Wheel" Enlarged: or, Elder Graves, its Builder, Daguerreotyped, by way of an Appendix. To which are added Some Personal Explanations.* Nashville: Published for the author, 1857.

———, *A Political Register, Setting forth the Principles of the Whig and Locofoco Parties in the United States, with the*

Life and Public Services of Henry Clay. Also an Appendix Personal to the Author; and a General Index. Jonesboro: Jonesboro Whig, 1844.

————, *Sketches of the Rise, Progress, and Decline of Secession; with a Narrative of Personal Adventures among the Rebels* [*Parson Brownlow's Book*]. Philadelphia: George W. Childs, 1862.

Burnett, J. J., *Sketches of Tennessee's Pioneer Baptist Preachers.* Nashville: Marshall & Bruce Co., 1919.

Cartland, Fernando G., *Southern Heroes or the Friends in War Times.* Cambridge: The Riverside Press, 1895.

Coale, C. B., *The Life and Adventures of William Waters, the Famous Hunter and Trapper of White Top Mountain, embracing Early History of Southwestern Virginia, Suffering of the Pioneers, etc., etc.* Richmond: G. W. Gary & Co., 1878.

Cole, A. C., *The Irrepressible Conflict, 1850-1865.* New York: The Macmillan Co., 1934.

Collins, Lewis, and Collins, R. H., *History of Kentucky.* 2 vols. Covington: Collins & Co., 1882.

Coulter, E. M., *The Cincinnati Southern Railroad and the Struggle for Southern Commerce, 1865-1872.* Chicago: The American Historical Society, 1922.

Dealings of God, Man, and the Devil: as Exemplified in the Life, Experience, and Travels of Lorenzo Dow, in a Period of over a Half a Century: Together with his Polemic and Miscellaneour Writings, Complete. Middleton, Ohio; Glasener & Marshall, 1849. Two volumes in one.

Diary of Gideon Welles, 3 vols. Boston: Hougton Mifflin Co., 1911.

Du Bose, John W., *Life and Times of William Lowndes Yancey. A History of Political Parties in the United States from 1834 to 1864.* Birmingham: Roberts & Son, 1892.

Fertig, J. W., *The Secession and Reconstruction of Tennessee.* Chicago: University of Chicago Press, 1898.

Fite, E. D., *Social and Industrial Conditions in the North during the Civil War.* New York: The Macmillan Co., 1910.

Fitzgerald, O. P., *John B. McFerrin: A Biography.* Nashville: Publishing House of the M. E. Church South, 1889.

Fleming, W. L., *The Sequel of Appomattox.* New Haven: Yale University Press, 1919.

Gorrie, P. D., *Episcopal Methodism, as It was, and is;* . . . Auburn, New York: Derby and Miller, 1852.

Graves, J. R., *The Great Iron Wheel; or, Republicanism Backwards and Christianity Reversed,* 17th ed. Nashville: Graves, Marks and Rutland, 1856.

————, *The Little Iron Wheel, A Declaration of Christian Rights, and Articles Showing the Despotism of Episcopal Methodism by H. B. Bascom, D.D.* Nashville: Graves, Marks and Rutland, 1856.

Hale, W. T. and Merritt, D. L., *A History of Tennessee and Tennesseeans,* 8 vols. Chicago: Lewis Publishing Co., 1913.

Hall, C. R., *Andrew Johnson, Military Governor of Tennessee.* Princeton: Princeton University Press, 1916.

Heiskell, S. G., *Andrew Jackson and Early Tennessee History.* 3 vols. Nashville: Ambrose Printing Co., 1920-1921.

Hodgson, Francis, *The Great Iron Wheel Reviewed: or A Defense of the Methodist E. Church against the Caluminous Assaults of Rev. F. A. Ross and Rev. A. Converse, D.D.* Philadelphia: Thomas Stokes, 1848.

Hooper, W. S., ed., *Fifty Years as a Presiding Elder by Rev. Peter Cartwright.* Cincinnati: Hitchcock and Walden, 1871.

Humes, T. W., *The Loyal Mountaineers of Tennessee.* Knoxville: Ogden Brothers & Co., 1888.

Jillson, W. R., *The Big Sandy Valley. A Regional History Prior to the Year 1850.* Louisville: John P. Morton & Co., 1923.

Johnson, R. U., and Buel, C. C., ed., *Battles and Leaders of the Civil War,* 4 vols. New York: The Century Co., 1887-1888.

Jones, J. S., *Life of Andrew Johnson.* Greeneville: Greeneville Publishing Co., 1901.

Journal of Rev. Francis Asbury, 3 vols. New York: Eaton & Mains, n. d.

Journals of the General Conference of the Methodist Episcopal Church, vol. I (1796-1836). New York: Carlton & Phillips, 1855.

Kirke, Edmund [J. R. Gilmore], *Down in Tennessee and Back by Way of Richmond.* New York: Carleton, 1866.

Lapsley, A. B., ed., *The Writings of Abraham Lincoln,* 8 vols. New York: G. P. Putnam's Sons, 1906.

*Life, Travels and Opinions of Benjamin Lundy, including his Jour-
ney to Texas and Mexico; with a Sketch of Contemporary
Events and a Notice of the Revolution in Hayti.* Philadelphia:
William D. Parrish, 1847. Compiled under the direction and
on behalf of his children.

M'Caine, Alexander, *A Defense of the Truth, as set forth in the
"History and Mystery of Methodist Episcopacy," being a
Reply to John Emory's Defense of our Fathers.* Baltimore:
Sherwood & Co., 1850.

M'Ferrin, J. B., *History of Methodism in Tennessee,* 3 vols. Nashville: Southern Methodist Publishing House, 1888.

McPherson, Edward, *The Political History of the United States
of America during the Great Rebellion,* 2nd ed. Washington:
Philip & Solomons, 1865.

————, *The Political History of the United States of America
during the Period of Reconstruction.* Washington: Solomons
& Chapman, 1875.

Mell, P. H., Jr., *Life of Patrick Hues Mell.* Louisville: Baptist
Book Concern, 1895.

Memoirs of Henry Villard, Journalist and Financier, 1835-1900,
2 vols. Boston: Houghton Mifflin Co., 1904.

Milburn, William Henry, *The Pioneers, Preachers and People of
the Mississippi Valley.* New York: Derby & Jackson, 1860.

————, *Ten Years of Preacher Life: Chapters from an Autobiography.* New York: Derby & Jackson, 1859.

Milton, George Fort, *The Age of Hate. Andrew Johnson and the
Radicals.* New York: Coward-McCann, 1930.

*Minutes of the Annual Conferences of the Methodist Episcopal
Church for the Years 1829-1839,* 2 vols. New York: T. Mason
and G. Lane, 1840.

Moore, Frank, comp., *The Rebellion Record: a diary of American
events, with documents, narratives, illustrative incidents,
poetry, etc.,* 11 vols. New York: G. P. Putnam's Sons, 1861-
1868.

Moore, John Trotwood, and Foster, Austin P., *Tennessee, the
Volunteer State,* 4 vols. Chicago: S. J. Clark Publishing Co.,
1923.

Nicholay, John G., and Hay, John, eds., *Complete Works of Abraham Lincoln,* 11 vols. New York: Francis D. Tandy Co., 1894.

Norwood, J. N., *The Schism in the Methodist Episcopal Church.* Alfred, New York: Alfred Press, 1923.

Noted Men of the Solid South. See *Why the Solid South?*

Oberholtzer, E. P., *A History of the United States since the Civil War,* 4 vols. New York: The Macmillan Co., 1917-1931.

Ought American Slavery to be Perpetuated? A Debate between Rev. W. G. Brownlow and Rev. A. Pryne, held at Philadelphia, September, 1858. Philadelphia: J. B. Lippincott & Co., 1858.

Patton, J. W., *Unionism and Reconstruction in Tennessee, 1860-1869.* Chapel Hill: University of North Carolina Press, 1934.

Perambulations of Cosmopolite; or Travels and Labors of Lorenzo Dow in Europe and America. Rochester, 1842.

Phillips, U. B., *A History of Transportation in the Eastern Cotton Belt to 1860.* New York: Columbia University Press, 1908.

Price, R. N., *Holston Methodism from its Origin to the Present Time,* 5 vols. Nashville: Publishing House of the M. E. Church South, 1903-1914.

Private and Official Correspondence of Gen. Benjamin F. Butler during the Period of the Civil War. 5 vols. Privately printed, 1917.

Randolph, T. J., ed., *Memoir, Correspondence, and Miscellanies, from the Papers of Thomas Jefferson,* 2nd ed., 4 vols. Boston: Gray and Bowen, 1830.

Riley, B. F., *A History of the Baptists in the Southern States East of the Mississippi.* Philadelphia: American Baptist Publishing Society, 1898.

Ross, Frederick A., *The Doctrine of the Direct Witness of the Spirit, as Taught by the Rev. John Wesley, shown to be Unscriptural, False, Fanatical, and of Mischievous Tendency.* Philadelphia: Perkins and Purves, 1846.

————, *Slavery Ordained of God.* Philadelphia: J. B. Lippincott & Co., 1857.

Sala, G. A., *My Diary in America in the Midst of War,* 2 vols. London: Tinsley Brothers, 1865.

Scott, Allen M., *Chronicles of the Great Rebellion.* Cincinnati: C. F. Vent & Co., 1867.

Secession or Prose in Rhyme and East Tennessee A Poem by an East Tennesseean. Philadelphia: Printed for the author, 1864.

South in the Building of the Nation, The, 13 vols. Richmond: The Southern Publication Society, 1909-1913.

Stevens, Abel, *History of the Methodist Episcopal Church of the United States of America,* 4 vols. New York: Carlton & Porter, 1867.

Strickland, W. P., ed., *Autobiography of Peter Cartwright the Backwoods Preacher.* New York: Carlton & Porter, 1857.

Stryker, L. P., *Andrew Johnson. A Study in Courage.* New York: The Macmillan Co., 1929.

Summers, L. P., *History of Southwest Virginia, 1764-1786, Washington County, 1777-1870.* Richmond: J. L. Hill Printing Co., 1903.

Sweet, W. W., *The Rise of Methodism in the West.* Nashville: Smith and Lamar, 1920.

———, *The Story of Religion in America.* New York: Harper & Brothers, 1930.

Temple, Oliver P., *Notable Men of Tennessee from 1833 to 1875.* New York: The Cosmopolitan Press, 1912.

Trowbridge, J. T., *Cudjo's Cave.* Boston: Lee and Shepard, 1893.

Warmoth, H. C., *War, Politics and Reconstruction. Stormy Days in Louisiana.* New York: The Macmillan Co., 1930.

Wender, H., *Southern Commercial Conventions, 1837-1859* (Johns Hopkins University Studies in History and Political Science, ser. XLVIII, no. 4). Baltimore: Johns Hopkins Press, 1930.

Why the Solid South? Or, Reconstruction and its Results. Baltimore: R. H. Woodward & Co., 1890. By various authors; binder's title, *Noted Men of the Solid South.*

Wightman, William W., *Life of William Capers, D.D., one of the Bishops of the Methodist Episcopal Church South; including an Autobiography.* Nashville: J. B. McFerrin, 1858.

Winston, R. W., *Andrew Johnson, Plebian and Patriot.* New York: Henry Holt & Co., 1928.

Worden, R. B., *An Account of the Private Life and Public Service of Salmon Portland Chase.* Cincinnati: Wilsach, Baldwin & Co., 1874.

INDEX

Abingdon, Va., 4, 7, 21, 55, 57, 61, 162
Abingdon District, 17
Abingdon Virginian, 41, 42
Abolition, of slavery, 79, 80, 89-92, 109, 95-108, 119, 120, 126, 129, 130, 132; condemned by Brownlow, 136, 137, 152, 214, 215
Abolitionists. *See* Abolition
Abraham, slaveholder, 96, 102
Academy of Music, New York City, 225, 226, 241
Academy of Music, Philadelphia, 231
Adairsville, Ga., 346
Adams, J. Q., supported by Brownlow, 111, 112
Aesop, 394
Africa, slavery in, 102, 103; seizure advocated by Brownlow, 104, 105
Alabama, 2, 20, 65, 87, 96, 98, 102, 128, 141, 163, 258
Alden, A. E., in Nashville election, 343
"Alden Ring," 343
Alexandria, Tenn., 250
Alexandria, Va., 208
Alleghany City, Pa., 219
Alleghany Mountains, 219
Altoona Pa., 219, 221
American Bible Society, 32
American Board of Commissioners for Foreign Missions, 33
American Colonization Society, 94
American Education Society, 33
American Home Missionary Society, 33
Americanism Contrasted . . . , by Brownlow, 124
American Party. *See* Native American Party
American Sunday School Union, 32
American System, 115
American Temperance Society, 33
American Tract Society, 32
Anderson, Isaac, 55

Anderson, Robert, 208
Anderson County, 155
Anderson District, S. C., 24
Andrew, James O., 27
Andrew, John A., 229
Anti-Masonic Movement, 21
Appalachia. *See* Southern Appalachia
Arkansas, 51, 98, 127
Armenian Magazine, founded, 57; mentioned, 62
Arnell, Samuel M., Brownlow's friend, 280; fears Klu Klux Klan, 356
Asbury, Francis, visits East Tenn., 7, 10, 11; on slavery, 90; mentioned, 399
Asheville, N. C., 86, 88, 384
Asheville District, 17, 18
Ashley, Henry M., slain, 356
Astor House, New York City, 225
Athens, Ga., lecture at by Brownlow, 93; mentioned, 273 n
Athens, Tenn., 57, 89, 205, 294, 330
Athens Circuit, 21
Athens Synod, 57, 62
Atlanta, Ga., 86, 89, 249, 273
Auburn, N. Y., 321
Augusta, Ga., 86, 249, 266
Augusta, Maine, 98

Baltimore, Md., visited by Brownlow, 26, 259; mentioned, 90, 130
Bangs, Nathan, 13
Banner of Peace, 129, 139
Baptism, contentions over form, 14, 15, 74-79
Baptism, with Reference to its Import . . . , 78
Baptist Publishing Society of North Carolina, 70
Baptists, development in East Tennessee, 7, 8, 13, 14, 15; first attacked by Brownlow, 18, 19; attack Methodists, 66-71; repelled by Brownlow, 67-81; early attitude on slavery,

kind treatment of by Andrew Johnson, 308; encounter with T. B.
Kirby, 356; mentioned, 116, 358 n,
390 n

Brownlow, Joseph A., 1

Brownlow, Susan, defends flag, 159;
accompanies Brownlow on tour of
North, 223; presented with revolver,
231; presented with United States
flag, 231; named Martha in book
about her, 244; misnamed Maude in
book about her, 245

Brownlow, William Gannaway ("Parson"), birth and early life, 1, 2;
farmer boy, 4; in school, 4; becomes
Methodist minister, 6; circuit-
rider, 17-34; love of nature, 18, 19;
first contact with Baptists, 18; conflict with Humphrey Posey, 22, 23;
sees Tallulah Falls, 24; on Nullification, 24-25; delegate to General
Conference in Philadelphia, 25-27;
writes his autobiography, 27-28;
writes book against Presbyterians,
27, 28; general attack on Presbyterians, 30-34; "locates," 34; mar-
ries, 34; settles in Elizabethton,
35; becomes newspaper editor, 35;
conflict with L. C. Haynes, 36-38,
39, 43, 48, 58; moves to Jonesboro,
38; quarrel with J. M. Smith, 40-
42; clubbed by unknown assailant,
43-44; sets up *Jonesboro Quarterly
Review,* 45, attacks in newspaper
John Tyler, 45, 46; moves to Knoxville, 46; conflict with Knoxville
editors, 47-52; quarrels with W. S.
Swan, 48; answers F. A. Ross, 57-
65; begins *Jonesboro Monthly Review,* 58-61; speaking campaign
against Ross, 61-62; challenges Ross
to debate, 62-63; attacks Ashbel
Green, 63-64; answers J. R. Graves,
71-81; writes *Great Iron Wheel
Examined* . . . , 71-72; attacks
Baptist form of church government,
73-74; tells anecdotes on close communion, 74 n; attacks immersion
and defends sprinkling, 74-79; attacks Graves as a Northerner, 79;
writes *"Little Iron Wheel" Enlarged* . . . , 80; attitude toward

slaveholders, 92-109; makes trip
through South, 92, 93; visits Southern commercial conventions, 93-94;
on Harriet Beecher Stowe, 95; sermon on slavery, 95-97; challenges
North for debate on slavery, 97;
debates Abraham Pryne, 97-108;
advocates exploiting Africa, 104,
105; on office-seeking, 110; hates
Andrew Jackson, 111, 113-14;
changes mind on Jackson, 125, 131;
supports J. Q. Adams, 111; becomes
a Whig, 111, 112; idolizes Henry
Clay, 112, 113, 115, 116, 117, 118,
119; writes life of Clay, 113; runs
for Congress and is defeated, 113,
117; contempt for Democrats, 114,
115, 122, 124, 126-28; opposition to
Andrew Johnson in ante-bellum
politics, 117, 120-22; opposes Taylor
as Whig nominee for presidency,
117-18; advocates Fillmore for
Whig nominee in 1848, 119; issues
prayer against Andrew Johnson,
121; writes *Political Register* . . . ,
113; opposes Catholics, 123, 124;
writes *Americanism Contrasted* . . . ,
124; joins Know-Nothings, 124, 125;
s u p p o r t s Constitutional Union
Party in 1860, 127, 130, 132; writes
letter to Jordan Clark, 127-28; opposes idea of Southern confederacy,
129, 130; opposes secession idea,
130-33; encounter with W. L.
Yancey, 132; fights secession movement, 135-53; attacks Cotton South,
135; opposes Abolitionists, 136, 152;
blames South Carolina for secession,
140-42; blames churches for secession, 144-46; opposes Sovereign
Convention, 146-47; runs for
governor in 1860, 149-51; rumor
that he would support Confederacy,
152; supports Union, 135-53; member of Knoxville convention for
East Tennessee statehood, 155;
member of session held in Greenville, 156-58; erects United States
flag on home, 159, 160; castigates
C o n f e d e r a t e officials, 160-62;
maligns Confederate soldiers, 163-
65; incites bridge-burners, 168-70;

420 INDEX

East Tennessee Relief Association, 255, 256, 271

East Tennessee University, Library, 381

Ebenezer, 21

Edmunds, George F., 389

Egypt, 96, 131, 389, 394

Eleven Years' War, 55

Elizabethton, Brownlow moves to, 35; mentioned, 38, 53, 85, 170, 384

Elizabethton Circuit, 27

Elizabethton Whig, The, set up, 35-36

Elks Club, 353

Ellsworth, Oliver, 208

Emancipation Proclamation, 289

Embre, Elihu, opposes slavery, 91

Emory, John, 13, 23

Emory and Henry College, 8, 49, 63

England, 73, 208, 229, 237, 344

"Entire Swine Party, The," 114

Episcopal Church, charged by Brownlow with helping to bring on secession, 144; mentioned, 129

Episcopalian, 55, 57

Etheridge, Emerson, East Tennessee Unionist, 154; greets Brownlow at Nashville, 210; speaks in Nashville, 211; becomes Conservative leader, 278; nominated for governor, 328; in campaign, 336, 337, 339; mentioned, 393

Europe, 104, 237

Evarts, William M., 225

Evensham, Va., 23

Everett, Edward, 127, 130, 256

F alling from grace, 30

"F. A. Ross Corner," in *Jonesboro Whig,* 61

Farragut, David G., 3, 321

Fayette County, Tenn., 357, 367

Fighting Parson, origin of term, 30 n

Fillmore, Millard, 118, 119, 125

"Financial Board," 376

First Congressional District, East Tennessee, distinction, 167

Fisk, John F., 215

Fleming, John, East Tennessee Unionist, 154

Fletcher, A. J., secretary of state, 266; opposes carpetbaggers, 289; in race for United States senate, 346; on Brownlow proclamation, 362; open break with Brownlow, 371-72; mentioned, 358

Florida, 140, 141, 228

Floyd, John, 194

Foote, Henry, S., 360

Ford's Atheneum, Washington, 233

Forney, John W., 315

Forrest, Nathan B., on Negroes, 334; leader of Ku Klux Klan, 354; mentioned, 258, 273, 360, 363, 378, 383, 384, 395

Fort Donelson, 213, 244, 257

Fort Sumter, 147, 208

Fort Warren, Boston, 229

Fourteenth Amendment, ratification of by Tennessee, 312-15; mentioned, 311, 316, 324, 369

Fowler, Joseph S., United States Senator, 276, 316, 351, 365

France, 229

Franchise laws, of Tennessee, 269-70, 283-87, 330

Franklin, Benjamin, 220

Franklin, N. C., 22, 32

Franklin, Tenn., 335

Franklin Circuit, 21

Franklin County, 339

Frazier, Thomas N., judge, 314

Freedmen's Bureau, 290, 292, 309, 311

Free Lovers, 107

Free Soilers, 107

Frémont, John C., 125, 247

French Broad Circuit, 18

French Broad District, 17

French Broad River, 11, 21, 27, 46, 85, 86, 87, 384

French Spoliations, 388

Frierson, Speaker of Tennessee house, 324

Fry, David, aids bridge-burning, 170

Furies, 354

G allaher, James, 9 n, 28

Gallatin, Tenn., 335

Gamble, John E., tried for treason, 274

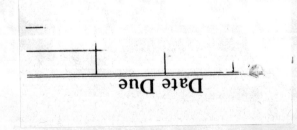
Date Due